P9-EKE-317

The Battle of Adwa

The Battle of Adwa

AFRICAN VICTORY IN THE
AGE OF EMPIRE

Raymond Jonas

The Belknap Press of Harvard University Press

Cambridge, Massachusetts · London, England

2011

Library of Congress Cataloging-in-Publication Data

Jonas, Raymond Anthony.
The Battle of Adwa : African victory in the age of empire / Raymond Jonas.
p. cm.
Includes bibliographical references and index.
ISBN 978-0-674-05274-1 (alk. paper)
1. Adwa, Battle of, Adwa, Ethiopia, 1896. 2. Italo-Ethiopian War,
1895–1896. 3. Menelik II, Negus of Ethiopia, 1844–1913. 4. Taitu, Empress,
consort of Menelik II, Negus of Ethiopia, d. 1918. 5. Italy—Foreign relations—
Ethiopia. 6. Ethiopia—Foreign relations—Italy. I. Title.
DT387.3.J67 2011

963'.043—dc22   2011014346

For Mark Jonas

Contents

Maps and Illustrations

The Battle of Adwa

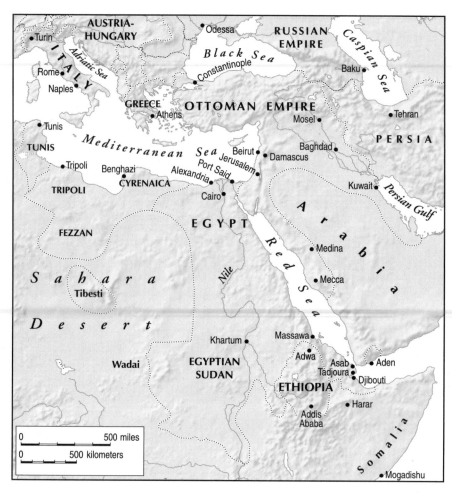

Northeast Africa and the eastern Mediterranean (adapted from *Scottish Geographical Magazine*, 1885)

Introduction

THIS IS THE STORY of a world turned upside down. On the first of March, 1896, not far from the Ethiopian town of Adwa, an African army won a spectacular victory over a European army. Africans had defeated Europeans before—at Isandlwana, for example—but these proved to be mere setbacks in otherwise inexorable conquests. Ethiopian victory over Italy at the battle of Adwa was decisive: it brought an Italian war of conquest to an end. In an age of relentless European expansion, Ethiopia alone had successfully defended its independence.

Inevitably, Ethiopian victory was interpreted in racial terms, for not only had an African army defeated a European army, but a black army had defeated a white army. Adwa thus cast doubt upon an unshakable certainty of the age—that sooner or later Africans would fall under the rule of Europeans. Adwa is not only the founding event in the history of modern Ethiopia, and not only a founding trauma in the young life of the modern Italian nation. Adwa is, I would argue, part of our global heritage. It was one of those events we call "world-historical" because we can readily imagine the world—*our* world—taking a different path had events gone differently. Adwa opened a breach that would lead, in the aftermath of world war fifty years later, to the rollback of European rule in Africa. It was an event that determined the color of Africa.

The story of Adwa has at its core a number of compelling personalities. Chief among them is Menelik, a provincial monarch who claimed a biblical ancestry originating with the liaison between King Solomon and the queen of Sheba. Menelik parlayed these assets into a claim on the Ethiopian throne. Menelik had more than inspired ancestry in his favor; he had an acute strategic imagination. In a manner reminiscent of Otto von Bismarck of Prussia, Menelik used aggressive external belligerents to subdue his rivals and so to lay claim to the title of emperor of Ethiopia.

A key collaborator was Taytu Betul. In her youth a prophecy told her that she would wear a crown. She had already gone through at least two husbands before marrying Menelik at the age of thirty, making good on the prophecy. Her quick wit and shrewd political sense brought balance to Menelik's cautious and deliberate leadership style. She also brought geographic balance. When Menelik and Taytu met, he was merely king of Shoa, a province in southern Ethiopia. His marriage to Taytu gave him a smart, energetic political partner with a power base in the north, confirming Menelik as a leader with a claim to truly national credentials. Taytu was a strong personality who didn't shrink from harsh measures, whether against the encroaching Europeans or against rivals for Menelik's affection. Second at court only to the emperor himself, Taytu led a faction that opposed Menelik's tentative embrace of the Europeans, favoring a bold and aggressive military response. A blend of Taytu's ardent maximalism and Menelik's brilliant gamesmanship culminated in the triumph at Adwa.

Ethiopian triumph owed almost as much to the soft power of propaganda as to blood and steely might. By appealing to sympathies abroad, Ethiopia pioneered the defining strategy of modern anticolonial struggles—the campaign for hearts and minds. The drive to abolish the slave trade decades earlier had shown that European public opinion could be engaged in the fate of Africa if offered a compelling story. Before a single shot was fired, Menelik and Taytu waged a savvy public opinion campaign in Europe. Since 1878, Menelik had relied on the Swiss engineer Alfred Ilg—his trusted advisor and factotum—for advice in dealing with Europe. In the 1890s, Menelik repeatedly deployed Ilg to Europe to help shape the emperor's image and that of Ethiopia. In a series of brilliant strokes, Ilg assimilated Ethiopia to European landscapes and conventions. Ilg touted mountainous Ethiopia as "Africa's Switzerland," a representation boosted in a postcard campaign. The card featured a collage of pleasing sketches—Menelik in regal profile, Ethiopia's rugged high mountains, *tukul* rendered with suspiciously Swiss orderliness. Ilg also secured the key markers of durable sovereignty so rare in Africa—postage stamps and coins—embossed with Menelik's likeness.

Ilg's collaborator, the freelance journalist Casimir Mondon-Vidailhet, had been promoting Menelik and Ethiopia since 1892 via features in the European press. Mondon-Vidailhet is a classic example of a European going abroad to refashion himself; sources refer to a shady past he sought to escape in Ethiopia. Described as slippery by his enemies and adroit by his friends, Mondon effectively functioned as Menelik's chief publicist. His dispatches fed European readers with a comfortable blend of the alluringly exotic and the reassuringly familiar. His descriptions of the Ethiopian court conjured a romanticized medieval Europe. "Sometimes I ask myself if our own chivalrous Middle Ages . . . haven't risen from the grave to seek, on this airy Ethiopian plateau . . . a final and safe refuge," he wrote. Besides appealing to European medieval nostalgia, Mondon's characterization quietly suggested that Ethiopia would, in the fullness of time, mature into a comfortingly familiar European present.

Mondon also underlined Ethiopia's Christian heritage. His features celebrated Menelik's triumphs over his Muslim neighbors, thus assimilating Ethiopia's struggles to those of Christian Europe and the larger global community of Christendom. "The Cross has defeated the Crescent," he wrote jubilantly following a brutal campaign against the Muslim Welayta. When Italy moved against Ethiopia the following year, Mondon appealed to European sympathies on behalf of Ethiopia. "The Ethiopian Emperor understands European public opinion," he wrote. "He counts on feelings of justice shared by all Christian peoples." The official portrait of Menelik circulated by what could be called his public relations team featured a serene head of state—the antithesis of the clichéd barbarian African—with a large crucifix worn high at the neck. European newspapers obligingly printed the portrait as they played up a sympathetic image of "Africa's Christian monarch." Against all odds, these efforts helped to turn Menelik and Taytu into celebrities in Europe and America. By the turn of the century, Menelik had his own tableau in wax at the

Musée Grévin in Paris, a sure marker of notoriety in popular culture. *Vanity Fair* profiled Menelik as the subject of one of its famous color lithographs—a distinction that put him in the company of such figures as Charles Darwin and Benjamin Disraeli. Félix Potin, the pioneering chain store merchant, featured Menelik and Taytu in a collectible card series of bankable fin-de-siècle personalities, doled out one card per visit.

Adwa's aftermaths matter, too. The scope of the disaster of Adwa was such that someone would have to pay. In Italy, the government of Francesco Crispi fell; his political career ended. General Oreste Baratieri, the commanding officer who had the misfortune of surviving Adwa, was put on trial even before he left Africa. Baratieri's trial played as a scripted drama on the themes of hubris, race, and betrayal.

Hundreds of Italians were taken prisoner after Adwa. It was a racial turning of the tables that put whites at the mercy of blacks in significant numbers for the first time. The prisoners were billeted upon the Ethiopian population for nearly a year, opening the door to retaliation and cruel revenge that never came. Instead, many prisoners developed close relationships with their guardian/captors, becoming friends and, occasionally, lovers. A surprising number of them left memoirs; a few of them were excellent observers. These accidental anthropologists will have their say, as will the entrepreneurs—Greeks, Armenians, Jews, Swiss—who operated as independent agents in Ethiopia, selling arms to Menelik and confounding our understanding of imperialism as a coordinated enterprise of statesmen, soldiers, and merchants.

Indeed, the story of the drive to conquer Ethiopia subverts much received wisdom about how imperialism operated and what drove it. Ethiopia made no sense as a settlement colony, as an outlet for investment capital, as a source of raw materials, or as a market for surplus production. It yielded no tangible political advantages among an electorate largely indifferent to the lure of imperial grandeur. The Italian bourgeoisie ridiculed the vision of Italian East Africa, notably through its journalistic mouthpiece, the Milan-based *Corriere della Sera*. They rightly diagnosed "Africa italiana" as a pathological projection of the ambitions of Italy's political leaders, who preferred to spend millions in pursuit of imperial glory while they ignored the urgent but more prosaic need for investment at home.

A close examination of the failed conquest of Ethiopia reveals not the operation of vast impersonal forces but the convergence of individual vanities and ambitions. The pursuit of empire is shown to be driven by distinct personalities: frustrated careerist administrators, ambitious officers, failed characters seeking sanctuary or redemption in overseas exploits, privateer merchants in pursuit of the killer deal, and, most crucially, political leaders seduced by the idea that empire was where both personal and national greatness could be found.

Around the globe, Adwa gave the lie to the inevitability of European domination—both political and racial. Fin-de-siècle culture in Europe and in the United States confidently predicted Africa's future in terms redolent of Manifest Destiny. In 1896, on the eve of the battle of Adwa, the *Atlanta Constitution* noted that Africa was already "carved up and possessed by the different governments of Europe." The Europeans, the *Constitution* observed, "are all repeating in Africa the work of colonization which has made America populous, and before them the negro must go, as did the Indian in America."[1] Assumptions about political domination and racial superiority were thus entwined. By setting back one, Adwa shattered pious certainties about the other. Nearly a hundred years before the abolition of apartheid, Adwa set in motion the long unraveling of European domination of Africa, just as it provoked a rethinking of seemingly settled issues about race.

Figures throughout the African diaspora grasped the significance of Adwa, Menelik, and independent Ethiopia. Some, such as Benito Sylvain of Haiti and Joseph Vitalien of the West Indies, saw in Ethiopia a beacon—a kind of Zion—and made the pilgrimage from the Americas.[2] Others—such as Booker T. Washington, Ida B. Wells, and W. E. B. Du Bois—became "virtual pilgrims" who visited and elaborated an Ethiopia of the imagination. In so doing, they anticipated the real and virtual pilgrimages taken by the Rastafarians a generation or so later.

In the aftermath of Adwa, it was tempting for some Europeans and Americans to explain away the exception of Ethiopian victory—and to soothe the sting of white defeat—by discounting Italy as a worthy and capable colonial power. But empire was never an exclusive big-power game. Portugal, Belgium, and the Dutch had carved out their pieces of empire; why not Italy?

History loves exceptions. This book seeks not to explain away the exception of Adwa but to embrace it. Patterns abound in history, and it is tempting for us to discern in an accumulation of instances an otherwise inscrutable underlying pattern. Exceptions create that rare opportunity to separate the contingent from the inevitable, to recognize in discrete choices and chance occurrences the branching paths of human endeavor. The story of Adwa represents one such opportunity, for in pitting one of the most integrated of African states against a latecomer to the scramble for Africa, it strips away the gloom of inevitability and—like the battle itself—puts history back into play.

PART I

The Road to Adwa

CHAPTER 1

Courtly Ambitions

I T WAS AN IMPROBABLE BEGINNING to one of the great political partnerships of modern times. Inside an oversized hut of branch and straw
construction, the young, charismatic king of Shoa sat cross-legged on a
carpet-draped dais. A black silk cape with white embroidered trim covered his shoulders; a bandana of fine white silk wrapped his head from
brow to nape, where it tied. Menelik combed his beard with his fingers as
he sat alone under a royal canopy; lieutenants in lion's mane headdresses
and red-trimmed tunics stood at either side, leaning on lances.[1] The
only illumination entered the room from doors on opposite sides. In the
somber light, Menelik could make out the features of the engineer sent to
him by Escher and Furrer, a Swiss firm operating out of Aden. The man
was young, tall, and broad-shouldered; he sported a long, full beard in
the style of an Alfred Tennyson or a Friedrich Engels. His name was
Alfred Ilg.[2]

Although barely thirty-five at the time of the meeting in 1879, Menelik
looked older than his years; his skin was deeply pitted, the traces of a
bout with smallpox. It was a useful mask—a hardened look that belied
the subtle, sensitive spirit within. Menelik was not a handsome man, but
those who met him remarked on the warmth, kindness, and quiet power
in his face. When the French geographer Alphonse Aubry met Menelik

in the 1880s he noted, as everyone did, the obvious scarring on Menelik's face. But he also commented on Menelik's expressive eyes, which he described as "quite beautiful, intelligent, and kind."[3] Captain Longbois, on mission to Menelik from the French Ministry of Foreign Affairs during the same years, offered a similar description to the French Geographic Society, suggesting that the smallpox scarring gave the king "a hard air" that was softened by his intelligent face and large black eyes full of tenderness and goodwill.[4] The British journalist Augustus Wylde couldn't see past the wide-brimmed black felt hat the young Menelik made his trademark; Wylde dismissed it as an affectation, "a two shilling black wideawake."[5] Whether Menelik was aware that in Ireland the wideawake was an emblem of anti-imperial resistance, we will never know; it may simply have been a sartorial preference.[6] Years later, the British diplomat Sir Rennell Rodd met Menelik at court in Addis Ababa and recalled his face as being "full of character and quiet power," his manner "dignified and at the same time cordially unreserved."[7]

As for Ilg, he might have passed for a gentle schoolteacher with his wire spectacles and fair alpine complexion. In his early teens Ilg had left Frauenfeld, his hometown in the foothills of northern Switzerland, for secondary schooling in Zürich. He was barely twenty-five when he departed for the Red Sea in May 1878, in the company of two craftsmen from Zürich.[8] The journey from the Somali coast to his meeting with Menelik in Ankober must have given him pause. It certainly tried his patience. He was stuck on the coast at Zeyla for weeks waiting for a caravan into the Ethiopian highlands. The delay was a standard business practice on the coast, said to facilitate the emptying of the wallets of bored and impatient travelers. Once the journey was under way, it took a month and a half to make the climb through territories controlled by Afar tribesmen eager to exact tribute from travelers.[9]

Alfred Ilg was lured not only by the promise of work but also by a sense of mission. He had taken inspiration from Werner Munzinger, a fellow Swiss of an earlier generation who had made a career for himself in Egypt. Munzinger had labored to fulfill Khedive Ismail's modernizing ambition for Egypt, serving the khedive first in Cairo, then as governor of territories from the Red Sea to the Sudan in the 1870s.[10] Where Munzinger had a romantic penchant and fell hard for Ismail's vision of expansion and

Menelik in 1888. From Guèbrè Sellassié, *Chronique du règne de Ménélik II, roi des rois d'Éthiopie*. Paris: Maisonneuve Frères, 1930.

monumental grandeur—the renaissance of Egyptian imperial glory—Ilg's temperament was pragmatic. As an engineer, he tended to see modernization in technical terms, a set of discrete practical problems to be mastered.

So did Menelik, the young monarch who hired the solemn Ilg to lead the technical modernization of his realm.[11] Patient, practical, and open to the world, Ilg rapidly adapted to life in Ethiopia. He was an engineer but also a realist; he soon reconciled his penchant for precision with the

Alfred Ilg. From *L'Illustrazione italiana,* 29 March 1896.

elastic standards of Ethiopia, where, he noted, "time is a loose concept."[12] Ilg shaved his Tennysonesque beard, took an Ethiopian wife,
started a family, and mastered Amharic. By the time he turned thirty, in
1884, he had completed a slew of projects for Menelik.[13] He was fast becoming royal architect and minister of bridges and roads.

Ilg showed a knack not only for public works but also for adapting
Menelik's modernizing ambition to his resources. Soon Menelik and
Taytu were giving Ilg shopping lists for his trips to Europe; he returned
loaded down with the bric-a-brac of modern life and European technology—a printing press, wide-brimmed hats, a cartridge reloader, soap, a

sturdy plow, fine footwear. Although Ilg's missions to Europe were largely matters of state, Empress Taytu didn't hesitate to write to modify her wishes, to remind Ilg of her preferences, or to inform him of her shoe size. (She wore a European size 39.)[14] But she was far from frivolous and was just as likely to follow up with a note about agricultural machinery. Either way, whether pursuing public interest or private passion, she signed her letters "Empress Taytu, light of Ethiopia."[15]

By the time of Menelik's accession to the Ethiopian throne in 1889, Ilg had assumed additional functions as councilor of state. He put his formidable language skills—French, German, Italian, English, Amharic—to work, never once hinting at ambitions beyond those of his patron and friend. The public works continued—in 1894, he completed a water conduit from Entotto to the imperial compound—but by then he was effectively operating as chief of staff.[16] After Adwa, Menelik would turn to Ilg for guidance in the negotiations for the Italian prisoners.[17] By turns builder, translator, arms merchant, and diplomat, Ilg was indispensable. He would serve Menelik for life.

The partnership established between Menelik and Ilg would be decisive for the future of Ethiopia. By the time of their meeting, the fate of Africa seemed clear. Inspired, in part, by the expansion of the United States and the Manifest Destiny that took European settler populations from sea to shining sea, European powers came increasingly to see Africa as *the* outlet for Europe's ambitions and its population. After a period of retrenchment during the revolutionary and Napoleonic wars, European expansion had begun anew. European settlement in south Africa recommenced after 1815; the conquest of north Africa began with Algeria in 1830. Even though the Atlantic slave trade was in decline by the second half of the century, King Leopold of Belgium found that great wealth could still be extracted from the Dark Continent and employed the most brutal methods in doing so. Along with Portugal and the Netherlands, Leopold's Belgium showed that even small powers could pursue grand ambitions in Africa. Meanwhile, Henry Morton Stanley turned African adventure into a manly sport, creating a book and lecture market for audiences primed for vicarious thrills.[18]

All the same, it was the great powers who were amassing the greatest territory. Britain would eventually lay claim to land stretching from Cairo to the Cape. France, encouraged by Bismarck to seek compensation abroad after defeat in the Franco-Prussian War of 1870, duly established interests in North and West Africa and defended toeholds on the Somali coast in the east. In 1884, Bismarck would convene a conference founded on the strong presumption that Africa's future would be European. When Menelik and Alfred Ilg met in 1878, that future was already closing in.

The Campaign against Tewodros: Blueprint for Conquest

Ethiopia in the nineteenth century was a collection of provinces ruled by kings, presided over by an emperor. Although principles of succession favored the eldest legitimate son of the previous emperor, there was plenty of room for interpretation and mischief. Prior to Menelik, Ethiopia had two great emperors in the nineteenth century—Tewodros and Yohannes. Both had risen from local power bases using tactics that often dressed blatant acts of banditry in the language of kingship. The image of the *shifta,* or bandit, looms large in the history of Ethiopia; it has even been said that the path of the *shifta* was "the sure way to political power."[19]

Tewodros, a *shifta* who was the son of a *shifta,* had clawed his way into power. The man who would become Emperor Tewodros was born with the name Kassa Hailu in 1818 near Gondar, in the west. Tewodros was abandoned by his father and raised by his mother. Rivals mocked his lowly origins. They liked to point out that his mother had eked out a living selling *koso,* which rids the digestive system of worms.

As a young man, Tewodros adopted a classic strategy of rebellion followed by accommodation. He ratcheted his way up as a regional figure, then used regional power and marriage to push aside rivals for the throne. He became emperor in 1855.[20] Tewodros set for himself the task of unifying Ethiopia and establishing Christian Ethiopia as a regional power. The thirty-three-year-old British consul, Walter Plowden, encouraged him in this regard, writing earnest letters back to London about the man who would "civilize and improve this distracted country."[21] Tewodros had decreed the abolition of the slave trade in Ethiopia, Plowden noted, just as he had outlawed the soldierly practice of taking trophies—via castration—from the bodies of fallen enemies. Such a sovereign, Plowden gushed, "shall merit the support and friendship of Her Majesty's Government."[22] Plowden apparently also encouraged the idea that Ethiopia and Britain might form an alliance of Christian brothers against Muslim Egypt.

Tewodros was seduced by the vision of Ethiopia as a unified Christian power whose authority stretched from the Ethiopian highlands down to the Red Sea. In 1856, he led his forces against the southern province of Shoa, whose king submitted and subsequently died of illness. The king's son, the young Menelik, was taken by Tewodros for safekeeping. (He later escaped.) The campaigns of Tewodros against the Muslim Oromo were less successful, and his armies never seriously threatened the Muslim towns and villages along the Red Sea coast.[23]

The *shifta* heritage of Tewodros ultimately worked against him. Contrary to Plowden's high hopes for Tewodros, his exercise of power rarely rose above the predatory. Tewodros and his armies were relentless in their campaigning—scarcely distinguishable from organized banditry—as they fed themselves from crops and livestock in their path. When farmers appealed for a lighter touch, Tewodros was blunt: "Soldiers eat; peasants provide." Tewodros relished his roguish image and took delight in his nickname, "Abba Bazbez" (Taker of Booty Day after Day).[24] Farmers learned to thwart Tewodros by driving off livestock and hiding the fruits of their harvest, and they tipped off their neighbors by lighting signal fires, warning of his movements. As his efforts at centralizing authority foundered, Tewodros became frustrated.

Tewodros also suffered slights from European powers—a letter sent in 1862 intended for Queen Victoria languished, unanswered, in the British Foreign Office.[25] And he became irritated by the presence of European missionaries, understandably so, for they seemed quite redundant in Christian Ethiopia. What Tewodros really wanted was "a cannon-founder, a gunsmith, an iron smelter, a heavy artillery man and a gunner."[26] Tewodros put the missionaries to work in the construction of roads and a massive siege gun christened "Sebastopol."[27]

He also detained the British consul and, in this, overplayed his hand.[28] Negotiations for the release of the consul and the missionaries led to deadlock; in 1867 Tewodros simply ignored a British ultimatum for their release. The following year, the consul and the missionary hostages became the object of a rescue mission undertaken by a British expeditionary force led by General Robert Napier.

In late January 1868, a fleet of transport ships began to unload their cargo at Zula, on the Red Sea coast just south of Massawa. The cargo included thousands of colonial troops from India, thousands of European

The Napier expedition. From Roger Acton, *The Abyssinian Expedition and the Life and Reign of King Theodore.* London: Illustrated London News, 1868.

British soldiers, and nearly two hundred Chinese laborers for road building—more than twenty thousand bodies in all, not counting three thousand pack animals, including forty-five Indian elephants.[29] The diverse composition of Napier's expeditionary force amounted to a demonstration of the global military might of the British Empire.

A few weeks later, the force began to move from the coast into the highlands. As the elephants lumbered along steep switchback trails, they carried disassembled Armstrong field guns strapped to their sides and backs. The elephants were piloted by colonial troops from India.

Tewodros might have adopted guerrilla tactics, harassing Napier's forces as their supply lines stretched. Instead, on 10 April, Good Friday, he put his infantrymen armed with rifles and spears in the open field against Napier's artillery and sharpshooters. The results were predictable and devastating—hundreds of Ethiopian dead versus twenty wounded

Le Petit Journal

SUPPLÉMENT ILLUSTRÉ

Huit pages : CINQ centimes

DIMANCHE 29 MARS 1896

S. M. TAÏTOU
Impératrice d'Abyssinie

Empress Taytu. From *Le Petit Journal*, 29 March 1896.

An early photograph shows a woman with high, full cheeks, full lips, and a narrow jaw. She wore her hair in cornrow braids that followed the arc of her ears and were collected in a ponytail at the back. She was famous for her slender fingers and her light complexion—a gift of her Oromo "Arab" descent. She was also known for her wealth, including holdings in farmland and pasture. She was connected to an extensive network of wealth and power through relatives.[47]

among Napier's men. Having failed at a show of force, Tewodros tried negotiation. He released some of the hostages and made a gift of a thousand cattle and five hundred sheep in peace and friendship.[30] Napier declined any peace offer that did not include the emperor himself. As Napier's expeditionary force closed in on the imperial redoubt at Magdala, Tewodros's authority vanished. When British forces moved up the mountainside and raced to free the hostages, Tewodros put the barrel of a pistol in his mouth and pulled the trigger.[31]

Britain had no interest in the conquest of Ethiopia. There was no ulterior motive, no secret plan to occupy Ethiopia. Britain's gripe was with Tewodros, not the Ethiopian people. After the rescue of the hostages, Napier packed up his things and left.[32]

When the British departed, they left behind two things—weapons and a blueprint for conquest. Kassa of Tigray, a local collaborator, had offered safe passage to Napier's forces and secure supply lines in the pursuit of Tewodros. The predations of Tewodros had created a population that was ready for a champion, and Kassa found that the role of champion suited his imperial ambitions. The departing British rewarded Kassa with a healthy stock of rifles and ammunition.[33] With Tewodros out of the way, the British gift of guns and ammo was enough to tip the ensuing succession battle in Kassa's favor.

But although the British were themselves not interested in Ethiopia, Napier's mission set an example for Egypt and Italy, who were. The British had shown how to take down an Ethiopian emperor by allying themselves with an internal rival. By using Kassa against Tewodros, the Napier mission drafted the blueprint for subsequent campaigns. One might add that the relative ease of the Napier rescue mission gave a quite false impression of the tenacity and fighting skills of Ethiopians, a misapprehension that would cost others dearly.

Egypt Moves against Ethiopia

Over the next three years, and thanks to his hefty arsenal, Kassa consolidated his power and dispatched his rivals. In January 1872, he assumed the imperial throne. He took the title of Yohannes IV when he received the crown in a coronation ceremony in the holy city of Axum.

While Ethiopia was distracted by the Napier mission and its aftermaths, Egypt pursued its vision of grandeur. Khedive Ismail imagined a modern Egypt that would recapture the glory of ancient Egypt through aggressive expansion into Sudan, Ethiopia, and the Somali coasts. Egyptian forces pushed south along the Red Sea coast, seizing Massawa in 1865. Ismail installed Werner Munzinger, a Swiss adventurer, voyager, and agent for hire, as governor of Massawa.[34]

Following Napier's lead, Ismail sought an internal Ethiopian ally who might challenge Yohannes. Menelik had already demonstrated a stubborn independence, withholding recognition of Yohannes and his claim to the title of emperor. And Menelik's location—at Yohannes's back as he faced the Egyptians in the north—would distract Yohannes as the Egyptians maneuvered against him.[35] Menelik would serve nicely as an ally to Egypt.

In 1875, the Egyptians occupied Harar, a major trading station and the end point of caravans coming up to Shoa from Djibouti. With Harar, Egypt had control of Menelik's main outlet to the sea. Very little left Shoa except by way of Harar, and very little entered. The Egyptians thus had considerable leverage over Menelik. At the same time they began to offer Menelik the firearms that would be useful in his ongoing quarrel with Yohannes, they consolidated control over a position that could choke off Menelik's access to the wider world.

Yohannes represented a significant obstacle to Egyptian ambitions, both because his power base was close at hand, in northern Ethiopia, and because Yohannes took seriously his role as defender of the Christian faith. Yohannes cast the Egyptian incursions both as territorial aggression and as the return of a conquering Islam. And, indeed, Egypt went after areas—Massawa, the Red Sea coast, Harar—where Islam had been durably established.

In 1875, Egypt organized a large force against Yohannes. It consisted of some fifteen thousand Egyptian soldiers commanded by veterans of the German wars of the 1860s (Danes, Germans, and Austrians) as well as veterans of the American Civil War.[36] The objective of this force was to bring about the downfall of Yohannes by threatening the area north of the Mareb River and west of the Red Sea—roughly speaking, the territory that would become Eritrea.[37]

At the same time, Werner Munzinger, Egypt's governor of Massawa, accompanied a shipment of firearms to Menelik. However, Munzinger's group

of four hundred never reached Menelik. On 7 November 1875, Munzinger and his party, including his Ethiopian wife and child, were annihilated by Afar, who preyed on trade to Shoa.[38] The very same day, the Egyptian force invading from the north was checked by Yohannes at Gundet.[39]

A few months later, Yohannes's advance guard, led by a bright and brave young commander named Alula, engaged the Egyptians at Gura. The Egyptians suffered a devastating defeat—a rout and a massacre—losing half their men in battle.[40] Defeat at Gura shattered Ismail's dream of an African empire for Egypt. Indeed, it set in motion events that would lead to his downfall three years later. It solidified Ethiopia's claim on what would become Eritrea.

Victory at Gura secured Alula's reputation as Ethiopia's fiercest defender.[41] Yohannes conferred upon Alula the lofty title of *ras* and installed Alula in the town of Asmara, in the highlands above Massawa, thus making the man and the town the hub of his defense against any future threats.[42]

Then Yohannes turned against his perceived enemies. Egypt's Muslim strategy made him wary of Ethiopia's Islamic minority. In 1880, he issued a proclamation in which he invited Ethiopian Muslims either to convert to Christianity or leave.[43] Then he moved against Menelik and forced him to pay homage. Yohannes sealed the deal by marrying his son to Menelik's daughter in 1882. This patched up relations, though the animosity never really subsided. Menelik never renounced his ambition to topple Yohannes and rule Ethiopia. Rather, Menelik pursued the imperial crown by other means. At about the time that Menelik was marrying off his daughter to the son of Yohannes, he began to court the woman who would serve as his most important political ally.

Ethiopia's Power Couple: Menelik and Taytu

Taytu Betul had a restless heart and an iron will. When Menelik courted Taytu, he was merely king of Shoa, but he articulated loftier ambitions. Menelik laid claim to the Ethiopian throne thanks to lineage reaching back to King Solomon and the queen of Sheba.[44] According to the *Kebre Negast*, a compendium of tradition and law, Ethiopia must be ruled by someone of such descent, so Menelik was both conforming to tradition and staking a claim, as had Tewodros and Yohannes before him.[45] As for Taytu, marriage to Menelik would fulfill a prophecy of royal destiny.[46]

The partnership between Menelik and Taytu was one of the great political unions of modern times. That Menelik and Taytu had a mutual
affection no one would deny—candid photos taken of their domestic life
years later show a level of comfort with each other that would be difficult
to fake. They made a point of eating meals together, and their interac-
tions were described as attentive and tender.[48] But as it was not the first
marriage for either of them, any romantic illusions had been tempered.
By the time Menelik met Taytu, the marriage with his first wife, the prin-
cess Altash, daughter of Emperor Tewodros, was over. It was a marriage
whose utility died with Tewodros. Menelik moved on to the courtesan
Bafena, a woman whose extraordinary beauty clouded Menelik's judgment, blinding him to her intrigues against him, until Taytu entered the
picture.[49] When Menelik and Taytu sealed their union on Easter Sunday
in 1883 it was a carefully considered act.

It was also a union of destinies. In Menelik, Taytu saw a vehicle for
her ambitions. In Taytu, Menelik saw wealth, political smarts, and connections in a part of the country he would have to win over if he was to
rule Ethiopia. If Menelik and Taytu were running for office in an American presidential election, it would be said that Taytu brought geographical balance to the ticket. The north had been the home of Ethiopia's most
recent emperors—both Tewodros and Yohannes had been from the
north—so there was a strong presumption in favor of northerners when
it came to imperial succession. Taytu was born in Semien, near Tigray,
a large, rich northern province; the family had contacts throughout the
north, including Tigray and Begemder.[50] Menelik was from the south,
so Taytu brought him a kind of local legitimacy.

In politics, Taytu's quick wit and acute political sense brought balance to Menelik's cautious and deliberate leadership. Although Taytu
was of Oromo—and thus Muslim—heritage, the family had converted in
the eighteenth century, confirming both the ideal of Christian Ethiopia
and the savvy opportunism of her family. Since then, the family had ac-
cumulated significant property.[51] Taytu gave Menelik a shrewd, wealthy,
energetic political partner with a power base in the north, confirming
Menelik as a leader with a claim to truly national credentials.

Taytu made the most of her position of power. Although she could
tolerate the company of Europeans and made sure to invite them to royal
events, her mistrust of Europeans was visceral. It was said that she could

not abide their odor.[52] At court, she anchored the anti-European faction. In policy discussions, she could always be counted on to define political choices in trenchant terms, framing the debate. Some credited her with choosing the site for Menelik's new capital, Addis Ababa. She took an active interest in the life of the capital, seeing it as an extension of her home and the most important theater for courtly performance and the display of political power. Under her watchful and benevolent eye, Addis became the venue for the dispensing of both justice and royal largesse.

She kept a close watch on Menelik's companions. Menelik was far from faithful, and while Taytu would tolerate his infidelities, she would not put up with rivals. Taytu was credited with the death by poison of one of his lovers; rumors circulated that it was not an isolated event. Her methods could be pitiless, but her anxiety was not unjustified. As one of her prominent critics observed, "The queen today may be only a woman tomorrow."[53]

Taytu's self-regard was legendary. It was remarked more than once that she composed her inner circle carefully, choosing women with darker complexions, the better to show off her own light coffee skin. Whether in Ankober, Entotto, or the new capital, Addis Ababa, Taytu was rarely seen without her full entourage. Taytu went about the city astride her mule with the royal red umbrella that both shielded her from the sun and announced her royal presence. As she moved about the city, custom demanded gestures of obeisance. These were sometimes offered perfunctorily or nullified by muttered insults—"hyena" and worse.[54] In time, her vanity became a political liability. As her public gestures of Christian devotion crossed the line from exemplary to ostentatious her motives became suspect, as if piety had become simply another vehicle for self-promotion.

Such criticism was to be expected of a woman who exercised power confidently. In the end, even her critics accorded her respect, however reluctantly. Nicola D'Amato didn't like Taytu, but he couldn't help admiring her. And he acknowledged that her unfavorable image owed something to "her political perspicacity" and her "rare, quick wit."[55] But animosity toward Taytu wasn't simply a reflection of the grudging respect accorded a powerful woman. Taytu was anything but a pleaser; she seems genuinely not to have cared whether she was liked. In the end, her understanding of power owed something to Machiavelli—it was said that while the gentle Menelik was loved, Taytu was feared.

CHAPTER 2

Listing toward Adwa

Il Giardino d'Italia was packed. Most of the soldiers had been in Naples only a few hours, having arrived over the course of the day from barracks across Italy. There was plenty of camaraderie, some genuine, some driven by drink and the need for companionship in the face of the unknown.

Naples was Italy's largest city, and it thrived on trade and shipping. It was a grand public occasion in Naples when soldiers shipped out. After arriving at the train station, soldiers made their way to the barracks at Granili, just south of the docks. Naples is a city that lives outdoors; by night, the glow of Bengal lights beckoned. The men packed the bars and cafés of Naples, spreading conviviality and cash. They were intent on a grand goodbye—the *bicchierata di congedo*. The *bicchierata,* a close relative of the pub crawl, was an unofficial military tradition. At the Giardino d'Italia, namesake of the nearby gardens of the Palazzo Reale, a final round of toasts marked the end of the evening.[1]

The next morning at Granili, the men dressed for their departure. Gherardo Pantano remembered being overcome by a feeling of serene contentment as he stood before the mirror and inspected the gold braid on his jacket sleeves. The look was right, he recalled, but the feeling was wrong, given the uncertainties ahead. In the end he chalked up his

serenity to his appetite for adventure and to his admittedly vast ignorance of Africa.[2]

Enlisted men marched to the dock looking sharp in white button-down
tunics, white pants, boots, and tan spats; they sported diagonal sashes
across the chest. From balconies there were shouted goodbyes and flut-
tering handkerchiefs. An army band played as families followed their
men—fathers, sons, brothers—to the grand waterfront promenade. Like
the other officers, Lieutenant Pantano surveyed the scene as men adjusted
helmets decorated with ribbons, braids, and jaunty feathers, white or
black according to regimental tradition.

It was a fine fall day, and Pantano was in good company. Umberto
Partini, a mate from school days in Modena, would share Pantano's cabin
on the journey. Neither had seen Africa, and they were full of questions
when they joined the conversation of a group of veterans of earlier campaigns. These included Lieutenant Borra, who wore a medal for valor
earned in the splendid victory against the Dervishes at Agordat, and Lieutenant Caruso, a veteran artillery officer who was fluent in Arabic. Also
with them was Luigi Mercatelli, a seasoned African correspondent with
the pro-Africanist newspaper *Tribuna;* Mercatelli had the distinction of
being one of the first embedded journalists of the modern media age.[3]

Pantano shipped out on the *Po,* a three-masted steamer, in mid-
September 1894. When Italy shipped soldiers to Africa, it often relied on
common carriers for troop transport; Pantano's vessel, the *Po,* was no
different. Pantano and his men would make their voyage in the company of
other paying passengers—performers, soldiers, salesmen—pursuing their
dreams by way of Africa. A traveling circus show featuring the Guillaume
sisters, a famous equestrian act, followed Pantano up the gangplank, adding a hint of the carnivalesque. The Guillaumes headlined a troupe that
would open in Alexandria, then push on to other venues, playing wher-
ever talent and fortune would take them. They represented the vanguard
of European circus/cabaret entertainment. They would reach out to audiences along the Red Sea, all the while trolling for novelty acts to add to
their show before returning—just back from the Orient!—for a triumphant
European tour.

Cranes hoisted mail sacks, costume wardrobes, ammunition crates,
and caged exotic animals. As they waited for the *Po* to push off, Pantano
and Partini shared deck space in the sun with the Guillaume sisters and

their entourage, including magicians, gymnasts, knife throwers, tight-rope walkers, and jugglers. Bears and monkeys sulked in cages nearby. Pantano stared in pity while the slouching bears—trapped in boredom—chewed neurotically at their bellies.

The *Po* was a stand-in for Italy itself, a vessel auspiciously named for the country's mightiest river. In conversation among officers on board, one heard the dialect of bourgeois Milan—*il dialetto meneghino.* Among rank-and-file soldiers and NCOs, the chatter was Sicilian, the vulgar tongue of the *lazzaroni.*[4] After she pushed free from the dock, the *Po* made for the gap between Sorrento and Capri, spewing smoke and soot. The great ancient port city anchored a fine panorama; the glories of the bay embraced them. The gleaming fishing villages of Procida and Ischia were to starboard. Sullen Vesuvius was to port.

As the fat, crenellated turrets of Naples's Castel Nuovo faded astern, Pantano began to notice what a rusting heap, "an old carcass," the *Po* truly was. Stair treads groaned. Red-orange stains streamed from decaying fixtures and casings. At the rails, flecks of paint peeled to the touch and fluttered to the sea. The *Po* turned south, then headed toward the Straits of Messina. Pantano noticed that he was leaning. He closed one eye and tried to align the line of the stern with the horizon. The journey was under way, but the *Po* would list visibly to starboard all the way to Africa.

The trauma of leaving can create vivid memories; while Pantano remembered warm sun and camaraderie, other soldiers begged to differ. Naples is an ancient city, and in the nineteenth century it was frequently prey to cholera, a disease as symbolically rich as it was deadly. Naples's gay spirit sometimes evoked revulsion, notably among officers from the north, who easily saw in Naples everything that was wrong with the Mezzogiorno—frivolity, indolence, and moral lassitude. A decade before Conrad's Marlow imagined his gleaming city as a "whited sepulcher," Naples conjured "vanity, filth, and immorality." When Major Marcello Prestinari made his departure from Naples in 1894 in the company of an operatic troupe, he complained that the entertainers made the crossing a display of vulgar dissipation.[5] Vico Mantegazza, who had made the voyage years before, in the 1880s, remembered leaving Naples on an inauspicious day—the Day of the Dead.[6]

Others enjoyed departures closer to the clichéd image of Italy, good-byes performed to the sound track of an accordion playing the tarantella.

The *Minghetti* departs from Naples. From *L'Illustrazione italiana,* 2 February 1896.

Luigi Goj was with his regiment in Milan when he heard he would be shipping out. He ran home to say goodbye to his family, then hopped on a bicycle and rode around Milan telling friends and acquaintances that he was on his way to Africa. He cut quite a figure on his bike—a modern novelty—racing around Milan in his military pants, jacket, and bright fez. At six in the evening he rendezvoused with his battalion at Santa Prassede. By the time they marched to Milan's central station, a crowd had already assembled in the piazza in front.[7]

"Ciao, mamma," he remembered calling from the train to his parents on the platform. His father's eyes were damp with tears. A brass band struck up a march as the train lurched. Looking back from the outskirts of the city, Goj saw the lights of Milan dim in the January night. After a night on the train and a night sleeping on straw in the barracks of Naples, he was on his way to Eritrea.

The passage to Massawa took about twelve days—plenty of time for talk. Soldiers gathered on deck, under canopies set up to shield voyagers from squalls and sun.[8] Pantano turned to his fellow soldiers for conversation, peppering the veterans with questions about Italy's Red Sea colony of Eritrea. One by one his misconceptions about Africa—a land of deserts, jungles, unrelenting heat, and dangerous wild animals—collapsed. Pantano learned "with great wonderment" that there are no deserts in Eritrea, nor leafy jungles, that meeting ferocious wild animals was quite uncommon, that the highlands had a springlike climate. "Thus crumbled," he recalled, "our vast erudition acquired from the newspapers."[9]

The passage was also a crash course in power and the global economy. In the waters off Port Said, at the Mediterranean opening to the Suez Canal, Pantano noted that ninety-five out of a hundred vessels were flying the Union Jack. And it wasn't just British commercial seapower on display. As vessels dropped anchor at Port Said, a transitory floating market took shape. Small craft bobbed and darted like pilot fish among the ships, hawking wares. Everything was for sale. Soldiers lowered baskets with cash and hauled up fruit, fish, bread, rum, cognac, and cigarettes.[10]

Once through the Suez Canal and into the Red Sea, the mood on board became more somber, a function of boredom and damp heat. Flying fish provided occasional comic relief. From time to time, one of the mules on board might succumb; the carcass would be hoisted to the gunwale and pitched into the sea. The night brought no relief. The heat remained so oppressive that the soldiers slept in the nude.[11]

Luigi Goj's first glimpse of Massawa was by night. Along with many other soldiers, he found a place near the prow and watched the lights of the city come into view, defining the port. Reflected illumination lent Massawa a mysterious, dreamlike quality. "We imagined ourselves in an enchanted land," he recalled, admitting the role that excited imaginations played. The dazzling glow of the lighthouse struck him as a "splendid magic lantern." But fantasyland would have to wait. The first to disembark were the heat-stressed mules, quickly offloaded by cranes.[12]

Massawa: Capital of Empire?

Proximity to the water is everything in Massawa, where heat and humidity suffocate and winter is the best season. Meanwhile, the city's architecture took on an archeological aspect; its buildings—durable markers of fleeting power—bore witness to the layers of a city's past. The oldest and wealthiest residences were nearly a mile offshore, on islands connected to the mainland by a causeway. Along with the peninsulas of Gehrar and Abd-el-Kader, these islands provided a protective embrace for ships making port. Old commercial families lived in large white houses whose *mashrabiya* and latticed windows shielded families from prying eyes but allowed cooling breezes off the Red Sea to push through. Empires would come and go, but the old Arab, Indian, and Turkish families that had settled in Massawa generations earlier provided the only truly lasting power, an informal dynasty of commerce.

The island of Tawlud was where Werner Munzinger, the Swiss who governed Massawa on behalf of the khedive of Egypt, had built the Governor's Palace in the 1870s. When the Egyptian bid for empire collapsed, the Italians moved in.[13] Italy's occupation in 1885 required fewer than a thousand men, and the Governor's Palace was easily the most important symbolic prize.[14] This magnificent structure was known locally as the Serraglio Palace—a term that evoked Istanbul, the intimacies of the harem, and the intrigues of Ottoman rule. As befit a political residence, it was the most imposing structure in town. All gleaming white, in Oriental style, the Serraglio's two stories of arcaded Moorish arches faced the sea. A monumental pair of staircases—worthy of Florence or Fontainebleau—ascended to the second floor, where a single arch, half again as large as the arches of the arcade, signaled the ceremonial entrance. Two red signal lights beamed from the roof, creating an effect that was "both solemn and fantastic."[15]

Next door was the Officers' Club, the social hub of the Italian colonial enterprise.[16] It was a single-story structure, also in white, with ornamental flourishes. The location of the Officers' Club facilitated official receptions at the Governor's Palace next door. Men gathered at the club in their officer's whites, boasting and teasing over cool drinks, thanks to block ice delivered aboard ships from Scandinavia.[17] From the club, they ascended a set of stairs to the large, deep veranda that faced the sea from the second story of the Serraglio. There, on grand occasions, the broad *terrazza* could accommodate dozens as moonlight scattered on the Red Sea and a waltz played. Rosalia Pianavia, a colonel's wife, remembered the glittering evenings when as many as 150 guests would gather to mix, dance, and gaze out to sea.[18]

Although the red-beaconed Serraglio seemed to beckon from the water, enlisted men and NCOs would rarely see it up close. The lowly ranks were housed in barracks on the peninsulas of Gehrar and Abd-el-Kader, where soldiers might rest a few days before pushing on to the cooler high plains.[19] As enlisted men were shuttled to shore in launches, they came face-to-face with the astonishing diversity of the port cities of the Middle East. "Italians, French, Greeks, Indians, Egyptians, Sudanese, Arabs, Nubians, Syrians, Armenians, English, Germans . . . a crowd as multicolored in its skin as its clothing," noted Cesare Pini.[20]

The first real contact came from dockside peddlers—blacks, Indians, and *moretti*—whose opening gambit consisted of a hearty "Salam!" or an ingratiating "Viva Italia!" while offering dates, cigars, knickknacks, and caramel treats.[21] They competed for space with dogs, water porters, and mules bearing wealthy women across town.[22]

Orientation to life in Africa was cursory. Officers warned soldiers not to bathe in the sea, lest they contract a skin disease or, worse, attract sharks.[23] For some soldiers, their acquaintance with Massawa never got beyond the waterfront, where Greek-owned cafés dominated, serving smoky white *mastika* over ice.[24] Those with a bit more time—or a veteran of Massawa as guide—probed deeper.

On the Town

For enlisted men and NCOs, two cafés served as headquarters of social activity in Massawa in the late 1880s. Though they certainly bore Egyptian names at one time, following the arrival of the Italians in 1885 they reinvented themselves as the Caffè Montebello and the Caffè Garibaldi—good Italian names, though the premises were owned and operated by Greeks. Even after the consolidation of Italian rule, the Greek café owners retained a prudent polynational, even cosmopolitan outlook. They studiously avoided decor or behavior that would offend any national sensibilities; they took care to embellish their café walls with portraits of all the European heads of state. As in other port cities, such as Suez or Port Said, café musicians were instructed to play patriotic hymns or folk tunes drawn from the national musical traditions—Italian, French, British, Russian—of clients as they arrived, fending off any idea that they served only a particular national clientele.[25] Just the same, Italian soon rivaled Arabic as the lingua franca of commercial life in Massawa.

By chance, the most important merchant in Massawa was an Italian national. Alessandro Seror was born to Jewish parents in the port city of Livorno but emigrated to Egypt in search of his fortune. In Cairo, he Ottomanized his name as "Skender" in a nod to local sensibilities. Eventually he landed in Massawa, where he built a reputation for fairness among Red Sea pearl divers. Soon he was the preferred go-between for buyers and sellers—Skender Seror, the pearl merchant of Massawa.

Colonial powers come and go, but by all accounts Seror was the unofficial mayor of Massawa—the "dean," as he was known. It was a status he earned long before the Italians arrived; he liked to joke that the Italian occupation of Massawa meant that he had gone home without leaving. In a place where many men went about naked from the waist, Seror scrupulously conformed to business attire, including pants and jacket, summer or winter. As he strolled about town, he sometimes carried his latest acquisitions with him—rolling pearls in his mouth, as if to finish the work begun by nature.[26]

Seror knew that the Italian presence was good for business in Massawa. Although the initial Italian toehold consisted of a triangular patch of territory around Massawa of less than four square miles, Italian construction betrayed larger ambitions. In short order the Italians had rebuilt the harbor, constructing new quays to serve vessels of deep draft—up to thirty-five feet. The stone facing on the quays—worthy of Civitavecchia or Piombino—suggested a long-term investment. A hospital followed, as did an arsenal and ice machines.[27] A rail station was built, serving a line that climbed into the highlands.[28]

As the economy of Massawa boomed, vendors and retail merchants warmed to the European presence. Like the gold rush merchants of California and the Klondike, in Eritrea it was the provisioners who prospered. Massawa was entirely without trees or shrubs, and by day its public spaces were inhospitable, so cafés, barber shops, and taverns also traded in shade. Little moved at the peak of the day, and little was heard beyond the call to prayer from Massawa's mosques. Families retreated indoors or to covered and latticed rooftops. In the morning and late afternoon, the streets bustled. Most women went about with faces covered, distinguishing themselves instead by bracelets and anklets of silver and necklaces of colored glass.[29]

Soldiers who ventured forth from their simple wood-plank barracks to the main settlement entered a warren of narrow streets among two- and three-story coral stone buildings. Sergeant Darli had been in Massawa for two months, working in the commissariat. That was enough to make him an old hand and an esteemed guide to the pleasures of Massawa. "Nobody knows it better!" he boasted.[30]

First stop—food. "A bite to eat and then a tour!"

The restaurant looked more like a barracks than an establishment catering to a European clientele. Alla Trattoria Napoletana barely recalled its namesake. Its walls were part stone and part wood, with woven reeds for wall covering. It featured decent pasta but bad fish served with Sicilian wine that was hardy but also heady in the heat. A fan system moved the air: a boy pulled a string that wagged a piece of cardboard hinged to the ceiling.[31]

Any tour of the city would have to include the two main piazzas—renamed Baratieri and Senafe by the Italians after victories in 1895. There, iron tracery dressed up the façades of the main buildings and the arcaded covered walkways.[32] The Indian Quarter featured low-ceilinged shops of stone and mortar with stoop entrances where Greeks, Arabs, and Indians produced jewelry and knickknacks—mostly rings and bracelets for the local market of Arabs and "Abyssinians." Wisps of smoke drifted from the tiny forges used in the shaping of metal. Only garlic and pepper could compete with the smoke, giving the quarter its olfactory signature.[33]

At the market square near the new Caffè Orientale a crowd of street vendors, mostly Indians, sold mats, blankets, and bundles of ostrich-quill pens; nearby, black Africans sold cigars, clumps of garlic, dates, and lemon water. The air swirled a delirious mix of odors—fruit, spice, dung. At the Arab bazaar a bit farther on, there were stalls of a more permanent sort—stitched-together hides were draped over tall wooden frames to provide shade and, incidentally, a kind of rustic, frontier ambience. In the middle of the square a woodworker stood by his wooden bed frames, which were lashed together and ready to go. Locals in loose garments chatted; uniformed soldiers strolled, mostly deaf to pitches from carpet merchants and spice vendors.[34]

The entertainment grew more elaborate at the Caffè Garibaldi, where black performers—a man and a woman—sang a set of Italian melodies with lyrics adapted to the circumstances. "L'Italia resta in Afreca!" went one dialect-inflected tune, "Italy will remain in Africa!"[35]

The optimistic lyrics matched the upbeat melody, but it was the female vocalist's uncanny mastery of Neapolitan vernacular that seduced the crowd. Her stage name, Italì, showed that she understood her audience and the arts of self-promotion. Night after night she delivered a mix of easy feelings, slipping from patriotism to nostalgia. Pretty, graceful, spirited—she was the African version of the *napoletana,* the swarthy, indomitable maid of Naples. If the idealized future could dance and sing, it would be her— African and Italian, exotic but approachable, spirited and aloof but alluring and attainable. No wonder that she was courted by officers and bourgeois, whom she played like fools.

If the men could afford it, the evening might end at Donna Carmela's. There a system of credit for known customers created a cordial air of abundant possibility and privileged ease, where money never seemed to intrude. Musical performances and gaming rooms offered ostensible entertainment—a pretext—in a private setting designed to stimulate the senses. Wispy, draped fabrics—abetted by sea breezes that pushed against the lingering heat of the day—suggested spirits easily roused from languor, while a rainbow of ready companions—white, Turkish, black, Egyptian, Ethiopian—offered distraction and easy conversation.

Rank-and-file soldiers might seek more casual entertainment strolling the quays. The sound of male chatter drew women from the shadows. "Salam, salam!" they greeted. "Salam a voi!" answered the men. The women bared their breasts. A few of the men approached appraisingly, made their selection, then disappeared into the darkness. Others begged off, claiming—out of modesty, preference, or mock refinement— to be repelled by the odor of camel fat.[36]

When soldiers tired of the café and bar, they might be ready for community theater, drawing on dramatic talent among the soldiers. They commandeered the Officers' Club as a performance venue and drafted the military band as a pit orchestra. Lieutenant Bignami was an accomplished gymnast and a reliable opening act.[37] He tumbled and performed pratfalls dressed in a clown suit. A group of officers calling themselves the Philo-

dramatists put on the main event. Melodramas, sketch comedies, and caba-
ret acts featured stock characters—the dandy, the professor, the nun, the
fool, the sweet maiden, the scalawag, the hero, the bishop.[38] Drag performances of female roles heightened the stakes for the players and tested their
range.

Pearl of the Red Sea or the gates of hell? Massawa lacked a chamber of
commerce, which surely would have expressed a preference. In time,
Massawa lived up to both.

CHAPTER 3

Italy in Africa

S OMETIMES HISTORY lies not in archives or libraries but beneath our feet. Tourists exiting the central train station in Rome spill out onto the Piazza dei Cinquecento, the Plaza of the Five Hundred. Travelers, distracted by taxis and touts, are unlikely to give the name much thought; those who do assume that it is yet another prideful nod to Italy's place in the Renaissance, the 1500s, in abbreviated form the Cinquecento. Auto enthusiasts could be forgiven if they guessed that it referred to the Fiat Cinquecento, an economy car that signaled the postwar automotive renaissance of Fiat.

But the correct answer has nothing to do with cars or the Renaissance. The five hundred in question are soldiers who died in the first great military disaster of Italy's African adventure. They fell in combat at a place called Dogali.

The road to Dogali was prepared by a decaying Ottoman Empire. Empire abhors a vacuum. The largely coastal territory west of the Red Sea, between Djibouti and Sudan, came under Turkish imperial rule following the conquests of Suleiman I in the sixteenth century. Ottoman rule endured for nearly three hundred years.

The appointment of Ismail Pasha as khedive (viceroy) of Egypt in 1867 opened a critical phase in the history of Egypt. Ismail modeled his vision of Egypt on the European powers of his day. He rebuilt Cairo on the model of Paris under Louis-Napoléon. He endowed it with a great opera house and commissioned Giuseppe Verdi to create a new opera—*Aïda*—to debut there.

Meanwhile, the opening of the Suez Canal in 1869 had dramatically changed the significance of the Red Sea coast.[1] It also inspired Ismail to undertake a program of imperial expansion at the expense of Egypt's African neighbors to the south, Sudan and Ethiopia. The Nile originates in Ethiopia and flows through Sudan before reaching Egypt. Ismail's moves would consolidate Egypt's control of the Nile and the great Red Sea waterway that now, thanks to Suez, linked Europe with Asia. Egypt would become the dominant regional power. Egypt moved into Sudan, establishing a presence at Darfur in 1874. In Ethiopia, Egypt occupied the trade hub of Harar in 1875 before being stopped by Ethiopian forces at Gura in 1876 and Sahati in 1883.[2]

The khedive's vision of a European-style Egypt—complete with colonies, a modern capital, and a grand opera house—exceeded his resources. By 1878, European creditors, anxious for their investments, forced the khedive to appoint Europeans to key positions in his government. Ismail Pasha's authority faded.

The rapid decline of Egypt in the 1870s and 1880s created an opening not only along the Red Sea coast but also in the interior, especially in Sudan, where it coincided with the rise of a millenarian Islamist movement known as Mahdism. Muhammad Ahmad, hailed as the Mahdi—the promised one who would wage war against the enemies of Islam—had successfully mobilized Muslim resentment of Western rule. In this case, Western rule was represented by British administrators in Egyptian Sudan. The Mahdi's preaching, along with his demonstrable piety and zeal, served to rally numerous believers who, in 1881, followed the Mahdi's lead and moved against Anglo-Egyptian garrisons and positions. The British colonel William Hicks was given command of an Egyptian force and sent against the Mahdists. Hicks and his men were destroyed in November 1883, as was a force sent to rescue Khartoum under General Charles Gordon.[3] With a rapidity that suggested divine favor, the Mahdi and his followers found themselves in control of western Sudan.[4]

Britain needed friends. In 1883 Britain sent Admiral Sir William Hewett to Ethiopia. Hewett's mission was to recruit Ethiopia—situated on the

Mahdists' eastern flank as they pushed northward—as a check on the forces of the Mahdi. Hewett met with Ethiopian emperor Yohannes at Adwa, a commercial crossroads town and political capital in the Ethiopian north.[5] Hewett found Yohannes open to persuasion.

Yohannes's motives were complex. He was a sincere and devout Christian and feared Mahdist influence in Ethiopia; in 1880 Yohannes had issued a proclamation that invited Ethiopian Muslims to either convert to Christianity or leave. He was also worried about his northern frontier with Egypt and Sudan.[6] And he was concerned about a northern outlet to the sea at Massawa, not only for the export of Ethiopian goods but also for the import of firearms.

Alexander Macomb Mason was an American Civil War veteran who had refashioned himself as an Egyptian civil servant.[7] Mason was a mere twenty-five years old in 1865, but he felt unprepared to return to civilian life in the United States. He decided to look abroad and offered his services to Egypt as a consultant, an expert in strategic and military matters. As an employee of Egypt in the 1870s, Mason helped train Egyptian troops. He also traveled hundreds of miles in Egypt and Sudan, surveying and drilling in search of water. By the 1880s, he had tired of field work. He settled into a desk job as bey (resident representative) at Massawa.

Massawa was a hub in a trading network for ivory, gold, pearls, slaves, ostrich feathers, and civet.[8] Caravan trade reached not only the Ethiopian highlands but across Sudan toward western Africa. Via boat, goods crossed the Red Sea to India, Arabia, and the Middle East. Massawa was critically important to Ethiopian trade and, in fact, was claimed by Ethiopia. At one point Yohannes tried bluff and bluster to make good on his claim to Massawa ("I must send down my troops!"), but Mason responded with mockery.[9] Massawa was a trade hub that belonged to Ethiopia no more than it belonged to any of the countries whose markets it served.[10] Ethiopia could have access to Massawa and its markets, but it would not own it.

Mason joined Yohannes and Hewett in signing the Hewett Treaty at Adwa in June of 1884. By the terms of the Hewett Treaty, Yohannes would apply military pressure on the Mahdists with an aim "to facilitate the withdrawal of the troops of His Highness the Khedive" from imperiled positions held by British and Egyptian forces. The British, in turn, recognized Ethiopia's territorial claim to Bogos, on its northern periphery. Crucially, Mason and the English guaranteed "free transit . . . to and

Yohannes IV. From Lincoln de Castro, *Nella terra dei negus, pagine raccolte in Abissinia*. Milan: Fratelli Treves, 1915.

from Abyssinia for all goods" through the Red Sea port of Massawa, then under Anglo-Egyptian control.[11]

Almost immediately there were misunderstandings. In late July, the merchant ship *Corsica* unloaded fifty crates of firearms—destined for Yohannes—at Massawa. Customs clearance was denied. The ink on the Hewett Treaty was barely dry, yet some eight hundred rifles remained sealed in their shipping crates at Massawa. Alula, Yohannes's lieutenant, protested via letter to Mason. Three months later, in October 1883, Yohannes was still writing angry letters, protesting the violation of the treaty, "I am keeping the treaty. I have not broken it. [It] is a disgrace to break a treaty." He promised to send troops against the Mahdi to fulfill his treaty obligations, but the promise contained a veiled threat that his troops just might march all the way to Massawa.[12]

Egypt Wavers; Italy Moves In

The corvette *Garibaldi* shuddered to a halt along the dock at Massawa. As the sun set on the fifth of February 1885, the *Garibaldi* and a companion vessel, the *Amedeo,* disgorged an Italian force of eight hundred men. As the Egyptians had never evacuated Massawa, the city remained at least nominally under Egyptian authority. That evening, the Italian flag went up alongside the Egyptian flag at the Governor's Palace.[13] The display announced a period of transition from Egyptian to Italian rule.[14] A proclamation to the people of Massawa promised peace and good order from an Italian government that claimed the friendship "of England, of Turkey and Egypt, no less than that of Abyssinia."[15]

Italy was inspired by Napier's mission against Tewodros in the 1860s, but also by King Leopold of Belgium, who since the late 1870s had been establishing a personal colonial empire in the Congo.[16] For King Umberto of Italy, the example of Leopold was apt, for it showed that even small nations can accomplish great things.[17] Of course, it was a precedent not lost on the Ethiopians, who were eager to avoid the fate of the Congo. Leopoldo Traversi set up a "scientific station" at Let-Marefia in Shoa on behalf of the Italian geographic society.[18] Two scientific missions in the Stanley mold, one led by Giuseppe Giulietti in 1881 and another led by Gustavo Bianchi in 1883, had ended in disaster: both parties were massacred on the climb to the Ethiopian highlands from the coast.[19]

Although the massacres were not carried out on Ethiopian soil, they occurred on routes normally accorded protection by authority of the Ethiopian emperor. These massacres had an emphatic intent, namely, to discourage such exploratory voyages, which inevitably led to larger and more permanent incursions. They set the price for European encroachment at a level that was despairingly, unacceptably high.

In the Italian case, they failed to have a deterrent effect. The massacres of the Giulietti expedition in 1881 and the Bianchi mission in 1883 served as pretexts. The security of Italian persons and Italian interests—a security the Ethiopians were manifestly unwilling to provide—became the justification for Italian occupation. It also established a pattern whereby each setback (there would be others) provided an occasion to move balky Italian political leadership along toward a deeper engagement. In telegraphed correspondence with Italian ambassadorial representatives in Constantinople in January 1885, Pasquale Stanislao Mancini, the Italian minister of foreign affairs, emphasized security concerns.

"The massacre of the Bianchi expedition," he wrote, "added to that of the Giulietti expedition, has obliged us to strengthen our authority and affirm our prestige by sending a garrison."[20] In the following days, the Italians prepared the transition from Egyptian rule to Italian rule at Massawa.

Pushing into the Highlands

Yohannes was livid. The Hewett Treaty, negotiated only months earlier, allowed free transit of goods, including arms, through Massawa. In the eyes of Yohannes, it was an arrangement that implicitly recognized Ethiopia's historical claim to Massawa. At the time of the treaty, Ethiopia allowed Massawa to remain in Egyptian hands, with the understanding that if Egypt departed, the port would revert to Ethiopian rule.[21]

However, well-placed British agents believed that Ethiopia simply couldn't be trusted with a Red Sea port of such strategic significance as Massawa.[22] In fact, following the completion of the Suez Canal in 1869, *any* major port on the Red Sea became a matter of preoccupation. During the Scramble for Africa, unoccupied territory generated anxiety that it would be occupied by a rival; in this case, an unattended Massawa might be added to Djibouti as part of France's Red Sea presence.

The possibility of Egyptian withdrawal from Massawa created an opening for Italy. If the Egyptians were incapable, the Ottomans unwilling, the Ethiopians untrustworthy, perhaps the Italians could serve.[23] While the Italians were not exactly British proxies, they were happily tolerated as placekeepers. If the Italians occupied Massawa, the French could not.[24]

Augustus Wylde, who had represented Britain in the Red Sea region, called British conduct toward Ethiopia and Yohannes a vile "bit of treachery." "England," he confessed, "made use of [Yohannes] as long as he was of any service, and then threw him over to the tender mercies of Italy."[25] Yohannes was displeased when Italy occupied Massawa, but he was a realist. He was not ready to move against Massawa, let alone occupy it. In discussions with an Italian representative, Yohannes stipulated that he would tolerate the Italian occupation of Massawa, provided that the Italian presence went no further.[26]

It was an idle promise. Italy's presence in 1885 was barely a toehold—the Italians controlled less than four square miles—a fifth of the area of Manhattan. In late 1886 and early 1887, the Italians pushed toward the Ethiopian highlands, creating a fortified position at Sahati. In response, Yohannes's intrepid commander Alula led repeated attacks on Sahati on 25 January. It was a classic colonial confrontation—lightly armed Africans attacking entrenched colonial defenders. The results were predictable. Hundreds of Alula's soldiers were maimed and killed by artillery fire; Italian casualties were virtually nil.

Fortunes changed abruptly. The following morning, Colonel Tommaso de Cristoforis led a column of 540 Italians and fifty native soldiers to reinforce Sahati. Alula was anxious to avoid a repeat of the tragedy of the previous day, so when he learned that Italian reinforcements were on their way, he resolved to intercept them before they could reach the safety of the fortifications at Sahati.

Alula chose his terrain well. About two-thirds of the way from Massawa to Sahati, the route, which follows a dry creek bed, passes between undulating hills. The hillsides are dotted with shrubs, providing a natural camouflage. Alula ordered some of his men to take cover on either side of the Italian route, concealing the remainder of his five thousand among the natural features of the hills.

When the leading edge of the Italian column came within range, Alula's men rained down a devastating convergent fire from the hillsides. Italian infantry saw little more than puffs of smoke. At the rear of the column De Cristoforis heard the gunfire, but he did not halt his men until, a few hundred feet further on, he realized that he was facing a much larger force. By then, withdrawal was not an option.

The young Alula. From Lincoln de Castro, *Nella terra dei negus, pagine raccolte in Abissinia.* Milan: Fratelli Treves, 1915.

The Legend of Dogali. From *La Tribuna Illustrata,* 26 January 1895.

De Cristoforis and his forces sought the advantage of a nearby hill, which gave them a commanding view, but the summit was too small for them to deploy fully. They formed a compact target and soon found themselves encircled. With the Italians outnumbered ten to one, the outcome was never in doubt. According to Alula's chronicler, for Alula and his men the eager rush of combat was "like a bridegroom going to the wedding." As the Italians fell wounded, Alula's forces closed with rifle, sword, and spear. All but eighty of the Italians died.[27]

Alula's soldiers begged him to follow up his success at Dogali with a march on Massawa. Alula hesitated, then decided to withdraw.

In Italy, shock was followed by speeches, prayer vigils, and memorial masses. There was myth building, too, centered around an unconfirmed report that the final victims at Dogali had abruptly stopped fighting and stood at attention, presenting arms in final salute to the fallen, whom they soon joined. Reconstructions of this patriotic tableau appeared in engravings, in cheap prints, and cut into sapphire jewelry.[28]

Improbably, Dogali was compared to Thermopylae, where King Leonidas and three hundred Spartans died in combat against an invading Persian force. Colonel De Cristoforis, the Italian commanding officer, was the new Leonidas.[29] It seems not to have occurred to anyone that Alula and his men were the defenders and that the five hundred Italians more closely fit the Persian role of invaders.

In Rome, there were calls for a monument in the Italian capital to honor the five hundred dead—the *cinquecento*.[30] The piazza in front of the train station was chosen for the memorial site and renamed in their honor. The architect of the Dogali monument rescued an Egyptian obelisk unearthed near the station and made it the focus of his monument.[31] The obelisk was an inspired choice. It had been hauled back in triumph to the imperial Rome of antiquity. On the Dogali monument it suggested continuity between old Rome and a new Rome being born. The obelisk sat on a plinth on which the names of the five hundred were inscribed. The dedication of the monument at the Piazza dei Cinquecento took place on 5 June.[32] It became the site of annual ceremonies of remembrance, which also served to stoke the fires of imperial ambition.

Italy sought to use the massacre at Dogali as a means to press expansionist claims. If nothing else, the five hundred dead could be traded for territorial compensation. Yohannes was in no mood to be generous. Dogali had hurt his standing among Europeans, who saw it as ungentlemanly—an African Little Big Horn. Yohannes had virtually no leverage on European public opinion, and now he was being cast in the role of savage and ruthless predator. He protested by letter to Queen Victoria that Dogali never would have happened if the Hewett Treaty had been respected. "[A] man came from the Italians as a friend," he wrote, "writing affectionate letters, and [bearing] some presents, to spy out my own country, but when he came where the Egyptians had been, he said, 'We shall occupy this.' Then I said, 'What have you to do with my own country?' "[33] Yohannes had done what any patriot would have done.

Yohannes backed Alula, who after Dogali was subject to sharp criticism: although Alula had more soldiers than the Italians, Alula had ambushed them, surrounded them, massacred them. Yohannes refused to make an example of Alula. As Yohannes explained to Victoria, Alula had done no wrong. "They came by force and made in two places forts. . . . Ras Alula went down to inquire, 'What business have you to do with other people's country?' "[34] It could hardly be stated more clearly: Dogali was a legitimate response to a blatant act of trespass. It was an act of defense.

Still, Italy pressed for compensation. Sir John Savile, writing to London from Rome, offered a brutally honest appraisal of the Italian position. If negotiations for compensation broke down, Italy threatened to send an army of more than twenty thousand in pursuit of Alula but, Savile wondered, to what end? "Ras Alula," Savile noted, "is not likely to await quietly the lesson the Italians wish to give him; they may be compelled to follow him into the interior, where it will be easy to prepare against them surprises like that of Dogali." And even if they managed to punish Alula, what would Italy have accomplished?

Savile noted that Italy was also using the promise of trade with Ethiopia to cover a policy of expansion. Italy, Savile noted skeptically, "spoke of opening [an expanded] Italian frontier to Abyssinian produce; but what does Abyssinia produce? A few hundred kilogrammes of coffee exchanged for a few bales of calico will certainly not enrich [Italy]." The only way to make money was by selling arms to Ethiopia, a trade Italy was unlikely to encourage. Moreover, Savile rightly noted that Italian public opinion was hardly keen on the idea of Italian expansion into

Africa. With tepid public support, dim commercial prospects, and daunting military challenges, what was the point?[35]

Britain dispatched Gerald Portal, from Her Majesty's legation at Cairo, to patch things up.[36] Britain wanted to keep expectations modest; a memo candidly described Portal as "of no very high rank." Portal was perfectly calibrated to his task. This Eton-educated gentleman had joined the diplomatic corps at twenty-one and was posted to Egypt three years later. He was still in his twenties when he was sent to Ethiopia.[37] Not only was it his first mission of consequence, it was the very first he would lead.

Portal was tall, fair, and well groomed. His full, waxed mustache curved up at the ends. He wore his hair parted in the middle, so that it repeated the line of his mustache, dipping slightly as it crossed his brow on either side.

Portal approached his mission partly as duty, partly as exotic voyage. He took careful notes of his journey. Later, he would publish his story in a volume that would feed the voracious Victorian appetite for adventure stories drawn from real life.

Portal's diplomatic mission got off to a rocky start, particularly since Yohannes, following the unraveling of the Hewett Treaty, had good reason to mistrust British intentions. The Ethiopians saw Portal, and the British more broadly, not as honest brokers but as a mouthpiece for Italian reparation demands after Dogali. A letter sent to Yohannes over Victoria's signature claimed that Italian moves toward the Ethiopian highlands were intended merely "for the protection of caravans" and pointedly argued that Ras Alula had attacked "unjustly."[38]

Portal arrived at Massawa in October 1887. He carried a summary of the Italian position, which insisted on territorial compensation including Dogali, Sahati, and more, lands that, according to the Italians, had "never been recognized as Abyssinian." As the road to Yohannes led through Ras Alula, Portal made the journey into the highlands, to Asmara, where Portal found the legendary fighter.

Alula was one of the great patriots of Ethiopian history. A rare photo shows a slender man of medium height with a round head, hooded eyes, and full face. The young Alula stands among his men, bare-headed but otherwise decked out in military regalia—silk tunic over cotton pants and a lion skin draped over his shoulders and tied at the chest. His shield was richly decorated in silver; he held a rifle in his right hand.[39]

Augustus Wylde, a British Red Sea diplomat, journalist, and author, was among Alula's earliest and most ardent admirers. Wylde's admiration, at least on a superficial level, amounted to an act of assimilation to European standards. For Wylde, Alula was "more like a brown Englishman than anything else." He was "very good-looking, [with] good eyes, well-shaped nose, and very white and perfect teeth, and had short, black, wavy hair." Wylde's appreciation went well beyond his looks. Alula was "charming," a fine storyteller, with a keen sense of humor and broad-minded views. Alula's vision was inclusive; his inner circle included both Muslims and Christians.[40] Wylde and Alula would remain good friends until Alula's untimely death a few months after the battle of Adwa.

But Portal was not Wylde. Alula was in no mood to charm. He could see no good coming from Portal's mission, which he saw as, at best, an attempt to paper over British treachery following the Hewett Treaty. At worst, Portal was an agent of Italian interests.

The audience took place at Alula's compound at Asmara. Alula's main building was a circular hut forty-five feet in diameter; massive posts supported a conical roof of branch and straw. At the top of the roof was a red wooden cross topped by an orb, good for warding off the evil eye.

Portal stooped as he entered, but as the room was illuminated by only two doors, he saw nothing at first. When his eyes adjusted, he could discern the outlines of a formidable reception. Ras Alula sat cross-legged on a divan draped in red cotton, flanked and backed by a court of no fewer than seventy people. Along the walls were animal horns from which weapons and shields were hanging.[41]

Portal had prepared for his meeting by dressing in full diplomatic attire. Like Portal, Alula dressed to impress; he had draped himself in purple silk with gold embroidery. A Martini-Henry rifle sat within reach, as did a curved sword, but Portal was most deeply impressed by Alula's face. Portal noted that Alula was darker than most men of Tigray; he was transfixed by Alula's bright hazel eyes and gleaming teeth, which he recalled in language that smacked of the exotic and feral. "I had seen such eyes in the head of a tiger and of a leopard," he noted, "but never in that of a human being."[42] Where Wylde had seen an Englishman, Portal saw trouble.

Portal observed the diplomatic custom of gift exchange by setting out a gift-boxed Winchester repeating rifle—a clear step up from Alula's

Martini-Henry—and five hundred rounds of ammunition, just to get him started.[43] Alula feigned indifference.

Although Portal's mission was to negotiate peace with Yohannes, Alula wanted to do everything in his power to undermine it. There could be no peace that did not repudiate Alula and his actions at Dogali. As for the Italian claim on compensation, Alula's message was emphatic. Presuming to speak for Yohannes and thus on behalf of Ethiopia, there would be no occupation of Sahati, outside of the quid pro quo that "the Italians should come to Sahati only if [Alula] could go as Governor to Rome."[44] After this first interview, Alula detained Portal as a virtual prisoner for ten days, which Portal feared might be his last. Alula knew better than to harm Portal, but he was deadly serious about detaining him. Peace would be impossible if Portal never reached Yohannes.

In due course, Alula received a message that he must allow Portal to proceed. Portal prepared to meet Yohannes at Lake Ashenge as the Ethiopian emperor and his army moved northward in early December.[45] Portal and his group took up a position by the side of the road and watched *for four hours* as the army went by. His account of the experience is instructive:

> Beech and I made a most careful calculation of the numbers of persons who marched past us that morning, counting first the numbers who passed a certain spot in a minute, and then taking the time in which the whole army passed; at a very low estimate we calculated the numbers to be not less than between 70,000 and 80,000 persons. About the middle of the throng rode the king himself, surrounded by a picked body of cavalry. He was mounted on a handsome mule, and was dressed in the usual Abyssinian red and white *shamma,* or toga, a fold of which concealed all the lower part of his face, the only distinguishing mark of royalty being the fact that he kept the rays of the sun from his august head with a red silk umbrella.[46]

Not only was it was Portal's first glimpse of Yohannes, but it was his first glimpse of an Ethiopian army at full strength. It left him with no illusions about Yohannes's intention to fight.

At their meeting, Portal presented a Winchester rifle and a very large telescope "suitable equally for astronomical and terrestrial purposes."[47] Portal's gift from Yohannes was a complete Ethiopian outfit—a pink embroidered undershirt, an embroidered *shamma* of fine cotton, a lion's mane stole to drape over his shoulders, with lion hind and forelegs pinned so as to drape down the front and back. Sword and scabbard were attached, in the Ethiopian manner, to the right hip, and a shield completed the armaments. The outfit was so impressive that upon his return to Cairo, Portal went immediately to a photographer's studio for a portrait in full Ethiopian regalia.

Peace negotiations went poorly. "I am the aggrieved," Yohannes observed. "Why, then, should I be punished?"[48] By December, Portal was back in Massawa, his mission in tatters. Meanwhile, Yohannes marched his army as far as Ginda, on the road from Asmara to Massawa and mere hours from Italian positions at Sahati.

As Yohannes prepared to settle with the Italians once and for all, he learned that the Mahdi had invaded the western provinces of his empire. Tekle Haimanot, the king of Gojjam, had been defeated on 21 January 1888.[49] Mahdist forces had marched on Gondar, an ancient Ethiopian capital, and torched much of the city, including dozens of churches. Against the advice of Alula, who insisted on a showdown with the Italians, Yohannes wheeled, taking his army and Alula with him. By April 1888, not only Sahati but Asmara itself had been evacuated.[50]

The Italians were preparing another challenge for Yohannes. At about the time that Ras Alula was entertaining Gerald Portal in Asmara, Italian agents were in the south, at Addis Ababa, wooing Menelik with the promise of firearms and a tacit alliance against Yohannes in exchange for land in the north and a special relationship with Italy.[51] Menelik, for his part, courted the Italians by observing that while avenging Dogali would cost Italy millions, he himself might be useful in that regard—a gift of rifles and cartridges could easily do the job.[52] For different but complementary reasons, Menelik and the Italians were hoping that Yohannes would stumble and fall. They would soon get their wish.

Menelik, as king of Shoa, offered Yohannes only a provisional loyalty. He aimed to replace Yohannes as emperor of Ethiopia at the first opportunity—at the death of Yohannes if need be, sooner if possible.

Yohannes harbored no illusions about Menelik; in the 1870s he had had to move militarily against Menelik to impose his authority. Since then he had enjoyed only grudging respect from Menelik. When Yohannes mobilized in the north against the encroaching Italians, he had to worry about Menelik at his back in the south. The Italians, for their part, harnessed their own ambitions to those of Menelik. One day Menelik would replace Yohannes, putting a compliant friend of Italy on the imperial throne.

Augustus Wylde, a friend of Ethiopia with a strong moralizing streak, had no kind words for Menelik. For Wylde, Menelik was an "intriguer" who "would stop at nothing" to topple Yohannes.[53] All of this was no doubt true. But the key question was not whether Menelik could be paid but whether he could be bought.[54] It was a distinction the Italians were about to learn.

With the vengeful Italians in the north and a slippery Menelik to the south, Yohannes opted first to go west and take on the Mahdi.[55] Augustus Wylde long afterward suspected Menelik of colluding with the Mahdists, pushing them to attack Ethiopia and Yohannes—a charge tantamount to treason.[56]

At first the fighting went well for Yohannes and his army, but then a Mahdist rifle round wounded Yohannes in the abdomen. The loss of Yohannes took the fight out of the Ethiopian army. A circle of followers rallied around the dying Yohannes, defending his body in retreat. The Mahdi's soldiers caught up with them the following day; they seized the emperor's corpse and took the head of Yohannes as a trophy. It was displayed in Khartoum atop a pike.[57]

Who would succeed the unfortunate Yohannes? As he lay dying, Yohannes recognized Mangasha as his son and heir.[58] This dying gesture gave Mangasha a claim on the imperial crown. Now he would have to earn it.

CHAPTER 4

The Price of Liberty

A DDIS ABABA was abuzz with news of the emperor's imminent return from a war of conquest. Menelik had defeated the Welayta people, and 18 January 1895 would be a day of splendor in the capital.

In fact, the emperor had arrived on the outskirts of the capital the day before. He might well have descended from the heights directly into his capital were it not the eve of Timkat, the Epiphany festival. To have entered Addis in celebration on a day of fasting would have been more than bad form; it would have been interpreted as a bad sign, an evil portent. Entry on the day of Timkat suggested a convergence of the sacred and the profane, the splendor of Timkat enhanced by the splendor of victory.

Crowds lined the road as the ceremonial entry began. Precedence put clergy at the head of the procession. Their solemn demeanor clashed with the rainbow colors of their parasols and vestments. They murmured prayers as they bore the *tabot*—a replica of the Ark of the Covenant—wrapped in colored fabric. As the clergy passed, the fervor of Timkat gave way to the joy of triumph. Some thirty mounted drummers and trumpeters led the way, followed by light cavalry astride mules adorned with rich fabrics of bright colors and fine decorative stitchery.

The emperor's party composed the heart of the procession. Menelik's *afa negus*—part attorney general, part Supreme Court justice—led with his pages, then Menelik himself, surrounded by his commanders arrayed in embroidered silk.[1] Horns of brass and wood let out a noise that blended bleats and moans, soon to be drowned out by celebratory gunfire. Cries of joy rose from the women at the first glimpse of the husbands, sons, and brothers who had been on campaign since November.

As in the triumphs of ancient Rome, the event was an occasion for mutual admiration. The victorious ruler and his soldiers displayed all they had gained by triumph of arms. The people could, in turn, bask in the glory of such a vivid display of their collective superiority.

Vivid it was. The Welayta are a pastoral people, and Menelik's loot included thousands of heads of cattle. Next came the captives, at least fifteen thousand of them, eyes downcast except for furtive attempts to glimpse the joyous crowd lining the route. They would be enslaved and distributed as compensation to the troops—part of the yield of the expedition. So extensive was the booty that three days passed before the parade of soldiers and captives ended.

The grandest trophy of all was Tona, the Welayta king. He had led his people in a brilliant but desperate war of resistance; he had the wounds to prove it. He had healed sufficiently to participate in the grand and tragic procession. His presence proved that Menelik's triumph had been total. It also served as an object lesson: this was a king brought low by his failure to protect his people—the most fundamental of sovereign compacts.[2]

Once in Addis, Tona's ordeal continued. The king of the Muslim Welayta followed through on his promise to convert to Christianity. Then he sat—unsmiling—for a photo portrait. He was dressed as a king for the occasion; his white silk tunic and black silk cape were gathered high around his neck and fastened just below his chin. He wrapped his head in a pair of scarves, in the manner of Menelik himself, except that he wore them pulled low in front, over his brow. The scarves served as a platform for a beaded and scalloped crown that sat atop his head. He wore an indecipherable expression on his face.[3]

Tona would soon return home. Menelik might have simply placed one of his lieutenants on Tona's throne, but he thought better of it. The Welayta country occupied a vast and rich area, more than eleven hundred square miles. It was also densely populated—Menelik claimed that there

were more inhabitants in the Welayta lands than in the entire area between Addis Ababa and Massawa. No wonder that it made such a tempting target.[4] Tona had been a fearless opponent, but he knew he had been
defeated. Menelik reckoned it would be easier to leave Tona in place and
tap him from time to time for tribute than to try to extract a surplus from
his people by brute force. Serving as Menelik's agent, Tona would funnel his people's wealth to Addis in the form of regular payments.

However successful as a military campaign and a harvest of resources,
the war against the Welayta was a disaster in terms of Menelik's global
reputation. For someone who had acquired such a sure grasp of the role
of public opinion, it was an uncharacteristic blunder. Perhaps Menelik
thought that an intra-African war would be of little interest to Europe.
Perhaps he never believed that Europeans would care about the Muslim
victims of Christian might. He certainly misunderstood the intentions of
Jean Gaston Vanderheym, the French company agent whose dispatches
to Europe during the campaign were catastrophic for Menelik's image.

Menelik had no one to blame but himself that such a capable witness as
Vanderheym shadowed him on campaign. Vanderheym came to Ethiopia
in the early 1890s, hoping to drum up business for French exporters; by
the summer of 1894, he had become a fixture in town and at court. When
planning for the Welayta campaign got under way in earnest, Menelik
began to work on Vanderheym, hoping he would join the campaign. He
provided Vanderheym with a modest entourage of twelve men, two boys,
and two women. And Menelik fed Vanderheym's penchant for gadgets,
allowing him to filch a compass and barometer from the royal treasury so
that he could log the campaign's progress. With his notebooks and a compact Express Détective camera built by the renowned Parisian photographer Paul Nadar, Vanderheym could fancy himself a one-man journalistic
team.[5]

In the run-up to the fall campaign of 1894—and in after-the-fact
justifications—Menelik presented the war as a kind of crusade and a long-
postponed payback. In the seventeenth century, Ahmad ibn Ibrahim al-
Ghazi had been the scourge of Welayta Christians, who had prudently
converted to Islam. Ethiopian Christian lore was full of improbable feats
performed against Muslim oppressors and wily rescues defying impossible odds.[6] In the end, the Muslim Welayta were represented paradoxically

both as a plausible if unlikely threat and as a conquered people ripe for religious reconversion.

The emphasis should lie on "plausible." The Welayta, least of all under Tona, were hardly prepared to threaten Menelik of Shoa and his burgeoning Ethiopian empire. When Menelik announced his campaign, he had already amassed East Africa's largest and best-armed fighting force. In size, the Shoan army easily surpassed that of Emperor Yohannes on the eve of his death. Menelik could effortlessly field a force of eighty thousand and—thanks to the Italians and French as well as independent arms merchants—most of them would carry Wetterly or Gras bolt-action rifles into action. Against such a force, the Welayta were hardly a menace.

Despite the overwhelming odds, the campaign began in a fit of anxiety. Worrisome signs—unspecified but numerous ominous auguries—drove Taytu to implore Menelik to call off his campaign. She beseeched Menelik's advisors to do the same. Taytu's appeals continued until the empress fell ill, sick with worry. Menelik took the opportunity to leave, promising to return in a few weeks.[7]

Menelik's Campaign against the Welayta

It was mid-November, the end of the rainy season, before Menelik's campaign got under way. Menelik assigned the role of advance guard to Ras Michael and his troops. Michael was a convert to Christianity from Islam, although it is unclear whether he was chosen out of concern for Muslim sensibilities, as a test of Michael's own conversion, or as a portent of what awaited the Welayta once conquered. At least half of Michael's force of seven thousand men carried good rifles of recent manufacture, with which to take on Tona's defenders. Once Michael's men had moved out, the imperial party followed with another thirteen thousand to eighteen thousand men.[8]

It was a forest of lances and rifles and tent poles. Each *ras* and every chief—however modest—had his entourage and his fighting men. Chief followed *ras*, and *ras* followed Menelik. The baggage train consisted of donkeys and mules loaded with supplies, as well as women who carried butter, *berbere,* honey, and other provisions.[9]

As Menelik's army moved south, the campaign began with spectacular violence, even before combat began. Pressed by the need to feed his vast army, Menelik ordered the dynamiting of a river, sending dozens of stunned fish floating to the surface—providential fishes, if not loaves.[10]

Although the emperor had promised Taytu a swift campaign, it was mid-December before the capital received any word from him. The campaign had bogged down. Part of the delay was due to unrealistic expectations— the Welayta, it was said, lived an idyllic, almost biblical existence on rich red loam, and Menelik had expected little resistance from a people known for farming, not fighting.[11]

But the greater credit goes to Welayta leadership. King Tona had done what any defender facing overwhelming force would do—he organized a guerrilla campaign. When Menelik's forces arrived in Welayta territory, Menelik called on Tona to surrender on behalf of his people. "Do not exterminate your people," Menelik said, according to the Ethiopian chronicle of his reign. "Do not lose your country. Submit and bring me tribute." Tona would have none of Menelik's bluster. "Christians will never enter my country," he is said to have responded. "I will not submit; I am ready to fight."[12]

Resistance started with a system of traps along the invasion route. At choke points Welayta fighters set sharpened stakes in camouflaged holes. The traps injured horses and men and slowed the Ethiopian advance. Menelik and his men halted to fill the traps laid for them, also to fell trees, level roads, and construct fords. This was public works with military intent.[13]

As Tona and his men retreated in the face of the Ethiopian advance, they avoided defeat but left the population vulnerable. Menelik's army countered with classic anti-guerrilla tactics, targeting a civilian population presumed to support the resistance. Soon the inhabitants of the villages vanished, too, for fear of reprisals. Ras Michael ordered his men to set fire to abandoned Welayta settlements and their characteristic beehive huts.

Other villages threw themselves upon Menelik's mercy. They surrendered to the approaching Ethiopian forces en masse, carrying tree branches in a sign of capitulation.[14] Raids and defections produced informants, who were induced to provide intelligence and to serve as guides. These ultimately led to Tona.

Once Tona's position had been established, Menelik's forces moved to prevent his escape. Leaving behind supplies and camp followers, Ethiopian forces undertook a night march along parallel routes to the east and west of Tona's camp, in a massive strategy of envelopment. After six hours, Menelik's men had pushed as far as Lake Abaya, nearly two hundred miles south of Addis, behind Tona's position. They were ready to close the trap. Deprived of a path of retreat, Tona and his men could no longer avoid a pitched battle; Ethiopian numbers and firepower could do their work.

On 11 December, Tona's forces squared off against Ethiopian marksmen, arrayed around artillery commanded by the eunuch Baltcha. In peacetime, Baltcha served as one of Menelik's key administrative lieutenants, entrusted with control of the imperial treasury. In war, Baltcha applied his accounting skills to the ammunition and personnel of the imperial artillery. Although the Italians later would make much of the idea of a eunuch serving as head of artillery—his impotence a metaphor for the reputedly limp Ethiopian gunnery—Baltcha's guns spread havoc and confusion in Tona's army. Tona's men crouched behind leafy cobas trees. When they left protective cover to launch their spears, they were cut down by Ethiopian rifle fire, falling to multiple wounds.[15]

Tona was captured on the thirteenth, but the fighting continued for several days, eventually shading into a pacification operation. By 18 December the fighting was over. Brought before Menelik, Tona adopted a contrite tone. "I listened only to my pride!" he moaned. "I should have submitted to you rather than see my country devastated and my subjects massacred. May the death of my countrymen be upon me."[16]

It was a generous statement. Tona was shouldering responsibility for Welayta suffering, although the cruelty and rapaciousness of the campaign shocked even veteran Ethiopian soldiers, men who had participated in earlier campaigns in Harar and Keffa.[17] The brutality of the conquest was heightened, in part, by the frustration of Ras Michael's men and the casualties they suffered, thanks to the effectiveness of Welayta guerrilla tactics. The conquerors had little mercy on Welayta men they captured, and had to be restrained by Menelik. The Ethiopian chronicle of Menelik's reign—occasionally given to boasting—relates that the Welayta "were exterminated in a single day." While manifestly this was not true— Menelik hoped to rely on tribute from the Welayta for years to come—

Menelik tallied eighty thousand Welayta killed or taken prisoner. The official Ethiopian chronicle puts the number higher, at an improbably precise 118,987. Vanderheym thought the true figure much lower.[18]

What is certain is that, in Africa as in Europe, war feeds on war. Wealth wasn't just incidental to the campaign; it is what drove it. Ethiopian soldiers were compensated in the form of what they could herd, prod, or haul away. Vanderheym detailed the booty amassed in a day of raiding—chickens, cabbage, pumpkins, horses, donkeys, goats, cattle. The day's take included women and children, too—thousands were enslaved. A livestock epidemic beginning in 1888 had depleted not just Ethiopian livestock but the Ethiopian population.[19] The loss of population in Shoa was devastating, as high as one-third.[20] Thus there was a "rape of the Sabines" dimension to the Welayta campaign as Menelik and his army forcibly transferred population as well as wealth in the aftermath of victory.

Menelik had his pick of the bounty of war. Of the thirty-six thousand cattle seized, Menelik took half, sharing the remainder with his soldiers. Menelik took one in ten slaves, for a total of eighteen hundred, which puts the number of enslaved at eighteen thousand. Menelik tagged his share with the sign of a cross, burned in acid on the hand. Thus indelibly claimed for the emperor, they were free to mingle during the slow procession back to Addis.[21]

On 29 December, still days from the capital, Menelik's forces staged a victory parade. A makeshift review stand was built. Menelik, dressed in ceremonial finery, took his place on the platform beneath a sunshade of woven branches. His head was framed by a lion's mane headdress. King Tona and his conquered Welayta chiefs sat in front of Menelik as the emperor's cavalry paraded in review. The cavalry passed at a gallop, followed by running infantry. Before departing for Addis, Menelik left his mark on the land, ordering that a residence be constructed on a hilltop. It offered a territorial view of the conquered region.[22]

The View from Abroad

Menelik's Welayta campaign was a resounding military success. It raised money desperately needed for the defense of Ethiopia. It allowed Menelik to test his army in real military action on the eve of the confrontation with Italy. The conquest of the Welayta turned green recruits into combat veterans.

It also allowed him to try out his weapons in combat. Menelik had bought fifteen thousand Gras rifles from the French businessman Léon Chefneux. A surprising number of them jammed after firing six or seven rounds, sometimes with fatal consequences. The jammed bolt-action rifles left Ethiopian soldiers temporarily disarmed as they struggled to drive the bolt home.[23] Welayta fighters fell upon them with their older but more reliable technology of lance and sword.

But the campaign had been costly in other ways. In the European press, Vanderheym's chronicle of the pitiless campaign threatened to undo Menelik's carefully cultivated image as a wise, humane, and Christian African leader. In fact, it threatened to erode Menelik's high moral ground in the looming battle with Italy by exposing an indigenous African impulse to conquer. Vanderheym's accounts of Welayta families being apportioned among Menelik's men also gave the lie to Menelik's public stand against the slave trade. Or, more precisely, it exposed a peculiar casuistry whereby the ban on slavery did not extend to spoils of war, domestic servants, or Muslims.

Menelik learned of Vanderheym's articles and their devastating impact in Europe after his triumphant return to Addis Ababa. Menelik mobilized Casimir Mondon-Vidailhet, whose breezy defense appeared in *Le Temps* in April. Mondon pitched the story of the Welayta conquest in historical and religious terms. The Welayta country was "a former province of the Ethiopian empire." Thus it was not a conquest but a reconquest of a province lost "for several centuries." Moreover, the Welayta remained "of Christian tradition," although "strongly touched" by Islam; Menelik had merely brought them back to the bosom of Christendom. "Today the Cross has won out over the Crescent," he concluded. "The former provinces . . . return to the Christian fold, thanks to Remington and Gras rifles. Force has submitted to force. So it was written."

As for European public opinion, Mondon spoke for Menelik here, too, invoking a common Christian bond: "European public opinion matters a great deal to Emperor Menelik; he expects . . . a feeling of justice, a sentiment he regards as dominant among Christian people."[24]

While Mondon carried out damage control, Menelik let it be known that Vanderheym was no longer welcome at court. Vanderheym quickly packed his bags and announced he was leaving for Harar, where he hoped to pass a few weeks, perhaps to rehabilitate himself and eventually return to court.

Menelik played the gracious host, but he prepared a trap. He provided Vanderheym with a letter of introduction to Makonnen, governor of Harar. Normally such a gesture guaranteed a warm reception and accommodations worthy of a guest of the emperor. But Vanderheym learned via back channels that the court had sent a messenger ahead with special instructions for Makonnen. By way of friends at court, Vanderheym learned that "unpleasant surprises" awaited him at Harar.[25]

Vanderheym organized his departure, including an armed escort. Once en route to Harar, Vanderheym announced a sudden need to deliver an important letter. He would forgo his visit to Makonnen and head straight to the coast. He offered his escorts double pay if they accompanied him. They bypassed Harar and made straight for Djibouti.

CHAPTER 5

Black in Service of White

THE WORDS "Dogali" and "the five hundred" became shorthand in Italy for the horrible cost that imperial ambitions could bring. At the same time that the monument in Rome sought to place the sacrifice of the five hundred on a path leading to a future that would justify it, Italian political leadership hit upon a new scheme. Why place Italy's sons in harm's way when there were Africans ready to take up arms in the service of Italy as professional soldiers?

When the Italians turned to the African population for recruits after Dogali, they followed local precedent. When Egypt sought to invade Ethiopia in the 1870s, it hired foreign officers, including veterans from the American Civil War, as well as Danes, Germans, and Austrians who had fought in European wars of 1864 and 1866.[1] These veteran officers commanded Egyptian soldiers as well as mercenaries drawn from the Ethiopian periphery.

Similarly, when the Italians wished to expand their military might in East Africa, they put out a recruitment call. Word passed from village to village. At the appointed time, dozens of potential recruits gathered. Their origins were diverse—men from the Red Sea coastal villages, men from the Sudan, men from the Ethiopian highlands as far away as Gondar and Shoa.[2] Recruiters did not discriminate by language or creed—Muslim and Christian were welcome.

Selection was pitiless. After the recruits mustered, a European officer would stride among the ranks, sending half the men on their way with a word or a gesture—too young, too old, too thin. Then a brutal endurance test would begin. An officer mounted on horseback would lead the aspirants at a slow gallop over hills and across streams. The sole purpose of the cross-country trek was to winnow the field; as the distances mounted—three, six, nine, twelve miles—men fell behind and the field thinned. At the end, four or five might remain. They were the elect, the chosen, the few.

A brief medical examination came next, then a bath and the distribution of clothing—a white tunic and calf-height white pants. These outfits were a dressed-up version of the everyday wear typical of East Africa—a belted white smock over white pants that are generous at the hips but tight at the upper calf or ankle.

For many recruits, these might be the finest clothes they had ever worn. It was only the beginning of the transformation. The ensemble was completed by a short jacket with embroidered arabesque flourishes and, for the head, a red tarbush or fez. Last came the tools of the soldier's trade—a rifle, a bayonet, and a cartridge pouch of red leather.

Forming the Askari Battalions

Recruits were assigned to distinct units, identified by a sash worn around the waist. The first four battalions were distinguished by sashes of red, blue, purple, and black—the First, Second, Third, and Fourth Native Battalions, respectively.[3]

As Italy pushed out of Massawa up into the highlands, its military needs grew. By the 1890s, four battalions were added, increasing the count of native battalions to eight, each of just under one thousand men. The new units adopted sashes of Scotch plaid, green, white, and yellow.

These soldiers, known as *bashi-buzuk* (an old Ottoman term) or *askari*, looked sharp in their uniforms of white linen or cotton. A smart uniform was part of the appeal of military service, but motives for joining varied. Some recruits were escaping a criminal past. Others—refugees from the slave trade, for example—saw it as a way to start life over.[4] For everyone, soldiering meant security—food, clothing, and steady pay.

A soldier signed up for a one-year term, in exchange for which he received 1.5 lire per day. While the sum was not huge—a mere fraction of

Askari recruits. From *L'Illustration*, 21 December 1895.

what a European soldier would have received—it represented a fine wage in Africa. For a young man, it was enough to support a wife—whom the smart uniform helped to attract—start a family, and, after a year of savings, buy a mule or other work animals.[5]

In addition to a stable income in an economy that was otherwise precarious, service offered prestige. The status of the soldier or warrior is very high in Ethiopian society and in East Africa generally. Most askari reupped after their year of service. Military service offered reliable income, local esteem, and social ascent.[6] A year or two of soldiering could buy a farmer's life. A soldier was someone with a future.

What the Italians got in return were soldiers who would fight for Italy, even though they were not Italian. The askari were foot soldiers of uncommon speed and endurance. Except for the coastal lowlands, Eritrea and Ethiopia are at high elevation—above six thousand feet. It wasn't easy for European troops to adapt to the thin air and extremes of temperature at altitude.[7] Even after acclimation, European soldiers never matched the speed and agility of native troops. Askari units led by Italian officers mounted on mules or horseback could move with astonishing speed compared to European infantry standards. Paul Lauribar recounts having received orders to move his native battalion, stationed at Asmara, to reinforce Italian positions at Agordat, some 118 miles away. Lauribar's askari, led by mounted officers, completed the journey in three days, averaging well over thirty miles a day in marches of nine, twelve, and fifteen hours.[8] Napoleon's armies, noted for their speed among European armies, might on occasion achieve twenty-five miles a day.

Such mobility put Italian forces on par with Ethiopian forces, taking away the speed advantage the Ethiopians enjoyed when matched against Italian soldiers. During the military campaigns of 1895, when Italy vastly increased the area of land under its rule, speed meant that the Italians could pursue, overtake, and defeat Ethiopian forces, even when the latter were in full retreat. Such a feat would have been simply unattainable by European units.

Askari battalions were always commanded by European officers, but askari could enter the leadership ranks as noncommissioned officers. These subaltern or noncommissioned officers were chosen from among the more seasoned and dedicated askari; they were distinguished by a red fez topped with a tassel or pompon whose color varied according to battalion.

Thanks to the askari, Italian commanding officers enjoyed a level of attention typically enjoyed only by Ethiopian chiefs. Just as the tent of an Ethiopian leader would form the center of any camp, so the tent of a European officer would constitute the core of an askari battalion camp. As soon as the day's march was concluded, the first duty of the askari was to prepare the tent of their commanding officers. They also served as bodyguards, never letting the officers out of their sight. If local inhabitants approached with an offer of food or drink, the askari would see that the local first sampled his own food or drink, to ensure that it was fit to be consumed.[9]

And while it may seem strange that the askari would take up arms against other Africans and even fellow Ethiopians, for many loyalty was personal and local, rather than national or "Ethiopian." Banditry was common in East Africa, and relations between neighboring regions and settlements could as often be predatory as cooperative. In such circumstances, the bonds of status, income, military service, and even friendship could trump all others.

When askari battalions returned from a mission, they remained a team. Askari lived with their families in *tukuls* rather than in barracks, but the huts were grouped around the residence of their commanding officer and the entire battalion-level settlement was enclosed by a palisade.[10] In an obvious sense, the existence of the askari was organized around their identity as soldiers. Strong bonds formed.

Italian military policy was, in its own way, family-friendly; this tended to encourage a broad identification with the European occupiers.[11] The spouses of the askari were permitted to go on campaign with their husbands, and frequently did so. Children were the inevitable result of such policies, and it was not unusual for entire families, in effect, to join the service, even to fight beside husbands and fathers and support them in combat. In the fighting at Mekele, askari family members served as runners, dodging Ethiopian fire to bring up ammunition. One askari spouse died in such a role, cut down bringing rifle rounds to her husband.[12]

Italian officers were surprised—but pleased—to hear askari sing patriotic Italian songs as they marched or built fortifications.[13] The archival record and memoir literature are full of statements of praise and affection from Italian officers. "Our faithful askari" is a recurring phrase in the historical record. With few exceptions, it does not appear to be an exaggeration.[14]

Askari were encouraged to learn Italian for both military and cultural reasons, with limited success. A survey of some thirty-six hundred askari revealed that more than half could neither speak nor understand the language. Hierarchies of command reflected hierarchies of race. When General Antonio Baldissera proposed that European and African troops serve side by side in mixed units, the idea was shot down by Rome.[15] Baldissera's innovative proposal suggests that racial ideas were still in flux; its rapid demise shows that such categories were rapidly hardening.

The Italians were indifferent to religion when they recruited askari; religious difference seems not to have interfered in the formation of strong soldierly bonds between askari of Christian and Muslim background. Soldiers followed their own religious traditions when it came to the butchering of meat, for example, or the consumption of wine, from which Muslim askari refrained. Both Muslim and Christian askari declined to consume preserved Italian meats, which would not have been prepared according to Islamic or Ethiopian Orthodox rules.[16]

Love in Africa

If askari men found it normal to combine military service and domestic partnership, the situation was somewhat different for European men on duty in Africa. By the end of 1895, there were more than ten thousand Italian soldiers on campaign. Many more served in support roles, with still more arriving each week.[17] Only the wives of high-ranking officers were permitted to follow their spouses; fewer still agreed to do so.[18] Rosalia Pianavia followed her husband to Eritrea, where she lived during his three-year tour of duty, but her situation was exceptional: her husband was a colonel, second in command of Italian forces.

What this meant for the sex lives of Europeans and Africans is interesting to imagine but difficult to document. Memoirs and diaries are largely silent on the issue. One is left only with tantalizing but inconclusive passing references. What, if anything, should we read into the fact that a certain Sergeant Finiello was known around the barracks as *la signorina* (the miss)?[19]

When the Italians returned in 1936, they would issue strict regulations aimed at safeguarding Italian "racial purity."[20] In the 1880s, they articulated no such concern—a measure of how far race had yet to travel as a concept and a boundary. Prostitution certainly existed at Massawa, as in any port city, and at Asmara, too. But many Italian soldiers established longer-term relationships with Eritrean women, whom they supported in roles situated somewhere between the courtesan and the spouse. These women were known as *madamas*—a title typically reserved for spouses.[21] General Giuseppe Arimondi, who would die at Adwa, had a *madama* of legendary beauty.[22]

Although the relationship between soldier and *madama* had a status approaching that of marriage, the bonds of marriage could be loosely interpreted. Like any marriage, these relationships produced their share of drama. Cesare Nerazzini spent years in Eritrea as a high-level diplomatic representative; he had his *madama* when he was in residence at Assab, on the Red Sea coast, but both Nerazzini and his *madama* had other lovers. When Nerazzini discovered Moka, a dancer at a nearby village, he had a shack built for her in Assab not far from where Nerazzini lived with his *madama*. Meanwhile, Nerazzini's *madama* took lovers of her own. Among them was Rosentretter, a Swiss machine installer posted briefly to Assab to set up a water distiller on behalf of a German manufacturer. When Rosentretter returned to Europe he was replaced by a handsome Florentine named Nozzoli. His purpose in Assab is unknown, but the affable Nozzoli made the most of his time there, befriending Nerazzini's *madama*. His sojourn in Assab ended abruptly, however: he was last seen leaving by way of the window when Nerazzini came home early one day.[23]

In many cases, the *madama* relationship was regularized, even institutionalized. Chris Prouty, in her fine work on this period, argued that many native families, especially impoverished ones, saw that to place a daughter in a relationship with a European could represent a significant opportunity. The European was expected to supply a home (a *tukul*), adequately furnished, along with grain and cash. The soldier's consort might also receive a mule, richly adorned with colorful tack. Above all, she received the title of *madama*, a status that conferred prestige. It also gave her a place in the hybrid European-African society, with a social rank commensurate with that of her patron. Thus the *madama* of the captain could lord it over the *madama* of a lieutenant.

Within local society, the *madama* was seen as married—a common-law spouse—with all the honor and respect pertaining thereto.[24] The elevated status of the *madama* remained with her even after her Italian partner returned to Europe. The goods she acquired meant that she was notably better off than she might otherwise have been; culturally, she enjoyed significantly higher status. Newly single, she was free to start over with another European or to "marry up" within local society.[25]

Far more ambiguous was the status of the offspring of these relationships.[26] In similar contexts, such children have been rejected as unpleasant reminders of collaboration with an occupier—one thinks of the children born to French women who had relationships with German soldiers during the Nazi occupation.[27] But this was not always so—Anglo-Indians acquired a particular status during the British Raj, although that status

Italian soldier with Madama. From SAI Archive at the University of Naples
"L'Orientale"; Silvana Palma, *Archivio storico della Società africana d'Italia;
Raccolte fotografiche e cartografiche.* Naples: Istituto Universitario Orientale, 1997.

certainly became more ambiguous after 1947. In Eritrea, at least in some
cases, the blended children resulting from these relationships were
welcomed—sometimes even embraced—by the surrounding community.

The Ethiopians had some experience in these areas, including European-
African relationships that were far more casual. When Augustus Wylde

arrived in Ethiopia to write a series of articles for the *Manchester Guardian* about the burgeoning Italo-Ethiopian conflict, he spied "a nearly white woman and her daughter, who was nearly as fair," living among the local population. He surmised, and was later able to confirm, that the woman was the product of a liaison that had occurred during the 1868 English expedition against Tewodros. The woman "would have passed as an English woman" and, in fact, was known locally as "the Englishwoman" (the *inglese*). She was born after the brief English campaign and raised within the Ethiopian community.[28] She eventually married and, by the time she was spotted by Wylde, had a daughter of her own.

Similarly, at least some of the children of Italian-Eritrean couples readily found a place in African society. When Major Pietro Toselli died in combat late in 1895, he left behind his *madama* and a newborn boy. She remarried; her new husband adopted Toselli's son as his own. The couple named the boy Petros in honor of his natural father.[29]

Other sources present a more complicated picture. Some photographs from the period depict European-African couples posing for studio portraits very much like those one would expect of European couples, the picture of domestic bliss—which tends to validate the image of the *madama* as the social and sentimental equivalent of the spouse. Other photos depict Eritrean women posing naked or nearly so alongside their European spouses. They are surrounded by props—animal skins, cheap jewelry—biased toward exotic sexual allure rather than cultivated domesticity.[30]

Locale mattered, too. The somewhat elevated status of the *madama* was a better fit for the relatively circumscribed community of the highlands, especially Asmara. In the more transient world of Massawa—as in port cities everywhere—casual relations predominated. Theater productions, of which the Italians seemed inordinately fond, sometimes featured half-naked costumed local women who functioned more as props than as performers.[31]

Rosalia Pianavia—an officer's wife and therefore a European *madama*—was troubled by the number of mixed-race infants in Eritrea and their insecure status. The role of the Italian fathers in the lives of these children ended either with their death in combat, as in the case of Toselli, or with the completion of their tour of duty. Pianavia admitted disgust at the thought of black and white living together, but the offense was not so much that of racial mixing as that these couples were heedless of the consequences of a union fated to end. Sooner or later their children would be fatherless.

Rosalia Pianavia made the care of these children a personal crusade, relying on a blend of compassion and guilt to drum up funds for on-going care. Her first case was Abadie, who had lost her mother. Her father, an Italian officer, entrusted Abadie to Pianavia when he returned to Italy. Pianavia accepted responsibility for the child, renaming her Mariannina.

Pianavia decided to create a home for orphaned children. It took work to persuade colonial authorities to grant permission for her initiative. The risks to the partisans of empire were considerable. Creating an or-phanage meant acknowledging colonial practices—sexual practices— that flouted moral conventions, and it highlighted the imbalances of power inherent in the colonial enterprise.[32] In time, Pianavia's venture was approved.

Mariannina became the first of many children consigned to Pianavia's care. The little girl was followed by Angelina, Vittorina I, Vittorina II, Lucchino, Oreste, and Giovannino, the latter two brothers.[33]

Rosalia's genius was to spotlight the responsibility of fathers and turn that responsibility into support for their children. In effect, it was a guilt tax. With the approval of Padre Bonomi, the military chaplain, Pianavia held collections in Eritrea to raise funds.[34] She used the proceeds to found an orphanage—the Institute of the Little Innocents—where aban-doned and orphaned children could find food, shelter, and care. The humanitarian core of her project—which the term "Little Innocents" bril-liantly captured—garnered support in Italy, where fund-raisers yielded additional funds. The city of Genoa hosted a festival, with proceeds dedi-cated to Pianavia's institute.

Genoa's benefit raised 28,000 lire, which financed the construction of buildings at the institute and staffed them with caregivers, both African and European. Pianavia secured the charitable engagement of a female religious order. The nuns served both as guardians and teachers.[35]

Pianavia's Institute of the Little Innocents could only be a palliative; it never addressed the contradictions inherent in empire. In fact, the stories of the askari and the *madamas* are in some ways analogous, showing the powerful forces at work to encourage African collaboration with European occupiers. As long as the European presence seemed permanent, realism as well as access to money and prestige argued in favor of accommodation.

CHAPTER 6

Africa in Italy

WHAT MANGASHA LACKED in intellect, he made up for in looks. He was tall, with fine skin and delicate features. His wide-set doe eyes had a seductive quality. A trim mustache, a soul patch, and a short beard added a dash of style and gravitas. His hair, often braided, alluded to his soldierly qualities.

Mangasha was a dandy and, like all dandies, was blessed with a knack for self-presentation. A photo portrait shows him in the classic aristocratic cape of black silk, which contrasted with the fine white fabric rolled loosely about the neck. Although pictures capture his penchant for jewelry—he wore small looped earrings—they don't capture the aroma. Mangasha loved perfume, a rare affectation in Ethiopia. Perfume was brought from the coast by Muslim merchants and so had infidel associations, especially among Christians of an older generation.[1]

Perfumed, vain, effeminate—Mangasha could brush off such criticism. What gnawed at him was his thwarted ambition—his claim on the imperial throne. Mangasha was the illegitimate son of Emperor Yohannes, the product of a casual liaison between the emperor and a lover whose name is lost to history. Mangasha claimed that Yohannes—mortally wounded in battle with the Mahdi in 1889—had recognized Mangasha as his son and successor on his deathbed.[2] In the succession struggle that ensued, however, Mangasha was outclassed. If Mangasha was to challenge Menelik and succeed Yohannes as emperor, he would have to earn it.

His greatest asset was Alula, a man who had served Yohannes faithfully and who, upon the emperor's death, shifted those loyalties to the son without hesitation. Alula was a legendary fighter. In the 1870s, he had defended the Ethiopian highlands against the incursions of the Egyptians, defeating them at Gura and Sahati. He did no less to the Italians in the 1880s, perpetrating the massacre at Dogali and earning Italy's grudging respect. Alula, to the Italians, was the Ethiopian Garibaldi. It's hard to imagine a higher compliment than to compare the fierce, falcon-nosed Alula to Giuseppe Garibaldi, the father of modern Italy.

But even with such talent at his side, Mangasha could never quite carry the role of pretender. In fact, beside Alula, Mangasha faded. It was a classic triumph of talent over lineage. While Mangasha's claim to power rested on his lofty birth, Alula was an upstart, a man who owed his American-style ascent from obscure but no doubt hardscrabble origins to his fighting skills and political realism. Alula would be known to history as "the best native general and strategist that Africa has perhaps produced in modern times."[3] Mangasha was propped up by Alula's skill and dogged loyalty. It was a compliment to Alula, but a cruel slam at Mangasha, that Alula was known to be both "mind and arm"—the intellect and the might—of the dim and vain would-be emperor.[4]

No one was better prepared to exploit the death of Yohannes than Menelik. The king of Shoa had been plotting against Yohannes for years, building up his army and conspiring with Italy against him. The Italian emissary Pietro Antonelli first visited Ethiopia in 1879, at the tender age of twenty, and he had been cultivating ties at court ever since.[5] In 1885, the Italian occupation of Massawa gave Menelik and Italy a common enemy in Yohannes, and the bond deepened. Just as the British had used Yohannes against Tewodros, Antonelli knew that building up Menelik would distract and weaken Yohannes.

For his part, Menelik was more than willing to be used, just as he made use of the Italians. Italy became a major source of firearms, with which Menelik would both challenge Yohannes and expand his domain. In a transaction that captured the essence of their relationship, in the aftermath of Dogali Menelik promised Italy revenge against Alula and Yohannes in exchange for ten thousand Remington rifles and four hundred thousand cartridges.[6]

All the while, Menelik fed Antonelli's image of Ethiopia as riven by factions. Not only Menelik himself but also Tekle Haimanot of Gojjam and Ras Michael of the Wollo Oromo were depicted as restive and ready to break with Yohannes.[7] It was not a picture wholly discordant with reality or with history. Traditions of banditry and the habitual jockeying of regional chiefs easily sustained the illusion that Yohannes was the sole stabilizing force in an Ethiopia seething with discontent.

Antonelli imagined that sponsoring Menelik while occupying the Red Sea ports of Massawa and Zeyla—thus limiting Menelik's access to the sea—prepared the way for Italian predominance in Ethiopia. Antonelli deeply admired Yohannes for having forged an Ethiopian empire, but he foresaw that the death of the emperor would unleash hell, a civil war where "a thousand pretenders will fight over an empire that no longer is." Italy, having backed Menelik, would be in a position to exploit and dominate a divided Ethiopia.[8]

By the late 1880s, Antonelli was shuttling between Rome and Addis, working out the details of a pact with Menelik. Italy was ready to enter a military alliance with Menelik in which Italy would support Menelik against Yohannes. If Yohannes attacked Menelik, Italy agreed to respond immediately by pushing up from the coast to the highlands, occupying Asmara. Such a move would threaten Yohannes from the north at the same time that it secured land for Italy. In effect, Menelik was buying allies with land, condoning Italian encroachment on territory Yohannes claimed for Ethiopia. When Yohannes had learned about the plotting of Menelik and the Italians, he sought to rally Menelik to his side under the banner of Ethiopia. "If the two of us remain united," he wrote to Menelik, "with the help of God we will win."[9]

Menelik was playing a high-risk game, and he was not without his critics, some of them powerful. If Menelik could see how Antonelli and the Italians were useful, Taytu could barely restrain her contempt. As a northerner, she headed the Tigrayan contingent at Menelik's court, greeting Antonelli "with a mix of ill humor and sarcasm."[10] But Menelik would not break with Antonelli and Italy as long was Yohannes was alive. And

he was taking no chances. At the same time that he cultivated his relationship with Italy, he was courting France at the very highest levels. Encouraged by Ilg, he wrote to Jules Grévy, president of the French Republic,
presenting himself as an honest broker, the benevolent peacemaker in a
dispute between Yohannes and Italy.[11]

Somehow, the part of Menelik that conspired against Yohannes could
get along with the part that was an Ethiopian patriot. Just as Menelik
could take money and weapons from Italy without being bought, he felt
he could undermine Yohannes without undermining Ethiopia. Yohannes
had good intelligence about Menelik's dealings, and he was unafraid
to act against those who were insubordinate; he had punished Tekle
Haimanot for such scheming, sending Ras Alula as his avenging angel.
Alula humiliated Tekle Haimanot, forcing him to seek refuge in a mountain hideaway.[12] One thing saved Menelik from a similar confrontation
with Yohannes in the fall of 1888—the remoteness of Shoa, relative to the
nearer threat of Mahdi invasion.

While Yohannes prepared for war against the Mahdi—the quasi crusade that would end with his death—Pietro Antonelli was arriving in
Addis Ababa with letters, gifts, 4,700 Remington rifles, and 220,000
cartridges. By then, Menelik had already campaigned with an army of
more than a hundred thousand soldiers, demonstrating a might rivaling
that of the emperor. Italy had helped to build Menelik—its client—into a
major regional player.

In March 1889, Menelik and Taytu were in the town of Wichale, visiting one of Taytu's properties, when news of the death of Yohannes reached
them. It was the moment Menelik had been waiting for. He immediately
claimed for himself the imperial title of *negusa negest*, king of kings. It
was a title Mangasha regarded as rightfully his, as the son of Yohannes.
Not only did Mangasha have lineage in his favor, he had precedent as
well. Historically, Ethiopia had been ruled from the north, from Tigray.
Bolstering that precedent was a strong antipathy among northerners
against the south and Shoa.

It hardly mattered. Now, with Menelik claiming the throne, power
shifted abruptly to the south. Addis Ababa, which had barely existed
a decade earlier, became the new capital of Ethiopia. More to the point,
when Yohannes died, the army Menelik had created to challenge him
was ready to intimidate even the stubbornest of rivals.

Pietro Antonelli, who had assumed responsibility for courting Menelik, building him up and cultivating him as a client for the day the throne was vacant, couldn't believe his good fortune. This turn of events made him look brilliant. He was the mastermind behind a dogged, long-term strategy that was finally paying off. He had backed a winner. He immediately set about formalizing the relationship.

The result was a treaty, signed in Wichale (in Italian, Uccialli) on 2 May 1889. The treaty reaffirmed the abolition of the slave trade in Ethiopia (article 14) and gave preference to Italians in trade and commerce with Ethiopia (article 18). However, the most important piece was article 17. According to Italy, this article obliged Ethiopia to accept Italian representation of its interests abroad, tantamount to an Italian protectorate over Ethiopia. Even though a separate article (article 19) proclaimed the Italian and Amharic versions of the treaty to be "in perfect concordance with each other," disagreement over the Amharic version of article 17 would become the cause—or at least the pretext—for the war that would culminate in the battle of Adwa.[13]

Antonelli signed on behalf of King Umberto of Italy; Menelik signed for himself. It was a measure of the respect Ethiopia had garnered in Europe that the Treaty of Wichale existed at all. A state-to-state treaty negotiated between sovereign European and African states was a rare thing in the nineteenth century.

The treaty's consequences were many. For Menelik, the agreement was insurance for his throne. He was making good on his promise to swap land for power. Mere months after the signing, in August 1889, the Italians moved up from Massawa into the cool highlands and occupied Asmara, where their presence would distract Mangasha and vex Alula. Just as Italy had preoccupied Yohannes, so it would preoccupy Mangasha, keeping him pinned in the north, where he could do little mischief.

Menelik set about consolidating his authority in other ways. Like Napoleon, he used family members as trusted local rulers, holding them personally accountable. Taytu's brother, Wele, immediately received the title of *ras* and sovereignty over additional territories worthy of his new title. Makonnen, Menelik's cousin, remained governor of Harar, east of Addis Ababa. Menelik demanded—and received—gestures of loyalty from other local rulers throughout Ethiopia, with the predictable exceptions of Mangasha and Alula.[14]

Meanwhile, an Ethiopian delegation was to visit Italy later that year, with the aim of ratifying in solemn ceremony in Rome the agreement concluded at Wichale. It was a plum assignment, but also one bearing great risk—someone would have to assume leadership of Ethiopia's first overseas diplomatic mission of modern times. Menelik chose his cousin Makonnen.

Makonnen, Governor of Harar

Menelik, who was forty-five when he claimed the title of emperor, had come to rely heavily on his young cousin. In 1887, as Egyptian power waned, and while Yohannes and the Europeans were distracted by Dogali, Menelik seized Harar, two hundred miles east of Addis. It was a move of great strategic importance. Sir Richard Burton, who is thought to be the first European to have entered the city, repeated a Harari saying he heard in 1854: "He who commands at [the coastal town of] Berbera, holds the beard of Harar in his hand."[15] Not only was Harar a major market town, it was Menelik's gateway to the sea. Menelik knew that his independence depended on it. As soon as his soldiers had secured the place, Menelik installed Makonnen, then a mere thirty-five years old, as governor.

The walls of Harar—made of stone bound by ochreous clay—vary from five to fifteen feet in height. Five heavy gates and fifteen towers create an impression of security that soothed harried travelers arriving from the Somali coast by way of the Afar desert.[16] One relieved visitor exclaimed that Harar seemed "built of chocolate."[17]

Inside the walls, Harar teemed with life. The residents of Harar itself, Burton claimed, made up "a distinct race."[18] The steady arrival and departure of caravans kept things lively, as did the diverse population that lived there or arrived on market days. The rural population of the Harar region is largely Oromo, and in addition to that language and Adari, which was the language of Harar itself, one could regularly hear spoken Amharic, Arabic, Greek, Hindi, Italian, French, English, Turkish, Armenian, and from time to time German.[19] The population of Harar numbered in the tens of thousands; its narrow, rain-rutted earthen streets funneled the population toward its public squares, giving the town an intensely urban feel.[20] In market squares and on adjacent streets, everything was for sale. Millet, lentils, and barley were displayed in mounds. Jujuba, bananas, and citrons were stacked on tables alongside fine locally hand-woven cloth.[21]

Ras Makonnen. From Guèbrè Sellassié, *Chronique du règne de Ménélik II, roi des rois d'Éthiopie*. Paris: Maisonneuve Frères, 1930.

Porters shouldered heavy loads of coffee in goatskins.[22] Vendors touted honey, butter, and the stimulant qat. In the dry season, dust swirled in the sun's glare, mixing with the smells of coffee, rotten fruit, and dung. Stray ostriches startled and bucked.[23] Goats and cattle were sold and butchered in the open squares, their gaping necks adding odor and color to the trade. The spectacle of crowds shuffling over blood-washed earth, speaking in tongues, gave Harar an apocalyptic quality.[24]

The hierarchy of trade descended from ground-floor shops, followed by wood-framed merchant stalls butted up against walls and shaded by makeshift awnings. In the squares, "shops" were no more than wares spread over blankets; nearby, peddlers worked the crowds and neighborhoods on foot. Most vendors disappeared at dusk, which arrives promptly at six-thirty, thanks to the equatorial latitude. That was when the hyenas moved in via gaps in the walls. Harar had no formal waste removal, other than nature itself. By night, the hyenas entered, scavengers taking what suited their appetite, leaving the remainder to be washed by seasonal rains.

Today Harar has much of the look and feel of a North African town, though a bit worse for wear. In the nineteenth century, it was little different. European visitors noted the resemblance, finding the town both picturesque and a little barbaric by North African standards. The fact that Harar had been fought over by Egyptians and Shoans surely had something to do with its well-used appearance. The Shoan occupation of Harar was brutal, and Menelik had moved quickly to put his stamp on the town. After the conquest Menelik announced, "This is not a Muslim country, as everyone knows."[25] Makonnen had the main mosque torn down, as if to drive the point home; he replaced it with an Ethiopian Orthodox church designed by an Italian architect.[26]

Harar was a gem, the terminus for caravans from the coast and the commercial capital of a rich agricultural region—an Eden for some—specializing in coffee.[27] But whether it was Eden or something else (for Burton it was Tuscany, which perhaps amounts to the same thing), Harar was the jewel in the imperial crown created by Menelik's aggressive expansion to the west, south, and east. Like the conquest of the Welayta, the incorporation of Harar could be justified as a strategic necessity, an Ethiopian realpolitik without which Adwa would have been impossible. Just the same, like the Egyptian expansion it displaced, Menelik's aggressive annexations bore witness to an indigenous African colonialism.[28] Menelik was determined to extract as much as possible from his conquest. A special tax was imposed; some members of the European population were forced to provide loans.[29] Menelik got what he wanted, but it took years for the business climate to recover.

Incorporating Harar was just a beginning. As governor of Harar, Makonnen operated as Menelik's viceroy. At an elementary level, Makonnen's job was to preserve order and forward tribute extracted from the coffee and coastal trade. In reality, his work was immensely complex. He had to manage what was easily Ethiopia's most cosmopolitan city. Plus, as the first Ethiopian official most visitors met, he was the face of Menelik's Ethiopia for official delegations making their way to the capital.[30]

Visitors of state were greeted on the approach to Harar, as much as a day's journey out. Mounted troops in parade dress formed the escort, their horses trimmed with silver tack. The riders themselves wore capes of purple velvet or embroidered silk and carried animal skin shields. Music—horns and flutes—added to the pageantry.[31] The transition in vegetation from the Afar desert is so abrupt that the impression is all the more intense. Grassy pasture and meadowland comes into view, and soon steep hillsides turn abruptly to gorges where fig trees thrive. The terrain stabilizes, and natural hedges of rosebush and euphorbia frame patches of land devoted to coffee cultivation. Harar itself sits in a basin; as caravans cleared the pass a mile away, its minarets, its wall, and its flat-roofed buildings came into view.[32]

As the only two-story structure in town, Makonnen's Governor's Palace stood apart.[33] Its gleaming white walls and tall windows with Roman arches presented an unmistakable profile to visitors as they approached the town. Awnings on the windows and a scalloped finish running along the top of the foot-thick walls softened an otherwise fortresslike façade. Banners fluttered from its gatelike entrance. On balance, the imposing structure served to accentuate the gracious reception of the host. Despite his reserve, Makonnen managed to communicate warmth. He unfailingly received emissaries and merchants with style and tact. On official occasions he received guests cordially, though formally, in a black silk shirt with colored piping, usually with a matching black silk cloak fastened with a gold clasp at the neck.[34]

Makonnen had a long, thin face, a full mustache, and a goatee described as "too long for a man of the African race."[35] Many visitors noted his dark, lively, somewhat mournful eyes.[36] Makonnen had lost his Oromo wife at a young age; he never remarried. While piety was not unusual among his contemporaries, fidelity was; it was said that his fidelity to his Oromo wife mirrored his fidelity to Harar and endeared him to the people of the region.[37] Makonnen was not above making informal appearances in public, and he ventured outside the Governor's Palace often. Unlike Menelik or Taytu, who rarely were seen without a full retinue, Makonnen frequently went out in the company of a single advisor, a gesture of trust on his part, and a measure of his popularity and esteem.

By all accounts, Makonnen's was an extraordinary intellect. Even his enemies credit him with intelligence, tact, and discernment. He left a vivid impression on everyone he met. "A perfect gentleman," Sir James Rennell Rodd recalled.[38] Others recalled him as "subtle," "cultivated," "enlightened, courteous, polished," "a man who wielded power in a quiet way." Behind the polish, some discerned a personality at once "smart, hypocritical, [and] wily," but no one doubted that he was a formidable figure.[39] He was voted by acclamation "the most intelligent man in Ethiopia," "alert and intelligent," a "quick intelligence"—there is no shortage of high regard.[40] This delicately attractive man possessed a "musical voice" and cordial, dignified manners.[41]

Until his death in 1906, Makonnen was widely seen as Menelik's successor.[42] He passed on many of his features to his son, Tafari Makonnen, who, as Ras Tafari, would assume a legendary and lofty status as the focus of the Rastafarian cult in the African diaspora. Though Makonnen would never rule, his son would succeed Menelik in the fullness of time, ascending the throne as Haile Selassie in 1930.

Makonnen's Harar was more than a diplomatic gateway. Harar was a cultural hub, a hinge between the coastal towns of the Red Sea, which had been steeped in the culture of Islam for generations, and the Ethiopian highlands, where Christianity tended to dominate. Both in architecture and in dress the city seemed to belong more to the Middle East than to sub-Saharan Africa. Chalk-white stone-and-mortar dwellings took the place of branch and straw *tukul*.

The 1880s were an era of commercial pioneers.[43] French, Italians, Indians, Armenians, and above all Greeks sought, if not a killing, at least a living.[44] For many, the basic idea was to buy something for which a European market no longer existed—fabrics with patterns or colors deemed démodé, firearms a war or two out of date—and sell them to African buyers. A few, such as the French poet Arthur Rimbaud, represented European firms with offices in Aden or elsewhere, but many operated on their own account, trying to make a living in the import-export trade.[45] Many, including Rimbaud, did both.

Rimbaud had arrived in Harar in 1880, where he represented the Bardey firm of Aden, but by 1885 he was also acting as his own agent; he was convinced that he would make as much as thirty thousand francs selling a shipment of armaments to Menelik. Rimbaud soon discovered that he had no pricing power in a country where there was only one legal buyer of firearms, namely, Menelik. After losing months trying to organize a caravan up from the Somali coast, Rimbaud hauled his shipment of slightly out-of-date rifles to Menelik's court. There Rimbaud watched while the emperor took 10 percent off the top as a customs duty, then dictated the price for the remainder. He even had to accept Menelik's terms: he left his shipment in Menelik's capital in exchange for an IOU, and would be paid by Makonnen upon his return to Harar. In the end, Rimbaud felt lucky to have recovered his costs.[46]

Suitably fleeced, Rimbaud learned the hard way what many other merchants already knew: the better trade was not in direct sales to African heads of state but in retail sales on local markets. This was where the Greeks dominated.[47] As in the California gold rush, much of the real money was not in gold but in dry goods and liquor.

Another lucrative trade was in slaves. As Harar was the terminus for all trade between Shoa and the coast, it was inevitably a hub in the regional slave trade.[48] There were five jumping-off points for caravans to Harar from the coast, but only three were heavily trafficked—Zeyla, where the British vigilantly suppressed the slave trade, and Obok and Tadjoura, both occupied by the French and both on the Gulf of Tadjoura.

Ibrahim Abu Bakr and his twelve sons controlled the preferred coastal markets on the Gulf of Tadjoura and much of the 182-mile caravan route to Harar.[49] Thin and of medium height, with a high forehead and darting eyes, Abu Bakr received guests seated on an *angareb* draped in animal skins. His everyday dress included a bright tunic and a turban of white muslin. He served coffee to his guests as a gesture of respect but also, some wryly noted, as a display of largesse.[50] Abu Bakr drove a hard bargain; he had few friends among those who had no choice but to do business with him. Eyewitnesses—all of them European, it must be said—mention no endearing qualities. One bitter acquaintance called him "a registered thief." It is difficult to disentangle the generally negative accounts of his personality from high-minded disdain for his role in the slave trade and widespread resentment of his stranglehold on caravan routes from the coast.[51] His European guests most readily remembered two things about Abu Bakr—that he constantly worked prayer beads in his left hand and that he had the nasty habit of spitting from a gap between his teeth, heedless of where his spittle landed. One gets the impression that conversations with Abu Bakr tended to be brief.

Negotiations, on the other hand, could drag on. A camel could carry up to three hundred pounds of goods; a large inventory of, say, rifles might require a hundred camels.[52] It could take a while to round them up, as Europeans wilted in the intense heat of the Somali coast. A French caravan was stalled from May until October while sufficient camels were found. Arthur Rimbaud, eager to sell his load of rifles to Menelik, cooled his heels at Tadjoura for a year.[53] Such delays were simply another form of negotiation, as additional camels could always be found at a price.[54]

Since members of the Abu Bakr clan rarely left the coast, Makonnen had no direct dealings with them. Conversations went through third parties, including the caravans to Harar and back. Both parties had strong incentives to keep the caravans moving without incident. Abu Bakr, whose most lucrative business was in enslaved people intended for markets across the Red Sea, depended on a steady supply of captives from the highlands. Menelik not only required an outlet for goods of all kinds but also needed to import firearms. Even with the best of intentions regarding the slave trade—and the record is mixed—Menelik had little choice but to do business with Abu Bakr.

With the British shutting down both the arms trade and the slave trade via Zeyla and other Red Sea ports, Abu Bakr and Menelik needed each other to survive.[55] So strong was the presumption that both parties needed a smoothly operating caravan trade that when anything untoward occurred—a massacre, a robbery—there was the strong presumption of complicity. The massacre of the Barral-Savouré caravan in 1886, for example, might or might not have been payback for a French naval commander's criticism of Abu Bakr's involvement in the slave trade. It might simply have been a way to hike up caravan rates by underlining the risks.[56] Either way, no one presumed Abu Bakr innocent.

Abu Bakr was a cultural broker as much as a merchant. On the coast, he lived among ethnic Somalis, but his Afar descent gave him entrée among the Afar people who controlled the routes the caravans took from the moment they left the Gulf of Tadjoura until they arrived at Harar. Following Abu Bakr's death in 1885, his sons carried on a thriving trade, bringing goods to Shoa and returning with caravans—frequently of enslaved boys and girls bound for the Arabian Peninsula and beyond.[57]

For Makonnen, dealing with the slave trade was one of his prickliest tasks as governor of Harar.[58] With Menelik's complete confidence, he controlled who and what entered Menelik's kingdom.[59] Coffee, firearms, ivory, slaves—nothing moved without his tacit approval. Both Makonnen and Menelik were aware of the disfavor in which the slave trade was held. Menelik had disavowed the trade, as had Tewodros before him, but the simple fact remained that enslaved people were a key export commodity. As caravans were rarely homogeneous—most featured disparate commodities shipped together for security—indirect complicity in the trade was nearly unavoidable.[60] And Menelik could ill afford to antagonize those who operated his trade link to the outside world. Moreover, as long as Menelik's soldiers remained largely unpaid, booty—including property, livestock, and slaves taken from among the defeated—would remain part of the soldier's life. Richard Pankhurst, in his magisterial *Economic History of Ethiopia,* cites a source to the effect that a slave caravan left Shoa every three months in the 1880s. By the mid-1890s, Menelik was actively suppressing the trade, destroying notorious slave market towns and punishing slavers with amputation. Even then, slavery persisted as a feature of the gift economy: enslaved people remained a staple of imperial largesse under Menelik—as wedding gifts to friends of the court, for example—as late as 1903.[61]

Managing commercial and moral transactions tactfully was part of Makonnen's charge at Harar. As merchants jockeyed for access and advantage, missionaries elbowed in, too. Father Louis Taurin Cahagne, a Capuchin friar, arrived in 1881 to develop the Roman Catholic missionary presence in the region. For a time, he combated the slave trade by buying slaves to save them not only from human bondage but also from eternal damnation. Taurin bought enslaved boys, mostly in their teens, for as many as fifty thalers and as few as thirty, took them on as his wards, and prepared them for conversion to the Catholic faith.[62] Some of them enjoyed successful careers, thanks to language training in mission schools.[63] In exceptional cases, such boys might themselves become missionaries, carrying on apostolic work among their own people. Taurin was assisted and eventually succeeded as bishop by André Jarosseau, who arrived in 1884. Fifty years later, in the 1930s, Jarosseau was still there.[64]

As for Makonnen himself, his work in Harar amounted to a kind of diplomacy school, an internship in dealing with Europeans. Long before his departure for Italy, Makonnen had acquired a cosmopolitan polish that would qualify him as Ethiopia's premier statesman. Anyone who could preside over the complicated affairs of Harar—not to mention the Europeans, Afar, Arabs, merchants, missionaries, slavers, and weapons merchants who made up its many constituencies—was an asset indeed. Later, Menelik would tap him to serve as his representative on missions to Rome, St. Petersburg, Paris, and London. When the French newspaper *Le Temps* referred to Makonnen as "the second personage in the empire"—that is, second only to Menelik—there was surely grumbling in Addis and elsewhere.[65] Anyone as smooth and talented as Makonnen was bound to have jealous detractors. But for Menelik himself there was really no doubt. When it came time to send an emissary to Rome to finalize the relationship embodied in the Treaty of Wichale, there was no hesitation. He sent Makonnen.

The Grandeur of Italy

When Makonnen and the rest of the Ethiopian delegation stepped off the train in Rome on 27 August 1889, it was already a victory for Africa. It marked the beginning of the first high-level diplomatic encounter between sub-Saharan Africa and Europe of modern times.[66]

Five years earlier, Otto von Bismarck, chancellor of imperial Germany, had convened an international conference on Africa at Berlin. At the Berlin Conference of 1884, the future of Africa lay in the hands of the attending European powers. As the fate of Africa was considered not to be in the hands of Africans, no one had thought to invite any. In its own quiet way, Makonnen's diplomatic mission was a rejoinder to the arrogance of Berlin. A more emphatic rejoinder would come in 1896 at Adwa.

Makonnen's delegation included translator Joseph Negussié, Orthodox priest Welde Michael, and five other high-ranking figures; they were supported by thirteen bodyguards and twenty-one personal servants. Makonnen and his delegation left Harar in July 1889 in the company of Pietro Antonelli and Luigi Capucci. Together, they made their way to the port city of Zeyla, where they boarded the *Colombo.*[67] The vessel was a fitting namesake for the mission Makonnen had undertaken: his voyage of discovery was leading him to the Old World.

Although the *Colombo* was Italian, and therefore flew Italian colors, Makonnen made a quiet independent gesture. From the foresail mast, a flag of horizontal green, yellow, and red bands fluttered in the wind; on the flag's middle band a proud Lion of Judah strutted, holding a cross in his forepaw. It was the first recorded use of this immortal symbol of Ethiopian sovereignty.[68]

Much was at stake for the Italians. As they understood it, the Treaty of Wichale linked Italy and Ethiopia in a protectorate relationship. It was incumbent upon them to show their capacity to shelter and protect. The voyage offered plenty of symbols of menace. After the *Colombo* had passed from the Red Sea to the Mediterranean by way of the Suez Canal, it headed for the Strait of Messina, legendary home of the monsters Scylla and Charybdis. As the vessel steamed among the Aeolian Islands, Stromboli obligingly spewed smoke and stray bits of lava—a convenient metaphor for danger—at which point an Italian naval squadron arrived as escort. From Stromboli to Naples, the squadron nestled the *Colombo* and its passengers in its protective embrace.

After landfall on 21 August, the Italian display continued. Naples was not only Italy's largest city by far—with five hundred thousand inhabitants, it was half again as large as Milan—but also the home of the Italian Geographical Society, ardent patron and promoter of an Italian colonial vision.[69] The dockside reception was grand, with diplomats, a cabinet-level official, and high-ranking officers of the army and navy receiving the delegation in the August heat. An infantry detachment fired off a rifle salute. The Ethiopian delegation clambered into carriages that raced up the Via Toledo to the grand palace at Capodimonte.

Capodimonte was one of the official residences of the Bourbon monarchy that had ruled Naples and Sicily until the arrival of Garibaldi in the 1860s. It was now being put to use to flatter Italy's new African partner. White tents with blue conical tops dotted the lawn, providing the guests with an alternative to lodging in the rooms inside. The strangeness of it

The Ethiopian diplomatic mission to Italy, 1889. From SAI Archive at the University of Naples "L'Orientale"; Silvana Palma, *Archivio storico della Società africana d'Italia; Raccolte fotografiche e cartografiche*. Naples: Istituto Universitario Orientale, 1997.

all was unsettling to the Ethiopians; most chose to bed down outdoors, and the entire delegation slept with swords at the ready.[70]

After settling in, Makonnen's group was treated to some of the region's best—a night at Teatro San Carlo, the opera house of Naples, for a performance of *Il Barbiere di Siviglia,* and a trip to Caserta to see yet another palace, the Bourbons' stunning Versailles-inspired country retreat.[71] After a week in Naples and Campania, Makonnen's delegation took the train north, arriving in Italy's capital on 27 August 1889.

It had already been an eventful summer in Rome. In June, members of the government invited controversy when they attended the solemn inauguration of the Giordano Bruno statue in Campo dei Fiori. It was a deliberate snub to the Vatican, whose predecessors had burned Bruno as a heretic in 1600 on the very spot.[72] Back in Africa, with the Makonnen mission en route, Italian troops moved from Massawa into the highlands and occupied the town of Asmara, on the pretext—laid out in a letter to Menelik—that Italian soldiers needed to be housed in a place "not so warm as Massawa."[73] Such a move could only have been prearranged. It was an act that paralleled the Makonnen mission and, like it, signaled the deepening Italo-Ethiopian collaboration.

However, it also ignited a public debate about the government's colonialist enterprise.[74] Aware of the public's doubts about empire, the government had been careful to couch its steps toward expansion in peaceful terms—the occupation of Asmara was only a means to escape from the heat of Massawa. The press wasn't buying it. The Vatican newspaper noted that what had begun as a purely commercial enterprise aimed at securing a port in the Red Sea ("Massawa . . . and nothing more") now looked like a strategy of conquest. Even the normally pro-government *Tribuna* pronounced itself "averse to colonial expansion" and pointedly accorded "all merit" but also "all responsibility" to those who had engineered Asmara's occupation.[75]

By the time the Makonnen delegation stepped down from its rail car in Rome shortly after three in the afternoon, Roman public opinion was primed; while some favored the government's policy, still others remembered and resented the massacre at Dogali. Most vocal of all were the anticolonialists, who used Makonnen's arrival to protest what was called, oddly, Italy's "pro-African" policy.

Rome tends to empty in the summer, but a small crowd, mostly workers, was on hand when Makonnen saluted the crowd from the platform by touching his hand to his mouth and forehead before extending his hand to the gathered onlookers.[76] He shook hands with General Emilio Pallavicini and a government representative.[77] A much larger and more boisterous crowd—their angry shouts and whistles could be heard inside the station—waited outside, where a woefully inadequate cordon of *carabinieri* struggled to hold them back. (The *carabinieri* captain responsible for the fiasco was later given a dressing-down.) There were more shouts, whistles, and cries of protest before the delegation was rushed into waiting landaus, where they sat immobile while the crowd surged to block their path. It took a charge by mounted *carabinieri* to clear the way. The press called it "an uproar" and "indecorous."[78] The carriages whisked the delegation past the Dogali monument to the Via Venti Settembre, through the Porta Pia, and on to the calm, lush grounds of the Villa Mirafiori.

At verdant Mirafiori, every need had been anticipated. Sheep and cattle had been set to pasture on the Mirafiori lawn, ready to be butchered according to Ethiopian custom. Inside the villa, a special low table—under two feet high, to accommodate Ethiopian dining customs—was set out in the dining room. The villa's pantry was well stocked. A curious press reported every activity of the delegation, down to the last detail of food and drink—salad, rice, lobster in mayonnaise sauce, Velletri wine, cognac, cigars, coffee, Benedictine.[79]

Sightseeing began the following afternoon. Makonnen visited the Pantheon and paid his respects at the tomb of Victor Emmanuel II. Under Agrippa's vaulted rotunda, Makonnen signed the guest book on behalf of Menelik.[80] Security was tight; the scandalous disruptions at the train station would not be repeated.

"I Ask the Protection of Your Majesty"

Makonnen's real work began on the twenty-ninth, when he ventured to the Quirinal Palace to meet Umberto, the king of Italy.[81] At the piazza in front of the palace, troops and a military band were ready in full parade dress in front of monumental statues of Castor and Pollux. There was a wide security screen, courtesy of the *carabinieri*.[82]

The Ethiopian delegation was escorted inside the palace and up the grand staircase to the throne room, where not only Prime Minister Francesco Crispi but also all the key ministers—army, navy, state—were present. Beside Umberto's throne were the many individuals who had cultivated the relationship with Menelik over the years, including Pietro Antonelli, Augusto Salimbeni, Cesare Nerazzini, Luigi Capucci, and Leopoldo Traversi. Standing in front of the throne was Umberto himself, in military dress. Makonnen prostrated himself before Umberto, as required by Ethiopian royal protocol. Once Makonnen rose, Umberto politely inquired about Makonnen's voyage.

The core of the ceremony come down to mere words, but as the existence of a protectorate would later be disputed, the words matter a great deal. Makonnen went first. Speaking through his translator, Joseph Negussié, Makonnen addressed Umberto on behalf of "His Majesty the king of Ethiopia" and acknowledged a mutual interest in "a treaty of friendship and commerce." Makonnen again invoked Menelik's name, then uttered on Menelik's behalf the phrase "I ask the protection of Your Majesty, so that

Umberto receives the Ethiopian diplomatic mission. From *L'Illustrazione italiana,* 1889; Widener Library, Harvard College Library, ICAF019.

peace and tranquility reign in Ethiopia and in the neighboring Italian possessions." Anyone listening would have been forgiven for thinking that Makonnen was invoking a protectorate in the name of Menelik.

"I have heard your words with great satisfaction," Umberto responded. "I hereby pledge myself to the treaty drawn up for the common good of the two kingdoms, and to the protection that I and my government grant to your country with which we sincerely desire peace and prosperity."[83]

Italy argued that the Treaty of Wichale, which Makonnen's presence was to ratify, established an Italian protectorate over Ethiopia. Even though the word "protectorate" appeared nowhere in the treaty, Makonnen's invocation of Umberto's protection, followed by Umberto's extension of protection in response, seemed to validate the Italian claim.[84] The word itself was splashed on the front page of newspapers reporting the event, coverage that would have been impossible for the Ethiopians to miss. If there had been a misunderstanding, there was ample opportunity for Makonnen to clear it up.

Was it all part of a ruse? The story was only beginning.

After the remarks of Makonnen and Umberto, there followed a parade of gifts from Menelik: shields, drums, lances trimmed in gold and laced with gems, two horns filled with *tej* (honey wine), five Oromo saddles, thirty oversized elephant tusks, and one live baby elephant.[85]

With the diplomatic and courtly formalities behind him, Makonnen embarked upon a tour of Italy. It was a hit parade of Italian cities—Genoa, La Spezia, Pisa, Monza, Turin, Bologna, Milan, Modena, Venice— designed to showcase Italy and justify its status as protector. The Ethiopians were treated to military reviews and cavalry maneuvers. They were feted with fireworks and Bengal lights on the canals of Venice. King Umberto and Queen Margherita hosted another royal reception at their grand palace in Monza. Makonnen pronounced himself seduced by the charms of Italy. Turin, he exclaimed, was the "kingdom of heaven." At Lake Como, quite understandably, Makonnen pronounced Italy wicked because, after seeing it, "one doesn't ever want to leave."[86]

Somehow Makonnen pulled himself away. On the nineteenth of September, he and his delegation returned to Rome, where he negotiated an addendum to the Treaty of Wichale, the Additional Convention, signed at Naples on the first of October. For Italy, this addendum recognized de facto Italian authority in lands they occupied, according to the principle of *uti posseditis*—"as you possess."[87] Since Italy had spent the late summer occupying the Ethiopian highlands from Asmara to the Mareb River, this provision recognized a blatant land grab.[88] For Ethiopia, the agreement provided scarce capital in the form of a loan of four million lire, guaranteed by the Italian government. Half of the funds were to be made available to Ethiopia immediately, with the remainder to be established as a credit line, to be used against purchases made by Ethiopia in Italy. In effect, the line of credit was also a kind of export subsidy for Italian business. As collateral, Makonnen put up the customs payments collected at Harar. If Ethiopia defaulted on the loan, Italy was entitled to take over customs operations at Harar until the loan had been made good.[89]

Although the Additional Convention entailed risk, it was risk both parties were willing to accept. On balance, it was a sweet deal for Italy. For Ethiopia, the stakes were much higher, but the country had little choice. It was struggling to preserve its sovereignty as the European powers circled menacingly; it was starved for resources as agrarian crisis and famine deepened at a moment of supreme peril. In exchange for cash, it offered recognition of what was about to be proclaimed as the Italian colony of Eritrea, carved from lands historically claimed by Ethiopia. Although it would later be disputed, Menelik—or at least Makonnen on his behalf—seemed to be recognizing Italy's annexation not only of Asmara but also of the regions of Bogos, Hamasen, and Akale-Guzai—at least fifty square miles in all. It also received the promise of two million lire in sales to Ethiopia (via the credit line) and the right to occupy Harar should Ethiopia default on the loan.

Ethiopia was betting the bank, trading land for time and money. With Italy ensconced in Eritrea in the north and the Harar trade hocked as collateral in the south, everything was at risk. If Ethiopia lost control of Harar through loan default, it would be utterly at the mercy of Italy.

About the time that the Makonnen delegation was getting ready to leave, an unusual news story broke. Menelik's gift baby elephant had gone into a rage, busted up its stall, and then, with relentless pounding from its trunk, shattered the door and escaped. It took twenty men to corral the animal and return it to its pen.[90] It was a timely reminder that life is full of surprises and that no one can predict, let alone control, the future.

CHAPTER 7

"Something Humiliating
for My Kingdom"

THE BREACH WAS GENTLE, but also somehow ominous: "I have discovered something humiliating for my kingdom."

Menelik was writing to King Umberto of Italy. The letter was dated 27 September 1890, about a year after Makonnen's journey to Italy. In November of the previous year, Menelik had been crowned emperor by Abuna Matewos, the metropolitan of Ethiopia, at the Church of Mary at Entotto, in the hills above Addis Ababa. Sometime later, Menelik wrote to the various European heads of state, announcing his coronation. In late February 1890, both Britain and Germany responded that, by the terms of Ethiopia's protectorate status, they should have been informed through Italy, which, as protector, handled Italy's diplomatic relations.

The replies sparked a vigorous protest. Had Ethiopia agreed to protectorate status? At an elementary level, the question turned on a translation. The Treaty of Wichale was drawn up in Amharic and Italian. In his letter of protest to Umberto, Menelik complained that while the Italian version of article 17 seemed to oblige Ethiopia to have recourse to Italy in its dealings with other states, the Amharic version merely gave Ethiopia the option to do so.[1] When Britain and Germany insisted upon receiving communications from Ethiopia by way of Italy—and indeed replied by way of Italy—the confusion had become evident.

But had the confusion been deliberate? Discussions of the causes leading up to the war between Italy and Ethiopia have tended to take the story of article 17 at face value—that the misunderstanding and subsequent hostilities emerged from a simple error of translation or a "dishonest interpretation."[2] Certainly the language of the treaty could have been clearer. The word "protectorate" appears nowhere in the document. It is only the implication of the language of article 17 that establishes it.

Still, there is plenty of reason to believe that the ambiguity of article 17, the "mistranslation," was something Menelik was aware of and was willing to live with for a time. After all, Menelik signed the treaty in early 1889; Britain and Germany both communicated with Menelik via Italy later that year, but it was only late the following year that Menelik made his formal objection. Certainly when Makonnen made his voyage to Italy to sign the treaty in late summer of 1889, the language of protectorate was everywhere. The newspapers used the language of protectorate in their coverage, on occasion resorting to headlines blaring out the single word *protettorato*. In the several weeks that Makonnen and his delegation toured Italy, the message could hardly have escaped them; there were plenty of opportunities to clear up any confusion. More to the point, both Umberto and Makonnen, in their formal addresses to each other, spoke specifically of a relationship of "protection." In addressing Umberto, Makonnen stated, "In the name of my king, I ask the protection of Your Majesty," to which Umberto replied, "I hereby pledge myself . . . to the protection that I and my government grant to your country."[3]

Makonnen was no fool. Although there were those at court who sometimes doubted his loyalty, who feared he would betray Menelik in order to replace him, Menelik's trust in his cousin—whom he sometimes called simply "brother"—was unwavering.[4] Could Makonnen have deceived Menelik and the court by speaking one language—the language of protectorate—at Rome while speaking another at home? In the age of modern newspapers, available and read in both capitals, such a feat was impossible.

Instead, for Menelik, the "mistranslation" of article 17 was a convenient fiction. It allowed Makonnen to go to Rome, sign the Treaty of Wichale, negotiate the Additional Convention and the all-important loan of four million lire, and return to Ethiopia a friend of Italy. Then, more than a year later and from the safety of his secure imperial throne, Menelik could begin to disentangle himself from the partnership with Italy that had facilitated his rise.

It was not yet a formal rupture. In his initial protest, Menelik used the language of a gentle friend who had been hurt, and he mostly communicated through official channels. He was in no hurry to bring down the edifice he had helped to create—for one thing, until Mangasha had been crushed as a rival to the throne, he still needed the Italians to keep arms from reaching Mangasha by way of Massawa.[5] It would be more than a year before he would formally, officially renounce the treaty. By then, he was ready to face whatever consequences this step might bring.

Antonio Baldissera could see where this was going.[6] As commander of Italian forces in Africa, he argued that Italy needed to rethink its policies and alliances in the face of Menelik's rise. It was fine to back Menelik when he was the young southern upstart plotting against Emperor Yohannes. According to the same logic, however, with Menelik now on Ethiopia's throne, it was time to find another internal ally, someone who could help to keep Menelik off balance and preserve Italy's margin for maneuver.

Not everyone agreed. Everything turned on one's view of Menelik. Pietro Antonelli, who had invested years in cultivating the Menelik relationship, argued that Menelik's ascendancy was also Italy's. Italy had backed the winning horse and was about to cash in.[7]

Baldissera saw things differently.[8] Menelik had played Antonelli—and through him, Italy—as long as he was the scrappy underdog. Now that Menelik was on top, he no longer needed Italy, hence the burgeoning "misunderstanding" about article 17 of the treaty. Italy shouldn't waste any time trying to clear up the misunderstanding, Baldissera argued, Italy should find a new scrappy underdog to sponsor against Menelik— for example, Mangasha, the son of Yohannes. *Divide et impera,* he was fond of saying in weighty Latin, redolent of Roman imperial grandeur, "divide and conquer."[9]

Baldissera got nowhere. Partly it was a matter of momentum. Italy had invested in Menelik and Shoa for so many years, it was hard to remember why it had done so. Partly it was a matter of lingering resentment. Backing Mangasha against Menelik would mean reconciling with his lieutenant Alula, the commander at the massacre of Dogali. But reconciling with Alula was politically difficult for Italy.[10] In frustration, Baldissera resigned.

The Creation of Eritrea

Baldissera, who led the Italian forces that occupied Asmara in August 1889 without firing a shot, stepped down in December, mere days before a signal date in the history of East Africa. On 1 January 1890, Italy announced the formation of the colony of Eritrea. Eritrea derived its name from the Greek word *erythros,* "red," thus explicitly referencing the Red Sea. The name conjured memories of classical antiquity, including, inevitably, the glories of the Roman Empire, whose renewal the new colony seemed to promise.[11]

Baldissera's replacement as commander of Italian forces in East Africa, General Baldassare Orero, took up residence in Asmara, now the capital of Eritrea.[12] In General Orero, Menelik and Ethiopia acquired a true friend. The question was, did they want one? Almost immediately after establishing himself in Eritrea, Orero began to think about what a good ally of Menelik would do. He hit upon the idea of marching into Ethiopia—the neighboring restive province of Tigray would do—and pacifying it for Menelik. In a letter to Rome, Orero wrote that he was contemplating a march on Adwa, where, having secured the city, he would await the arrival of Menelik. Such a move would demonstrate to Ethiopia Italy's power and value as an ally.[13] Menelik could even use the occasion to have himself crowned in the historic holy city of Axum.

Rome responded that Orero should focus on fortifying Eritrea, to which Orero replied that the best way to defend Eritrea was by securing Tigray. At this point, Antonelli could see that the years of work that had gone into cultivating his relationship with Ethiopia were in jeopardy; he threatened to resign. But before anyone could restrain Orero, he pounced. The next time Rome heard from Orero, it was 26 January 1890 and he was writing from Adwa.[14]

Orero's Adwa adventure was a disaster. Less than one month after Italy announced the creation of Eritrea, Orero had carried out a new invasion of Ethiopia. If there was anyone left in Ethiopia who was unsure of

Italy's expansionist intentions, those doubts crumbled. It also brought home to Menelik just how risky his pro-Italian policy had been. Although Italy had helped him to arm himself, to build his treasury, and to maneuver against Yohannes, he now risked appearing to be a stooge of Italy. Certainly, had he accepted Orero's invitation and met the invading Italian forces or, even worse, had himself crowned at Axum as the Italians looked on as patrons, he would have suffered irremediable damage. He stayed away.

Instead Menelik extracted what he could from the episode. The pacification of Tigray and the submission of his rival Mangasha were worthy goals—provided he could keep his distance from the Italians. He marched his army northward through the Enderta region, as if heading to meet Orero, but proceeding at a stately pace. Along the way, Menelik encountered significant resistance from farmers reluctant to feed his army.[15] Menelik continued to push northward, brutally relentless, providing a vivid demonstration of what awaited Mangasha and Tigray when he arrived. Menelik's display of determination convinced Mangasha to give in. He was about to be crushed between Menelik, driving northward, and the Italians, pushing south; he despaired at the destruction and suffering. In late February he set out, accompanied by an entourage of three hundred, to meet Menelik before the latter reached Tigray. He was received with honors and made his formal submission, carrying a rock on his shoulder as a symbol of his subordinate status. The battle to succeed Yohannes was over; Menelik had won.

Orero was sacked. His clashes with Antonelli and his rash behavior revealed him to be a liability. By April, a mere four months after his appointment, he was gone.[16] By June, Oreste Baratieri was in Eritrea—along with his prize horse, Trentino—beginning an ascent that would give him executive authority in both military and civic matters for the entire colony.[17]

By 1890, Baratieri had already enjoyed a stellar career as an Italian patriot and soldier. He was born in the alpine region of Trentino-Südtirol in 1841, when not only Trentino but also much of what is now northern Italy was under Austrian rule. Although Trentino is an area of hybrid Italian and German culture, the Baratieri family identified with Italy. Oreste attended a monastery school where he was taught by brothers of the Order of St. Francis.

Oreste Baratieri. From Museo Storico Trento.

The young Oreste was an excellent student, a fine writer, and a spirited young man with a romantic sensibility. He was seventeen when he joined Giuseppe Garibaldi's Red Shirts, an insurgent band determined to unite Italy. He was part of the legendary Red Shirt expedition that landed in Sicily in May 1860 and fought to bring Sicily and the southern Italian peninsula into modern Italy.

Success inspired Baratieri to pursue a military career; he became a captain in the army. He was wounded in the fighting that drove Austria out of

Venetia and paved the way for Italian unity in 1870. He was promoted to the rank of major in 1876; he ran for election in Brescia, won, and began a twenty-year stint in the Chamber of Deputies in Rome. With the idea of "Italy" as his guide, he had become an accomplished military and political leader. He was barely thirty-five years old.[18]

Baratieri, Umberto, and the Example of Leopold's Congo

If Baratieri ever sensed the eerie parallel between Ethiopian efforts to be rid of Italy and his own efforts to rid Italy of the Austrians, he didn't write it down. By the time he shipped out to Massawa, he had moved ever deeper into Italy's budding imperialist circles. As a result of his travels and his military service in North Africa, Baratieri came into the orbit of the Geographical Society, which in Italy, as everywhere else, was an incubator of colonialist sentiment.

Baratieri made an effective colonial advocate. He had honed his writing skills as editor of *Rivista militare*, Italy's major military periodical, which helped to get him elected to the governing council of the Geographical Society. There he came to admire the work of King Leopold of Belgium. In the 1870s, Leopold had asserted that tiny Belgium was "small, happy, content," yet by the 1880s, Leopold was well on his way to carving out a vast African enterprise for himself in Congo.[19] The example of Leopold fired imaginations in expansionist circles by showing that even small countries could accomplish grand colonial feats. Soon King Umberto was emphasizing commercial and maritime themes.[20]

Baratieri was an avid reader. By the time he arrived at Massawa in 1890 he was already an amateur African ethnologist, seeking to gain tactical advantage over Ethiopian adversaries by exploiting their differences.[21] As he rose in authority, he sought out partnerships with local chiefs in Eritrea, playing on both their resentment of Mangasha's heavy-handed rule and their fear of Menelik and rule from the south. In each case, his pitch was the same: Italian rule was better—less burdensome, more liberal— than any local alternative.[22]

The showcase figure was Bahta Hagos. For years prior to the arrival of the Italians in the highlands, Bahta had lived the life of a *shifta*, a bandit. He and his men pounced on caravans making their way between Massawa and the coast. As the authority of the Ethiopian state expanded, first under Tewodros, then under Yohannes and Menelik, his room for maneuver became constrained. The arrival of the Italians provided a counterweight to Ethiopian authority, which had encroached on his autonomy and his income. A courtship of mutual interest began. Italy struck a deal with Bahta, recognizing his regional authority, including an administrative capital at Saganeiti.[23] The ascent of the *shifta* had begun.

Bahta's collaboration brought him power and legitimacy. His service as Italian regional administrator came with authority to mobilize a military force numbering in the hundreds. This made Bahta powerful, but as he was now Italy's ally, the deal also increased Italian firepower at minimal additional expense. In exchange for his administrative and military service, Bahta was authorized to exact a tribute of 10 percent—a tithe, in effect—on the population in his region. It was even said that Bahta had converted to Roman Catholicism. The Italians were proving themselves adept at expansion and consolidation via co-optation of local leaders.[24]

Bahta entertained lavishly. Rosalia Pianavia, who confessed to a fascination for Bahta, remarked on his pride, his imposing presence, and his air of mystery. She was less admiring of his methods as a ruler—Bahta was "more feared than loved."[25] The fascination was mutual. Bahta developed an infatuation for Rosalia, even though—or perhaps because—she was the spouse of one of the ranking Italian officers. Mimetic desire requires no translation. Bahta visited Rosalia in great pomp, preceded by soldiers and musicians blasting out a tune on their *meleket* horns. Bahta followed on a white mule whose pink saddlecloth was embroidered in silver. Rosalia was flattered by the spectacle, and Bahta left "enchanted."[26] More cordial visits ensued, and Bahta's fascination did not abate. Politics would soon dampen his ardor.

Eritrea, Settlement Colony

On 10 November 1893, nine Italian families—fifty individuals in all—arrived in the highlands of the new colony of Eritrea. The event represented the fulfillment of a cherished vision: to find an outlet for Italy's burgeoning population. In 1891, just a year after the noisy proclamation of Eritrea as a colony, a parliamentary commission had set off for Massawa. Its task was to determine the suitability of Eritrea for settlement. Every year thousands of Italians left Europe for a new life in the Americas, where they started over as Brazilians, Argentinians, or Americans. For some political leaders, finding an outlet for all of this youthful vigor became a national priority. A member of the Chamber of Deputies, Leopoldo Franchetti, became the leading advocate for the vision of Eritrea as a settlement colony.[27]

Franchetti soon encountered resistance—not so much, at first, from Africans, but from the Italian civil and military authorities. Franchetti's vision of colonial Eritrea was populist. If landless Italians were being lost to the Americas, he argued, then it was the landless who should be invited—and subsidized—as farmers and settlers in the new colony of Eritrea. Unless the colony was properly settled by family farmers, Franchetti argued, well-capitalized investors would seize the best land and simply reproduce the quasi plantation system, the vast latifundia, that hampered the development of southern Italy.

Franchetti's idea of subsidized settlers faced resistance on a number of levels. Eritrea was a huge drain on Italy's budget. Any funds had to be coaxed from a legislature that was skeptical of the value of colonial enterprise. Unless new money was found, Franchetti's subsidies for settlers would be diverted from other colonial interests, including the army. The army was already starved for resources; it viewed resettling landless Italian peasants in Eritrea as a luxury, even a burden. What the army wanted above all were stable, well-capitalized large-scale farmers who would be allies in the conquest and pacification of Eritrea—something closer to the stable, wealthy *colon* settler communities the French were establishing in North Africa.[28]

Franchetti's vision won. The work of building a settler's Eritrea began. Franchetti's settlement plan offered generous inducements, the Italian equivalent of forty acres and a mule. Each family was promised twenty hectares (nearly fifty acres) in perpetuity provided they occupied and cultivated the land for five years. Start-up costs—travel to Eritrea, seed, tools, a dwelling, and an advance on the first year's crop yield—were provided in the form of a loan, payable in cash or in kind, at an interest rate of 3 percent.[29]

From his position as the head of the Office of Settlement, Franchetti was tireless in his advocacy. Between 1893 and 1895, some four hundred thousand hectares (nearly a million acres) of the finest farm and pasture-land in the Eritrean highlands was set aside for settlers and ruled off-limits to the local African population. Rather than try to create an organic community from scratch, colonial administrators transplanted parts of existing communities. The first settler families were drawn from two villages. Seven families were from the Lombard town of Magenta; the other two hailed from the Sicilian town of Pedara, near Catania.[30]

Adi Ugri, a site about thirty miles south of Asmara, was chosen for the settlement.[31] The new village was baptized Umberto I, after the king of Italy. Its layout tells us something about what were considered the essentials of Italian village life. The village of Umberto was laid out in a grid around a central piazza, which featured a windmill and a communal oven.

Upon arrival each family was assigned two *tukul*—the native huts of straw and wood typical of the highlands. Likewise, each family received a livestock allotment of eight cattle, ten chickens, and a piglet. Nine farming plots, one per family, were laid out around the perimeter of the settlement. By the time of the official inauguration of the village of Umberto in May 1893, furrows had been cut, irrigation canals dug, vines planted, and coffee plants started.[32]

A large tent was set up near the fields for Catholic Mass. Father Bonomi, the army chaplain, used the occasion to offer words of encouragement and to prepare the intrepid settlers for the inevitable disappointments of settler life. Then the village was duly blessed. Father Bonomi, dressed in his most colorful vestments and bearing a monstrance, led a benedictory procession around the perimeter—just as he might have in Italy—blessing the fields and the *tukuls*. A few weeks later, in late July, Rosalia Oldani, Eritrea's first settler infant, was born.[33]

Despite such a promising display of fecundity, the settlement would come to an abrupt end. Public opinion in Italy remained skeptical. The contrast between the bleak poverty of the Italian countryside and the generous subsidies offered to the families of Umberto—four thousand lire, a princely sum—fed claims of a colonial boondoggle.[34] What might those lire buy if properly invested in the farmers of the Mezzogiorno, Italy's impoverished south?

But the real pressure came from displaced Africans. What could be more arrogant than to push a population abruptly from a million acres of the best land? Some land had been abandoned—how much we'll never know—as the highland population of Eritrea and Ethiopia struggled with the consequences of rinderpest, a viral disease that killed cattle. Since the introduction of rinderpest—most likely by way of cattle imported from India via Massawa—the highlands population had languished. Without cattle for dairy, meat, and farm labor, the Ethiopian population had endured years of famine and illness, from 1888 to 1892. Estimates of casualties range from one-tenth to one-third of the Ethiopian population.[35]

From Rome, Francesco Crispi urged Italian military leaders to treat underfarmed land as abandoned and "at the mercy of the first occupant," namely, Italian settlers. Building on Franchetti's populist vision, Crispi imagined an enrooted peasant-soldier—an African Cincinnatus—eager to defend his land and, with it, Eritrea.[36] Instead, the boldness of the Italian settlement initiative aroused the local population, which could now plainly see what was in store for them.

A few weeks later, at nine o'clock on the morning of 2 June 1894, Menelik's archrival Mangasha entered Addis Ababa accompanied by his lieutenants, including the formidable Alula. As they approached Menelik's palace, each shouldered a stone—a sign of repentance and submission. They had submitted before, in 1890, but this occasion occurred in new circumstances and with additional pomp. Drums and horns played from the imperial closure, the clamor exceeded only when Mangasha crossed into the royal compound with his (unarmed) soldiers and his clergy; Menelik's troops fired their rifles into the air in celebration. Mangasha and his lieutenants approached Menelik's throne. Mangasha removed the stone from his shoulder and placed it at Menelik's feet. Then he and his entourage prostrated themselves in front of the emperor, completing the ritual of submission.[37]

From a naive point of view, it was a triumph not only for Menelik but also for Italy, his partner. In fact, the ceremony of June 1894 signaled a decisive moment in the creation of modern Ethiopia. Tigray, through Mangasha, bound its fate to that of Ethiopia. Mangasha had no alternative but to accept Menelik's leadership in the face of Italy's encroachments. By the end of the year, the revolt against Italy would begin.

Francesco Crispi. From John Grand-Carteret, *Crispi, Bismarck et la Triple-alliance en caricatures.* Paris: C. Delagrave, 1891.

Against the Bite of the White Serpent:
Bahta Hagos and Mangasha

In late December 1894, Bahta Hagos attended a dinner at the home of the chief Italian resident at Saganeiti. At the end of the evening, as he and his companions rose to take their leave, they turned on their host and tied him up. "Go ahead, [but] Italy is great!" shouted the resident defiantly. Bahta shot back, "Ethiopia is greater still!" Bahta—the slippery bandit, the convert, the collaborator—had chosen Ethiopia.[38]

Bahta's men beat the drum—the *chitet*—in a call to arms. They also seized two Italian telegraph specialists. In a gentlemanly gesture, Bahta assured his captives that their arrest was "nothing personal." The colonial settlements had set him off. Italy was taking the best land; worse, Italy's soldiers were taking the women, too, as *madama*.[39] Nation, land, women— the loyalties were hard to disentangle, but the choice of revolt was clear. And there was the prickly matter of race. When an associate asked why he rebelled, Bahta offered a colorful analogy: "When the white serpent has once bitten you, you will search in vain for the cure."[40]

Three days later, Bahta was dead. His men had answered his call for an uprising, but they were no match for the forces sent against him. As for the general population, they had their resentments against Italy, but Bahta's reputation was tarnished, too, leaving the locals confused in their loyalties and thus largely passive. Major Pietro Toselli had been ordered to Saganeiti along with fifteen hundred men to investigate.[41] As Bahta could counter with a force of seven hundred at most, the failure of his revolt was sealed. To his great credit, Bahta released his hostages, rather than take their lives in a vengeful gesture. Bahta himself fell in a hail of bullets at Halai.[42] He ascended to whatever paradise is reserved for bandit heroes.

Bahta's revolt was only the beginning. The day after Bahta's death, Mangasha rallied his forces at Entisho, to the east of his capital at Adwa. He offered a peaceful explanation: the Muslim Dervishes were on the move again, and he was preparing to defend against them. However, as Mangasha's forces, estimated at nineteen thousand men, massed menacingly near the frontier of the newly proclaimed Italian colony of Eritrea, Mangasha's Dervish cover story was greeted with skepticism.

Oreste Baratieri, commander of the Italian forces, assembled nine thousand men and marched southward. He didn't confront Mangasha's forces directly. Mangasha had left Adwa, his capital, undefended. Baratieri marched toward Adwa unopposed and on 28 December entered the town.[43]

There is nothing quite like a triumphant entry into an undefended capital to make a point—a leader who cannot defend his people or the seat of his power is no leader at all. In Adwa, Baratieri received gestures of support and submission, notably from the clergy. However, Mangasha was anything but through. His army was intact, and Eritrea lay before him. Just as Baratieri had ignored Mangasha and marched directly to Adwa, Mangasha was in a position to march on Asmara, or even all the way to Massawa and the coast. Like Sherman's march through the South, Mangasha might simply ignore his enemy, push past him, and shatter the myth of colonial Eritrea with a single devastating march to the sea. Such an exploit would have made Mangasha a national hero and bolstered his claim to his father's throne. In fact, just such a nightmare scenario for Menelik prompted wild rumors in Addis; it was said that Mangasha had defeated Baratieri and was well on his way to Massawa.[44]

These were only rumors, of course. Still, after three days in Adwa, the thought of Eritrea at the mercy of Mangasha chastened Baratieri; he withdrew back north as Mangasha began a tentative move into Eritrea. Given that Mangasha's forces outnumbered his own by more than two to one, a direct confrontation was out of the question. Baratieri shadowed Mangasha and his forces as they moved north, waiting for an opportune moment to attack.

Late in the afternoon on 12 January 1895, Baratieri's scouts located Mangasha's forces, encamped near Coatit. Baratieri's men occupied a dominant position overlooking Mangasha's camp, while Mangasha remained unaware of their arrival. Fighting began the next day with neither side victorious, though Mangasha's forces suffered greater casualties. On the fourteenth, Mangasha withdrew toward the south, toward home, under cover of darkness. At dawn on the fifteenth, Baratieri and his men awoke to find Mangasha's camp vacant.[45]

Having turned back Mangasha's invasion, Baratieri sought to turn Mangasha's retreat into a rout. Although Mangasha had at least a six-hour lead, Baratieri's forces pursued, making up twenty-five miles in less than a day. Late in the afternoon, they came upon Mangasha encamped at Senafe. Within minutes, Italian artillery deployed and opened fire, wreaking havoc on Mangasha's camp, including a direct hit on Mangasha's tent.

Mangasha survived the attack and fled with his army, leaving his camp in shattered disarray. Mangasha's tent, damaged by artillery fire, became a trophy for Baratieri and his men. Its contents, including a chest that served as Mangasha's mobile archives, would yield precious intelligence.[46] Weeks later, on 1 March 1895, Mangasha tried to explain away what had happened in a repentant letter to Baratieri. "The animosity was the work of Satan," he wrote, suggesting that when he invaded Eritrea, he had simply been possessed by a very bad idea.

Mangasha's captured archives showed otherwise. They contained an extensive correspondence that showed that Mangasha was anything but a rogue performer. He certainly wasn't possessed by the devil; rather, he had been incited to act by Menelik himself. Among the trove of correspondence was a letter from Menelik telling Mangasha that "his enemies" the Italians continued to talk down Mangasha at court, repeating "brazen calumnies."[47] There was also evidence that the revolt of Bahta Hagos had been coordinated with the full knowledge not only of Mangasha but also of Menelik.

If the Italians had any remaining illusions about Menelik, they now dissipated.[48] Their protégé, the man they had supported in an attempt to harry Yohannes, the man whose ascendancy they had counted as their own, was now without a doubt their most formidable enemy.

Moreover, in attacking and routing Mangasha, the Italians both achieved a great military victory and inflicted upon themselves a catastrophic strategic defeat. Mangasha had been the only credible rival to Menelik's authority; it was said that he and Alula had been ready to deal with the Italians against Menelik, an arrangement that would have given Italy great leverage to use against Menelik.[49] Instead, by defeating Mangasha, Baratieri had done Menelik's dirty work. Mangasha was now "reduced to a bandit in the hills of Tembien."[50] The remark, attributed to Cesare Nerazzini, captured a sad truth: Mangasha had been humiliated, reduced to a mere *shifta*. But it missed a still greater truth: that Ethiopia itself had been pushed into Menelik's arms along with Mangasha. The nation at large knew that Ethiopia now had only one credible defender—Emperor Menelik, king of kings, Lion of the Tribe of Judah. As for the Italians, the next time they would see Mangasha would be on the battlefield at Adwa, fighting as part of Menelik's army.

While still basking in the glory of his victories, Baratieri filed his expense sheet for the campaign against Mangasha; his costs came to 500,000 lire—a bargain, well under $100,000.[51] By comparison, American Civil War costs typically exceeded $1 million *per day*. When George

Berkeley translated Baratieri's 500,000 lire figure into terms his reader could understand, he came up with £19,000—"a price often paid for a house in London."[52] This truly was empire on the cheap.

Baratieri's secret, of course, was the askari mercenaries. By hiring Africans to fight Africans, Baratieri avoided the cost of mobilizing, training, and paying European troops. The commanding officers at Coatit and Senafe were Italians, but the men lobbing shells into Mangasha's tent were Africans, paid at African rates. Baratieri also avoided the political cost of reporting the deaths of European soldiers. After one of his engagements with Mangasha's forces, Baratieri duly reported his casualties to Rome— eleven dead and thirty wounded. None were white. Not only were Baratieri's victories cheap, but they cost little in European lives.[53]

The final irony was that Baratieri's victories of late 1894 and early 1895 lay the foundation for his defeat at Adwa. They did so by creating expectations that were completely unrealistic. The rapid suppression of Bahta's chaotic revolt and the comic collapse of Mangasha's forces in flight underpinned an invalid assessment of Ethiopian military valor. Meanwhile, the cheapness of the campaign encouraged Italian political leadership to underestimate the cost—both in terms of cash and in European lives—of the full-scale war Menelik was already preparing.

Baratieri Pushes into Ethiopia

Baratieri's campaigns against Bahta Hagos and Mangasha vaulted him to celebrity status. In Italy, avid colonialists reached back to the glories of ancient Rome for a proper comparison. They hailed Baratieri as the new Scipio Africanus, after the general of Roman antiquity who had defeated the Carthaginians in North Africa. In Eritrea, Baratieri's successes led to calls to follow up his victories with a campaign into the northern Ethiopian province of Tigray. Such a campaign, it was argued, would consolidate Baratieri's victory by permanently weakening Mangasha. It would also give Eritrea a more defensible natural frontier. Mangasha and his army had descended into Eritrea from the higher elevations of Tigray. Italian control of a line of mountains from Adwa to Adigrat would form a natural defense from which Eritrea could repel any invasion. The only catch was that such an occupation of Tigray was sure to raise hackles in Addis. If Italy took

Tigray, what would Menelik do? Without waiting to answer this question, Baratieri moved. Two days after Mangasha's contrite "work of Satan" letter, on 3 March 1895, Italian forces occupied the town of Adigrat.

Adigrat is a market town set in a fertile valley; it sits almost on top of East Africa's great watershed. East of Adigrat, the rivers flow to the Red Sea. Rivers west of Adigrat drain to the Nile. Of all the regions and settlements to fall into Italian hands in 1895, Adigrat was the most alluring. Besides being the capital of the Agamé region, at more than eight thousand feet it stood aloof of the malarial lowlands and its temperature was mild, even at near-equatorial latitudes.

Caravans to Adigrat could count on a seven-day journey from Massawa. From a military point of view, that was a long way, but Italy now had a series of fortified positions—Massawa, Ginda, Asmara, Gura, Coatit, Senafe, Barakit, Adigrat—all the way up from the coast. A fort at Adigrat, which the Italians immediately set about building, could be provisioned and reinforced with relative ease.[54] Baratieri wrote a lengthy report to Rome, praising the settlement prospects of Adigrat and the Agamé region. It is "very rich and very productive," he wrote, adding that it is "just right for Italian colonization."[55]

But Mangasha remained an irresistible lure. Adigrat had fallen into Italian hands, but Mangasha—by either dumb luck or wily evasion—managed to remain at large, always just out of reach. Baratieri took the bait. He dispatched an askari column to pursue Mangasha as far as Mekele, while Baratieri himself went westward to occupy Adwa and the Tigray region.[56] In early April, Baratieri received homage and gestures of submission from the clergy of Adwa and Axum, but he misread their accommodation as gratitude for the Italian presence.[57]

The challenge for Baratieri was to know where to stop. The lure of Mangasha, the irresistible bait, would drive Baratieri to push as far south as Amba Alage, nearly doubling the area under Italian control. But it did nothing to make Eritrea any more secure, and it seems never to have occurred to Baratieri how he would hold, much less administer, such a vast territory.[58] Years later he would concede that it was a mistake.[59] At the time, in the heady aftermath of victory, he adopted the tone of a conqueror. "Tigray awaits Italian occupation," he told Rome, casting Tigray in the role of impatient maiden, with Italy playing gallant suitor.[60]

Baratieri set out a systematic plan for occupation and colonization of the new territories in seven typeset pages. The newly conquered lands of Tigray, Agamé, Enderta, and more were to be Italianized. Ethiopian farmers would be bought out (in order not to create ill will) to make way for an Italian settler population. Once the settler communities were established, askari veterans would be settled on farmland around the periphery of the Italian settlements as a reward for faithful service, but also to create a security buffer. There would be churches, schools, clinics, Italian language classes—an entire cultural infrastructure.[61]

Baratieri's grand vision soon ran into political and economic realities. Resistance to colonialism, both in the Chamber of Deputies and among the general public, forced Crispi to rein in spending. When Baratieri asked for thirteen million lire, a mere pittance, Crispi told him to make do with nine million, telling him that "Napoleon made war with the money of the defeated."[62] It was a remark that combined the grandiose with comic irony—when Napoleon made war with the money of the defeated in the 1790s, he was looting the wealthy provinces of northern Italy, not the plague- and war-depleted provinces of northern Ethiopia.

Baratieri was frustrated and asked to be replaced. In May 1895, Crispi refused Baratieri's request for replacement. Instead, he recalled him to Italy, to discuss plans and budgets in person.

Baratieri returned to Italy in July 1895. He was feted at banquets hosted by pro-colonial groups. Medals were struck in his honor as "the hero of Coatit and Senafe." Baratieri used such occasions to drum up public support for his vision of a resurrected imperial Rome. "Give me ten million lire and I will haul Menelik to Rome," he promised.[63] It was an allusion to the Gallic wars of Julius Caesar, who famously defeated the Gallic chieftain Vercingetorix and had him brought to Rome in chains.

Costly colonial wars were a tough sell, not only to a diffident Italian public but also in Italy's Chamber of Deputies. In Rome, Matteo Imbriani, a patriot who, like Baratieri, had fought with Garibaldi, pushed back. On 27 July, as Baratieri sought to conjure Roman glories, Imbriani presented a legislative motion rejecting the government's "colonial war of conquest." He called on Prime Minister Francesco Crispi to abandon it. Crispi shot back, portraying Italy's land grab as a necessary act of defense, one that justified a long-term presence. "If fortune of arms has given us the territory we now occupy, we cannot abandon it," he argued before the deputies.[64] Like it or not, the new territories were a fait accompli.

The next day, Baratieri met with Crispi and his ministers of finance, war, and foreign affairs. He had reduced his original request for thirteen million lire to ten million, but Crispi still would go no higher than nine.

Afterward, Baratieri went on vacation. He visited his family in Trentino for alpine picnics and boating.[65] He mulled over his choices. In September, he visited with Crispi once more, then headed for Brindisi, where he departed for Africa.

Prey to vanity, self-doubt, and a blind patriotism, Baratieri had given in. He was deeply attached to his status as military commander in chief and governor of Eritrea. The thought of resigning in the face of unacceptable constraints, as Baldissera had done before him, was foreign to his rigid sense of duty. Italy—his *madre patria* (mother fatherland), as he repeatedly referred to it—claimed every ounce of his filial piety, all of his devotion. He couldn't say no.

PART II

The Battle

CHAPTER 8

Menelik's March

I T WAS A SATURDAY—market day in Addis Ababa—in September 1895. Two heralds made their way to the top of a mound overlooking the market. Each carried a staff topped by banners of red and green. A horn sounded; people gathered round to hear an imperial proclamation. The emperor was calling the nation to arms.[1] Ethiopia was going to war.

Sometimes being a leader means knowing what *not* to do. When Menelik learned of Mangasha's defeat in January 1895, he did nothing. And when he heard in March of the Italian occupation of Tigray as far south as Lake Ashenge, Menelik did not race to drive them out.

In Africa and in Europe, Menelik's failure to respond immediately was taken as a sign of cowardice. "Menelik is a myth," a remark attributed both to Tekle Haimanot and to Major Pietro Toselli, summed it all up.[2] After all, Italy had just taken a Connecticut-sized bite out of Ethiopia, but Menelik dawdled at home in the south. Although Italy made no explicit territorial claims, from Axum to Adigrat to Amba Alage it now occupied an additional seven thousand square miles of Ethiopian territory, an area bigger than Belgium or Ecuador. Moreover, the occupied area included the ancient holy city of Axum, reputed home of the Ark of the Covenant and the historic coronation city for Ethiopia's rulers—the equivalent of Charlemagne's Aachen. No self-respecting ruler of Ethiopia could let such an affront stand.

In fact, nearly a year would pass between Mangasha's humiliating rout at Coatit and Senafé and the first Ethiopian rejoinder at a place called Amba Alage. Yet Menelik knew that while his power could withstand the doubts of those who saw fear in his hesitation, it could not withstand defeat. Moreover, Tigray, the northern province now claimed for Italy, was a restless land; Menelik, a southerner, had only nominal authority there. Although six years had passed since he had laid claim to the emperor's title, he had never visited Tigray. He ruled the province only through rebellious lieutenants.[3] Menelik would have to demonstrate his authority in a place where it had never been secure.

Ethiopia Rising: The Mobilization

What should Menelik do? At court, pressure to respond vigorously was acute. Empress Taytu, her brother Ras Wele, and her fellow northerners Mangasha and Alula wanted immediate action. But war would have to wait. Military campaigns are shaped by the seasons. Heavy, sometimes violent rains fall in the summer months in Ethiopia, impeding all but the most determined travelers. Menelik waited, and behind the scenes he prepared. In April 1895 he ordered a special tax to pay for rifles and cartridges. He courted the Muslim Dervishes, sending gifts of horses and coffee. Menelik played down their long standing religious differences, emphasizing instead a common racial heritage: "I am black and you are black—let us unite to hunt our common enemy."[4]

Finally, in September 1895, at the end of the rainy season, Menelik issued his call for a national mobilization. He also ordered all Italians expelled from Ethiopian territory.[5]

Ethiopia did not have a national army. What it did have was a strong military tradition that made service in the national militia an obligation both patriotic and religious. The organization for this militia has been called feudal; given the personal nature of the military service obligation, the claim has an element of truth.[6] In effect, the order passed down the chain of command from the emperor to the *ras* and regional governors and thence to the heads of district.

The call to arms started with drumming, which stopped all work and all conversation. Then the proclamation was made.[7] Within minutes, men were riding off in all directions to relay the news. Shield, lance, rifle, and ten days' supply of food—these were the requirements of the soldier. Women prepared thick breadcakes. Horns were filled with red pepper and butter. Cartridge belts were slipped over the shoulder or around the waist. Rifle muzzles were stuffed with scraps of wood or a rag to keep out dirt on the march.[8] Swords were strapped to the right hip, following Ethiopian custom.[9] All able-bodied men answered the call to arms, and from the local district they moved toward established rendezvous points on the appointed day.

Ad hoc recruitment served Ethiopia well, notably in its struggle against Egyptian expansion. The risk in such an informal system, of course, was the threat of disloyalty. Menelik was the king of Ethiopia, a position he had clawed his way into from his secure base as king of Shoa. As emperor, he relied upon a web of relationships that depended variously on blood, marriage, trust, and fear. In the end, the success of the mobilization would depend on the strength of those relationships. Menelik's closest supporters included his cousin Makonnen; Wele, brother of Empress Taytu; and Michael, a convert from Islam and viceroy in the land of the Wollo Oromo. But he also needed Mangasha, the resentful son of Emperor Yohannes and restless governor of Tigray; Tekle Haimanot, the king of Gojjam and rival for the throne; and Alula, a patriot who resented Menelik's dealings with the Italians.[10] These relationships would be tested on the march. Some would fray. Up until the eve of Adwa, Italian strategic assessments crackled with speculation about who might peel away from Menelik, leaving his army—and Ethiopia itself—exposed to fatal division.

Menelik would lead a march northward from Addis Ababa, starting on 11 October. Troops in the south were instructed to converge on Warra-Ilu, 155 miles northeast of the capital, while subordinates farther north were to join him en route at Lake Ashenge and Mekele, respectively 250 and 310 miles north of Addis.[11] These northerly assembly points would save the men the trouble of marching south to Addis only to march north. They would also reduce the colossal footprint of Menelik's army. Ethiopian peasants were happy enough to produce tribute for Menelik on his way north, but there could be no mistaking the devastation the passing of the emperor's army could inflict. There were limits to hospitality. When Menelik's army eventually headed south again after the battle of Adwa, villages would be far from pleased to see the emperor again.

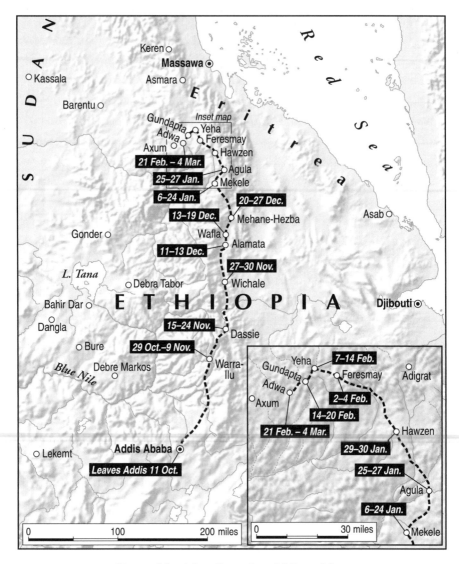

Route of the Adwa Campaign, Addis to Adwa

The March Begins

Menelik and Taytu traveled with the pomp but also the purpose of a Renaissance court. Theirs was no conventional military campaign. With every step, the imperial couple would be testing public opinion and the loyalty of those who had pledged to join the defense of Ethiopia.

The imperial court proceeded at a stately pace. As Menelik's men pressed onward they marched surrounded by the din of drums, horns, and song.[12] The sheer scale of the Ethiopian army—among the largest Africa had ever seen—gave the impression of an irresistible flow. Whenever the terrain allowed it, the troops of Ras Michael and Ras Wele peeled away from the main army, flanking Menelik's troops in columns on either side. These dispersed movements minimized bottlenecks, enhanced security, and reduced the impact on the population. These parallel armies widened trails as they went, undaunted in their progress. As they crossed adjacent passes, securing the way of the emperor, they formed a spectacle of billowing *shammas* and bobbing rifles and lances, the mark of this citizens' army. One chronicler captured the pageantry of the event, recounting how drums beat and trumpets blared, as if to say, "Courage" and "Fortune is yours," while minstrels sang in mock astonishment, "O wonder! They came to conquer Abyssinia, crossing the sea on a boat."[13]

Taytu gloried in a march that radiated splendor and power. Her entourage dwarfed all but the emperor's, which she followed on the march. A mounted soldier sounded a shrill horn to announce her imminent arrival. Then came a military guard, followed by the empress herself—veiled and mounted on mule or horseback. Taytu's mount was led by Baltcha, a trusted lieutenant and eunuch who—along with the jobs of imperial treasurer and chief artilleryman—had the honor of holding the imperial reins. She was followed, at a distance, by a formation of women, also mounted and arrayed in a semicircle. Each member of the empress's entourage carried a brightly colored umbrella, forming a throbbing cluster of color at the heart of the march.[14]

Taytu's group included thousands of soldiers armed to the teeth. But the ladies of the court added color, and Taytu's musical detail alone numbered over a hundred—men and women, singers and performers. Thanks to them, the empress never lacked for a sound track. Taytu preferred the music of the *masenqo*, a fiddlelike instrument common to East Africa, though to compare it to a fiddle misrepresents the scale of this instrument. The single string of the fretless *masenqo* is typically played with a bow by a seated musician who holds the instrument between the knees, somewhat like a cello. As such, the *masenqo* was not well adapted to marching. Instead, Taytu's musicians plucked a marching melody on

Taytu on campaign. From *L'Illustration,* 14 March 1896.

an eight-stringed guitarlike instrument. As Taytu's group moved out, her performers played and sang a musical motif that repeated after four measures.[15]

The end of the day was no less brilliant. It began with a harbinger, the group charged with the task of transporting and setting up the royal tents. They carried the *desseta,* the emperor's tent of red velvet; the *el-fign,* the tent of the empress; and the *adderach,* the tent used for royal audiences. The location of the *desseta* ("joy," because seeing it meant that the day's march was over) determined the layout of the mobile court. Everything else in camp followed from the position of the *desseta*—the placement of other tents, even the direction of the next day's march, which was indicated by the orientation of the tent door. If the tent was dismantled before sundown, the march would resume in the morning; if it remained, the following day would be a day of rest.[16]

Once the red tent was in place on the high ground dominating the camp, hundreds of royal servants flew into action. Their task was to turn the royal campsite into a fully functioning imperial court. The empress's tent, the *elfign,* was set up behind the red tent. If important business was to be carried out, or if the emperor would be entertaining, the emperor's great tent, the *adderach*—twenty feet high—was set out in front of the *desseta.*[17] Fabric for the tent roof was stretched across. Carpets were laid down on the ground, the emperor's divan was assembled, and cushions were set out. Tent walls of fine silk—transported by fifteen mules on the march—were unloaded and hoisted into place. Green, yellow, and red pennants flew from the top. In less than an hour the imperial court was ready for business.[18]

The imperial complex was enclosed by a screen of fabric six feet high, the openings to which were guarded by soldiers bearing spears and staves, controlling access to the imperial couple.

Topology was taxonomy in the imperial camp. Proximity to the court was an honor; the placement of tents relative to the imperial core reflected the imperial hierarchy. The treasury tent was nearby; so was the imperial wardrobe.[19] Then came the tents of the royal guard and the clergy. Beyond them were the mules, horses, and tack. Then came the working spaces of the royal servants—hundreds of them—charged with operating the royal kitchens, which included a tent for the royal bread, the sauce tent, the tent for royal drink (*tej,* beer, Fernet-Branca, cau de vie), and more besides.[20]

Royal provisions included grain, flour, and honey as well as hundreds of animals for slaughter—some provided by locals, some driven with the march. The production of *enjera*—the pancakelike bread that is a staple of the Ethiopian diet—was a major preoccupation, requiring a mobile bakery, including several open-fire stoves *(mitad)* that operated through the night. In the morning more than two hundred mules would be loaded up with *enjera* that had been baked, stacked, and packed into crates. The crates, in turn, were locked, covered with an animal skin to keep out dust, then strapped to the mules. Hundreds of mules were harnessed to the needs of the royal household and kitchens—the full army required thousands.[21]

Beyond the tents of the servants, guards, and key services came the tents of the major figures at court: Ras Mangasha and Ras Makonnen, as well as the *afa negus*—in effect Menelik's attorney general, but a man with a considerable military force at his disposal.[22] Beyond them came the rank-and-file soldiers and their vast city of tents.

Although Ethiopian armies could move with awe-inspiring speed— faster than any European army on foot—the stages in the northward movement were brief. Typically, the army marched for no more than five hours, and the pace was modest, about five miles per day on the opening stage from Addis to Lake Ashenge.

Menelik was in no great hurry. Plenty of sacrifices lay ahead, and speed now would only thin mules, horses, and men at a time when they needed to protect a healthy reserve. Speed risked injury, too.[23] The passing of the imperial army and the court was the occasion for the completion of important public works—roads were widened and washouts were restored. Even so, Ethiopian roads were not kind to wheeled vehicles. There would be no royal carriage. Menelik traveled astride a mule.

But there were political and ceremonial reasons for their stately pace, too. Menelik and Taytu knew that the mobilization was a kind of national plebiscite. They took reassurance from the size of the force that answered their call, as well as from the vast tribute they received in the form of livestock, grain, and drink along the way.

They gave as well as they got. Menelik and Taytu made a point of halting at Taytu's hel at Erguebo, where she hosted a feast; storehouses were opened and great quantities of food were distributed. September is the month of the chickpea harvest, and these were distributed liberally along with flour, honey, butter, oil, and *berbere*, the characteristic spice mixture of Ethiopia.[24] Taytu's properties were also famous for the quality of honey they produced—and the *tej* made from it. The variety of flowers on Taytu's land produced honey with various taste qualities. The royal couple were *tej* connoisseurs; they especially relished a white honey that made a clear and fine *tej*.[25]

Feasts boosted morale. They also confirmed the status of Menelik and Taytu as generous patrons of the army and the nation—parents, even— who could be counted on to protect and provide for the children of Ethiopia. By the time the emperor's red tent was erected at Lake Ashenge in mid-December, Menelik had amassed a force of more than a hundred thousand. Confident, in high spirits, equipped with modern firearms—

including artillery—and outnumbering Italian forces by more than four to one, Menelik's army was already rewriting the rules of colonial warfare.

At the same time that he built up his army, Menelik carefully crafted the image he wished to project. Lowball estimates of the size of Menelik's army were leaked.[26] These were eagerly picked up by the Italians. Menelik's court also produced rumors of rancor—that Makonnen would betray Menelik for the emperor's crown, that Tekle Haimanot would bolt with his army before he would fight. It was even put about that Menelik had been hit by lightning and struck dumb, or perhaps killed. Every scrap of news reassured the Italians and bolstered their confidence that they would face a small, fractured, and demoralized opponent.[27]

CHAPTER 9

Amba Alage

Pietro Toselli was seventeen years old when he graduated from the Accademia Reale in Turin as a *sottotenente*, the first rung on the officers' ladder of military rank. The Accademia, one of Italy's top military training institutes, normally didn't even admit students under the age of sixteen, but Toselli had shown unusual promise. He tore through the three year curriculum for artillerymen, finishing in 1878. Toselli opted for additional training in military engineering, and within two years he had ratcheted himself to the rank of first lieutenant.

Then his career stalled. After such an auspicious beginning, Toselli had only one promotion in the next eight years. Toselli had a nervous temperament and by disposition he favored action, so he became restless. The Italian occupation of Massawa in 1885 reconfigured his options. Toselli began to see colonial service as an outlet for thwarted ambition—the answer to a stalled career—and he asked to be assigned overseas. In 1888, he set foot in Massawa, ready to make his career as a colonial officer.[1]

Toselli endeared himself to his men—his "golden boys," as he called them.[2] He greeted them with *buna seira,* "good evening" in dialect, at all times of the day, including sunrise.[3] His personality—that of a gentlemanly, quirky, but highly competent senior officer—comes through in

Pietro Toselli and friends. From *L'Illustrazione italiana*, 5 January 1896.

photos. They show him striking an exaggerated pose, the chain of his watch dangling from his jacket pocket, but it is clear that he delights in the company of his fellow soldiers.

Toselli flourished in Eritrea. The colonial environment provided an outlet for energies and abilities that simply wasn't available elsewhere. It also paid well.[4] Toselli rose rapidly in the ranks, from lieutenant to captain to major in just a few years. He credited his rise to his "stubborn star" and his hard work. He reveled in a setting where a glorious future beckoned, but he was discouraged by the overwhelming indifference of Italian public opinion to the call of empire and the sacrifices the army was making in its behalf. He wondered whether in years to come, when northern Ethiopia had been Italianized despite popular apathy, anyone would remember or express gratitude for his sleepless nights and tormented days.[5]

By the early 1890s, Toselli was back in Italy, sharing the dream of an Italianized East Africa with anyone who would listen. But he remained frustrated in his ambition to arouse a spirit of conquest in the Italian people. He became an evangelist for colonial expansion, seeing in his own experience—vigorous adventure, practical engagement, rapid advancement—a model for what empire could mean for Italy as a whole.

Reaching back and conjuring an image of Italy's past, he adopted a simple pseudonym, "Un Eritreo," and wrote a book whose three-word Latin title served as a stirring call to the Italian people to recover the lost glories of imperial Rome. Toselli's *Pro Africa italica* not only advocated the development of Italian Africa but also invoked the memory of Scipio Africanus, the pacifier of the Carthaginians and founder of Italica, a colonial settlement in southern Spain.[6] Toselli would be a modern Scipio.

Back in Africa, Toselli played a key role in defeating Mangasha in 1895. At the urging of General Arimondi, a demanding and mercurial personality, Toselli and his men had pursued Mangasha, taking advantage of his humiliating rout at Coatit and Senafe to push deep into Ethiopian territory. The rapid—and exceedingly dangerous—expansion of Italian rule had been the work of Pietro Toselli as much as anyone.

Following the rout of Mangasha, Toselli had proposed pushing south with the intent of destabilizing Menelik's rule. Many Europeans imagined Ethiopians—especially in the north, in Tigray—as seething in resentment of Menelik's rule; the mere appearance of an alternative to Menelik would prompt a rebellion. Menelik's empire would collapse in the wake of a bold advance as local rulers peeled away. Toselli was one of those who believed that the Italian presence would encourage rebels among local chieftains, starting with the Muslim leader Sheik Thala.[7] Upon moving as far south as Amba Alage, however, Toselli found that the Italian presence made little difference. Sheik Thala joined him with a few hundred men, but as a rule, the local population proved indifferent, even hostile, in the face of the Italian presence. Toselli's forward position in the path of Menelik's advance was thus the result of his own initiative.[8]

The Ethiopian *amba* is a mesa or plateau—an elevated area of land that is flat or nearly so, with sides that are steep and clifflike. For Major

Pietro Toselli and his two thousand men, Amba Alage was an excellent choice for an advance position.[9] Amba Alage is a natural fortress that rises about ten thousand feet above sea level, a monster block of granite that towers over the surrounding countryside. It sits at a choke point on one of the main roads linking south and north, Shoa and Tigray, Addis and Adigrat. The steep approaches to Amba Alage—today, the highway through the pass has nearly a dozen switchbacks—give great advantages to the defender, as attackers must endure enemy fire and fatigue in any assault.

Nearly a year had passed since Mangasha's defeat and Toselli's mad southward dash, but no one had clarified what Toselli's role would be when Menelik got around to mobilizing his response. Once his soldiers were in place, Toselli's mission was unclear—engage, delay, or simply observe? Communications with General Arimondi, his commanding officer thirty-five miles to the north, were iffy in a part of the country where the population was unsure, to say the least, about the Italian occupation. Peasants doubled as insurgents, waylaying messengers and intercepting messages. Communications sputtered. Even worse, bitter personal differences intruded. Months earlier, relations between Toselli and Arimondi had reached the point where they communicated only when professional obligation compelled them; in April, Toselli wrote home that he and Arimondi had broken with each other. "Siamo in rotta," he wrote. By July, they were no longer even on speaking terms. Even so, Toselli remained confident. "[I don't] enjoy his goodwill—no matter. I'll do my duty."[10]

Toselli's determined optimism had to overcome more than Arimondi's hostility. Toselli's force of two thousand was minuscule compared to the size of the force that Menelik had organized. In fact, it was far from obvious that Ethiopia needed to "win back" Amba Alage at all. Menelik, had he wished to do so, simply could have marched his army of a hundred thousand past Toselli and Amba Alage. Bypassed and cut off from its lines of reinforcement, Toselli's force would wither and die. Amba Alage would simply cease to matter.

But Amba Alage would fulfill other objectives for Menelik, notably to test Makonnen and his men by putting him at the head of an Ethiopian attack on Amba Alage. At court, Empress Taytu was the core of an anti-European faction that doubted (or pretended to doubt) the loyalty of Ras Makonnen, Ethiopia's noted Europhile. Taytu, her brother Ras Wele, Mangasha, and Alula—in effect, those from Tigray, in the north— had no illusions about European intentions. As Tigrayans, they had witnessed the steady southward encroachment of Italy.

Makonnen, however, had a distinct admiration for Europe and things Italian. He had led Menelik's delegation to Italy in 1889 and toured the country, reveling in the glories of Milan, Naples, Venice, and Rome. In his capacity as Menelik's viceroy at Harar in the Ethiopian south, he had developed cordial relationships with the community of European merchants and traders there. In the event of Menelik's untimely death, Makonnen would be a clear contender for the succession—an eventuality the ambitious Taytu undoubtedly had pondered. There were even rumors that Makonnen might be a pawn, an Italian ally in a divide-and-conquer strategy.[11]

All the more reason to put Makonnen at the head of the advance guard. There, he would be the first to shed Italian blood. His men would be the first to fall. If Makonnen's loyalties were in doubt, what better test than to pit him and his men against the Italians?[12]

Cruel Awakening

Makonnen's arrival at Amba Alage was an eye-opener for the Italians. It was the first time that the Italians could see with their own eyes the monster they had conjured. Although some commentators argued otherwise, the dominant view expressed in Italian military and journalistic circles was that Menelik could raise a force only in the tens of thousands, perhaps no more than thirty thousand.[13] In April 1895, Italian intelligence in Addis was reporting two Ethiopian columns of twelve thousand each.[14] Other rumors had it that Taytu had stayed behind in Addis; that troops had been diverted to Gojjam to put down a rebellion by Tekle Haimanot; that Makonnen alone was marching northward with a few thousand soldiers—these were rumors the Italians were only too happy to believe.[15]

Similarly, it was argued that Menelik's support was insecure, that one or more of his allies—Alula, Mangasha, Tekle Haimanot, Makonnen— would betray him at a critical moment.[16] Such a presumption was not entirely wishful thinking. Menelik himself had proven an untrustworthy ally of Yohannes, although he owed him his loyalty. Would he, in turn, be betrayed by untrustworthy subordinates? It wasn't unreasonable to think that Menelik would prefer to negotiate, rather than test his army or the loyalty of his lieutenants. History was on the side of such arguments. Menelik had declared himself king of kings in 1889. Twice since then, the Italians had entered northern Ethiopia—in January 1890 and in December 1894—and Menelik hadn't moved.

This was what lay behind Toselli's dismissive remark that Menelik was a myth. But Menelik had had his reasons. He was still ostensibly an ally of the Italians in 1890, when they occupied part of Tigray and invited him to Axum to celebrate his solemn coronation. Wisely, he declined the invitation; to have accepted would have forever branded him a pawn of Italy. In 1894, the Italian entry into Adwa occurred in the context of the war with Mangasha, which did important work for Menelik by driving Mangasha into his arms. But it hardly required his presence and was over in a few days.

Things were different in 1895. Mangasha, Alula, and the other restless northerners had long since rallied to Menelik's side as the only possible defender of Ethiopia. By forming his massive army and marching it against the Italians, his erstwhile patrons, Menelik could only affirm his independence and his right to the imperial title.

Toselli, personally, expected to face a very modest force. As recently as July he had anticipated a force of no more than forty-five hundred— possibly led by Mangasha, whom the Italians had defeated, or perhaps Ras Wele.[17] In a cruel awakening, Toselli and his men watched in awe from the heights of Amba Alage as Makonnen's forces, nearly forty thousand strong, streamed over the passes into the valley opposite. In an instant, the situation confronting Italy changed radically. Toselli wrote in disbelief to Arimondi, "Sono molti, molti!"—"They are many, many!"[18] And it was only Menelik's advance guard.

On 5 December, Makonnen appealed to Toselli to evacuate his position. "I have come to make war," he wrote. "Friendship for [Italian commander in chief] Baratieri leads me to serve as a peacemaker." Makonnen even suggested he was being driven forward by Menelik, almost against his will. "I must advance because the emperor is at Lake Ashenge [some twenty-five miles to the south] and when I stop, his road is blocked."[19] Toselli would have to get out of the way.

Toselli understood the weakness of his position. If Makonnen attacked, Toselli and his men would die. Instead, Toselli appealed to Makonnen's self-interest, underlining the potential cost of war to Makonnen's ambitions. "To advance means war," replied Toselli, "the consequences of which no one can predict." Toselli hinted that defeat for Ethiopia might yet create an opening for Makonnen. "Consider that Magdala and Sahati determined the fate of two great Ethiopian emperors," he wrote, alluding to the defeats of Tewodros and Mangasha. Then, in an allusion to Makonnen's close relationship with Italy dating back to his visit in 1889, he added, "Today you would destroy your work of seven years."[20]

Toselli's bravado aimed to raise doubts in Makonnen—and to play on Makonnen's presumed imperial ambitions—but privately Toselli and his men had plenty of doubts of their own. Luigi Canovetti, a sweet and gentle native of Florence, wrote an unsparingly candid analysis of their situation to his sister Maria. Although he wrote with affection—signing with his nickname, "Gigi"—he barely concealed the gravity of the moment. "We are 1,000 against 20,000," he wrote, undercounting both Makonnen's forces and his own. "Our names will be written in history books," he noted presciently. "What better reward can there be?"[21]

Toselli could retreat or he could be reinforced, but he refused to give up such a strong position without explicit instructions to do so. "The situation is graver than we thought . . . there are at least 30,000 of them," he wrote to General Arimondi, his commanding officer. "I await your reinforcements."[22]

Although Toselli didn't know it, General Arimondi had already ordered Toselli's retreat. Toselli never received the orders.[23] That evening in his tent, Toselli scratched out a final note to Arimondi, a note that expressed his awe in the face of the vast Ethiopian encampment, along with his deep private misgivings.

> Tonight the enemy has put on a magical spectacle of lights. The camp is bigger than Mangasha's camp at Coatit [and Toselli

commanded a much smaller force than the one Baratieri led at Coatit] . . . it may be possible to gain a few days for [the defense of] the Colony, but we cannot resolve the situation and it will be necessary to pull back in order to prepare a counteroffensive and a large-scale war.

He closed with the hope that reinforcements would arrive at any moment. "Is everything prepared? Are many troops on the way?"[24] It was Toselli's final letter.

All day on the sixth, the Ethiopians prepared for battle. That afternoon, about four o'clock, Toselli received a final communication from Arimondi. A column of six companies and two artillery batteries were on their way south, having left that morning. Toselli was encouraged by the news. At a distance of about thirty-five miles, reinforcements likely would arrive sometime the next day, on the seventh.[25] The ambiguity in Arimondi's letter would prove fatal—he was only pushing these forces forward to cover Toselli's retreat. He had no intention of sending reinforcements all the way to Amba Alage.

The next morning, 7 December, Makonnen's forces began their attack with rifle fire on advanced positions at six-thirty. It was an attack that would build over the course of the morning, probing for weakness.

Makonnen knew exactly where to test for fractures. The core of the Italian position consisted of the Fourth Battalion—thirteen hundred askari led by Italian officers and supported by two artillery groups. The local chieftains Ras Sebhat and Sheik Thala, Ethiopians with grievances against Mangasha (in Ras Sebhat's case) or Menelik (in Thala's case), had sided with the Italians. Each added some 350 men to Toselli's force. Under the weight of Makonnen's attack, they and their men would feel acutely the gravity of the choice they had made. If they wavered, the Italian position would crumble. Thus Makonnen focused his initial attacks on Toselli's uncertain allies.

Toselli chose to protect his core forces, arraying his disciplined askari companies around Amba Alage and putting Sebhat and Thala on the periphery. Sebhat was posted on the Italian left, perched on high ground above the main road leading around Amba Alage to the north. If Sebhat gave way, Makonnen's forces could turn the Italian left and begin the encirclement of Toselli's position. Toselli positioned two companies in support of Sebhat.[26]

On the right, some four hundred men loyal to Sheik Thala occupied a position analogous to that of Ras Sebhat on the left. They covered the road that bypassed Amba Alage to the west, leading to Togora. Their role was to prevent a turning movement that threatened an alternative path of retreat. They were backed by indigenous Eritrean recruits commanded by Lieutenant Volpicelli.

Toselli, his four artillery pieces, and his reserve occupied the central position, the *amba* itself.[27] Pathways connecting the Italian left and right were precarious. In some places the paths were little more than goat trails on hillsides or along ridges above precipitous drops.

Makonnen chose his attack carefully. At seven in the morning, he sent a small force against the Italian right; it was easily repulsed. Makonnen then directed Ras Wele to lead his seven thousand men to test Sebhat's position on the Italian left. Despite Sebhat's dominant position, the disparity in numbers proved overwhelming; the resolve of Sebhat's men—built on animosity toward Mangasha—wavered as thousands of their countrymen advanced. Within two hours, Sebhat's forces were giving way. Toselli sent a company from his reserve in support, repulsing three renewed assaults.

By nine o'clock, Ras Makonnen was directing forces against the Italian center. Some fifteen thousand men advanced with high ground on either side. Terrain funneled them in front of Toselli's position, putting compact masses of men in front of disciplined artillerymen.[28]

Italian guns were capable of firing both shells and shrapnel, typically fused to explode in the air.[29] Shrapnel consisted of artillery shells packed with balls that were a fraction of an inch in diameter. Exploding in the air, the shell containing them rained down death for yards around, wounding dozens in a single, brilliant flash; when it was fired into hard ground, shot ricocheted up with brutal force, spraying lead into soft bodies. Attacking the center in force, Makonnen's men formed inviting targets for shrapnel and suffered heavy casualties, the heaviest of the day.

A little before ten, a third column of some fifteen thousand men, Tigrayans under the command of Mangasha and Alula, attacked the Italian right. Makonnen's battle plan, which applied pressure first to the

Italian left, then to the center, then to the right, aimed at rolling up To-selli's forces. Besides being a brilliantly simple plan—and correspond-ingly easy to execute—it represented a significant departure from stan-dard Ethiopian tactics, which typically sought envelopment by pressuring right and left flanks simultaneously. By rolling from Italian left to right, Makonnen broke Toselli's contact with his preferred line of retreat, north to Mekele, and his most likely path of reinforcement.

The sheer imbalance of forces—Toselli had four cannon and per-haps two thousand soldiers, a mere handful of men against Makon-nen's forty thousand—left little doubt about the outcome. In the end, Toselli could only cling to the illusory hope that General Arimondi would arrive with reinforcements before his forces were wiped out. In the meantime, Toselli resolved to make the Ethiopians pay for every foot of terrain. The rugged topography of the *amba* meant that the Ethiopians would have to endure very high casualties to reach the Ital-ian positions. Ethiopian troops clambered up the steep slopes, and those who survived the climb pressed on against Italian artillery posi-tions, taking horrific casualties as the Italians fired shot at fifty paces.[30] The carnage was unspeakable.

By twelve-thirty, Toselli had despaired of reinforcement; he had to think about retreat.[31] He shifted two artillery batteries to reinforce his right to protect his only remaining path of retreat. But the advantage of terrain shifted in retreat. Moving soldiers and material was a challenge where men and mules could move only in single file. A man who fell in retreat blocked the path completely. A false step could lead to a fall of a thousand feet.

As Toselli's men took aim to cover their retreat, the bodies of mules served as impromptu redoubts. When the situation grew more desperate, artillery pieces were pitched down the hillside rather than left to be cap-tured. In some cases, men threw themselves after. The tangle of guns, mules, and men became treacherous. One Eritrean soldier watched as a mule crumpled, hit by a bullet. The animal tumbled to the valley below, taking Lieutenant Marzio Manfredini and part of an artillery piece with him.[32]

By one in the afternoon the fighting was over.[33] The retreat turned into a massacre. Soldiers scrambled, trampling the fallen as they raced northward in panicked flight. Ethiopian pursuers picked off stragglers. When the chase broke off, villagers took over, harassing the retreating men and stripping the fallen.[34]

Amba Alage: The Turning Point

For Italy and its allies, Amba Alage would be a story of heroism, starting with Toselli himself, who enjoyed a kind of secular canonization following his death. Illustrations depicted Toselli at the moment of his death, at the center of a swarm of Ethiopians, being crowned in laurel by an angelic figure, as his body rose heavenward—an apotheosis. A singable tune—"Toselli's Song"—enjoyed a modest popularity, at least in military circles.[35] And indeed, by all accounts Toselli had fought bravely in a desperate situation, covering the retreat of his men until he himself was taken down. Gabra Iyasus—one of the better contemporary Ethiopian observers—noted that Major Toselli "never looked back" (in other words, he never considered retreat for himself) and "fought like a lion," parrying blows "like a hero" without tiring until he "fell where he stood."[36] Ras Makonnen made sure that Toselli's body was recovered and properly buried—a gesture of profound respect.

Newspapers in Germany and Austria dutifully respected the sentiments of their Italian ally—the story of Amba Alage was the story of a hero.[37] The French press, antagonistic toward Italy and especially toward Italy's francophobic prime minister, Francesco Crispi, didn't bother to conceal its sympathy for Menelik.[38] In Italy itself, Amba Alage revealed popular ambivalence about Italy's colonial enterprise. Italians certainly were moved by the tragic deaths at Amba Alage. In fact, the sentiments the defeat inspired—a desire for revenge and the retrieval of Italy's honor—were leveraged in the Chamber of Deputies into approval of additional funding for Eritrea.[39] Still, the purpose of the Italian presence in East Africa was no clearer and the cause no more popular. *Corriere della Sera,* the leading Italian newspaper, felt vindicated in its criticism of the government's colonial adventure. Meanwhile, students at the University of Rome—suspicious of militarism and colonialism—chanted "Viva Menelik!" to the horror of patriotic commentators.[40] It may well have been Europe's first anticolonial demonstration.

Makonnen, the hero of Amba Alage. From *Le Petit Journal,* 29 December 1896.

For Ethiopia, the story of Amba Alage was a story of triumph and confidence—a critical interim step that would culminate in victory at Adwa. After all, the speed with which Mangasha had been defeated just a few months earlier had raised doubts about Ethiopian effectiveness against European forces. These doubts were dramatically erased when the news of Amba Alage reached the main Ethiopian force at Alamata, more than fifty miles to the south. In a feat reminiscent of Marathon, one of Mangasha's men had run all night after the battle, reaching Alamata just as Menelik's army was breaking camp. As the messenger scrambled down the hillside, soldiers pressed around him. "Where are you from?" the men asked. "Give us news!"

"I'm sent by the *ras* [Mangasha]," he gasped. "I bear a letter. The Italian army at Alage is annihilated; their cannon and rifles are in our hands!"

"Pity on us!" the soldiers cried in mock disappointment. "Have we come all this way without a chance to fight?"[41]

At Amba Alage, the Italians had done Ethiopia an enormous favor by putting a smaller, beatable force in harm's way. However imbalanced the conflict, Ethiopian victory at Amba Alage showed that the Italians could be defeated—and defeated decisively. This paid dividends as local chiefs, some of whom had wavered in their support, now rallied to Menelik.

At his new camp at Wafla, Menelik received several local chiefs who previously had hesitated, unsure whom to back; now they pledged their loyalty and agreed to join the Ethiopian army, with their men, at Mekele.[42] Even Tekle Haimanot, who had vacillated, sent a force to Menelik after Amba Alage, with a promise of more troops to follow.[43]

Amba Alage also showed that Ethiopia's princes, its *ras*, could be trusted to overcome their differences in the name of Ethiopia. Amba Alage was the first time that soldiers from north and south, Tigray and Shoa, fought side by side. Despite rival ambitions that had split Mangasha from Menelik and regional prejudices that made Tigrayans wary of Shoans, these men fought together as Ethiopians.

In that sense, Amba Alage was a milestone in the creation of modern Ethiopia. As a national victory, it meant that personal, local, and regional interests and loyalties had to be recalibrated. Ethiopian particularisms didn't vanish, but they had to make way as national allegiances were added to the mix. As Menelik and his army continued their march, minstrels proudly sang a verse mocking the Italians: "O wonders! . . . They crossed the sea on a boat to conquer Ethiopia?"[44] The minstrels' skeptical query captured the confidence and pride of the army—did the Italians really think it was going to be that easy? And given that these troubles had started over the issue of a protectorate, it raised an obvious question: who needs a protectorate when the protected can defeat the would-be protector? When the Ethiopians marched north from Amba Alage to pursue their war of independence, they marched with the swagger of winners.

Fortifying Mekele

The story of Toselli's glorious martyrdom offered solace to the aggrieved, but it masked questions about military leadership and competency—starting with Baratieri himself. General Arimondi, the person most directly responsible for the disaster, shifted attention from himself by taking his disagreements with Baratieri public, feeding the Italian press with information that put Baratieri's judgment in doubt. Within weeks, critics asked publicly whether Toselli's men had died not with the thought "that their sacrifice had been useful to the fatherland" but instead with "the conviction that their death was the consequence of foreseeable errors."[45]

What kind of leader would put two thousand men in such an exposed position, miles away from reinforcement? What kind of leader would fail to give orders—or liberty of action—in the face of unforeseeable contingencies? Toselli's death may have been glorious by some standard, but if so, it was a tragic glory, the glory of men who died because of the incompetence of other men.

Italy now knew the full dimensions of the enemy it had conjured. Mobilization for the next confrontation began in earnest. Toselli's sacrifice inspired some volunteers in Italy to join the ranks, but in nothing near the numbers the Italian leadership now knew it needed. What patriotism couldn't provide, chance and duty would. The army created a lottery—a kind of random tax on existing units—plucking the men it needed from those already in uniform to create fourteen battalions. These newly amalgamated units, forty thousand men in all, began to ship out from Naples within days of the news of the disaster. Between 16 December and 5 January eleven steamships—provided by the pro-Africanist Rubattino shipping company—departed for Massawa. A second round of reinforcements began shipping out on 12 January and extended through 1 February, sending tons of equipment and supplies, along with an additional sixty-five hundred soldiers.[46]

Amba Alage was just the first stop in Menelik's campaign to restore Ethiopian sovereignty. Thirty-five miles to the north, the Italians had established a fortified position at Mekele. General Arimondi chose to evacuate most of his forces following the defeat at Amba Alage, rather than allow them to be entrapped at Mekele. But in the end he decided that the outright abandonment of Mekele was out of the question. It had a certain symbolic importance—it was said that once the Italian flag flew over the fortress, it could never be abandoned—but it had military significance, too, with the goal of slowing the northward progress of Menelik's army.[47] The thankless task of defending Mekele had been given to Major Giuseppe Galliano. As Baratieri scrambled to build up his forces, Galliano's assignment—and that of the twelve hundred men he commanded—would be to buy time.[48]

Long before the emperor's red tent went up outside Mekele, Galliano's soldiers understood the challenge facing them. In the late morning of 7 December, the men at Mekele had seen smoke spewing from Amba Alage, thirty miles distant as the crow flies; fighting had begun. Then the smoke stopped.[49] Had Toselli and his men turned back the Ethiopian attack? There was no word.

Shortly after midnight, the quiet of the night was broken by the wailing of women, the spouses of the askari, signaling grief as the first stragglers from Amba Alage arrived at Mekele, bearing witness to the extent of the disaster.[50]

"Dead! All dead!" the survivors gasped. "Majors, captains, lieutenants—all dead, everyone, everyone!"[51]

For an hour, wounded soldiers stumbled out of the night into the torchlight, safe at last in the fortress at Mekele. As the stream of survivors trailed off and the hope of more faded, sobbing women clawed at their faces and dragged rough stones across their skin in a bloody display of sorrow. Others pulled at their hair. Some sobbed as they crawled along the ground, faces buried in the earth. Dust mingled with streams of blood and tears, fashioning living masks of grief.[52]

Many of the survivors were clad only in rags; a few were naked, victims of civilians who had preyed on them, stripping them of weapons and clothing. Some had been castrated, including one who boasted that it had taken eight men to restrain him, arms and legs splayed. "The hands are still good," he bellowed. "When I am healed I want to mow down all the Abyssinians . . . !"[53]

Mekele was a city of some importance, having been the imperial capital during the reign of Yohannes. For much of the month of December 1895, Italian forces had built up defenses. A church was converted into an ammunition depot. Italian soldiers and their askari recruits sang Italian songs as they reinforced the 230-foot-long wall that would be their main defense.[54] When they were done, the walls of the presidio were substantial—six feet thick at the top and some sixteen feet at the bottom.[55] Ethiopian light artillery would have a hard time breaching them.

The defenders' hope was that the Ethiopian officers would send wave after wave of infantry in an effort to take the fort by sheer numbers. An Ethiopian infantry assault would allow Italian artillery to do its work. The Italians prepared for such a conflict in minute detail. They pulled down *tukul* near the fort that might provide cover for attackers and obstruct the line of sight of Italian artillery. They ran wire to establish a defensive perimeter outside the fort. Engineers dug deep trenches on either side of the main approach to the fort from the south. At the bottom of these ten-foot trenches—too deep to provide cover—they buried yard-long spikes at two-foot intervals. These would impale anyone falling in. The intent was to create a choke point. Ethiopian soldiers charging the fort from the south would be forced to converge on the road in order to bypass the spiked trenches. As they did so, they would make ripe, compact targets for eager Italian fire.

Any soldiers who survived to approach the walls of the fort would have to negotiate additional hazards. Ethiopian soldiers fight without shoes, so the Italians scattered broken glass and pottery shards. As the Ethiopians picked their way among these hazards, they would do so within range of Italian sharpshooters.[56]

A fort needs to be a self-sustaining facility but rarely is. On 9 December, a company of men left the fort in search of food for the men and feed for the animals. What they discovered on their foray was that much of the local population had vanished. This may have been simple prudence in the face of a requisitioning force or, more ominously, a vote of no confidence in the future of the Italian occupation. Either way, it made the work of the troops more difficult. Instead of persuading local peasants to trade, sell, or "donate" their goods, the soldiers were forced to discover where the peasants had stashed their food and feed.[57]

As these foraging missions went on, the radius of operations had to increase; eventually these forays extended six miles from the fort. There were other ominous signs as well. Communication with the north had become tenuous. After Amba Alage, the local population turned hostile. Couriers traveling by day were accosted. Only mail carried by night could get through.

Italian spirits were kept up by daily rations of wine, coffee, and rum. Cigars and loose tobacco were also available for the European soldiers.[58] Nerves and drink led to some boasting among the soldiers about how they would dispose of the Ethiopians when they arrived. "Come, Abyssinians! We'll help you find the road to hell!" boomed one.[59] At night, European officers gathered for what often turned into extended bouts of drinking. "Flasks of Chianti and bottles of Barbera rolled under the table," noted one officer. "Long live Italy! Long live the king! Long live Major Galliano! Long live Major Toselli!" Major Galliano filed a rosy report with General Baratieri: "Morale is as high as can be."[60]

The mood changed dramatically on 19 December. Mekele sits in a high-altitude basin several miles across, dominated by surrounding heights.[61] Around ten in the morning, a great dust cloud appeared on the southeast edge of the basin, where the heights descend to the plain. As the cloud approached, its base took the shape of an enormous column of men on foot and on horseback. It was the army of Ras Makonnen, fresh from its victory at Amba Alage.[62]

Makonnen's forces set up camp to the northeast of Mekele, occupying a high position relative to the fort. Their position also put them between Mekele and the main route north to Eritrea. There would be no evacuation of the fort—and no rescue—that didn't go through Makonnen.

Two days after his arrival, Makonnen wrote to Major Galliano, the Italian commander of the Mekele presidio. Despite the imposing forces at his command and their dominant position, his tone was almost apologetic; still, the objective was unmistakable. "How are you?" he wrote to Galliano.

> I am well, thanks be to God. Are your soldiers well? Mine are very well.

In the name of my emperor, I pray you leave this land, otherwise I will be forced to make war. It pains me to have to shed the blood of Christians. Please leave with your soldiers.

Your friend Makonnen[63]

Major Giuseppe Galliano—known by the whimsical name "Pinotto" to his family and friends—was skeptical of Makonnen's peace overtures. He believed that Makonnen was stalling, buying time until Menelik could arrive with the artillery that was critical to an assault on the fort. Galliano was somewhat skeptical about claims that Menelik was right behind Makonnen, at the head of tens of thousands of additional troops. He took comfort in a commonplace among some northern Ethiopians that Menelik would never risk his crown for Tigray. Galliano was equally skeptical of rumors that Menelik's artillery would be carried by African elephants; Menelik, Galliano observed, like the elephants, never seemed to arrive.[64]

Galliano responded to Makonnen's letter in mock-sincere tones.

To His Highness Ras Makonnen, commander of the Shoan advance guard, from the commander of the fort at Mekele.

How are you? I am well, thanks be to God; my soldiers are very well, as I hope yours are too.

My king has ordered me to remain here and I will not move. Do what you have to do; I assure you that I have fine rifles and very fine cannon.

Your friend Galliano[65]

A second set of letters was exchanged on the twenty-fifth, but the results were no different. The signs were not all ominous, however. On 30 December one of Ras Makonnen's soldiers appeared outside the fort bearing a white flag and a third letter from Makonnen. Makonnen was asking for medical help for some of the men wounded in the battle at Amba Alage. Galliano complied, sending Lieutenant Mozzetti, a physician, who spent a day in the Ethiopian camp caring for wounded soldiers.[66] Later Mozzetti returned, accompanied by an Ethiopian escorting force commanded by Ato Gheorgheos. While Mozzetti provided Galliano with firsthand information about the size and battle-readiness of Makonnen's forces, the Italian kitchen crew plied Ato Gheorgheos with food and drink. Generous quantities of brandy made Gheorgheos chatty, and in the course of conversation he revealed that Menelik would arrive shortly, augmenting Makonnen's forces with some one hundred thousand of his own. (If accurate, this meant the Ethiopian forces would total 125,000 and confirm the higher estimate of the size of Menelik's army.)[67]

As the brandy took hold—and before drifting off to sleep in the Italian fort—Gheorgheos assured his hosts that Menelik had artillery and that his aim was to enjoy a drink in the Governor's Palace in Massawa. In other words, Menelik's goal was to drive Italy not only from Tigray but also from Africa entirely.[68]

Days passed without an attack from Ras Makonnen, feeding speculation that Makonnen, as a friend of Italy, would not attack. Meanwhile, the askari took comfort from the fact that the flag flying over the fort at Mekele fluttered to the north—an auspicious sign, helped along by the prevailing winds.[69]

More ominous, surely, was the fact that Makonnen's forces were completing their occupation of the high ground surrounding Mekele. By 1 January, the encirclement was complete. In a defiant gesture that showed a wicked sense of humor, the defenders suspended a banner from the wall of the fort. On it was a jolly seasonal greeting: "1896 Buon Anno!"[70]

Even with humor intact, Galliano and his men were running out of options. Galliano ordered the destruction of the remaining houses and huts surrounding the fort. Squads of men worked their way through the settlements; whatever couldn't be hauled to the fort was torched. The burning went on for two days.[71]

The gentlemanly exchange of messages and envoys ended. Makonnen's message of 3 January was both blunt and grimly comic: "Remember Amba Alage and Toselli's end. Give me the fort. Don't waste any more blood. I will escort you to Massawa and send along your bags, too."[72]

A Kind of Epiphany

On 6 January, Galliano duly observed the Christian feast of the Epiphany in his journal, but the day brought a military epiphany as well. "Numerous columns" descended from the passes into the valley opposite the fort in "a kind of review."[73] The emperor had arrived, but the review was as much for Galliano's benefit—to cure his skepticism by displaying the might of the Ethiopian army. Inside the fort at Mekele, murmurs of "It's the *negus*" rose from all sides. Menelik's red tent went up to the north-west of the fort, just outside the range of the Italian artillery.[74]

That night, campfires rimmed the Mekele basin. Clusters of fires to the east and west gave off an ardent, imposing glow that streamed down the hillsides into the plain.[75] The next morning, a new supply of provisions arrived from Taytu's properties: butter, a great quantity of cattle, and five hundred sheep. Taytu had this providential bounty distributed to the army—a sign of her readiness to persevere until victory.[76] The siege of Mekele, properly speaking, had begun.

Very quickly, the confident mood in the fort took a sober turn. The Italians had established two observation posts outside the fort. Both of these fell to the Ethiopians following skirmishes on the seventh. The rapidity with which they succumbed surprised the Italians. Just the same, the Ethiopians suffered significant casualties in the fight. Taytu, Mangasha, Alula—even Menelik himself—upbraided Makonnen for not having attacked as soon as he arrived, before the fortifications were complete. Makonnen had wasted time in negotiations that produced nothing. There were murmured accusations of treason.[77] Makonnen would pay the price for his delay: his men would have to lead the assault on the fort.

On the eighth, Ethiopian artillery pounded the fort all day in hopes of opening a breach, without success. The Ethiopian quick-firing Hotchkiss batteries had better range than the Italian artillery, but their smaller caliber had little effect on the walls of Mekele's fortress.[78] Still, Galliano was impressed by the effectiveness of the fire from the twelve artillery pieces—two of them Italian guns seized at Amba Alage—that the Ethiopians trained on the fort. The Ethiopian artillerymen had mastered the art of correcting their aim after watching each shot fall. "Long, short, then just right," noted one of the Italian artillerymen admiringly. The aim of the Ethiopian batteries was so precise that Galliano became convinced that they were not operated by Ethiopian soldiers. "It's impossible that they're not European," he insisted.[79]

On the ninth, Makonnen's forces launched a major assault on the fort, taking heavy casualties. The loss of life pained Makonnen, but the reaction of the Ethiopian leadership was pitiless. Taytu, Menelik,

Makonnen's forces attack Mekele. From *L'Illustrazione italiana*, 2 February 1896.

Tekle Haimanot, and Abuna Matewos (the last of these the court chaplain and ranking cleric) turned on Makonnen and accused him of treason. "What do I have to do to prove my loyalty?" Makonnen pleaded—after all, Makonnen's soldiers were taking the heaviest losses. "You gave them time to build the fort," they answered. "It's up to you to take it down."[80]

Makonnen threw his forces into the fight with renewed vigor. He ordered three attacks on the night of the tenth—the first shortly after midnight, the second at two, and the third at four in the morning. Each time the Italians used flares to light up the night, and the attacks were repulsed.

The next day, the eleventh, Makonnen's men prepared scaling ladders to be used to climb the walls. At three in the morning the Ethiopians approached the fort under cover of darkness. They reached the walls apparently undetected, raised the ladders, and began to clamber up.

The Italians were ready, however, withholding their fire until the last possible moment, when masses of Ethiopian soldiers gathered eagerly at the foot of the ladders.[81] The effect of the opening volley was shattering, and dozens were killed. The rest wavered in confusion and panic. Many more fell in the fighting that followed, as stunned Ethiopian soldiers were picked off by soldiers firing from the walls of the fort. As the light of dawn rose on 11 January, more than six hundred Ethiopian fighters lay dead beneath the walls of Mekele.[82] When news of the tragedy reached Makonnen, he sought his own death by standing in full view of the fort, exposing himself to Italian fire. Ras Alula dashed over and forced him to take cover.[83] Coming from Alula, a critic of Makonnen, this was a redemptive gesture.

That day, 11 January, represented the nadir of Menelik's march. It was the moment when everything might have unraveled. The frustrations at Mekele were bringing out the worst in the Ethiopians—rivalries, mistrust, suspect motives—and putting the army and the nation at risk. All of the goodwill of Menelik's subordinates, all of the confidence gained at Amba Alage, had been put in jeopardy by a thousand men within the walls of Mekele.

Inside Menelik's tent the mood was somber. Menelik and Makonnen sat opposite each other; tears streamed down their faces. Outside, across the camp, the wives of the fallen wailed in grief; the cries might just as well have been for Ethiopia itself. Menelik spoke: "Today is a very sad day for Ethiopia." Then they resumed their silence as the tormented cries washed over them. Finally the two men stood. Menelik embraced Makonnen, then turned to address the court in his characteristically laconic form, saying, "This is my faithful subject."[84] It was a kind of absolution. There would be no more carping, no more recrimination.

Menelik called off the attacks on the fort. Perhaps Mekele could be taken without force. The great weakness of the Italian position was that the fort lacked an independent supply of water. There were two springs in the immediate vicinity, one to the north and another to the south, but neither was within the walls of the fort itself. The Italians had constructed a covered passageway to the closer of the two springs, offering protection from snipers, but the fundamental problem remained. Once the fort's water supply was taken, it would be very difficult to win back.[85]

In their frantic preparations for the arrival of Menelik's army, Galliano's soldiers had sought to address this weakness by constructing improvised cisterns. Captain Torquato Benucci supervised the excavation of two large pits—each capable of holding about thirteen thousand gallons—within the fort walls. Waterproof tarpaulins were laid in the pits. For a week soldiers, using empty wine casks, shuttled water from the springs to the reservoirs. They also ransacked the vacated homes of Mekele, seizing the clay bottles and pots used to hold *tej, talla* (beer from barley), and grain. The pots were filled with water and added to the fort's stores. A strict daily water ration allowed about five quarts of water a day for mules and horses, two for officers, and one for ordinary soldiers.[86]

It's not clear who among the Ethiopians thought to target the Italian water supply. One source—the official Ethiopian chronicle—credits Empress Taytu herself.[87] On 8 January, Ethiopian troops seized both of the springs, establishing the circumstances that would eventually force the Italians to capitulate. Water rations had to be cut almost entirely, with an exception made for the animals and the askari who used the water for the making of bread. In a move that undoubtedly improved morale at least in the short term, a wine ration took the place of water for the Italian soldiers.[88]

But the overall situation was bleak. The Ethiopians had control of the springs, and the Italians were unable to do anything about it. At the same time, the Ethiopians moved up their artillery pieces. With their surprisingly accurate fire they were able to prevent the Italians from leaving the fort at all, for any purpose. Given that the range of the Ethiopian guns was greater than that of the Italian artillery, the Italians had no effective response to the Ethiopian gunners. As the Ethiopians moved closer to the fort, they dug trenches to consolidate their gains. Under the cover of darkness Ethiopian infantrymen could advance as far as the wire perimeter. From there, they would shout to the askari, alternately encouraging them to defect and threatening them with terrible reprisals should they fight and lose.[89]

For the men in the fort, thirst became an equally formidable enemy. As of 13 January, water rations were down to less than a quart per soldier per day. Even at that miserly rate, the fort would fall one way or another by the twenty-first.[90] The quality of the water deteriorated as the reservoirs became muddy habitats for insects and moss. By the seventeenth, each soldier was receiving just two cups of polluted water.

The defenders of Mekele had turned back five attacks on the fort, but their situation was becoming desperate. The cherished illusion, of course, was that one day the defenders of Mekele would hear the sound of cannon fire coming from the north announcing their rescue.[91] It was an illusion shared by Galliano himself, suggesting he had only a vague notion of his true predicament. Rescue for Galliano and the Italian fort at Mekele was out of the question. It would have taken tens of thousands of men to challenge Menelik's army, and no such force was available. When Baratieri arrived at Adigrat on 9 January, he had two battalions. To these he could add the forces under the command of General Arimondi, as well as reinforcements moving up from Massawa. In all, he had some ten thousand men under his command.[92] This meant that Adigrat was secure, but any thought of rescue for Galliano and Mekele would have been sheer folly.[93] "Must the nation resign itself to another 7 December?" *Corriere della Sera* asked, referencing the date on which Toselli's forces had fallen at Amba Alage.[94] A repeat of Amba Alage wasn't out of the question, but it was an outcome Baratieri wanted to avoid at all costs. Negotiation was the only way out.

For Menelik, time was a factor, too. He didn't have pressing water supply concerns, but an army of the size he had created had to move or die. A lengthy siege imposed hardships that went beyond declining morale. He needed to keep his army in motion or lose it to hunger and attrition.

Devoured by the Lion of Judah

Italy dispatched Pietro Felter to negotiate an end to the siege. Felter was a merchant with long experience in Ethiopia, having first set foot there in 1881. He was known to all the principals at court—Taytu, Menelik, Makonnen. If he wasn't exactly a trusted figure, he was at least familiar. As the talks proceeded, Felter took Galliano with him to the Ethiopian camp to conclude the negotiations. When Felter entered Menelik's tent, he found the emperor much changed. In place of the amiable character he had come to know in Addis, he confronted a "dark and serious" man. The smallpox scars gave the emperor a hard, fierce look, a look now deepened by the stress of war. Galliano, who never before had been in the presence of the Lion of Judah, looked as if he thought he was about to be eaten.[95]

He might well have been. So many Ethiopian lives had been lost at Mekele that no one was more despised than Galliano. "Why did you bring this man into my presence?" Menelik asked. Felter adroitly reminded the emperor of the honor owed all men who fight heroically for their king. If one of Menelik's brave warriors were presented to the king of Italy, he would be received with full honors. Menelik paused, then whispered to one of his pages, who immediately left. He returned moments later, leading what Felter described as "the most splendid mule I have ever seen." The mule was outfitted with a collar of solid silver. Without a doubt, the mule came from Menelik's own stables.

"Dear Felter," Menelik began. "You know that we are a poor people . . . yet this gift must surely satisfy your commander [Galliano]." The emperor then covered his face, signaling the end of the audience. Galliano—who had uttered not a word—rode the mule back to Mekele.[96]

On 19 January, Menelik and Felter reached an agreement: if Galliano and his men abandoned the fort, they could go free, taking their weapons, ammunition, baggage, provisions, women, children, and wounded.[97] On 20 January, Galliano ordered the white flag of surrender raised over the fort at Mekele.

There were a few details to be worked out. Galliano's men would not immediately be free; they would travel under escort of the Ethiopian army. In fact, the escort was welcome—there was enough spilled blood and resentment to make the exit of Galliano's soldiers from the fort a dicey affair, with scuffles and threats.

Then there was the matter of transport. Galliano's men lacked adequate pack animals, so the Ethiopians loaned Galliano several hundred mules for the transport of their gear. It would later be revealed that the Italians had agreed to a hefty "rental fee" for the animals—twenty-five thousand thalers, to be precise, more than enough to buy them and then some. In effect, the Italians were paying, in the guise of a fee, a ransom for Galliano's men.[98]

The following day, the twenty-first, Galliano and his troops prepared to leave. After more than a month of hostilities—including five failed assaults on the fortress—tensions were high. As Galliano's men exited the fort, they marched between two parallel columns of Ethiopian soldiers—"two flanking walls," as one experienced it.[99] When the evacuation was complete, the yellow, green, and red pennants of Ethiopia were hoisted over the fort; the work of demolition began. Within hours, the fort at Mekele was gone.

When the news reached Italy, the reaction was one of relief and celebration. Italy had avoided another Amba Alage, another Dogali. "O brave young men! O heroic young men!" the weekly *Illustrazione italiana* commented. The news was greeted "as if it were a victory."[100] Major Galliano was promoted to the rank of lieutenant colonel.[101]

The foreign press was not so kind. In France, *Le Petit Journal* ran a full-page color political cartoon on its cover. It showed Francesco Crispi, in military dress, getting a black eye from Menelik. The cartoon was picked up by newspapers around the world.[102]

Italy's allies joined an orchestrated effort to save face. Kaiser Wilhelm II of Germany sent a telegram of congratulations to King Umberto, observing that Galliano and Baratieri were worthy successors to the ancient Romans.[103] Wilhelm asked Umberto's permission to decorate Galliano with a medal; the kaiser claimed to experience "great joy" when Umberto graciously consented. To be sure, Galliano had accomplished much with little. With barely a thousand men, he had held the mighty Ethiopian army at bay. He had broken the élan of the Ethiopians in the aftermath of Amba Alage. He had bought time for Baratieri to bring up the reinforcements that were arriving daily from Italy, concentrating them at Adigrat.

Menelik's northward march resumed on the twenty-second, with Galliano's men in custody. Mangasha's forces would take the lead, followed by Galliano and his men, while Makonnen and his soldiers served as rear guard. Menelik and the main Ethiopian army would follow at three hours' delay.[104] By 30 January, it was evident that the safe passage of Galliano's forces fit into a larger plan. After Mekele, there was nothing standing between Menelik, his army, and the forces Italy was concentrating frantically

Menelik, the Lion of Judah. Photograph taken by Alfred Ilg in 1896. From Völkerkundemuseum der Universität Zürich; credit: © Völkerkundemuseum der Universität Zürich, VMZ 805.01.001.

at Adigrat. A titanic confrontation loomed. Indeed, when Menelik left Mekele, he proceeded as if he intended to march on Adigrat. He paused for two days at Agula in late January, but then he shifted his path toward the west, as if to bypass Adigrat. By 29 January he was encamped at Hawzen, on a route that would take him west to Adwa, rather than north to Adigrat.

Menelik had absorbed the lesson of Mekele: attacking fortified positions was futile. Menelik had no intention of advancing on Adigrat. He was using Galliano's men as a shield to protect his army as it completed a risky passing movement, exposing his flank to Baratieri's forces as he moved past Adigrat.[105] Menelik's army would not be attacked as long as Galliano's troops were among them. Finally, on the thirtieth, Galliano's troops were released to rejoin Baratieri. Menelik held ten officers, including Galliano, for a few more days for safekeeping.[106]

Menelik's movement, along with the careful use of his hostages, telegraphed his strategic plan. He would bypass Adigrat and seek to turn the Italian position by moving past it. All the while, he openly advertised his position and his willingness to negotiate a definitive peace. Moreover, with every step he gave the lie to Italian claims on Ethiopian territory. His northward march shredded Italian assertions of sovereignty in Tigray and shielded a delicate maneuver under the guise of an honor guard. It played well in Europe, where Menelik, always with an eye to international public opinion, could now add shrewd strategist to his reputation as a patient and peace-loving statesman.[107]

On the fifth of February, he sent Barambaras Emmanuel to Baratieri with the announcement that he had moved his court from Hawzen to Gundapta, to the east of Adwa, where he would wait five days for an Italian envoy authorized to negotiate a peace treaty. Baratieri responded with a message that was either a brazen bluff or proof of a tragic state of denial. With Menelik poised to march into Eritrea with an army of more than a hundred thousand, Baratieri—who might soon have seventeen thousand soldiers at his disposal—acted like a man holding all the cards. He sent Major Tommaso Salsa to Menelik with the message that he would accept negotiations on the basis of two conditions: reaffirmation of the Treaty of Wichale and recognition of the Italian occupation of the new territories.

There was an admirable boldness in Baratieri's response, but it also antagonized the Ethiopian court. Taytu, her brother Wele, and the Tigrayans Alula and Mangasha were furious. Given the strategic realities, Menelik's reply was the picture of moderation. He would accept negotiations on the basis of two conditions: the return of the occupied territories and the complete modification of the Treaty of Wichale.[108]

Thanks to Amba Alage and Mekele, the strategic balance was now in Ethiopia's favor. However, *because* of Amba Alage and Mekele, the pressure on Oreste Baratieri for a victory of some kind was stronger than ever. Italy had been maneuvered into a strategic corner. With little leverage to use in negotiations, Baratieri's options were down to two: military victory—which looked increasingly doubtful—or humiliating retreat.

CHAPTER 10

Stalled at Sauria

A T THE SAME TIME that Menelik mobilized his army for the war of independence, he deployed Alfred Ilg on a parallel mission—a public relations campaign in Europe. Ilg's task was to tell Ethiopia's story, but in a European voice. The polyglot Swiss gave interviews in all the major European languages—in fact, he talked to anyone who would listen. Above all, Ilg wanted to humanize the Ethiopians, a critical step in building sympathy for Ethiopia in the war—and for marginalizing Italy.

Ilg was pitiless in his criticism of Italy, and he invited Europeans to identify with the cause of Ethiopian liberty. He denounced the Treaty of Wichale candidly as a fraud perpetrated by Italy. How, he asked, could anyone even dream "of conquering such an extent of land, with a tradition of independence that reached back centuries?"[1]

Ilg also prepared Europe for Ethiopian victory. He was keen to tell the people of Italy what their leaders wouldn't tell them, namely, that their young men were at risk. Ethiopia's military advantage was so clear that Ilg could see no point in concealing Menelik's plans. Menelik had no intention of breaking his army on the walls of Adigrat. Menelik would deny Italy the classic colonial military encounter it wanted.

Adigrat's vulnerability was strategic, Ilg noted. It didn't need to be taken by force. He depicted Adigrat as a meaningless fortress, dangling at the end of a precarious link to the coast. "Provisioning troops is already very difficult," Ilg noted. "Everything has to come from Massawa." Menelik would simply ignore Adigrat, push past it, and threaten Eritrea. Such a move would isolate Adigrat, turning it into another Mekele—besieged, starving, helpless. Adigrat would be cut off and left to die.

Ilg didn't seek to deny Ethiopian vulnerabilities, especially the quarreling in the Ethiopian court. Yes, there were jealousies, even rivalries. But Ethiopia had overcome these rivalries, and it owed it all to Italy. "It's like two dogs fighting over a bone. If a hyena arrives and tries to join the fight, the dogs unite against him."[2]

By laying out the strength of the Ethiopian position, Ilg was trying to build pressure for a negotiated settlement. It would be far better for both sides if combat could be avoided. But if a showdown couldn't be avoided—if fighting ensued and lives were lost—at least Ethiopia occupied the moral high ground, defending itself and its sovereignty. Finally, Ilg appealed to the sympathy of Europeans, asking them to identify themselves with Ethiopia and the Ethiopians. "No European nation would submit to Abyssinian rule," he stated, inviting his readers to supply the corollary: that Abyssinia would never submit to European rule.

Colonial warfare in the nineteenth century was governed by a few simple principles, and by the 1890s these were known by both sides. Numerical superiority always gave an advantage on the battlefield. European colonial armies tended to be small, while African armies could easily overwhelm them in numbers—advantage Africa. But that assumed that the soldiers being counted were equivalent in other ways. What the Europeans lacked in numbers they compensated for elsewhere, in firepower and in discipline—advantage Europe.

It was as if Menelik, in preparing the defense of Ethiopia, had taken the checklist of European military advantages and crossed them off one by one. If the Ethiopians lacked the training and discipline of European armies, they were nevertheless far from being raw recruits. They lacked the snappy uniforms of the European soldiers—warfare for the Ethiopians was strictly a come-as-you-are affair—but they had enough experience and training to avoid foolish mistakes in combat. Menelik's campaign against the Welayta, followed by the victories at Amba Alage and Mekele, had turned his army into a confident, battle-hardened force.

The Ethiopian army was also better organized than in previous campaigns. Baratieri was among the first to admit it. When he was pressed by the Italian government to explain why he hadn't attacked Menelik as the Ethiopians moved north toward Eritrea, Baratieri snapped back testily: "There is a great disproportion in the size of our forces—the enemy is shrewd and his organization has greatly improved since 1888 [when Yohannes had led a large Ethiopian force into Eritrea, only to turn back], obliging us to exercise maximum prudence . . . in order to take advantage of any error."[3]

Nor were they necessarily at a disadvantage with respect to arms and firepower. Menelik had been careful not to concede the high ground of military technology to the Italians. The soldiers Yohannes had marched into Eritrea carried ancient muzzle-loaders; many of Menelik's soldiers had breech-loaders.[4] Baratieri's European infantrymen were issued magazine-fed repeating rifles, for the most part. The askari recruits, however, were given hand-me-down rifles, no longer adequate for combat in Europe but deemed good enough for colonial warfare. These were no better than—and sometimes inferior to—the rifles carried by Menelik's soldiers. Menelik's French-made Hotchkiss artillery pieces, properly operated, were superior to the mountain guns fired by Baratieri's European and askari batteries.

Another critical variable was position. Menelik had refused to give the Italians battle where they most wanted it, at Adigrat, where Menelik's thousands would bloody themselves storming the walls of the fortress. Instead, he skirted Adigrat, moving west and to the north—a play that threatened not only Baratieri's lines of communication but also the colony of Eritrea itself. This left Baratieri with a difficult choice. He could abandon Adigrat and withdraw into Eritrea. This would shorten his supply lines and keep his army between Menelik and Eritrea. But this would mean evacuating the lands seized following the defeat of Mangasha the previous year. It was tantamount to conceding defeat.

The alternative was to leave a defensive contingent in Adigrat while moving his main forces westward in pursuit of Menelik. On 1 February, just two days after Galliano's troops had rejoined him, Baratieri occupied the Alequa Pass, about ten miles west of Adigrat on the road to Adwa. As Menelik continued his westward move away from Baratieri and Adigrat,

Baratieri followed, advancing another fifteen miles. Two days later, on the third of February, Baratieri set up camp near Enticho, at a place called Sauria. On the fifth, Menelik sent word that he had established his headquarters at Gundapta, where he would await peace overtures.

Thus, by early February 1896, Ethiopian and Italian forces had positioned themselves halfway between Adigrat and Axum. Terrain in this part of Ethiopia can be varied and complex, but the landscape between Menelik's camp at Gundapta and Baratieri's camp at Enticho is mostly flat. It is a high plain two miles wide from north to south and at least five miles wide east to west. The plain is bounded by hills, creating a high-altitude elliptical bowl.

Ethiopian and Italian forces faced off across this vast expanse. Menelik spread out his army at the western edge of the bowl, on the fields and hillsides of the Gundapta plain. If the Italians advanced on him, he would have plenty of room to deploy his forces. For Baratieri, it was just the opposite. Moving his forces across the bowl into the open field would expose his flanks and play into the envelopment strategies the Ethiopians preferred.[5] He needed a confined space where he could deploy his troops, with their disciplined artillery and rifle fire, to maximum advantage. He established his camp on slopes on the eastern edge of the bowl, backed up against high ground, looking west toward Menelik. It was a natural fortress, "a field cut by five or six mountains that guard it in place of towers."[6] He immediately set his forces to work digging trenches and constructing fortified positions. If the Ethiopians attacked, his "towers" would funnel them toward his artillery and entrenched soldiers.

Baratieri fully understood the risks entailed in attacking Menelik at Gundapta. He summarized the standoff in a note to Rome: "The enemy occupies a strong position between Entisho and Gundapta, five hours from our camp. . . . Our position is strong, but intricate terrain makes advancing difficult without exposing our flanks."[7] And so stalemate ensued. Menelik no more wanted to attack the Italians in their entrenched position at Sauria than Baratieri wanted to engage Ethiopian forces in the wide valley in front of Gundapta. Peace negotiations began halfheartedly and broke down within a week. Then a sudden betrayal decisively shifted the balance in Ethiopia's favor.

The End of Divide and Conquer: The Defection
of Ras Sebhat and Hagos Tafari

Baratieri had reason to believe that time was on his side. Troops called up after Amba Alage were on steamships making their way across the Mediterranean to Eritrea. Thousands were disembarking at Massawa each week. In the last ten days of January alone, six vessels—the *Singapore,* the *Adria,* the *Gottardo,* the *Washington,* the *Rubattino,* and the *Minghetti*—landed at Massawa. They disgorged almost four thousand soldiers and officers. In February, vessels were leaving Naples at a rate of nearly one a day, bringing thousands more.[8]

But the Italian position had its challenges, too. Feeding tens of thousands of men in the Ethiopian highlands was no joke. Much of what was needed could not be found locally, not in Asmara, not even in Massawa. At times meat on the hoof was brought in from India on contract; virtually everything else had to be brought in from Italy. Getting it to Massawa was just the beginning. From Massawa, supplies had to be moved first by narrow-gauge rail most of the way to Asmara and then by caravan to Adigrat. The ascent from Massawa to Adigrat took a week under optimal conditions.[9] Along the way, caravans were delayed when pack animals pulled up lame; there were bandit raids. The difficulty of it all is conveyed in the litany of places through which the supplies moved, a list almost as long as the route itself: Massawa, Ilalia, Mahio, Adi Caie, Senafe, Barakit, Adiguden, Adigrat.[10]

And Menelik's army was not the only one vulnerable to defections. Baratieri relied on important native allies—Hagos Tafari and Ras Sebhat—whose allegiance was "conditional" and held a nasty surprise for Baratieri.

Hagos Tafari and Ras Sebhat had joined the cause of Italy and Eritrea after a fallout with Mangasha in 1895. The men were rivals. They came from families that historically ruled in Agamé, a region north of Tigray. When Mangasha need to appoint a new ruler in Agamé, rather than choose between them, he chose neither.[11] This might have been the end of it, but in the rough-and-tumble world of Tigrayan politics, Mangasha also sought pacification. He invited the defeated rivals to visit him at Adwa. Hagos Tafari, smelling a trap, decided to stay away. Ras Sebhat accepted

Mangasha's invitation and was magnificently received. Midway through the festivities, Sebhat was seized, tied up, and hauled away. Mangasha had him imprisoned on a remote hilltop called Amba Alage. He would remain a prisoner of Mangasha until released by the Italians in October 1895.[12]

Mangasha's high-handedness earned him Hagos Tafari's eternal enmity. It also brought Italy a valued ally—at least for a time. Hagos Tafari joined the Italians, fought Mangasha alongside them, and shared in the booty after the victories of 1895. After the defeat of Mangasha at Senafe, Hagos Tafari hauled away weapons, animals, women, and treasure from the rubble of Mangasha's camp.[13] Weeks later, Ras Sebhat also joined the Italians when they drove off Mangasha, setting him free. Thus by late 1895, both men were allies of Italy.[14]

Winning over Sebhat and Hagos Tafari had been a brilliant move. It was a perfect execution of Italy's strategy of divide and conquer. By cultivating the support of Mangasha's disgruntled lieutenants, Baratieri could weaken Mangasha while adding to the forces at his disposal. Moreover, these forces knew the terrain and the enemy intimately. Baratieri thought the relationship would hold. In his dispatches to Rome, Baratieri referred to Hagos Tafari as "our friend."[15]

But Hagos Tafari was an opportunist, not a traitor. His loyalty lasted only as long as the illusion of Italian inevitability did. By the middle of February 1896, after Amba Alage and Mekele, it was clear that Menelik had taken the initiative. Baratieri was playing defense, reacting to Menelik's moves.[16] Hagos Tafari and Sebhat could see how the coming conflict was going to turn out. As one of Ras Sebhat's soldiers bluntly put it, "[The Italians] were weak, while Menelik was strong."[17] Around eleven o'clock in the evening on 13 February, Hagos Tafari, Ras Sebhat, and their men quietly picked up their things—including Italian-issued firearms—and left the Italian camp, leaving behind mules, provisions, and tents.

Baratieri was stunned. He thought their move made no sense, and he said so in telegrams back to Rome. "Mangasha is their enemy," he protested. "He gave control of these lands to others." Baratieri missed the point. The defection of Hagos Tafari and Ras Sebhat was not about Mangasha. It represented a sober assessment of the balance of forces in the coming conflict. If Baratieri had been paying attention, he would have understood what it meant: Menelik and Ethiopia were going to win.[18]

When they arrived at Menelik's camp, the erstwhile traitors Hagos Tafari and Ras Sebhat were greeted as honored heroes.[19] And when the news reached Adigrat—Agamé's main city and the linchpin of the Italian occupation—the people celebrated spontaneously and shamelessly.[20]

The Italian Occupation Crumbles

The defection of Hagos Tafari and Sebhat represented a loss of five hundred men—not much in the great scheme of things. But what it portended was much more, including interruptions in communications, disrupted supply lines, and Agamé in revolt.[21] The departure of Hagos Tafari and Ras Sebhat threatened Italian morale as it rallied the broader population.[22] If, for a time, the Italians had deceived themselves into thinking that their presence was welcome, they could no longer. Even Baratieri had to concede that within days of their defection, Ras Sebhat and Hagos Tafari had tripled the size of their forces, thanks to volunteers from the surrounding population eager to join a burgeoning resistance.

With Menelik's encouragement, Ras Sebhat and Hagos Tafari wasted no time in putting their new recruits to work.[23] Hagos Tafari and Sebhat knew the disposition of Italian forces intimately. Baratieri's telegraph communication with the rear was cut, then restored, then lost again. On the eighteenth, only five days after they had left Baratieri's camp, the forces of Hagos Tafari and Sebhat were threatening the town of Barakit, a strategic position along Baratieri's supply lines thirty-three miles to the rear.

Italian troops escorting a supply caravan were attacked at Mai Maret, a point midway between Baratieri and the rear supply position of Barakit.[24]

Forays out of Adigrat or the encampment at Sauria frequently led to disaster. They were often accompanied by the atrocities that wars of insurgency can bring. A reconnaissance mission of 110 soldiers was ambushed and badly shot up on 14 February. That night, a rescue mission of thirty-five men set out. They were intercepted and massacred. The bodies of the dead were stripped.[25]

On 16 February, insurgents loyal to Menelik occupied the high ground around the town of Adigrat. When a contingent of a hundred Italian soldiers set out to greet a large caravan coming up from Asmara, they were set upon by forces greatly outnumbering them. The soldiers retreated toward Adigrat, leaving behind many dead and several prisoners, including two commanding officers. The Ethiopians seized the uniforms of the dead and the captured. The following day, they wore those captured uniforms as a part of a ruse to lure a rescue force of 140 men into an ambush.[26]

There were also reports of mistreatment of captured soldiers, wounded soldiers burned alive, and the disfiguring of the bodies of the dead—reports that troubled soldiers and undermined morale.[27] While Baratieri at Sauria was contemplating attack or retreat in terms of conventional warfare, on the roads leading to and from Adigrat one could make out the unmistakable signs of an incipient guerrilla war.

Baratieri considered shifting his supply lines away from Adigrat to a road that ran by way of Mai Marat and Debra Damo. But the revolt initiated by the departures of Hagos Tafari and Ras Sebhat included the entire Agamé region, and the high ground near the monastery of Debra Damo provided a hospitable refuge for the insurgents.[28] The Italians, who once claimed to have arrived to liberate the local inhabitants from Mangasha's arbitrary and divisive rule, were now facing a civilian insurrection actively supporting Menelik's defense of Ethiopia.

Troops loyal to Ethiopia harried caravans between Adigrat to Sauria. They watched as Italian soldiers, wary of ambush and with fixed bayonets, made their way along narrow paths. Supply convoy details—understandably eager to bring the ordeal to an end—pushed pack animals to the limit, but when fatigue set in they had to stop, sometimes hourly, to unburden the animals and allow them to rest. Some of the animals, utterly spent, would simply fall to the ground and die.

Campfires became part of an elaborate game of disinformation as Ethiopians and Italians sought to exaggerate numbers. At night, the campfires of the Ethiopian troops flickered from the surrounding hilltops. Luigi Goj's convoy built extra campfires to create the illusion of a large force and thus discourage attack.[29]

Convoys sometimes traveled at night in the hope of avoiding detection, but it left them prey to the fear of an enemy they couldn't see, concealed by darkness. Sometimes the soldiers couldn't help giving away their presence. The passes were so dangerous at night that the soldiers would set fire to dry shrubs, creating a small bonfire to light their way. Ethiopian scouts were witness to the eerie spectacle of soldiers and animals passing the flames one by one, their shadows bobbing and leaping against the mountain face.[30]

Soon the precarious situation began to have a bearing on supplies. Rations of flour, canned meat, and coffee continued, but there was no more wine, rum, salt, or sugar.[31] By the third week of February, soldiers were receiving flour, biscuits, and meat only every other day.[32] Things were no better for the askari; on the twenty-sixth, barley—what they considered to be animal fodder—was distributed to the askari in place of wheat.[33]

Hunger became a factor. Carlo Diotti, a corporal in the kitchen detail, witnessed fellow soldiers buying food from the askari. For the askari it was a profit opportunity; for the Italians it was a way of staving off hunger. Shortages had an impact on discipline. Luigi Goj saw soldiers break into food stocks; they stole a sack of flour and a case of biscuits while a sympathetic sentry looked the other way.

The shortage of food began to manifest itself in other ways. Soldiers began to grumble. Some left jackets unbuttoned, stopped shaving, or went shirtless. Some still looked like soldiers; others resembled bandits.[34] Baratieri's army was coming apart. Menelik had won. He had shown Baratieri and Italy that the victories over Mangasha the prior year were hollow. Power exists only where it can be defended. By marching unimpeded as far as Tigray, Menelik had demonstrated the emptiness of Italian rule.

Political leadership in Rome seemed to appreciate the gravity of the situation more acutely than Baratieri himself. The telegraph line crackled with notes of concern. "Sebhat and [H]agos occupy the mountains surrounding Adigrat and incite rebellion in Agamé," Baratieri wrote to Stanislao Mocenni (the minister of war) on 18 February—without specifying what he intended to do about it.[35] "Ministry preoccupied with consequences of rebellion," replied Mocenni in spare telegraphic language, "and invites Your Excellency [Baratieri] to communicate your views on the present situation. The ministry has decided to give you any other reinforcements necessary."[36] Mocenni was anxious about the strategic situation of Italian forces. Since the beginning of the year he had been shipping out battalions even in advance of Baratieri's requests. Meanwhile, Mocenni was doing battle with Sidney Sonnino, the minister of treasury, who wanted assurance that Baratieri's operations wouldn't break the bank. Would the campaign shatter the government's budget? Sonnino asked. Not if operations lasted only a month, responded Mocenni.[37] Italy needed a victory, and it needed it soon.

CHAPTER 11

Baratieri Chooses

A S A YOUNG PATRIOT, Oreste Baratieri had fought to drive an Austrian occupier from Italian soil, thus creating an independent
modern Italy. If it ever occurred to Baratieri to compare Italy's struggle
for independence with that of Ethiopia, he never mentioned it. That Italy
was Austria to Ethiopia's Italy seems not to have crossed his mind. Patriotism resolved the glaring contradiction. Great powers had empires, and
so if Italy was to realize its destiny in the modern world, it must acquire
an empire. The same patriotic impulse that had driven Baratieri to liberate Italy now told him to subjugate Ethiopia in Italy's name.

By February 1896 the grand continuity in Baratieri's life—the patriotic
thread that connected Trentino to Tigray—was at risk. For Baratieri,
Sauria was not only a military crisis but an existential one. Baratieri's bold
annexation of northern Ethiopia had cast Italy in the role of aggressor in
the eyes of international public opinion. Meanwhile, Menelik's measured
northward march was the embodiment of a prudent and just defense of
Ethiopian sovereignty. Ilg was right. No European nation would submit
to Abyssinian rule; why should Abyssinia submit to European rule?

Italy was losing the battle for public opinion. It was also losing the
battle on the ground. Not only was Italy's control of Tigray unraveling,
but Menelik's movement to the northwest, skirting a direct confrontation

with the Italians at Adigrat, manifested his military skill for the world to see. It showed that Menelik would deny Baratieri the thing he most wanted—a battle where Menelik broke his army attacking a fortified Italian position. Instead, Menelik had seized the strategic initiative leaving Baratieri to adapt to Menelik's moves. To the extent that Baratieri's fellow officers and rank-and-file soldiers understood the deteriorating strategic situation, it was humiliation for Baratieri.[1]

Baratieri's answer was to keep his men occupied. In the memoirs of Italian soldiers, the days at Sauria were days of drudgery, digging trench after trench. As it became clear that they were preparing for an Ethiopian attack that would never come, these labors consumed morale as well as strength.[2] Baratieri's brigadier generals expressed a sense of futility in the face of these exercises. General Giuseppe Arimondi, who seethed under Baratieri's command, saw an opening and seized it; in an elegantly vulgar slur he mocked these barren efforts as "the onanism of the military arts."[3]

It was also a situation that heightened the contrast between the Ethiopian and Italian ways of war. The Italians relied on conventional forms of supply and reinforcement. As Baratieri's lines of communication stretched in pursuit of Menelik, his supply caravans became that much more vulnerable to attack. As reinforcements arrived from Italy, bringing more mouths to feed, supply demands only increased.

In contrast, Menelik's army lived off the land. What his soldiers couldn't carry, they had to find along the way. This made Menelik's army speedy and mobile—there were no cumbersome caravans to delay their progress. But the system was far from perfect, especially for an army as large as that of Menelik. When a court travels, it is customary for it to be supported by those who live along its path. And while it is true that once the emperor's tent was set, among the first rituals was the presentation of gifts—animals, flour, drink—by the local population, these amounted to mere gestures for an army on the scale of Menelik's.

"Foraging" is the polite word for what happens when an army feeds itself off what it finds. From the point of view of the army, foraging is a fee for services rendered. After all, the army is defending the people who are being asked to feed it. But the burden tends to fall disproportionately on those who have the misfortune of living in the path of the army.

Requisitioning—for that is what it ought to be called—meant that the foragers had to move outward from Menelik's camp in an ever-widening arc as local supplies were exhausted. Following the march from Mekele, Menelik's forces settled into camp at Gundapta. The following week they moved on to the rich lands around Adwa.[4] As a practical necessity, Menelik's army had to keep moving to live.

Thus both armies contended with deepening sense of urgency. For Menelik, there was a growing desperation surrounding the question of food. For Baratieri, there was a deteriorating local situation—a growing rebellion—at the same time as he was getting political pressure from Rome to do something, anything, to bring the standoff to a conclusion. "My colleagues and I are sending you two additional brigades and everything that you have asked for. Remember that Amba Alage and Mekele were two military failures, however glorious, and that the honor of Italy and that of the monarchy are in your hands."[5] Francesco Crispi was writing to Baratieri in a manner that left little room for misunderstanding.

The Upstart and the Blue Bloods

The pressure wasn't coming only from Rome. Baratieri's generals were a constant source of carping and dissent. Of the four generals directly under Baratieri's command, at least three of them expressed doubts about Baratieri's leadership. For the most part, the generals had kept their peace while Baratieri was winning. However, as Menelik's forces rolled up the Italian positions—Amba Alage, Mekele, and now Tigray itself—there was plenty of room for second-guessing. All kinds of resentments came out, including social snobbery fed by some of the worst professional jealousies.

Baratieri's patriotism was unassailable. However, his unconventional path to command via Garibaldian populist insurgency meant that his social credentials remained open to question. All four of the generals under his immediate command in Ethiopia—Albertone, Arimondi, Dabormida, and Ellena—came from old patrician families of Piedmont, in northern Italy.[6] As elsewhere in Europe, the army was one place where the partisans of the old regime could still contest the authority of the new. The army's officer corps had been a preserve of the highborn—an honorable career for the sons of the aristocracy. Baratieri was the son of a mere magistrate. By birth and by training, he was a parvenu.

General Giuseppe Arimondi was an elegantly handsome man. He kept his hair short and brushed back from his imposing brow. He had steely eyes, a trimmed full beard, and a mustache that turned up slightly at the ends. He sat ramrod straight for his official portrait, with five medals pinned high on the chest of a jacket laced with officer's braids. He had the air of a man not to be trifled with.

Of all the officers under Baratieri's command, Arimondi was the one with whom he had the thorniest relationship. At forty-nine, General Arimondi was not a young man, but he was five years younger than Baratieri and had plenty of ambition. He chafed under Baratieri's leadership. In December 1894, when Baratieri was recalled to Rome to confer with the government, Arimondi set out on a campaign against the Dervishes. A victory at Agordat made a big splash in Italy, earning Arimondi a promotion, but it embarrassed and upstaged Baratieri. Relations didn't improve upon Baratieri's return. Within months, Arimondi was asking to be sent back to Italy, a request that Baratieri refused. Arimondi appealed to the minister of war, who also refused. In a bitter and rambling letter to his brother Francesco, Arimondi complained that Baratieri was an "omnipotent" figure whose power Arimondi attributed to a murky mix of politics, personal favor (Crispi), and ties to the Masonic order.[7] Paradoxically, he attributed real power in Eritrea to Baratieri's adjutant, Major Tommaso Salsa, whom he saw as a puppetmaster manipulating Baratieri the buffoon.[8]

One could hardly say that either man was warm and approachable. Baratieri was cerebral. With his narrow-set eyes and pince-nez, he gave off a professorial air that was complemented by a penchant for grand words and complicated syntax. Arimondi's aloofness was social, not intellectual—a mix of high birth and self-regard.[9] His brooding, sulky character was famous. Around camp, Arimondi was known as "Achilles in his tent"—a remark suggesting military prowess but also a prickly personality.[10]

In Rome, opinion of Arimondi was not high. "In general, he is little esteemed as a soldier," concluded an unsigned, undated memo written around 1895; "it would be better to replace him with an officer of lower rank who took greater care and had greater competence in the areas of service required." He occupied himself too much and in minute detail with things of only secondary importance. Baratieri, it was said, had little respect for him, consulting him only as a formality or in order to spread out responsibility for an unpopular decision.[11] Arimondi was described as vain and unwilling to let go of even small offenses. Major Toselli had strained relations with Arimondi, his superior, that spilled over into an open break. "Siamo in rotta," Toselli wrote in confidence to his brother. "We have broken with each other."[12] It was Arimondi who had failed to rein in Toselli's aggressive push to Amba Alage and who had not given Toselli clear orders to retreat in the face of overwhelming odds. Arimondi's mistakes had led to disaster.

Baratieri also saw Arimondi as a hothead, given to risky offensives, especially when it came to African troops under his command.[13] Askari were faster and had greater stamina than European troops, especially in the high-altitude conditions of Eritrea and Ethiopia. Given Arimondi's tendency to see any military problem as best solved by going on the attack, this was a dangerous combination. After Amba Alage, Baratieri was sufficiently concerned about the possibility of another disastrous mistake that he took Arimondi's askari and placed them under the command of General Matteo Albertone.[14]

Proud, nervous, chatty, intemperate, troublesome—General Matteo Albertone had a complicated reputation long before 1 March 1896. Albertone's official portrait highlights his high forehead. Epaulets trimmed generously with gold braid rest on wide shoulders. More gold braid swoops across his chest, drawing an emphatic arc beneath a spray of medals. A hard gaze—completely lacking in warmth—complements a regal air. The ends of a full, dark mustache curl up above a resolute chin. The portrait is of a man certain of his destiny.

Accounts of Albertone on the move with his troops in Ethiopia, as well as memos dashed off to the high command in Rome, suggest that Albertone had an impulsive personality. Zealous and impatient, he was mercurial in spirit, passing quickly from high emotion to sulky moodiness. He was easily convinced that his extraordinary talent was wasted.

Somehow Albertone's career hadn't reflected the grandeur of his self-image. Eritrea must have felt like a punishment when he arrived at the

Matteo Albertone. From *L'Illustrazione italiana,* 19 January 1896.

Red Sea port of Massawa, where midday temperatures pushed past a hellish 115 degrees. We don't know how Albertone earned a colonial post, but we know that it was not an assignment he coveted. The colonies were where frustrated soldiers went—or were sent—to revive flagging careers. Albertone first laid eyes on Eritrea in 1885. The experience left him a convinced anti-Africanist—an opponent of the vision of *Italia africana*. He deemed the soil too poor to produce much of value. He returned to Italy but was posted to Eritrea again in 1888 and once more in 1895, when he arrived with reinforcements in the final buildup.[15]

If General Arimondi was the one who was seen as reckless and dangerous, it wasn't obvious to contemporaries that Albertone was a model of composure. One contemporary observed that the askari preferred Arimondi to the excitable Albertone. Alessandro Sapelli recounted an episode that occurred one morning during the long face-off between the Italian and Ethiopian forces across the Gundapta plain. Sapelli was with Albertone as part of a forward observation group when they spotted an Ethiopian outpost on a hill opposite them. Albertone turned to Degiac Fanta, the leader of an Eritrean band supporting the Italian forces, and remarked, "Let's go over to those heights and take a look at the emperor's camp."

"But those hills are full of armed men," warned Fanta. "In a minute they would call thousands of men to their position."

"So what?" answered Albertone. "When they see us they'll scamper off."

"Don't say that, General!" cautioned Fanta. "These men have come from a place far, far away—as far as you have come—and they have come to fight."[16]

Albertone's remarks perfectly capture his disdain for Menelik's forces. He was not alone in thinking that Menelik's army would collapse at the first resolute use of force.

In some ways, General Vittorio Emanuele Dabormida was the most interesting of the generals under Baratieri's command. His name alone spoke volumes about his patriotic and noble northern Italian lineage—Victor Emmanuel, Dabormida's namesake, was the king who served as patron of Italian unity. The Dabormida family was so well connected that King Victor Emmanuel had served as godfather at Vittorio's baptism.

The adult Dabormida had a full mustache, stylishly upturned at the ends, and a tapered soul patch under his lower lip. A gold pince-nez completed the bookish look.[17]

Bookish he was. Dabormida was a scholar of strategy and tactics, a published author of books and pamphlets on military history and the principles of national defense.[18] His diplomatic experience was also impressive. In the 1880s, his aristocratic background made him the obvious choice as Italy's representative in discussions with imperial Germany about the Triple Alliance.[19]

None of this prepared Dabormida for the realities of leadership in combat. Dabormida's narrow and deep-set eyes gave him a forbidding aspect. His lofty, distant air made him seem unapproachable. "Pedantic," "absolutist," "excessive sense of self-worth"—the words his subordinates used to describe him are not kind.[20] He was abrupt with subordinates—the antithesis of the soldier's soldier. He expected his orders to be obeyed scrupulously; his keen sense of hierarchy and discipline made him unwilling to countenance any discussion of his decisions.[21]

Dabormida had no experience of Africa. In mid-January 1896—mere weeks before Adwa—Dabormida shipped out for Massawa even though he harbored private misgivings about the wisdom of the campaign in which he was engaged. In letters home he strikes the tone of a man trapped between a deep sense of duty and doubts about his mission. They were fighting, he wrote to his family, "to defend the honor of our country— rightly or wrongly engaged—but engaged nonetheless."[22] Dabormida's reservations about the enterprise of Italian East Africa were trumped by an aristocratic commitment to honor. His dedication to duty and country derived from what was called "the chivalrous spirit of the old aristocracy"—a spirit that wedded honor and family.[23]

"Do what you must do," his father had told him as a young man. It was a phrase redolent of weighty but vague responsibility. Dabormida took it to heart. No longer young in 1896—he had turned fifty-three just before leaving Italy for Eritrea—he still carried the burden of family. His illustrious name, or so he felt it, obligated him. "Would that I carried a name not enshrined in respect," he mused. He worried lest the family name lose any of the luster his ancestors had earned.

"A true ingenue" is how a close friend characterized him, implying naiveté as much as candor.[24] Dabormida's understanding of warfare was as good as that of anyone in the Italian camp, but it was entirely bookish and abstract. His first direct experience of combat would come on 1 March.[25]

General Giuseppe Ellena was the most recently arrived of the four generals at Sauria. In fact, he had been with them less than two weeks, having left Italy with a group of reinforcements on 25 January. Although the oldest of the group, at fifty-six, as a newcomer to Africa he was too respectful of the other generals to weigh in heavily during the discussions leading up to the battle. Just the same, his voice mattered in part because he was so recently arrived. Even if he had little understanding of Ethiopia or Africa, Ellena could express with greater authority than anyone else the mood of the political elites in Rome, who were impatient for victory and to avenge what had happened at Amba Alage and Mekele.[26] Ellena carried this impatience with him when he set foot in Africa.

Many of the rank-and-file soldiers were impatient, too. Soldiers who had been in Africa for a while had a realistic idea of what combat with Ethiopian troops might be like. Some of them had fought against Mangasha. Still others had been part of the siege at Mekele and had been released along with Galliano. They knew that warfare—especially colonial warfare—was no picnic. They respected the Ethiopian soldiers who tenaciously resisted the Italian presence. Some of them had seen what had happened to soldiers who were attacked while defending convoys coming up from Asmara—they had seen the stripped bodies and knew the Ethiopians rarely took prisoners.

New recruits had a slightly different attitude. The send-offs they had received in train stations and dockside at Naples often had been tumultuous. Italy may have been indifferent to the larger colonial enterprise, but Italians had no difficulty identifying with their sons.[27] Soldiers who had left Italy since Mekele and Amba Alage had a much clearer sense that their mission was one of vengeance. They represented a momentum that was driving toward combat and had little patience for a prudent commander such as Baratieri.[28]

Neither, apparently, did Francesco Crispi. By mid-February, Crispi and his government had lost confidence in their commander. The victories against Mangasha in 1895 had been a pleasant surprise, even though some members of the government saw Baratieri's pursuit of Mangasha as hasty and ill-advised. By early 1896, these concerns had been validated. The government understood as well as Baratieri himself just how overextended he was.[29] The campaign was ruinously expensive. When the Chamber of Deputies returned from its recess, anti-Africanists would be smelling blood and the government would have some explaining to do. The government wanted something—anything—that would justify the enterprise they had embarked upon.

Rome Dismisses Baratieri

In mid-February, an exasperated Crispi government decided to sack Baratieri. They offered the command to Antonio Baldissera, who had served as governor-general of Eritrea in the 1880s. Baldissera refused, pointing out the risks of removing a commander at such a critical moment. Such a move would make Italy seem desperate and might undermine diplomatic efforts to bring the conflict to a close without a fight.[30]

The government was adamant, and eventually Baldissera relented. The decision to demote Baratieri came on 21 February; General Baldissera would be named commander in chief of troops in Africa, though the decision was to be kept quiet. Two days later, Antonio Baldissera, dressed in civilian clothes, boarded a British vessel at Brindisi and began the journey to Africa.[31]

Four days later, Crispi wrote a sharply worded telegram to Baratieri. His irritation was evident as he characterized the campaign Baratieri had led. "This is military wastage, not a war," he wrote.

> Small skirmishes in which we always find ourselves inferior in numbers to the enemy, heroic gestures squandered without success. I don't have any advice to offer because I'm not on the scene. I simply note that your campaign has been conducted without any preestablished plan, and I would like you to make one. We are ready for any sacrifice to save the honor of the army and the prestige of the monarchy.[32]

It is unclear why Crispi sent this telegram, as Baratieri's fate was already sealed and his successor was on his way. Crispi's outburst served no political or military purpose. It served merely as a final slap at Baratieri, a measure of Crispi's frustration and his capacity for insult. Given what happened a few days later—Baratieri's ill-fated decision to march toward Adwa—some have argued that it was Crispi's telegram that drove Baratieri to act.

In fact, in the days leading up to the first of March, the option Baratieri championed in discussions with his staff was a strategic retreat to the north, back toward Eritrea—an obvious defensive move for a commander whose lines of communication were already dangerously overstretched. Baratieri recognized that Menelik's northward march had changed the stakes dramatically. What had started as an Ethiopian challenge to the Italian occupation of the province of Tigray now threatened Eritrea itself. To withdraw from Tigray into Eritrea might change the dynamics of the campaign by bringing Baratieri and his men closer to their supply lines, closer to the thousands of fresh troops arriving at Massawa every week. If Menelik could be induced to continue his campaign into Eritrea, it could shift the strategic balance in Italy's favor.

But circumstances were conspiring against such a course of action. Nearly every day new troops were arriving at Massawa, charged with the task of avenging their fellow soldiers after Amba Alage and Mekele. Then there were insubordinate officers. Arimondi's remark about "military onanism" showed that he held Baratieri in a contempt that he no longer bothered to conceal. Dabormida, who as a combat novice should have known better, gave in to the most optimistic scenarios of Italian victory. He imagined Menelik's army as numbering eighty thousand—a lowball estimate encouraged by Menelik's agents posing as informants. Menelik's army, Dabormida believed, was saddled with the burden of women and children—in all, some 150,000 mouths to feed. And he gave in to the fantasy that the Ethiopians would scatter if attacked. "I believe a surprise attack would prompt them to flee," he wrote. Dabormida surely was not alone in favoring the most optimistic intelligence—disinformation supplied by Ethiopian agents—to the effect that Menelik's men were hungry, discouraged, and homesick.[33] Many believed that Menelik's soldiers were "fearful" and "effeminate."[34] Such reckless talk did not bode well.

Dabormida and Albertone were eager for a showdown that would pit the full strength of the Italian forces against Menelik's army. After all, the main bodies of the two armies had yet to come face-to-face. Ambition also had its place. Gherardo Pantano would complain that some of Baratieri's generals "wanted their own Austerlitz"—a reference to a military victory that cemented the reputation of Napoleon Bonaparte.[35] But there were no Napoleons in the Italian camp.

For most of February, Menelik's forces remained encamped in the valley of Gundapta. Then, on 22 February, Menelik withdrew. He moved his forces westward, away from Baratieri's forces, into the valley near Adwa. What did it mean? On the face of it, the shift signaled weakness—an army retreats to avoid conflict. More realistically, however, Menelik's move—which opened new grounds for foraging—revealed a steely resolve to endure. More ominously, it raised the possibility of an invasion of Eritrea by a more westerly route. The road leading northward out of Adwa by way of Adi Abuna led directly to Eritrea. An invasion by that route would leave Baratieri in frantic pursuit as Menelik's men spread chaos and destruction.

The Meeting of the Generals

Menelik's move could be interpreted as a search for food, as prelude to an invasion of Eritrea, or even as a sign of weakness. The ambiguity was no doubt deliberate.[36] The next day, 23 February, Baratieri ordered preparations for a retreat northward to Debra Damo, a move that mirrored Menelik's by bringing the Italians closer to Eritrea on a parallel route. "Yesterday, the enemy moved to Adwa, breaking contact with our troops. In following this move, I have decided to post our corps of operation to Debra Damo."

Baratieri correctly understood the risks posed by Menelik's latest gambit, which was not a sign of weakness but a new threat. His officers saw it differently. Lieutenant Cesare Pini oozed disdain for Baratieri, whom he mocked as a commander intimidated by "an enemy who flees."[37] General Dabormida heaped scorn on Baratieri's announcement: "The enemy retreats and we do the same!"[38]

The military crisis, along with the carping and criticism, compounded a deep personal crisis for Baratieri. Captain Mario Bassi painted a grave and vivid picture in his journal. Baratieri had stopped eating. He had a constant fever. In addition to being "physically finished," Baratieri was "a wreck"—"the victim of great nervous exhaustion." Baratieri's crisis transcended the person. It was a crisis for colonialism itself. Baratieri's "dream"— his "embrace" of Ethiopia—had become "a deadly embrace for him and for Italy." Baratieri's symptoms, Bassi noted presciently, announced "the beginning of the end of the colonial farce."[39]

Baratieri recognized retreat as his only option, Bassi noted, and in this he echoed the views of Major Tommaso Salsa, the man some regarded as Baratieri's puppetmaster. Bassi fervently wished their cautious view would hold. The alternative to retreat, he predicted, would be "a great and truly grave catastrophe." Of all the views recorded prior to Adwa, Bassi most clearly articulated the choice between retreat and disaster. Sometimes there is no comfort in being right: Bassi would die at Adwa.

Rattled by criticism from his officers, Baratieri called off the retreat to Debra Damo a few days after announcing it. On 28 February, Baratieri summoned his generals to his tent for a candid airing of military options. Baratieri and the four generals—Albertone, Arimondi, Dabormida, Ellena—took their places around a small table. The only other person present was Baratieri's chief of staff, Colonel Gioacchino Valenzano. The small tent was claustrophobic in the stifling heat.

Baratieri invited a frank discussion.

> I haven't asked you to a war council, because the responsibility for any decision rests with me. I've asked you to open up your hearts [as I would in] an ordinary situation of troop movements or maneuvers. I ask you to give me, as is customary, information on the condition of the troops.[40]

Colonel Valenzano began with a report on the state of supplies. The news was not good. Since the defection of Hagos Tafari and Ras Sebhat and the opening of guerrilla warfare, supplies had become scarce.[41] Ration reserves for European soldiers were nearly depleted, and the remaining provisions were adequate for only three days. The askari, who were given money with which to buy food from the local population, might get by for a week.[42] Additional supplies were on the way, but it was unclear that they would arrive in time. In a few days, the army might have to retreat simply to procure food.

The discussion then turned to the army's course of action. Retreat, attack, or advance—these were the options. Each of the generals spoke in turn. As they did, it was clear that retreat was not the preferred option.[43] General Dabormida spoke first. "Never retreat!" he began. The soldiers would never understand such a move. "Troop morale is very high; a retreat would bring it down." No one, he argued, would be able to explain why the army had chosen to retreat after three months in the face of the enemy. Dabormida even put a price on honor: Italy would prefer a loss of two to three thousand men to a dishonorable retreat.[44]

A retreat would also be dangerous, Dabormida argued, and possibly more costly than defeat in open battle. The Ethiopians knew the roads and byways, and they would harass the retreat every step of the way.[45]

General Albertone supported Dabormida and laid out an argument in favor of an attack. He believed that he had solid information about the status of enemy forces, thanks to the scouting work of his speedy askari units. Menelik's army had been depleted. Part of it was away on requisitioning raids; another part had already begun a southward retreat. What remained was divided into two forces, the smaller of which—perhaps a mere fourteen or fifteen thousand men—was closer to the Italians. Far from being a daunting, overwhelming force, Menelik's army was beginning to sound like an attractive target.[46]

And that was not all. According to Albertone's information, dissension among the Ethiopian chiefs was beginning to take its toll on the combat readiness of Menelik's forces. Albertone, who had been in favor of a retreat after the defection of Ras Sebhat and Hagos Tafari, now believed that retreat was the greater danger because it would actually "provoke an enemy advance."[47] In effect, the Italians had exaggerated the cohesiveness and effectiveness of Menelik's forces. They faced a shriveled and dispirited enemy. The time had come to move against it.

General Arimondi—the sulky Achilles of the Italian camp—was the most fanatically aggressive. For Arimondi, there could be no talk of retreat. It was bad enough that the Italians had let pass two or three good occasions to attack. Conditions were ripe for battle, he argued, and he enumerated all the reasons to be optimistic about victory. Better arms, more ammunition, better marksmanship, better leadership, superior valor, more disciplined firepower—all of these would more than compensate for smaller numbers. And the time to act was now. To await reinforcements would mean the loss of precious time; it would let an opportunity slip away. He concluded his argument with the statement that the only way out of the present difficulties was to advance on Adwa and give battle to the enemy.[48]

Giuseppe Ellena was the last to speak. Given that he had been with the forces less than two weeks, he freely admitted that he was in no position to offer an independent opinion. He deferred to the judgment of his colleagues—Dabormida, Albertone, Arimondi—who advocated an attack.[49]

Baratieri closed the meeting with words that ought to have brought the generals back down to earth: "The enemy is valiant and despises death."

Then, upon being reassured that the morale of the Italian soldiers was excellent, he closed the meeting with the promise that he was awaiting further intelligence from informants, after which he would make a decision.

Baratieri had hoped the meeting would defuse tense relations with his generals—they would air their differences, then arrive at consensus. Instead, the meeting had made things worse, revealing his utter isolation. Baratieri reflected awhile, then called in his chief of staff, Valenzano, and asked his opinion. Until then, Valenzano had been an advocate of prudence, but he had been impressed both by the arguments and by the generals' unanimity. He decided that he agreed with them and said so to Baratieri.

When he recalled these fateful moments at Baratieri's court-martial, Valenzano emphasized the political arguments the generals had used. Italy wanted revenge, they agreed. Retreat would be worse than a disaster; "it would be a betrayal of the country."[50]

The following evening, 29 February, General Baratieri called the generals back to inform them of his decision. The army would advance toward Adwa. They would take up positions very close to Menelik's camp—an aggressive move that would invite Ethiopian attack. He handed out a map of the terrain they would occupy, and he explained the order and path of advance. When the generals were dismissed, Baratieri sought to impress upon them the seriousness of what lay ahead. It would be, he told them, "a matter of victory or death."[51]

CHAPTER 12

Armies Meet

M UCH OF ETHIOPIA exists above sixty-five hundred feet, a fact that goes a long way toward explaining Ethiopia's ability to resist incursions from the outside, whether they be zealous followers of the Prophet Muhammad in the sixteenth century or Europeans in search of empire in the nineteenth century. The high elevation and rugged terrain inspired some visitors to dub Ethiopia "Africa's Switzerland." The analogy was useful in countering the common European misconception of sub-Saharan Africa as a vast, damp, leafy jungle—the Congo writ large—but it brought confusions of its own. Ethiopia largely lacks evergreens, and it certainly lacks chalets and lederhosen.

In late February, before the rains resume, the high valleys and prairies of Tigray share a palette of tan, gray, brown, and black. When the dry season ends, heavy rains work the land, cutting breaks, ruts, and ravines. When the Italians marched west from their camp toward Adwa, they traversed a landscape that was a broad plain in essence, yet intricate in detail. Only two real paths crossed west from Sauria, leading respectively to two passes across the mountains separating the Gundapta plains from the town of Adwa. As they headed westward, a range of peaks loomed in the distance. The rugged, snowless profiles of three of them—Eshasho, Raio, and Semayata—served as markers for the soldiers' destination.

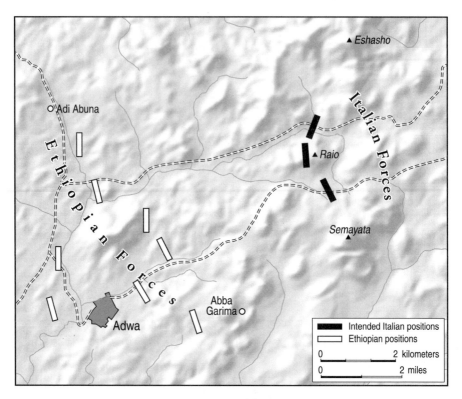

Baratieri's plan

Baratieri's plan was simple. The army would advance in three columns, followed by Baratieri and his staff and a fourth reserve column, led by General Ellena. The three columns were to take up positions holding the two passes over the mountains. General Dabormida's column, the army's right flank, would move to occupy the northern pass between the peaks of Eshasho and Raio. General Albertone's column, the army's left flank, would move to occupy the southern pass between the peaks of Raio and Semayata. General Arimondi's brigade, the army's center column, would occupy the ground in between, the western flanks of Raio. The advance would take place at night, to minimize the risk of detection and ambush.

Militarily, the march would accomplish a number of things. First, it would reduce the distance between the two forces. When the Ethiopians awoke on the morning of 1 March, they would find the Italians dug in at a very strong position at the passes, a mere five miles to their east. Such an aggressive move, although falling short of an actual attack, would make it difficult for the Ethiopians to refuse to give battle without losing face. Second, it would put the Italian forces in the dominant position, on high ground. The ground leading up to the two passes—the terrain Ethiopian forces would have to cover if they moved against the Italians—narrowed as one approached. This meant that the Ethiopians would have to approach the Italians on a funnel-like climb. As they neared the passes, fatigued and slowing from their climb, they would present compact targets for Italian riflemen and artillery.

The plan had its limitations, however. The passes are narrow and it wasn't obvious that the Italian forces would be able fully to deploy themselves there. Arimondi's column, in particular, would have to take up positions between the passes on the saddle of the western edge of Mount Raio. Could the Italian forces array themselves successfully in such uneven and confined space? Much would depend on execution.

And then there was the problem of communication. The brigades were ordered to remain in contact with one another and with Baratieri throughout the march, but the fact that three brigades would advance on two separate paths meant that one of them would have to trail the others. As it turned out, the Arimondi brigade had to wait while the Albertone brigade advanced, putting them hours behind.

There also seems to have been some confusion among Baratieri's generals about the objective of this movement. Baratieri's plan called for an aggressive movement, a provocative advance—not an attack.[1] The hope was that it would induce the Ethiopians to attack the Italians at last in a position that played to Italian strength. And even if the Ethiopians didn't attack, such an aggressive move would end the stalemate, salvage Italian honor, and prepare the moral ground for subsequent retreat.[2] It might even precipitate Menelik's retreat back to Shoa.

Giuseppe Menarini, a captain of a *bersaglieri* unit serving under General Dabormida, remembered meeting with the general on the eve of the army's advance. Dabormida entered "looking rather preoccupied." He barely responded to his officers' salutes, which was unlike him, and his somber expression made Menarini wonder whether a passing illness had returned. Dabormida removed his cap and sat down, putting his elbows on the table. He wiped his face with his hands before turning to Colonel

Cesare Airaghi. "Airaghi, we're not retreating anymore; we are advancing. Our movement begins this evening at nine o'clock."[3] Was Dabormida having second thoughts?

Advance by Moonlight

Orders to move out were not communicated to rank-and-file soldiers until the last possible moment, to minimize the risk of tipping off the Ethiopians. By the time the officers spread the word to prepare to move out, some of the soldiers had already turned in for the night. Others were just sitting down to a late dinner.

Ernesto Cordella was an artillery officer. He was ordered to Eritrea in December 1895 after the disaster of Amba Alage. When he arrived at Sauria on 27 February, the ascent from Massawa had taken twelve days. He and his men were assigned to the Third Mountain Battery, commanded by Captain Eduardo Bianchini; a feast to celebrate their arrival was planned for the night of 29 February. Umberto Masotto, the brigade cook and "emeritus chef in difficult circumstances," had put together a pasta dish that was judged "altogether ingestible." The call to move out interrupted them just as they were about to enjoy their evening meal. They gobbled down what they could, mounted their artillery pieces on the backs of their mules, and began to move out.[4]

Francesco Frisina had shipped out from Naples on Christmas Eve aboard the *Marco Minghetti* under circumstances more solemn than most. Like Cordella, his unit was dispatched to Africa in the aftermath of Amba Alage. The *Minghetti* arrived at Massawa on 30 January, and his group reached the encampment at Sauria in mid-February. On the evening of the twenty-ninth, having just barely settled into the camp routine, he was enjoying coffee and cake when the call to arms was trumpeted at eight-thirty. Like the others, he and his men were told they wouldn't be gone long; they left their camp intact.[5]

Carlo Diotti, a corporal in Dabormida's brigade, had already turned in for the night when he was called out for a brief speech by Major Secondo Solaro, commander of the Fourteenth Infantry Battalion: "Boys! The time for chatter is over. Tomorrow morning it's combat."[6] Another soldier—who lived to tell the story of the battle—believed that the plan called for a sneak attack on the Ethiopians.[7]

Such confusion about what was happening did not bode well. At the rank of major, Solaro was just a step or two away from Dabormida himself. Corporal Diotti had the conviction that he and his comrades were about to attack the Ethiopians. As Diotti and his comrades saw it, General Dabormida was itching for a fight, but Major Solaro confided to Diotti that he didn't share Dabormida's rosy outlook. Diotti himself felt confused. For days, he and other officers had promoted an optimistic view of the balance of forces, in order to boost morale: distress reigned in the Ethiopian camp, there was a shortage of food and internal divisions, Italian training would overcome Ethiopian numbers. Diotti hadn't known what to think, but in a personal sense it hadn't mattered, as he'd been assigned to the food detail and wouldn't be shooting anybody. Then, toward the end of February, he was reassigned from the kitchens to combat duty. Suddenly the prospect of battle was real.[8]

The Italian camps were on high ground. When the soldiers were ready, they descended to pass in review before General Baratieri and his staff. The askari units, as scouts, took the lead. Diotti and his comrades watched in admiration as the askari in the Dabormida brigade (officially known as the Native Company of Asmara) moved out smartly in their white pants and matching smocks with red embroidery on the shoulder. A woolen belt circled the waist, and a fez topped by a tassel completed the look.[9] The askari were in high spirits, laughing and chattering. Tassels bobbed as the askari set out, barefoot, on the road to Adwa.[10]

As the other units fell into line, including Diotti's Fourteenth Infantry Battalion, the order went round that they were to march in silence—without smoking, without flame—so as to pass undetected.[11]

General Albertone, encamped at a more westerly position, moved out a bit later. First, the Sixth, Seventh, and Eighth Native Battalions took the lead, followed by Cordella's Third Mountain Battery along with three other artillery units. Each mountain battery group consisted of four artillery pieces, dismantled for transport and packed on mules. These were followed by ammunition caissons—in fact not wagons but crates strapped on mules. There were thirty-six animals in all for each battery, carrying weapons, ammunition, and supplies. Nearly seventy soldiers, including eight officers, rounded out each battery.[12]

By nine forty-five that night, with the exception of support units, the entire Italian force was on the move.

The night was enchanted. The sky was clear; the stars and a full moon cast a silvery glow upon everything. For Giovanni Tedone, a soldier in a *bersaglieri* unit in Arimondi's brigade, the moon was "an immense street-light."[13] Giovanni Gamerra, commanding a battalion of askari, recalled the cloudless, moonlit night as the most beautiful he'd ever seen, and he welcomed it as an auspicious sign.[14] In spite of the good omens, the soldiers took every precaution. They marched without bayonets fixed for fear that the gleaming moonlight would reflect off the metal and give them away.[15]

Major Ludovico De Vito's askari battalion was out in front, serving as the eyes for the Dabormida brigade. They stopped at three in the morning. Finally at rest after six hours of marching, some battalions received orders to break out their reserve rations. The men had only a rough idea where they were; in the heavens above, the Southern Cross sparkled.[16] Glancing around, a few veterans recognized the area near Yeha and its high peak, a local landmark. The rocky profile at Yeha, when marked by afternoon shadows, forms a lion's head—the proud outline of the Lion of Judah.

There is no conclusive evidence to suggest that the Ethiopians had news of the Italian advance. However, there was some sympathy for what the Italian soldiers endured. Sometime after the events of 1 March, Gabra Iyasus compared the dogged determination of the Italians to a kind of pilgrimage. They were "loaded down for the entire night with a heavy pack on the back, a rifle on the shoulder, on the left hip an ammunition belt, on the right a water canteen . . . moving with difficulty in a strange land, like pilgrims to Lalibela."[17]

Albertone Overshoots

The rugged mountains separating the town of Adwa from the Gundapta plains are barren in February, the end of the dry season in Ethiopia. Three peaks—from north to south Eshasho, Raio, and Semayata—loom over the surrounding terrain. None is easy to overlook. Semayata is a classic, symmetrical volcanic cone. Both Eshasho and Semayata are nine thousand feet tall. At eight thousand feet, Raio is not nearly as high, but it is unmistakable. Its gnarly, bulbous profile bears a passing resemblance to

The rendezvous: looking south from Eshasho to Raio and, beyond, Semayata. From Eduardo Ximenes, *Sul Campo di Adua, marzo-giugno 1896.* Milan: Fratelli Treves Editori, 1897.

a walrus snout. Taken together, the three peaks define the surrounding geography. They serve as points of triangulation by means of which one can estimate distance and relative position for miles around. They are simply impossible to miss.

The map Baratieri distributed to his generals was the creation of Major Tommaso Salsa. It was amateurishly drawn and a little short on verisimilitude. It bore only an approximate resemblance to the geography of the area. Even so, it got the main landmarks right. The three peaks of Eshasho, Raio, and Semayata were clearly drawn; the artist even inserted brackets to mark the passes between them. Baratieri's tactical concept was there on the page, and the objective was clear: march to the passes and occupy them.[18]

The left and right columns would take up their positions at the passes at about the same time, with a third column, commanded by General Arimondi, occupying the ground between, on the western flanks of Raio. A

fourth, reserve column would be stationed to the rear. As with any disposition of military forces, the alignment of units depended upon the lay
of the land.[19]

Timing would be important. Should one of the columns arrive well in
advance of the rest of the army—and should its presence be detected—
fighting could break out before the Italian forces could take their positions. Security for the entire army depended upon establishing positions
at the passes before the Ethiopians could react.

Matteo Albertone, commander of Baratieri's left column, had a reputation for restlessness.[20] It was a quality the frustrations of the preceding
weeks had only made worse. Since September of the previous year, Albertone and the rest of the army had prepared for a decisive encounter
with Ethiopian forces that never seemed to arrive. The setbacks of Amba
Alage and Mekele had gone unanswered. Much of February had been
lost to a war of positions. Albertone, like the other generals, was critical
of Baratieri's extreme caution in the face of the enemy. Like the others,
he began to believe that Baratieri feared a decisive encounter.

Although the men under his command had doubts about this too impulsive general, Albertone had been given some of the best soldiers in
the Italian army.[21] These were the four all-askari battalions, veterans of
the victorious campaign against the Mahdi the year before. They were
known for their energy and boldness. The speed of the askari posed a
challenge to the coordinated movements of the army. Baratieri was aware
of the problem and ordered his generals to remain in communication.
Baratieri was particularly concerned about General Albertone's askari
battalions. Baratieri took Albertone aside, warning him "to proceed
with caution and above all not to push too far ahead."[22]

On the night of the move into the passes, Albertone's advance guard,
the First Native Battalion, commanded by Major Domenico Turitto, covered ten difficult miles in under three hours, arriving at Gundapta at
midnight. The pace was breathtaking. They were already halfway to
their destination with five hours to go. They waited at Gundapta for an
hour until the rest of Albertone's column could catch up. Turitto had a
slightly nervous personality. His narrow-set eyes darted fretfully, glancing from his men toward the pass and back toward the approaching
Albertone. Baratieri's plan called for him to wait at Gundapta until

two-thirty in the morning before pushing on, but Turitto was anxious to get going and insisted on leaving at two in order to be in position three hours later.

By three-thirty Turitto was already at the pass between Raio and Semayata, the assigned rendezvous point for Albertone's column. Turitto's askari advance guard had needed only an hour and half to cover the remaining distance to the pass. He waited. Half an hour later, the remainder of the column arrived.

General Albertone approached Major Turitto and asked the major why he had stopped. "This is Kidane Mehret," Turitto answered, using the local name for the pass. Albertone argued with Turitto; he told Turitto that he was wrong and that the real Kidane Mehret was farther forward. Certainly the speed with which they reached their objective might have made them wonder if they had gone far enough.

"Go ahead; I don't want any hesitation," Albertone barked. He fixed Turitto with a glare, then asked, "You're not afraid, are you?"[23] Albertone's bullying remark was all that was needed to end the discussion. Turitto rounded up his men and headed down the slope toward the valley below.

There were many errors contributing to the Italian disaster at Adwa, but Albertone's goading sealed the fate of the Italian advance and, indeed, the Italian army. It would later be remarked, in Albertone's defense, that the place name confusion was real. Yet it was Baratieri's explicit intent that his generals coordinate the occupation of the passes. The success of the operation depended on it. Although there was plenty of time, General Albertone did not seek clarification from General Baratieri, or even bother to communicate with him, although such routine (and required) communication would have forestalled disaster.[24] But Albertone didn't foresee disaster. Albertone, Turitto, and the four thousand men under their command pushed through the pass and plunged onward toward Adwa.

The descent from the passes is fairly steep, falling three hundred feet in the first mile. Today, the northern pass is a dirt and gravel road wide enough for a lane (unmarked) in each direction. On 1 March 1896, it was barely half as wide, while the southern pass—the one Turitto and Albertone took—was a footpath. With the slope now in their favor, it took only thirty minutes for the 950 men under Turitto's command to descend from the pass and reach the point where the landscape begins to open out on the approach to the town of Adwa. Although there are still plenty of minor hills and peaks, some of them six hundred feet or more above the valley floor, the confined spaces of the pass give way to rolling hills and broad valleys.

By five-thirty in the morning, Turitto and his men were abreast of the location Albertone had pushed them to occupy. All night they had marched by moonlight, but sunrise was three-quarters of an hour away and the sky was showing the first signs of dawn. They were a mile and a half or so ahead of the rest of Albertone's column. Proper military procedure would dictate that they await the arrival of Albertone and the three other battalions, to re-establish contact with the rest of the brigade. Instead, perhaps still driven by Albertone's stinging rebuke, they pushed on.

They descended another four hundred feet. In full daylight and with the aid of a pair of binoculars, they could have discerned the collection of huts and churches that made up the town of Adwa, due west. They would have been able to make out the thousands of Ethiopian tents in the Adwa plain and on the flanks of the mountain north of the town.[25] Instead, in the damp, yellow-blue light of dawn they nearly walked into the middle of an Ethiopian camp. Startled Ethiopian sentries fired warning shots and took cover. It was a little after six in the morning. The battle of Adwa had begun.

Menelik and Taytu Gird for Battle

It is unclear whether the Ethiopians were waiting for the Italians, though the preponderance of evidence suggests they were not. By the time Ridolfo Mazzucconi wrote his account of the battle in the 1930s, he could claim with confidence that Menelik was with Taytu in church when he received word of the Italian advance. According to an unnamed Ethiopian eye-witness, a messenger found the royal couple already deep in prayer at four in the morning. The messenger approached Menelik, who listened as the messenger whispered dramatic news: the Italian forces were on their way. Then, in a stunning gesture of piety, the Emperor turned his attention back to the service.[26] Only when the service had concluded did Menelik allow himself to prepare for battle. Horns sounded and commanders were alerted, and by five-thirty the entire Ethiopian army was ready for battle.

The story works well for both sides. Menelik and Taytu come off as suitably pious—in church before dawn—while the Italian defeat becomes a bit easier to understand: they weren't done in by jealousy and ambition but were betrayed by spies. They were defeated because the Ethiopians had had hours to prepare. However, there are good reasons to doubt this anonymous account, the best of them being that the official Ethiopian chronicle of the reign of Menelik—which misses no opportunity to cast the monarchs in a favorable light—makes no mention of it.[27] Nor does Joseph Negussié mention it in his detailed account set down shortly after the battle in a letter to Alfred Ilg. Negussié marks the beginning of the battle as gunfire exchanged with Turitto's men, at which point "Menelik the lion, girded with an iron belt . . . arrayed his whole army and came out."[28]

The Ethiopian chronicle does point out that the clergy of Axum were at Adwa with the royal couple on 1 March. They had arrived the day before, most likely to protest the repeated demands for grain that Menelik's army had made upon them and their city, in violation of a long-standing municipal privilege exempting the holy city of Axum from such exactions.[29] They were still at Adwa when the battle began—a providential sign—and they carried the altar tablets *(tabot)* of Mary, mother of Jesus, into battle in support of the army and the royal couple. It was said that Menelik never went on campaign without the *tabot* of St. George, whose feast day happens to be 1 March. The chance presence of the clergy of Axum and of the *tabot* of both Mary and St. George would later be used to support the claim that God intervened on the side of Ethiopia.[30]

Turitto needed no sacred signs to know that he was in serious trouble. He was on high ground, but he was at least a mile and a half ahead of Albertone and any supporting forces. As gunfire ricocheted among the hills, the entire Ethiopian army awoke to the sounds of combat. Turitto had stumbled upon Ras Mangasha's forces, but Empress Taytu had five thousand men, commanded by Baltcha, in the immediate vicinity, and they were quickly engaged.[31] Tekle Haimanot, king of Gojjam, had four to five thousand men a short jog away. Ras Wele, Taytu's brother, had another ten thousand nearby. Menelik's thirty-five thousand were encamped in the broad, sweeping valley that extended from the town of Adwa out to Abba Garima and north onto the slopes of Shelloda.[32]

"When a mouse wants to die, it goes and smells a cat's tail." It was thus that Gabra Iyasus, the Ethiopian diplomat, described the utter disproportion of forces engaged.[33] Nearly ten thousand Ethiopian fighters immediately converged on the 950 men in Turitto's First Native Battalion.[34] Within minutes Turitto's battalion was pinned down and facing encirclement.

When an advance guard is actively seeking an enemy in order to engage it in battle, its role is clear—it pins the enemy in place, hunkers down, and waits to be reinforced by the army's main body. Alternatively, an advance guard serves to protect the main force from surprise; if it engages the enemy, it withdraws to the main force.

Neither scenario, however, fit Turitto's situation. Goaded by Albertone's mockery or by his own high spirits, Turitto had allowed his men to get far ahead of the rest of Albertone's column and had lost communication with it. All the same, Turitto's situation was soon clear enough to Albertone. Albertone and his men heard lively gunfire shortly after six and could tell that Turitto's forces were seriously engaged. However, Albertone could not move forward to join Turitto without putting his soldiers seriously at risk—the distance was just too great.

Nor could Turitto and his men easily scamper back to Albertone. Albertone's forces were not yet in position, and to withdraw would risk drawing the Ethiopian forces upon Albertone's column before it could deploy. An army on the move is vulnerable, especially when it depends on its artillery and the artillery pieces are disassembled for the march. Normal field cannon in this period might be unlimbered and ready for action in little more than a minute. Mountain batteries were different—the cannon had to be taken down from the mules and assembled before they could be deployed. Until Albertone's artillery and infantry were arrayed and able to offer a covering fire, Turitto was on his own.[35]

While Turitto's forces were scrambling to hold on, the main portion of Albertone's column was arriving on a hillside called Adi Vecci, more than a mile behind. This high ground offered a number of advantages. It was about three hundred feet wide, leaving plenty of room for Albertone's battalions to take up their positions. In front of them was a valley,

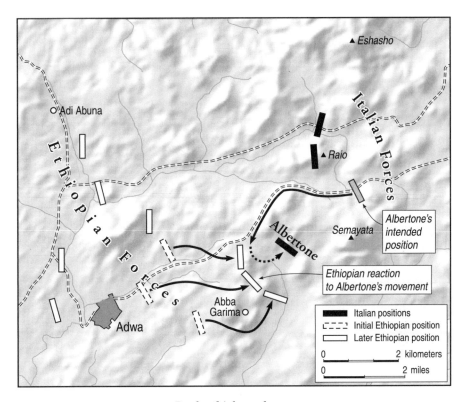

Battle of Adwa, phase 1

nearly a mile wide and long, across which attacking Ethiopian forces would have to travel in order to close with the Italians. Ethiopians moving against Albertone would be exposed to rifle and artillery fire with little cover.

Albertone had chosen well, as the Ethiopians were soon to discover. However, the position was framed by two mountains; if those were taken, the Italian position would become untenable, forcing a withdrawal. Albertone was convinced of the security of his position, believing the mountains on his right and left to be too high and steep for the Ethiopians to occupy. In this judgment he would be proven wrong.[36]

Albertone set to work positioning his forces, including his three remaining askari battalions. He ordered Major Rodolfo Valli's Seventh Native Battalion, with more than nine hundred infantrymen, to the left, sidling up to the steep hillside. Beyond them, a group of Eritrean irregulars covered their flank. Major Salvatore Cossu's Sixth Native Battalion, with 850 rifles, took up position on the right, holding the southern flank of Mount Gossosa. Major Giovanni Gamerra's Eighth Native would hold the center.[37]

Menelik ordered soldiers into position opposite Albertone. The Ethiopians occupied a saddle between two large hills.[38] The hills protected their flanks, and the saddle itself provided a natural platform for the Ethiopian artillery. Morning had broken, and Menelik could clearly see Albertone's forces arrayed in front of him. This was the fight that Menelik had wanted—army against army in the open field. If Italian training, discipline, and technology could overwhelm Ethiopian numbers, then so be it.

Although no one knew it at the time, this was a battle for more than Ethiopia. It was a fight for the future of Africa. There was a profound visual irony in the makeup of the forces, for the soldiers on both sides were African. Apart from a few dozen European officers and as many artillerymen— maybe a hundred in all—almost to a man Albertone's brigade was composed of askari recruits, that is, Africans. His main force consisted of four native battalions of just under one thousand African soldiers each; add to these nearly four hundred Eritrean irregulars. Thus, of the 4,076 soldiers squaring off against Menelik, perhaps one hundred were white. The opening shots in the battle for Africa would be fired by Africans—on both sides. The difference, of course, was that on Menelik's side, the soldiers were led by men who looked like themselves, Africans leading Africans. In Albertone's brigade one could glimpse a different future—Africans under the command of Europeans.

Albertone's mountain batteries trailed his infantry battalions. At six-thirty they were ordered to take up positions at the center of the Italian line. Artillerymen hauled the guns off the backs of their mules. While some men began to assemble the guns, others drove the mules up the slope behind them, and still others cleared away brush that would encumber the field of fire.[39] Ethiopian forces were already making their way across the valley; Italian rifle fire held them at bay. As the shattered remnants of Turitto's battalion attempted to scamper back, Captain Henry's First Mountain Battery was the first to open fire. It was seven-fifteen.

At first, the Ethiopian forces attacked the Italian center. Ethiopian riflemen, including Menelik's Imperial Guard, descended into the valley with the glare of the morning sun in their eyes. They started first in smaller numbers and then in concentrated masses, making easy targets for Italian rifle fire and shell.[40] Eventually all fourteen guns in the four Italian artillery batteries were ready. They opened fire at a range of five thousand feet. The first Ethiopian attacks were repulsed, but each time the Ethiopian infantry faltered, another charge would follow. Empress Taytu shouted praise and encouragement. In an unusual gesture, she approached her soldiers on foot and pulled aside her veil to speak. As an Ethiopian chronicler put it, "She abandoned her womanly nature and acted like a warrior, seasoned by combat." An unveiled empress going about on foot shocked and motivated the soldiers as much as her words: "What is going on? Courage! Victory is ours!" Other women joined Taytu. With their manly virtue at stake, the soldiers dared not show fear or hesitation.

From the Italian side, the artillery continued their slow, measured rate of fire. The fire was effective, but the repeated infantry assaults forced them to reduce their range as the Ethiopian forces pushed closer, finding cover from which to harass the Italian positions.[41] In three successive advances, the Ethiopians were relentless. As costly as these advances were to the Ethiopians, the arithmetic was unassailable. As long as the Ethiopians could continue to feed men into the attack, they would eventually close with the Italian forces.

Meanwhile, other components of the Ethiopian attack were coming together. The Ethiopian rapid-fire Hotchkiss artillery battery, which had already proven its effectiveness in the siege at Mekele, was firing on Albertone's forces from the saddle between the mountains.[42] The emperor himself appeared to inspire and encourage the artillerymen.[43] Taytu presided over the operation of five artillery pieces.[44] Then, as Ethiopian artillery found its range as methodically as it had at Mekele, Ras Makonnen and Ras Michael prepared to order fifteen thousand soldiers against Albertone's right.[45] At roughly the same time, Tekle Haimanot, Wagshum Gangul—the ruler of Lasta province—and Empress Taytu directed forces in a sweeping arc against the Italian left.[46] The classic Ethiopian strategy of envelopment was taking shape. It forced the Italians to scatter their fire across a wider arc, reducing its effect and providing some relief for Ethiopian forces advancing against the center.

Improvisation

Back at the passes, Dabormida's brigade had reached its rendezvous point—the pass between Eshasho and Raio—at five-fifteen in the morning. Soon they heard the unmistakable sound of gunfire down in the lowlands five miles to the west, as Turitto stumbled into the Ethiopian camp. Alberto Woctt, an infantry captain in General Dabormida's brigade, recalled that he and his soldiers reacted to the first sounds of combat with a mixture of disbelief and dread. "[Some of us] received the first sounds of gunfire [that morning] with incredulous chuckles, others with a moral effect that was clearly visible."[47] Despite talk of an attack as the troops left Sauria, many in Dabormida's brigade had not expected their nightlong march to end with a fight.

Around six-thirty, Oreste Baratieri arrived at the northern pass. What he heard and saw would have made his heart sink. Logistics are the heart and soul of a fighting force. An army that articulates clumsily is an army at risk. But instead of seeing his forces quietly consolidating their positions at the pass, as his plan intended, Baratieri was confronted with a situation that threatened his entire army. For thirty minutes already, the crackle of gunfire had ricocheted up from the valley below, with building intensity.

Baratieri and his staff moved up the flank of Eshasho, accompanied by General Dabormida, for a better view of the combat below. The sun was up by then and at his back, but the peaks at the pass were still casting deep shadows into the valleys. From Eshasho they could barely make out Albertone's position, partly obscured by the sloping terrain, but they could clearly see the developing Ethiopian attack on the facing high ground.

Albertone was nearly four miles ahead of the rest of the army, well to the west of the passes. His forces were sharply engaged. He would need help to extricate himself. Baratieri commanded Dabormida to descend from the pass and take up a position slightly behind Albertone and to his right, "forward from the pass, on the road to Mariam Shavitu."[48] Such a position would provide support for Albertone's brigade and offer cover for a retreat. At the same time, Baratieri sent orders to General Arimondi, moving up from Gundapta, to occupy the passes.[49]

What happened next is one of the great mysteries of the battle of Adwa. What Baratieri intended seemed clear enough: Dabormida should link up with Albertone and provide meaningful support by establishing a position to the right of and behind Albertone. Such a position, in echelon relative to Albertone, would both support Albertone's right and cover his retreat.[50] When Dabormida set out, his route took him west on the main road toward Adwa. If nothing else, the sound of rifle and artillery fire ought to have oriented him. However, a few miles west of the pass, the road splits, and instead of going left toward Albertone's forces, Dabormida turned to the right.[51]

Vittorio Emanuele Dabormida was a scholar of military science. He was also, like most high-ranking officers in the Italian army, a member of the Italian gentry. His lofty, distant air made him unapproachable, the antithesis of the soldier's soldier. His role was to lead, theirs was to follow.

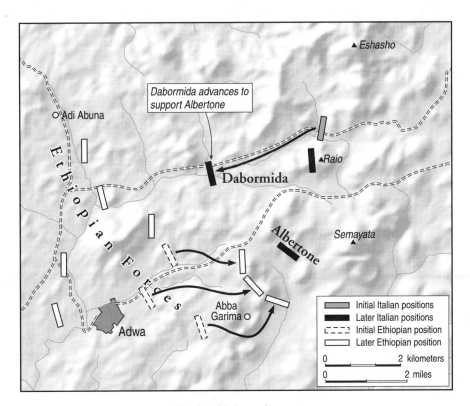

Battle of Adwa, phase 2

He expected to be obeyed. As Dabormida led his soldiers away from Albertone's brigade, they had no idea where they were going, and they dared not ask.

Mariam Shavitu is the name Baratieri attached to the route he wanted Dabormida to take. It is the name of a long, narrow valley significantly to the north—more than a mile and a half—of the position occupied by Albertone. In obvious neglect of Baratieri's tactical intent (though perhaps in dogged obedience to Baratieri's toponymy), Dabormida took himself and his men to a position not merely on the road to Mariam Shavitu but actually into the valley of Mariam Shavitu. It was a position where Dabormida and his men could be of little use to Albertone, except perhaps as a diversion, drawing Menelik's forces away from Albertone.[52]

"Reinforcements Would Be Welcome"

Baratieri had ordered his generals to remain in contact with one another and with him after leaving Sauria. Albertone ignored the order. Finally, at nine in the morning on 1 March—a full twelve hours after leaving Sauria—Baratieri received his first message from Albertone.

> At Kidane Mehret pass, the 1st Battalion remains seriously engaged. I have all remaining troops in position behind them. I seek to disengage the 1st Battalion. Large enemy force before me. Reinforcements would be welcome. 1–3–96, 8:15
>
> Major General Albertone[53]

The message is stunning for what it doesn't say. In reading it, one could be forgiven for thinking that only Turitto's First Native Battalion was involved in the fight when, in fact, by eight-fifteen Turitto's battalion had been destroyed and Turitto along with it.

A few minutes later, Baratieri received another bulletin from Albertone, in fact sent earlier than the first, at seven-thirty. It suggested a somewhat more urgent situation. It opened with a bold lie.

> Kidane Mehret pass was occupied without the enemy's knowledge at 6 a.m. The enemy is all around Adwa and behind Mariam Shavitu.

The 1st Battalion pushed beyond the pass and is energetically engaged . . . the 6th Battalion occupies a strong high ground on the
right; the other two battalions are grouped with the artillery. I can
foresee a serious engagement. Move up the Arimondi brigade in reinforcement. It would be quite opportune to move up the Dabormida
brigade, which would draw to itself a part of the enemy's forces.[54]

This bulletin probably best describes how General Albertone hoped
the events of 1 March would unfold. Albertone would engage the Ethiopian forces and draw the reluctant Baratieri into a decisive confrontation
with Menelik. With Albertone pinned, Baratieri would have no choice but to
move the rest of his forces forward. The decisive battle with Menelik would
ensue. The very tone of the message suggests that Albertone had assumed
command and issued orders to Baratieri ("move up the Arimondi brigade"),
wresting control of the battle from his superior.

This was Albertone's showdown scenario. The problem was that Albertone's very advanced position made it almost impossible to bring about.
Albertone's position was now analogous to that of his own advance guard,
Turitto's First Battalion. Just as Albertone could not risk moving his
forces forward to support Turitto directly, Baratieri could not chance
sending his men forward in support of Albertone.[55] And since Albertone
could not disengage and rejoin the main Italian body, the stage was set for
the piecemeal destruction of the Italian army.

Menelik Shoots the Gap

Albertone had only the vaguest idea of what was going on with the rest of
the Italian forces behind him. He had been so reckless in his advance
and so dilatory in his communications, he could only hope the battle
was about to be transformed by the imminent arrival of reinforcements.
In fact, his fate and that of his brigade depended entirely upon a retreat
the Dabormida brigade would cover, and there the outlook was not good.

Whatever the source of his error—confusion or willfulness—Dabormida
led his brigade away on a path that slowed his movement significantly.[56]
The path they followed—over a pass and then down into a valley—was so
narrow in parts that Dabormida's men could march only in single file.

Crates became wedged against trailside boulders and dense brush snagged packs, stopping mules in their tracks. Mules had to be unloaded to clear obstacles, then reloaded beyond.[57] Delays affected morale, too. The painfully slow movement of Dabormida's forces clashed with a deep sense of urgency that came from knowing that Albertone's brigade of four thousand was bearing the full fury of the Ethiopian army.

Men were showing signs of fatigue and extreme thirst. Before Menelik's soldiers abandoned their advance positions for Adwa, they had fouled the water around their camps at Yeha and Gundapta by leaving animal carcasses in streams and ponds. Italian officers had forbidden soldiers to take water without permission, but Dabormida's soldiers, thirsty and unsure when they would find water again, filled their canteens from sources that were almost certainly polluted.[58]

Finally, by a circuitous, slow, and difficult route, Dabormida arrived in position a full hour and a quarter after receiving his orders. He then dispatched a bulletin to Baratieri.

> Hour 9:15. Extensive [Ethiopian] encampment observed to the north of Adwa; a strong column heads from this encampment toward [Albertone's position]; I am reaching out to [Albertone], and am also holding a strong nucleus of troops amassed near the road that leads from the pass to Adwa and am also keeping watch on the heights to my right.[59]

Translation? First, Dabormida had completed his movement and now had his men in position; second, he was seeking contact with Albertone while facing a major Ethiopian force directly in front of him. He does not report that he had actually communicated with Albertone. Since his orders were to support Albertone's right and, if necessary, provide cover for Albertone's retreat, his mission already was compromised.

Menelik wasted no time exploiting the Italian mistake. The sheer sluggishness of Dabormida's advance stole any possibility of surprise— not that it mattered. The Ethiopians watched Dabormida's column take up positions in the Mariam Shavitu valley without linking to Albertone's forces. Seeing the strategic opening, Menelik ignored Dabormida's challenge and directed a column of fifteen thousand Ethiopian infantrymen into the gap between Albertone and Dabormida. This was the "strong column" Dabormida mentioned in his report to Baratieri at nine-fifteen.

The column consisted of troops under the command of Makonnen and Mangasha.[60] By nine-thirty, part of this column was engaging Albertone's right flank while another part began to push beyond, effectively dividing the Italian army into three now hopelessly isolated pieces—Albertone facing off against Menelik and Taytu, Dabormida at Mariam Shavitu, and the remainder of the Italian army at the passes. Although combat would continue into the afternoon, and sporadic fighting would go on until well after dark, by nine-thirty in the morning the battle of Adwa was effectively over.

CHAPTER 13

The Center Crumbles

W HEN MENELIK'S TROOPS ran the gap between the Albertone and Dabormida brigades, they won victory for Ethiopia at Adwa. Immediately Ras Alula saw an opportunity that was not to be lost—the utter annihilation of the Italian army. He dispatched a courier to Menelik with a message to send the Oromo cavalry to block the passes from the east, trapping the Italians by closing their line of retreat. For whatever reason—prudence or unwillingness to repeat Dogali on a massive scale— Menelik demurred.[1] It was a decision that saved thousands of lives and a few shreds of dignity for a defeated army.

Although the battle was effectively over, the fighting was not. Baratieri was improvising, desperately looking for a way to save his army. Baratieri's assessment of the situation told him that sending the army forward would put it at risk of destruction. Instead, Baratieri had ordered Dabormida's brigade into a position where he thought he could provide cover for Albertone in retreat. Then he arrayed his remaining forces at the two passes. If Albertone could successfully disengage his forces, they could seek safety in the secure defensive positions Baratieri had established.

Such a plan meant effectively occupying the passes and the flanks of Mount Raio. This Baratieri did by ordering Arimondi's brigade into position at around eight-fifteen. Arimondi's deployment at the passes was a scaled-down version of what Baratieri had intended for the entire army.[2] Now, with the Albertone and Dabormida brigades positioned well ahead, control of the passes would be the responsibility of Arimondi's men and Ellena's reserve. As Arimondi's troops took up their positions, the weakness of Baratieri's original plan became evident. The ridge that extended from Raio was quite narrow and steep on either side, making it very difficult for the troops to deploy effectively.[3] Some units took up positions that put them at an oblique angle to the line of attack.[4] The slope was so awkwardly steep that artillery had trouble finding a stable platform.[5] Moreover, the rise approaching the Italian positions was uneven and covered with shrubs, providing cover for advancing troops.

Baratieri himself took a position high on the flanks of Raio, giving him a commanding view of his own troops and one of the ascending valleys up which the Ethiopians would advance. General Ellena's reserve brigade, which was still arriving from Gundapta, was ordered to occupy a position toward the rear, to be moved forward as the fighting developed.

Arimondi's soldiers were lighthearted as they took up their positions. "They won't get away today!" shouted one.[6] Francesco Frisina, recently arrived from Italy, was typical of the youthfully exuberant soldiers gleeful at the prospect of proving themselves in battle against an enemy they woefully underestimated. Frisina's joyful attitude evaporated when he turned to look behind him. There he recognized General Arimondi sitting on the ground, elbows on knees, face in hands. Although Frisina would later see Arimondi confidently giving commands, the general had already telegraphed his misgivings.[7]

Stragglers and Pursuers

Just as Arimondi's men were settling in, their battle abruptly began.[8] At nine o'clock, African soldiers began running toward the Italian positions. They were not Ethiopian soldiers. They were askari in full retreat. Their flight marked the beginning of the collapse of Albertone's brigade.

Turitto's advance guard, the First Native Battalion, had come under withering fire after it walked into the Ethiopian encampment. When facing askari units, Ethiopian riflemen targeted their European officers—take away the head and the creature dies. The officers, recognizable as much by their complexion as by their uniforms, were among the first to fall; soon seven were on the ground, dying. Under intense fire, its officers depleted, the First Native Battalion began to break up sometime after seven o'clock, retreating in disorder back toward Albertone's position. Albertone's officers sought to rally them—and succeeded with a few. Others paused but eventually pushed through, racing east toward the pass, past Arimondi's forces on Raio and on toward the camp at Sauria.

By nine-thirty, Albertone and his men knew that there would be no reinforcements. They were likely still unaware of Dabormida's movement to cover their right and their retreat. They were in the final ninety minutes of their share of the battle of Adwa.

By fanning out and attacking the flanks, Ethiopian infantry had turned the fight against Albertone's brigade in their favor. The Ethiopian flanking movements were creating nearly a half circle of convergent fire, while the Italians were forced to spread their fire across a widening perimeter.[9] Ethiopian infantrymen took advantage of terrain, vegetation, dead angles, and speed to move up on the Italian right. They occupied the flanks of Adi Vecci and Monoxeito, conical peaks a mere two thousand feet from the Italian artillery batteries. From there, they opened fire on the artillerymen. A few well-aimed artillery shots chased them from their positions, but the distraction opened defensive holes at the center, where Ethiopian troops scurried closer to the Italian front lines.[10]

By ten o'clock, the situation on Albertone's left was becoming tenuous. For a moment some of the Italian soldiers thought the battle was about to enter a lull, but suddenly masses of fresh troops joined the assault on the Italian left. Ernesto Cordella, artillery lieutenant, spotted a hundred multicolored flags, accompanied by beating drums and the hearty cries of soldiers puffed up for battle.[11] For the Ethiopians, it was sheer joy to be engaged in a battle where numbers could finally make a difference. For the Italians, the effect was deeply demoralizing, for although they could force the Ethiopians to take heavy casualties, the supply of Ethiopian troops seemed limitless. Dozens would fall, but dozens more would take their places.

And that is how the end came for Albertone's brigade. As the Ethiopians attacked the flanks with renewed vigor, they created new opportunities for the Ethiopian center to advance. There was no shortage of targets for the Italians, but the sheer number of targets diluted their fire. Ethiopian soldiers were not famous for their marksmanship, but as Ethiopian infantrymen moved closer to the Italian positions, they fired with greater effect, picking off the men who operated the artillery and the infantry who defended them. Attrition began to set in on the Italian side: of personnel, as artillery officers were forced to work the guns themselves as their soldiers fell, and of ammunition, for there were plenty of targets but not enough shells. Lieutenant Ernesto Cordella took his place alongside Mohamed Aga Adam and Sultan Aga Amed, loading and aiming the guns as they fired their last rounds.[12]

From his perspective among the artillery pieces, Lieutenant Cordella watched the decay and collapse of the Eighth Native Battalion, which was protecting his position on the right. The Ethiopian envelopment was nearly complete. They were firing on the Italians from the front, from the sides, and even from high ground to the rear. By ten-fifteen, they were picking off the remnants of the Eighth Battalion.

When the order to retreat was given is unclear. Gherardo Pantano, a lieutenant fighting on Albertone's left flank in Major Valli's Seventh Native Battalion, claimed to have received an order to retreat around nine-thirty from Captain Pinelli. Pinelli had ordered a retreat by echelons not because the battle was lost but merely in order to disengage in favor of a position to the rear.[13] One wonders whether the time is correct, since the concerted assault on the Italian left didn't begin until ten o'clock. Other evidence and the flow of the battle itself suggest that the call to fall back came later, closer to ten-thirty. By then, a combination of casualties and departures had reduced the Eighth Native Battalion to mere remnants.[14] Sometime around ten-thirty, with both flanks verging on collapse, General Albertone gave orders for the Third and Fourth Mountain Batteries to hold their positions until their ammunition was exhausted. The remaining ammunition from the other batteries was put at their disposal. In effect, they were being asked to sacrifice themselves to cover the retreat.

With the Third and Fourth Mountain Batteries holding, what remained of the Eighth Native Battalion was ordered to retreat, followed by the Seventh and then the Sixth. By eleven o'clock, the artillery pieces were firing their final rounds. Cordella was taken prisoner, along with gunners Mohamed Aga Adam, Sultan Aga Amed, and Idris Tutai.[15] General

Albertone, wounded, was surrounded and gave himself up. His capture was one of the great prizes of the day.

Of those whose retreat they had bravely covered, many were cut down. Ethiopian marksmen consistently targeted Italian officers, so by the time the retreat began, rank-and-file soldiers had little guidance. By all accounts, the retreat was disorderly.[16] The men were exhausted, in shock, and hotly pursued as they raced back toward the passes. They blew past Arimondi's brigade, deaf to the bugle call to halt, indifferent to officers waving revolvers threateningly. Most followed paths back to the camp at Sauria and from there north toward Eritrea. More than two hundred would die along the way, victims of their pursuers and an insurgent population.[17]

Among the survivors, many were beginning a long journey that would end days later after many close calls. Sergeants Della Torre and Pepe endured a retreat that lasted more than two weeks. Their retreat began on 1 March and ended on the sixteenth when they stumbled into Asmara shoeless—indeed, naked from head to toe.[18]

The triumph over Albertone's brigade boosted Ethiopian confidence, but it came at a cost. Italian fire had had devastating effects on the Ethiopians. The number of bodies writhing in pain or falling silent in the broad plain that had once divided Albertone's forces from Menelik's provided ample evidence of the bitter contest and the body-shattering effects of Italian artillery. We will never know how many Ethiopians died. The bodies were not counted.

Albertone's men had suffered, too. Eduardo Ximenes was part of a mission to the battle site a few weeks after the event. He found more than 80 dead where Turitto's men had fought their desperate and solitary fight, 110 where Albertone's men had stood their ground, another 200 on the path of retreat—in all, more than 400 dead out of a brigade of 4,000.[19] While the Italian forces were quite literally decimated, the Ethiopians suffered higher casualties.

Defense and Collapse at the Passes

In retreat, Albertone's brigade followed the road that led to the northern pass, pursued hotly by Ethiopian infantry. Arimondi's men watched helplessly; they dared not fire on the Ethiopians for fear of hitting the askari, indistinguishable from their Ethiopian pursuers. The close chase meant that hundreds of Ethiopians would arrive within close range of the Italian center without facing hostile fire.[20] The fleeing soldiers were unstoppable in their panic, insensible to commands or threats.

In pursuing Albertone's fleeing ranks, the Ethiopians threatened to push beyond the passes and close off the path of retreat. At the same time, the strong column of Ethiopian forces that pushed between Dabormida and Albertone began to occupy a high hill—Zeban Daro—opposite the Italian forces on Raio.

How the importance of this high ground had been overlooked is unclear. It may be that the Italians simply discounted the possibility that it could be scaled until they saw the Ethiopians begin to scale it. Colonel Francesco Stevani ordered the Second Bersaglieri Battalion to contest the high

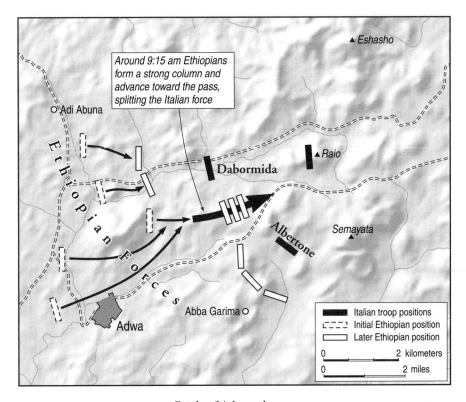

Battle of Adwa, phase 3

ground threatened by the Ethiopians, to no avail. They faced a murderous fire as they clambered up. A mere forty *bersaglieri* reached the summit, and the first was gored by a bullet to the face.[21] He fell backward, coming to rest with his face to the sky. The remaining soldiers returned fire before being picked off, leaving the Ethiopians in control of the hill.

Arimondi's left flank, where the Third Native Battalion of Colonel Galliano stood, was also challenged with a fierce assault and withering fire. Within twenty minutes, by ten-thirty, they had lost half of their officers to Ethiopian marksmen. Leaderless and presented with the example of headlong retreat by Albertone's askari, the Third Native Battalion collapsed in uncontrolled flight.[22] As the Third Native began their retreat, the Eighth Mountain Battery somehow managed to set up their guns and begin to fire, covered by a company and a half of *bersaglieri*.[23]

While this move momentarily shored up the Italian left and center, the Italian right at the northern pass—far more vulnerable—was coming under intense pressure. Relentless fire from Zeban Daro in front and enfilading fire from the flanks of Eshasho were having devastating effects. Ethiopian soldiers found good positions behind rocks and bushes on the high ground some three hundred feet above the Italian lines. Italian infantrymen returned fire from a kneeling position. Giovanni Tedone, sergeant in the *bersaglieri*, couldn't help noting how the Italian officers, who commanded standing beside their soldiers, made ripe targets. Their bright sashes of red or blue screamed officer to Ethiopian marksmen, who obliged by cutting them down.[24] Of 610 officers at Adwa, only 258 returned.

Italian fire was very effective, but sheer numbers were having their effect. As Ethiopians fell, others took their places with a courage that forced the Italians to remark, echoing Baratieri, that they "despised death." Ethiopians fired rounds with smokeless gunpowder from hidden positions. "There was a hail of bullets," recalled one soldier. Bullets "ricocheted from every direction, whistling, screaming, howling in our ears, such that we couldn't tell from where they came."[25]

The Italian position was rapidly becoming untenable. Colonel Stevani, in an admission that did nothing for morale, declared, "Today is a second Dogali!"[26] As the *bersaglieri* abandoned their position, they attempted an alternating covered retreat, whereby each company took turns covering the retreat of the others, but because they were deprived of many of their officers, coordination became difficult. Order soon broke down, and the retreat became a rout. As Tedone would later describe it, "It was no longer a fight, but a slaughterhouse."

It was not yet a slaughterhouse at the center, where by ten forty-five Baratieri was making his final demands on the reserve brigade commanded by General Ellena. With his right collapsing, Baratieri knew that the outcome of the battle depended upon Ellena and his reserves. If they couldn't halt the Ethiopian advance toward the pass, "we are all lost."[27] But much of Ellena's reserve had already been deployed, and a mere two regiments remained. They might slow the advance but would never halt it.[28]

By eleven o'clock, Ethiopian troops had pursued their envelopment to the point that they occupied positions beyond the Italian flanks. Ethiopian troops pushed through the southern pass at Kidane Mehret, driving east, then sweeping north toward the plains, threatening encirclement just as new Ethiopian contingents were taking up positions on the flanks of Eshasho, seeking to control the northern pass. It was eleven-thirty.

Seeing the danger—and seeing his officers fall wounded and dead around him—Baratieri ordered a flag unfurled as a rallying point. He raised his officer's saber, crying, "Viva l'Italia!" The signal for retreat was sounded, though heard by few over the din. Baratieri began making his way down the slope of Raio, his retreat covered by the Ninth Battalion, the First and Second Bersaglieri, and an artillery battery, which held out until noon. His retreat through the northern pass was covered for a time, and the movement of Italian troops retained some semblance of order for around two miles before breaking down under relentless pursuit from the Ethiopians.[29] Many of the Italians had not eaten in hours, nor had anything to drink. Thanks to their nighttime march, they had had little or no sleep. With their officers cut down, many units were leaderless. The retreat rapidly came apart, with clumps of soldiers doing whatever they could to escape the pitiless Ethiopian onslaught. Some headed east, back toward the camp at Sauria. Others went directly north to Eritrea. Even Baratieri's flight had all the marks of haste and panic. Pieces of his official correspondence fluttered over the plain at Gundapta—mute orders abandoned to chance.

Round Three: Dabormida's Battle

With Albertone's brigade broken and the army at the passes in retreat, the fate of General Dabormida's brigade was yet to be decided. From the moment around nine-fifteen that morning when Dabormida observed the strong column of Ethiopian soldiers shoot the gap between his position and Albertone's, he was cut off from the rest of the army. His day unfolded almost as an independent combat.

General Dabormida was an officer and a nobleman. Anything but the soldier's soldier, Dabormida thought it unnecessary to tell anyone the position General Baratieri had ordered him to occupy. His men might well have questioned him, had he ever given the slightest hint that he would allow it. The mysteries of that morning start with the fact that although Dabormida knew that Albertone's forces were engaged—an errant round landed near Dabormida's men as a timely reminder—the movement of Dabormida's brigade was painfully slow.[30] Why Dabormida chose the route he did—indeed, nearly everything about his behavior that morning—is information that he carried to his grave.[31]

By nine-thirty, Dabormida's men had taken up their positions in the Mariam Shavitu valley. Two artillery batteries stood at the center, protected by an infantry battalion on either side, the Fourteenth and Fifth Battalions, respectively. A little forward and to the left, the Sixth and Tenth Infantry Battalions, under Colonel Ottavio Ragni, defended adjacent high ground. The Thirteenth Infantry Battalion and part of the Third were held toward the rear in reserve.[32]

Although Baratieri's intent for Dabormida's brigade was clear—link up with Albertone in order to support him and cover his retreat—Dabormida's isolated position offered neither possibility. The valley of Mariam Shavitu is hemmed in on three sides. On the left and on the right are ridges that rise high above the valley. Behind them are the steep western extensions of Mount Eshasho.

General Dabormida had marched his men into the tactical equivalent of the bottom of a tin can. The tin can tips to the west, facing Makonnen's camp and the tens of thousands of Ethiopians eagerly preparing for battle there. The rise in elevation southward from of the valley—combined with the significant distance—rendered any link-up with Albertone's forces to the south difficult.[33]

Vittorio Dabormida. From *L'Illustrazione italiana,* 22 March 1896.

This simple fact was confirmed when Dabormida ordered a militia bat-talion, commanded by Major De Vito, to reach out to General Albertone and his forces on the left. The native troops under De Vito's command, impressed by their isolation and shaken by the size of the Ethiopian forces in front of them, could only ask, "Are the white troops coming?"[34]

The question captured the situation perfectly. The only way Dabormi-da's position made sense—given their isolation and the disproportion of forces—was if the rest of the army moved up to fill the gap between Alber-tone and Dabormida.

The Ethiopians attacked De Vito's battalion, seeking to decapitate it by concentrating their fire on the officers. De Vito himself was among the first to fall, and the battalion soon found itself overwhelmed. After a firefight of no more than twenty minutes, De Vito's battalion was obliged to fall back hastily toward the core of Dabormida's forces. They left behind twelve officers wounded or dead.[35]

The speed and force with which the Ethiopians pushed back De Vito's battalion ought to have told Dabormida that he would be of no use to Albertone in his current position. Emilio Bellavita, who fought under Dabormida's command at the battle of Adwa and lived to tell the tale, pointed out that the lack of contact with Albertone's forces—even visual—ought to have clued in Dabormida about his mistake. "A more agile mind," as he put it, might have recognized the error and corrected it. But Dabormida, Bellavita implied, was too stubborn to admit his error.[36]

But was it a mistake? It would be easy to dismiss Dabormida's behavior as incompetence, but it is not the only explanation, nor even the most plausible. Sometimes the best explanation is the simplest—that Dabormida was exactly where he wanted to be. That is, an impatient and frustrated Dabormida, like Albertone and perhaps in collusion with him, sought a decisive encounter with the Ethiopian army. He interpreted Baratieri's orders loosely by pushing on into the valley of Mariam Shavitu. The brigade-sized gap left between Dabormida and Albertone would serve as an invitation to Baratieri to fill it by sending Arimondi's brigade forward. Indeed, Albertone's bulletin of seven-thirty that morning ("Move up the Arimondi brigade in reinforcement. It would be quite opportune to move up the Dabormida brigade, which would draw to itself a part of the enemy's forces") had urged just such a course of action. Such a scenario would suggest collusion between Albertone and Dabormida to hijack control of the battle from Baratieri.

Alternatively, and less convincingly, it was surmised that Dabormida intended a diversion. Giuseppe Menarini, a captain who, like Bellavita, fought beside Dabormida at Adwa, suggested that Dabormida foresaw that a bold Garibaldi-style attack at Mariam Shavitu would draw Ethiopian forces away from the attack on Albertone's position.[37] Thanks to Dabormida's selfless diversion, the Ethiopians would have to divide their forces between the Albertone and Dabormida brigades, thus diluting their impact.

As it turned out, there were plenty of Ethiopian soldiers to go around. This rendered moot any notion of a selfless diversion. At the same time that Makonnen and Mangasha directed their strong column toward Albertone's right and beyond, they prepared to attack Dabormida's center.[38] Ethiopian infantry, covered by Oromo cavalry, charged Dabormida's artillery. This simple move pinned Dabormida in place like an entomology specimen, giving him no opportunity to reconsider his folly. With Dabormida immobilized, the Ethiopian army moved to defeat first Albertone and then Arimondi. Later they would turn their full force against Dabormida.

For the remainder of the morning, Dabormida's forces would acquit themselves reasonably well, in part because Ethiopian attention was focused elsewhere. While Ethiopian forces consolidated their positions in front of Dabormida and the high ground to his left and right—and Ethiopians and Italians continued to exchange rifle and artillery fire—Dabormida could reassure himself that he was in control of this sector of the battle. At 12:30 p.m. he wrote a bulletin to General Baratieri informing him that his forces had turned back two frontal attacks. Dabormida had no way of knowing it, but by that time Baratieri was on his way back to Eritrea. Dabormida and his men were orphans.

Toward one o'clock that afternoon, there was a noticeable lull in the fighting. Some of Dabormida's soldiers allowed themselves to believe that the battle was over. They ran about, firing their rifles and shouting, "Victory! Long live the king! Viva l'Italia!" But as their cries echoed across Mariam Shavitu, they were reminded that they were still isolated and without reinforcements. They wondered about the rest of the army, from which they had had not a word. Then, famished and thirsty, they drank from their canteens and cracked open meat tins.[39]

A few hundred yards away, the Ethiopians prepared their final attack of the day. They passed out ammunition and gathered all available forces. Ethiopian soldiers scurried forward, seeking cover behind bushes, deep ruts, and breaks. Then the fighting resumed.

Italian soldiers, shooting from kneeling or prone positions, complained that they couldn't even see their adversaries—the skin of the Ethiopians blended with the dry brown earth. When the Ethiopians opened fire, smokeless gunpowder made it hard to determine who was firing or from where. And the fact that the Ethiopians fired at will, rather than in volleys, meant that there were no auditory clues as to their whereabouts.[40]

The popping of rifles—like the bullets themselves—seemed to be coming from everywhere.

Ethiopian riflemen concentrated their aim on Italian officers, who commanded while standing, offering fine targets of themselves with their uniforms, plumed helmets, and colored sashes. Italians would later claim that the Ethiopians were poor shots, but it hardly mattered. Even when they missed, stray bullets hit the soldiers standing near them.[41]

And so the fighting of the early afternoon went. The Ethiopians were in no hurry. Having dispatched the main Italian force, the outcome of the day was ensured. The Ethiopians would seek to position themselves close to the Italian lines, using their advance positions to pick off officers and other targets, while the Italians, whose fire was effective at greater range, sought to prevent the Ethiopians—who crawled or scampered forward—from getting close. As a practical matter, this meant that the Italians were obliged to undertake bayonet charges from time to time in order to clear the ground in front of them. The Sixth and Tenth Battalions carried out successive bayonet attacks against forces threatening Dabormida's left flank. At the center, Colonel Airaghi led successive attacks, urging his men forward aggressively to clear the field of sharpshooters.[42]

For well-rested men, charging over such uneven ground would have been exhausting. For men who had been marched all night, it pushed them to their limits. By midafternoon, the fight had shifted decisively in Ethiopia's favor. Meanwhile, it was dawning on Dabormida that something was terribly wrong. He murmured to himself, "This is serious, serious!" and "Not a bulletin, not an order, no reinforcements, nothing!"[43] For the first time, Captain Menarini noted, Dabormida seemed nervous.

The sound of rifle fire to the left and slightly to the rear drew Dabormida's attention. Askari pointed toward the high pass Dabormida's brigade had used to enter the valley that morning. Oromo cavalry, having completed their pursuit of Arimondi's central column, were returning to the fight. Behind them one could see clutches of infantrymen—dozens, then hundreds—descending on a path that would soon bring them into the battle.[44]

Dabormida turned to Colonel Airaghi. "I want to attempt another charge. Who knows? Maybe reinforcements will arrive in the meantime!" Airaghi couldn't believe what he was hearing. It was sometime around three-thirty—more than six hours since the last contact with Baratieri—and Dabormida was holding out hope that reinforcements were on the way. Airaghi's look of disbelief prompted Dabormida to add, "And if reinforcements don't arrive, the assault will permit us to begin a retreat!"[45]

Airaghi passed the order on to his remaining officers. He knew that what his men were being asked to do was nearly beyond them. Horns sounded the assault. Airaghi raised his helmet and cried, "Savoy! Long live Italy!"

To their own surprise and the surprise of the Ethiopians facing them, the men found the strength for a final charge. Given that the outcome of the combat was in no way at stake, the Ethiopians gave way, then opened fire at close range.[46] Italian casualties were horrific. The long retreat began with cries from the wounded, begging not to be left behind.[47]

Ras Alula, Ras Mangasha, Ras Michael, and the Oromo cavalry were now threatening from the high ground on either side of Dabormida's brigade. The charge had put Dabormida's forces deeper into an Ethiopian pocket—it only increased the exposure of the Italian flanks, which now collapsed. Dabormida himself was soon surrounded in a whirl of hand-to-hand fighting. Basha Gabrè was in a group of soldiers who closed in on "the old man." He watched as Dabormida used his officer's revolver to shoot three of Basha Gabrè's comrades. Dabormida then turned to fire at Gabrè, but he took cover behind a tree. When Dabormida swiveled to face other attackers, Gabrè stepped from behind the tree and delivered the fatal shot. The bullet entered Dabormida's chest from the side, below the right shoulder, and tore his officer's sash as it exited the left.[48] Dabormida, who had expressed the desire to die rather than return to Italy after such a humiliating campaign, had gotten his wish.[49]

Dabormida's body was stripped. His white-handled officer's saber was one of the great trophies of the battle. Gabrè would later present it as a gift to Menelik.[50]

PART III

Aftermaths

CHAPTER 14

Despair, Panic, Pursuit

E ARLY IN MARCH 1896, a group of peasants from the village of
Ciacamte made a journey to the monastery at Debra Damo. They
returned with a strange and rich harvest: a ladle, a pair of gloves, a tiny
portrait frame, matches, a bouquet of dry carnations, a frying pan, a can
of shoe polish, several cans of tomatoes, a man's garter, and a book of
recipes entitled *The King of Cooks*. Back in their village, they spread their
unexpected bounty in front of a group of Italian prisoners. The apparently random and innocuous objects—in fact the debris field of an army
that had come apart in flight—brought on an unbearable sadness among
the prisoners.[1]

Melancholy was not the only emotional state induced by the bric-a-brac
of a shattered army. As Baratieri's army came apart on the first of March,
it brought elation to Menelik's soldiers, but it also whetted the appetite
for gain. Menelik's Ethiopia, secured by victory at Adwa, did not have a
conscription law, and Ethiopian soldiers were not drafted. But neither
were Ethiopian soldiers professionals. They were not paid. The army that
Menelik led against Italy had been created through his proclamation, which
called upon men to take up arms and assemble at designated places. In
practical terms, it was the equivalent of what the French call the *levée en
masse*—a taking up of arms by motivated citizen-soldiers.

Soldiers do not fight for nothing. In Menelik's Ethiopia, while soldiers were under arms they expected to be provided for by those who commanded them and ultimately by the head of state himself. And their relationship to war was entrepreneurial—as victors in battle, they expected to find their reward among the defeated. As the battle of Adwa turned from combat to rout, the soldiers' energies didn't dissolve into a celebration of victory. Instead, the soldiers redoubled their energy, seeing in the fleeing Italian soldiers a modest compensation for weeks of deprivation.

The effect on the Italian soldiers was all the greater given that they knew what was about to befall them—wounded or dead, they would be stripped and trophies would be taken. This knowledge had a devastating and demoralizing effect when the battle began to turn against the Italians.

Breakdown and Retreat

The breakdown of order occurred almost immediately with the collapse of Albertone's brigade, which had a cascading effect on the troops behind them at the passes. Albertone himself was captured, along with a number of his officers and soldiers, but many of his men were able to begin their retreat in semiorderly fashion.

Albertone's final commands called for some units to remain and cover the retreat, allowing other units to disengage. The problem for Albertone's men was that their pursuers were by no means limited to the forces in front of them. When the strong column of Ethiopian troops pushed into the gap separating Albertone from Dabormida, they were on the same path to the pass as Albertone's retreating soldiers. Pursuers and pursued became enmeshed and given that most of the retreating soldiers were askari—that is, African—confusion reigned. Arimondi and his men were still settling into their positions when Albertone's forces began their retreat. But even if the flanks of Raio had offered a more generous platform for deployment, they still would have been unprepared for what they now witnessed. A steady flow of men—some panicked, others with steely resolve—moved toward them. The scarlet flash of an askari fez or a glimpse of a (white) European officer confirmed that they were witnessing a retreat and not an attack.

But as the racing sea of men made their way toward Arimondi's positions, it became clear that the situation was more complicated. Ethiopian soldiers used sword and lance to claim victims among the fleeing soldiers. Others immersed themselves in the flow of running men in order to advance unimpeded to the pass and take aim at the officers at close range.[2] The collapse occurred almost instantly. Giuseppe Baudoin's *bersaglieri* battalion found that the time required to reload was sufficient for the Ethiopians to close with them. They were surrounded and disarmed.[3]

Luigi Goj witnessed an attempt by General Baratieri to rally the troops, including a handful of wounded *bersaglieri* and *alpini*. Baratieri deployed his flag as a rallying point and repeatedly cried out, "Savoy"— the seat of the Italian ruling dynasty. Baratieri wanted to guide the retreat back toward the camp at Sauria and the fort at Adigrat, a path that would lead to strength. But the soldiers would have none of it. They ignored the pleas of their officers and, once clear of the passes, headed due north, back to Eritrea and safety.[4] A short while later, Baratieri was seen spurring his mule northward, until he reached the head of the retreating Italian column.[5] At some point Baratieri lost his eyewear, which meant that, as a final humiliation, he had to take voice commands from Lieutenant Giuseppe Marozzi, who became his eyes, telling him to duck or to steer his mount around hazards left and right.[6]

Fear began to weigh in the decisions of Italian soldiers. The appearance of Oromo cavalrymen, known at the time as Galla, had a notably dispiriting effect. The Oromo were mounted infantrymen. They rode into position, dismounted, and fired. Oromo cavalry had achieved quasi-mythical status in the weeks leading up to the war thanks in part to a tendency on the part of the European press to sensationalize stories out of Ethiopia.[7] Stories on Oromo cavalry and illustrations with captions reading "Mow them down!" fed the imaginations not only of civilians but also of soldiers shipping out. There were skeptics. Giovanni Tedone criticized such depictions of the Oromo as "dangerous exaggeration." The Oromo, he explained, were simply "a motley collection of predators, naked, poorly armed, poorly mounted."[8] But since the Italians had no cavalry and, in retreat, were sometimes without weapons, the Oromo held a distinct advantage. Their lion's mane headdresses, which amplified their reputation for ferocity in combat, made them fearsome.

The Oromo functioned with such grim efficiency that they hastened the demoralization of the crumbling Italian army. Baratieri would later

Oromo cavalry. From *L'Illustrazione italiana*, 22 March 1896.

claim that fear of the Oromo—and the belief that the Oromo castrated only soldiers caught with weapons—prompted dozens of retreating soldiers to cast down their weapons *come pazzi*—like madmen.[9] One Italian soldier survived the combat but lost his mind. He had managed to retreat as far as Sauria, where he was seen wandering around the camp "with a strange smile on his lips" and murmuring, "Galla cavalry! Galla cavalry! Horror! Horror!"[10]

Giovanni Tedone, a sergeant in the *bersaglieri* fighting under General Arimondi's command, gave a vivid account of the role of the Oromo in the breakdown of Italian forces. Colonels Ugo Brusati and Francesco Stevani were part of a group of officers who tried to organize an orderly retreat. Just as his men rallied to slow the assault from in front, Tedone glanced to his left to see a large group of Ethiopian soldiers approach their position. It was as if "a high black sea had flowed into the immense valley." He and his men were nearly surrounded. Eugenio Dolciotti, like Tedone a member of a *bersaglieri* unit assigned to Arimondi, watched officer after officer fall—Lieutenant Agostino Chigi, Lieutenant Colonel Lorenzo Compiano, Lieutenant Gillio, and finally General Arimondi himself.[11]

Despair set in. For the Italians, the retreat was now deadlier than the battle, especially as they lost the discipline needed to halt the Ethiopian pursuit. Some chose individual strategies. Tedone watched Lieutenant Pastore put a revolver to his head and pull the trigger.[12] Francesco Frisina witnessed a man—wounded, disarmed, and unable to continue the retreat—toss himself from a high rock, a final cigarette still in his mouth.[13]

As Tedone and his men moved away from the passes, they found themselves surrounded by Oromo cavalry. Tedone's men were badly outnumbered in the ensuing firefight; they held the Oromo at bay as their ammunition and numbers dwindled. Tedone watched as his immediate superior, Lieutenant Garibaldi Pennazzi, chose death. Sensing the end of combat, Pennazzi turned his pistol on himself, firing a round into his chest. The wound wasn't fatal, so Pennazzi sat up and fired again, crumpling at Tedone's feet. Following Pennazzi's lead, Second Lieutenant Mazzoleni raised his revolver to his right temple and pulled the trigger, spraying Tedone with blood and grey matter. As the Oromo closed in on Tedone he fell, wounded by saber and lance blows.[14] His battle was over.

The Fate of the Dabormida Brigade

The fate of Dabormida's brigade followed the pattern of the others, though delayed by several hours—Dabormida's forces held out until sometime after three in the afternoon, when a bugle call sounded the retreat. Captain Mottino's four artillery pieces covered the retreat, while units of the

Tenth Infantry Battalion protected their flanks.[15] Mottino and most of his men would die among their guns.

As the Ethiopian forces were closing in from the Italian left as well as front, there was never any question of evacuating toward the passes. Dabormida and his men hadn't the slightest idea of the fate of Baratieri, Arimondi, and the others, but given that they had had no contact for more than six hours, they might have guessed. They at least knew that they could expect no help.

Dabormida's forces withdrew toward the northeast—essentially, the direction of Eritrea—but this route funneled them onto a narrow trail toward high ground. Men jostled one another and competed with panicked artillery mules for space along the path, all the while dodging fire. Men and animals clambered over one another, frantic to break free of the pursuing Ethiopians. Even vegetation conspired against them, as clothing snagged on thorny brush and acacia.[16]

The admirable discipline that had characterized Dabormida's forces throughout the day broke down. Dabormida's men abandoned their wounded as Ethiopian soldiers fell upon them, finishing them off with lances and sabers. Men who still possessed some strength after the march and the day's fighting pushed past the exhausted and the fallen. Colonel Airaghi called upon men to save the artillery pieces, to keep them from falling into enemy hands. His voice was lost in the surrounding cries and yells. Captain Palumbo, a portly man, gave in to exhaustion. He simply sat down, pointed his revolver at the pursuing Ethiopians, and waited to die. Lieutenant Campara took his own life, and Colonel Airaghi, now wounded, dragged himself in the general direction of retreat.[17]

It was not a single retreat, but as many retreats as there were men— each man seeing to his own survival. Alberto Woctt remembered some acts of heroism, though he recognized that they were few, for the circumstances favored self-preservation above all. Where the path of retreat narrowed to single or double file, the body of soldiers formed a serpent-like shape. Those making up the tail end of the retreat fell victim; they were like bones tossed to the pursuers, unwitting heroes slowing the Ethiopian pursuit. If some escaped that day, it was because others fell in unwilling sacrifice. Officers pulled revolvers on men deaf to command and discipline, but to no avail.[18] "No more orders, no more officers," was how one survivor put it.[19]

The path of retreat crossed a waterway that had carved a narrow but deep break in the earth. A few could jump in a single leap; most descended to cross and clamber up the other side. Still others, parched with thirst, stopped at the bottom and risked death to drink as bullets whizzed past. Both pursuers and pursued fell in the fight and the confusion. Alberto Woctt recalled seeing both black and white soldiers "facedown in the mud, fraternizing in death."[20]

Eventually the Ethiopians broke off their pursuit, choosing to focus instead on the rich spoils behind them. A light rain began to fall around six-thirty, teasing the retreating Italians as it vanished in the dry earth. As the rain continued, some soldiers stopped to raise rocks to their lips, drinking the drops that puddled in depressions on the stones.[21] Others stripped off their rain-soaked clothing, then raised it over their heads to wring drops of water into their parched mouths.[22]

Panic at Sauria

Some of the survivors made their way back to the base camp at Sauria. There they hoped to find food, water, and protection. Instead, they found a devastated camp. What transpired at Sauria during the day of the battle can be pieced together from fragmentary accounts. Support personnel at Sauria rose at dawn on 1 March. Their main task for the day was to deliver supplies. By now, they imagined, the columns had reached their rendezvous points and were consolidating their position at the passes; they would be ready for new provisions.

It took an hour and a half to prepare the convoy. Around eight that morning, a large caravan bearing food and ammunition set out across the Gundapta plain toward Zala. At the western edge, the terrain rises and narrows to the Zala pass, then widens again as it continues westward. Members of the supply caravan expected to be en route most of the day, catching up with Baratieri's forces in the late afternoon.

Then, at ten in the morning, a rider was seen crossing the plain at top speed via a southerly route parallel to the supply caravan. As he came into camp the rider, an officer, halted long enough to deliver the news that a battle was under way, then he spurred his horse again and continued on his way. A bit later, as if to provide proof, an askari walked into camp, his leggings soaked in blood. The timing of his arrival suggested either an early departure from battle or an astonishingly rapid retreat, likely both. He bore indisputable evidence of a fight—blood oozed from a wound to the thigh. He smiled as he offered the thought that he had done his part and was going home. Then he left.[23]

In a flash, the first Ethiopian pursuers appeared, coming from the south. They were mounted infantry, Oromo horsemen. Repulsed with rifle fire, they remained at bay until early afternoon.[24] Pietro Felter, an old hand in Ethiopian affairs, knew trouble when he saw it. He had his assistant saddle up his mule so that he would be ready to move out at a moment's notice. Then he took his place in the shade of some tall shrubs, sitting and looking intently across the valley to the west.

Just before eleven o'clock, he noticed movement out of the Zala pass toward the camp. As Felter watched, the movement grew "into a swirling human river" of askari, white infantrymen, officers, women, and children. They were the remnants of the Albertone brigade. Some were mounted, but most were on foot. As the horde grew, the pass became choked. The "serpent," as Felter called it, nearly came to a halt as bodies pressed against each other in panic. Once through the pass, the refugees fanned out, rapidly closing with the supply caravan, which was just then approaching the pass. The two collided, then the caravan melted into the crowd, joining it in a swirl of animals and men. The eastward momentum of panicked flight overwhelmed the caravan, and the two combined in a desperate exodus back toward camp.[25]

Once in camp, arguments broke out over what to do next. There seems to have been little discussion of whether to organize a defense of the camp. The only real question was the route of retreat. Arnoldo Nicoletti-Altimari, one of the ranking officers at Sauria, assumed the retreat would follow the supply line back toward Barakit by way of Debra Damo. Alessandro Sapelli, who had fought as part of the Albertone brigade, disagreed. Supply caravans on that road had been taking high casualties in the days before the battle. Why should anyone assume the route had become any safer? They parted ways, with only a handful following Sapelli.[26]

A much larger group followed Nicoletti-Altimari, many to their death. The group suffered casualties along their way and got caught up in a fight at Debra Damo. Of the eighty who followed Nicoletti-Altimari, only eight made it to the relative safety of Mai Maret.[27] Nicoletti-Altimari was badly wounded and captured.

Bad as their experiences were, both groups escaped the slaughter that befell the camp itself. The main Ethiopian pursuit reached Sauria by early afternoon. By the time they left, dozens of bodies were scattered about. The camp was thoroughly ransacked.[28]

Even as Menelik's forces called off their pursuit, a new set of threats emerged. In the days before the battle, the population of Agamé had turned increasingly assertive in its opposition to the Italian occupation, engaging in acts of sabotage and guerrilla warfare. In the aftermath of the European defeat, the population rose in open rebellion, seeking to drive the retreating Italians northward while stripping them of anything of value.[29] On the night of the defeat, the retreating soldiers, traveling alone and in groups, could see fires on the hilltops as peasants communicated the news of Ethiopian victory in a gesture that spread and accelerated the revolt.[30] In the early morning hours of 2 March, as stragglers raced northward in pursuit of safety, they were picked off, adding to the confusion and fear. Sudden attacks out of the darkness continued the horrors of battle.[31]

The better-organized groups of soldiers preserved enough discipline to set up sentries to allow halts for rest or water. In at least one instance, rescue came from loved ones. Alessandro Sapelli had fought with the Albertone brigade; he was joined in retreat by Degiac Fanta, leader of native Eritrean forces engaged at Adwa. The two men were exhausted not only from the day's fighting but also by the sleepless nights that preceded and followed it. On 2 March, Sapelli and Fanta finally felt safe enough to pause to rest. Sapelli dozed while Fanta stood watch, chewing cloves of garlic to stay alert. As Fanta scanned the horizon, he noticed a woman approach on horseback, accompanied by three servants. He roused Sapelli, who soon recognized the woman as Amlassu, his *madama*. She had heard the news of the battle—"How bad news flies!" mused Sapelli—and raced to his rescue, heedless of the danger. Amlassu intended "to bury me if I had died, to comfort me if I had been taken prisoner." She had packed food, medicine, and bandages. She also carried two hundred thalers—a small fortune, enough for bribes or ransom—concealed in her saddle. After a reunion we can only imagine, Amlassu guided Sapelli home. Her courageous exploit gave proof of a devotion that conquered all hazards, all risks.

Even after the pursuit ended, a persistent fear remained that Menelik might follow up his victory with a campaign to drive the Italians from Asmara, perhaps from Africa altogether. A shudder of panic rolled across Eritrea, stirring up phantoms from Dogali to Amba Alage. Were Menelik's thousands on the way? Would Alula reclaim his Asmara home? Would Oromo cavalry appear in a cloud of dust on the horizon? Would the population turn against Italy? Fear caromed from Saganeiti and Coatit to Asmara, then rolled down the Ginda pass toward the coast. Massawa itself was choking on refugees, as civilians who once had bought into Italy's vision of African paradise were no longer taking chances. Dreams of riches faded; they would settle for their lives.[32] Eritrea, the product of years, threatened to roll up in the space of days.

One soldier, grateful to have reached the safety of Massawa, sat down to capture the ordeal in a letter to his mother. It was a litany of woe, but in the end he found splendor in a dignified survival:

> [Captain Passamonte] was healthy, [Lieutenant Longagnani] had a head wound . . . ; of 103 soldiers [in our original unit] sixty-three remained. Plus, we had taken on twenty-five wounded [from other units] and five mules. Almost all of the soldiers are without shoes, although some have wrapped their feet in handkerchiefs or scraps of shirt fabric. Pants and jackets are shredded, torn to pieces. . . . But . . . all of the healthy soldiers [still] have their weapons and ammunition. Isn't it beautiful, Mamma?[33]

CHAPTER 15

The Harvest

A s NIGHT FELL over Adwa, some of the fleeing Italians experienced it as deliverance, because it brought an end to the Ethiopian pursuit. For others, it brought only a shift to the color-drained palette of night, illuminating a new set of horrors.

Here and there on the battlefield, Ethiopian soldiers set fire to the rain-damp grass. Amid steam, smoke, and sparks, flames climbed from the fields, bringing light back to the scene. Ghostly figures rose, too, emerging from the grass, rising with the smoke, stumbling among the flames, dragging shattered limbs, forming eerie profiles, and casting long shadows. It was as if the earth were giving up the dead, neither damned nor saved. These were soldiers—wounded or feigning death—who now rose to escape the flames, only to be seized in a final harvest of prisoners.[1]

At Adwa, bodies were stripped where they fell. Stripping the bodies of dead soldiers is an ageless if not time-honored practice. Armies on the move have to carry their wealth; it isn't unusual to find cash, coin, and other valuables on the dead.[2] Pieces of clothing can be used, traded, or sold. So can weapons. For some armies, especially volunteers such as the Ethiopians, such yield is the only source of income. It is how a soldier gets paid.

The bodies of the dead also yielded tokens of valor. Alberto Woctt was captain of the Third Africa Infantry Battalion in General Dabormida's brigade. By nightfall, he recalled, the bright moon of Adwa illuminated bodies fallen in retreat. "All around us," he recounted, "mutilated bodies [glowed with] a horrifying whiteness under the silver moonlight."[3] The mutilations in question were not the random disfigurements that occur to bodies in combat. These were deliberate acts, the emasculation of the dead and the dying.

Giovanni Tedone, a sergeant, witnessed the agony of a fellow soldier. Tedone didn't recognize him, but he knew the dying man had to be a member of the *bersaglieri*, not by his uniform—the man had been stripped and lay naked in the moonlight—but by the simple fact that the man called Tedone by name, begging for water. As Tedone approached, he saw that the man had been wounded with saber blows to the chest, legs, arm, and head. In a gesture of modesty, the man covered his genitals with his hand to conceal the wound created by his emasculation, which, Tedone hastened to explain, had taken the scrotum but not the penis. It left a yellowish patch, as Tedone described it, presumably referring to fatty tissue not obscured by blood.[4] And although some witnesses blamed the practice for the death, by loss of blood, of still-living soldiers, Tedone rebutted such claims. He noted that castration, properly performed, rarely led to great losses of blood. With a matter-of-factness that suggested a background in animal husbandry, Tedone described the procedure: "Two lateral cuts, and then a cut from the bottom up and that's it."

Tedone witnessed this scene as he was being marched, a prisoner of Menelik, back to the Ethiopian camp. He, too, had been wounded and had lost consciousness. He awoke with his arms tied behind his back. He had been stripped completely naked, except for the stylish black-feathered helmet characteristic of the *bersaglieri*; it was a dispensation Tedone regarded as mockery—a cock plucked but for the head. Nearby, two Ethiopian soldiers were fighting over his belongings, including his bloody jacket. He observed Tibaldi and Sportiglione, two fellow soldiers, lying on the ground—naked, bleeding, and weakened by wounds. They looked at Tedone and saw their fate mirrored in his: "Now they'll do that to us, too!"[5]

Luigi Goj, who had been deployed to Ethiopia only a few months prior to Adwa, surrendered and was captured by Oromo cavalry. As he was being walked back to the Ethiopian camp, he heard a voice call out "from a pile of black and white cadavers." "Acqua," the voice cried. As Goj moved closer he spied "one of ours" who was mortally wounded and "horrible to say it—emasculated."[6]

A Vexed History

The castration of the fallen, both dead and wounded, was a notorious problem in Ethiopian encounters with Europe. It stood in tandem with the slave trade as the pair of issues invoked as examples of "Abyssinian barbarism" and exploited as such to justify European pretensions to a civilizing mission.

Abolishing the slave trade and eliminating the practice of castrating vanquished foes remained high on the lists of issues raised by Europeans in their dealings with Ethiopia. In 1855, with the rise to power of Tewodros, Walter Plowden, British consul, wrote triumphantly to London that the new king of Ethiopia could be counted on to address both issues. "I have the honour to inform you," Plowden wrote in 1855, "that Dejajmatch Kasai has defeated and taken prisoner Dejajmatch Oobeay, and having thus vanquished his last and most formidable competitor, has been crowned with much pomp by the Aboona Salama and all the clergy as King of Ethiopia."

Plowden went on to say, in the charming language of Victorian England, that Tewodros had "signalized his career already by two great acts—the abolition of the Slave Trade and of the barbarous mutilation of fallen enemies."[7] Both claims turned out to be wildly optimistic; put differently, they "signalized" the good intentions of Tewodros but also the limitations of his authority. Issuing edicts was one thing. Carrying them out would prove far more difficult, as both the slave trade and emasculation would continue to vex Ethiopia through the reigns of Tewodros, Yohannes, and Menelik.

What did emasculation mean?[8] The answer is by no means simple, nor was the practice limited to situations of combat. Ethiopian criminal justice rarely called for incarceration or confinement. In most cases, punishment involved literal or symbolic restitution. The family of a murdered man, for example, could ask for the death of his murderer. But in cases where confinement was called for, prisoners were confined to the high mesas, called *ambas,* where nature has provided, by means of abrupt, unscalable walls, a near perfect arena for confinement—reachable only by treacherous goat paths or a rope dropped from the top of the *amba.* There, as Augustus Wylde explains, prisoners are guarded by eunuchs. Emasculation was a condition of employment; the position meant job security for life.[9]

In the military context, however, a different logic takes over. Manly reputations are made in combat. One way that Ethiopian men showed their prowess as fighters and killers was by braiding their hair. Augustus Wylde, a British journalist generally sympathetic to the Ethiopians, described meeting Asalafie Hailou during his visit to Ethiopia in the aftermath of Adwa. Wylde concedes that he "had already taken a strong dislike" to the Ethiopian. He goes on to explain that Hailou's hair was "plaited in strands, which were tied together at the back of his head, like that of all Abyssinians who have killed their man."[10]

Emasculation thus had its place among other signs of triumph. At the most basic level, the scrotum of the vanquished is a trophy and a mark of valor.[11] The man who braids his hair makes a claim not visibly substantiated; a body part validates the claim. In that sense, the excision of the scrotum is little different from the taking of an ear, a scalp, or a digit. It testifies vividly to the total domination of the body that yields its remnant. How else could such a relic be taken?

What sets a scrotum apart, however, is that unlike an ear or digit, it can only have come from a man.[12] Accordingly, to take the scrotum is much more personal, more than just a trophy. It is metonymy—a stand-in for the entire subjugated body of the vanquished. It can also be taken as a commentary on the lack of valor on the part of the losers. Defeat is a consequence of failure in the soldierly arts—even the absence of valor. Emasculation is commensurate with the lack of manly virtue in combat.[13]

Emasculation also lays claim to the future. The scrotum and testes perform no functions vital to coitus—even to ejaculation. The main result of castration is to render an adult man sterile. A mutilated foe will survive but not reproduce, making castration a gesture that exacts a price not only on a man but also on a people.

The practice was not alien to European culture. This was the punishment meted out to those involved in the Gunpowder Plot of 1605 in

England, which aimed to blow up Parliament and the king. The castration of the traitor vividly manifested his unworthiness to reproduce—a point rendered moot, however, by his subsequent execution.[14] During the religious wars in France, the body of Gaspard de Coligny, the Protestant admiral, was similarly mutilated—though after death—during the massacres of St. Bartholomew's Day in 1572 in Paris.[15]

Castration could be about intimidation, but also punishment. In medieval Paris, Heloise's lover, Abelard, was set upon by Heloise's guardian, eager to punish the seducer of his niece. A group of men broke into Abelard's home in the night, restrained him, and castrated him. Abelard saw his castration as a punishment from God. "God had struck me in the parts of the body with which I had sinned," he wrote. But his attackers were punished in a symmetrical fashion. The judgment against them specified that they, too, would be castrated as punishment for their crime.[16]

Castration was not uncommon in Jim Crow America. The message went beyond trophies and spoke directly to issues of sexuality and race. The ritual of lynching almost always involved castration and other mutilation, sometimes of a victim not yet dead. William Faulkner's vivid portrait of the Jim Crow South, *Light in August,* includes a castration scene as one of its core events. The remarks of Faulkner's perpetrator ("Now you'll let white women alone, even in hell") suggest the conviction that castration touched the victim eternally.[17]

Lynchings and dismemberments did not require a racial component and, whether racialized or not, functioned as a way to embody, or pretend to embody, local social norms. Italians were lynched in New Orleans, although perhaps Italians, like the Irish of the period, were not seen as entirely white.[18] Sexual dismemberments were not unheard of in France, especially during periods of intense social strife. In village France, arguments could end in lynchings, mutilations, and castrations.[19] Georges Clemenceau described a scene on 18 March 1871, during the outbreak of the revolt known as the Paris Commune, where he saw children "waving indescribable trophies" taken from officers and soldiers.[20]

A Potent Symbol

Castration not only signaled the judgment of men; it could also signify eternal damnation. The Bible addresses the issue quite explicitly. "No man whose testicles have been crushed or whose organ has been severed," states Deuteronomy 23:1, "shall become a member of the assembly of the Lord." Although we will never know for certain whether Ethiopian castrations functioned in such a condemnatory way, that is, seeking to deny the victim Christian fellowship and entry to paradise, the relevant passage would have been known in Christian Ethiopia.

Some Ethiopians apparently justified castrations through reference to a different passage in the Bible, saying that David had won the respect of King Saul with such acts against the Philistines. The passage usually referenced in this regard (1 Samuel 18:27) describes David as slaying two hundred Philistines and taking their foreskins in a gesture of appeasement, although this is sometimes interpreted as a gentle euphemism for taking the scrotum.

It is worth pointing out that while all of Menelik's soldiers were "sons of Abraham," not all were Christian. According to some accounts, the Oromo cavalry were particularly prominent among the perpetrators—and the Oromo were often Muslim. Giuseppe Tedone, traumatized by his experience of the retreat and quite possibly a victim of such practices, goes so far as to refer to Ras Michael, head of the Oromo, as "the head of the emasculators."[21] It is certainly the case that the Oromo, uniquely able in their capacity as mounted soldiers to pursue the fleeing Italians, were well placed to carry out such acts. Alberto Woctt praised the fighting ardor of the Oromo, referring to them as "bold," "beautiful" warriors and "stupendous horsemen" who "love war for war's sake."[22] In fact, it was the warlike reputation of the Oromo that made them particularly effective. Their mere appearance could undermine the confidence of the Italians, hastening their collapse into disorderly retreat.

Castration even had military advantages because fear of emasculation was itself a powerful weapon.[23] Baratieri claimed that the belief that the Ethiopians castrated only soldiers taken with arms prompted soldiers to abandon their weapons in retreat. The fact that some Oromo rode horses whose necks were decorated with daisy-chained scrotums only made them more fearsome. These trophies were the proof of past soldierly success.[24] They also served as a vivid, terrifying reminder of the fate of the defeated.

The Oromo were far from alone as perpetrators, however. Jean Gaston Vanderheym, an acute observer who traveled with Menelik and his army in

1894 and 1895, described the practice of castration as quite common among Menelik's soldiers in their campaign against the Welayta. The practice was "deeply rooted" both among "Abyssinians" and among the Oromo, populations he treated as distinct. "In spite of all the laws and edicts," he wrote, "Menelik can do nothing to abolish this ignoble practice." And he described castration as an act committed not only upon the bodies of the dead—that is, the taking of trophies—but also upon the wounded, as a lien against the future. Menelik's soldiers were quite clear in explaining their intent. "The Abyssinians explain themselves," he wrote, "by saying that this is how they bring a halt to the enemy's capacity to reproduce."[25]

All of this is confirmed by earlier sources. Edmond Combes and Maurice Tamisier were barely twenty-one when they visited Ethiopia in the 1830s. There were members of a visionary political sect known as the Saint-Simonians who believed, among other things, that the East would yield a female messiah. Put on trial in 1832 and convicted of publishing works offensive to public morality, some of the Saint-Simonians concluded that the moment had arrived to set out to explore the East.[26]

Everywhere they went in Ethiopia, they saw evidence of the practice: scrotums on lances, scrotums on shields, scrotums around the necks of horses.[27] At least one of their contacts claimed that the necklace of testicles around the neck of his horse gave it strength and vigor.[28] Aside from the talismanic, restorative, or therapeutic qualities attributed to the detached scrotum, above all it symbolized the defeat of the enemy. Combes and Tamisier reproduced the lyrics of a song they heard among the enemies of the Oromo at Dher. One line referred to the wives of castrated Oromo soldiers as "widows whose husbands are still alive," that is, as wives effectively widowed by the sterility of their spouses.[29]

This throws new light on what happened in the aftermath of Adwa, among the living and the dead. Most castrations likely occurred among the dead. Eduardo Ximenes, who was part of the mission to bury the Italian dead in the aftermath of the battle, observed that of forty bodies buried one day, "about twenty" had been emasculated.[30] However, a significant number of the wounded returning from Adwa were castrated. One historian puts the figure at 30 out of 461 Italian wounded, about 7 percent.[31] Ultimately, the castrations at Adwa cannot be reduced to a single explanation. In some cases, it was a symbolic attack on the enemy's capacity to reproduce. In others, castration seemed to be motivated by little more than the wish for trophies, a desire to collect and display these intimate objects as a sign of manly valor and incontrovertible evidence of mastery over a vanquished foe.[32]

It was this aspect of the practice that Menelik addressed on the eve of his campaign to liberate Ethiopia. "Bring me the man, not the testicles," Menelik warned. A prisoner was worth more; testicles could come from any man. His admonishment was largely ignored; the practice proved to be too deeply embedded in the warrior culture of Ethiopia.[33]

One might say that the physical emasculations inflicted upon Italian soldiers paled in comparison with the political emasculation of Ethiopia that Italian rule would have entailed. Without a doubt, Italian victory would have meant the subjection of Ethiopia, with all the humiliation that colonial rule would bring. So, in a sense, the barbaric cruelty inflicted upon the bodies of the fleeing Italian soldiers mirrored—at least at the symbolic level—what the Ethiopians would have suffered under Italian dominion. Even on the battlefield the distinction between real and symbolic gestures never entirely breaks down.

Solomonic Menelik

The night of 1 March was a night of celebration for Ethiopia. In the Ethiopian camp, *tej* flowed freely. Tall bonfires cast long shadows. There was music, drumming, and dancing. Boastful storytelling, shrieks, and celebratory rifle fire drowned out the sobs of those who had lost loved ones.

The Ethiopians had been complete masters of the day. In a few hours, the specter of defeat and occupation vanished. They had stopped the Italian incursions and rolled back the Italian claims to Ethiopian territory. By defeating the main Italian force and shattering it in precipitous retreat, they secured Ethiopian independence for more than a generation.

They also gave a stunning lesson to would-be conquerors. Ethiopia's victory established its status as one of the great African nations—a leader in a modern era of nations and peoples.[34] As a nation was born, it announced the end of an era in which foreign powers could colonize African territory at will.

As night fell, Ethiopian soldiers organized some of their prisoners to haul battlefield loot back to camp. Captured Italians were loaded up with rifles, jackets, canteens, and shoes, then guided like teams of porters westward toward the vast Ethiopian encampment surrounding the town of Adwa. North of town, on the road to Adi Abuna, was the camp of Ras Mangasha, illuminated by bonfires. After the humiliations of Senafé and Coatit, Adwa was his revenge. Farther west and to the south was Menelik's camp, where the court celebrated a victory that confirmed his status as king of kings.[35]

Hundreds of Italian soldiers were now at the mercy of their captors. As they were herded toward the Ethiopian camp, the Italian soldiers realized that the men they had sought to conquer had instead conquered them. An abrupt inversion of expectations added to the sense of disorientation. Giovanni Tedone, already traumatized by his evening among the wounded and the mutilated, described his approach to the Ethiopian camp in terms worthy of an Italian poet: "I completed the ascent of a high peak; the enemy camp opened out before me. It stretched on forever, like a city without end—an inferno with all of its horrors!"

Tedone recognized that his anxiety, exhaustion, and fear had deprived him of his capacity to comprehend.

> Between the sounds of the Ethiopian drums, the war dances, the assorted cries, the flames of the fires reaching up to the sky for several meters, the fantasy of it all—the cries and the continuous firing of guns in the end deprived me of my remaining grip on reason.[36]

As his Ethiopian captors drove him towards their camp, Carlo Diotti—exhausted from the night march and the day of fighting—had to be prodded with periodic shoves in the back with rifle butts.[37] Diotti, as a prisoner, suffered some of the standard abuse offered by victors. Ethiopian soldiers spit at him. Others gave out a mocking laugh of ridicule. It was dusk and there was just enough light for the horrors of the battlefield to form a tragic panorama—soldiers, naked, bleeding, mutilated. An Italian soldier wounded in the knee, cried out piteously while an Ethiopian goaded him to walk on. Later, the soldier was put out of his misery.

Even for the Ethiopians, all was not joy. Ethiopian soldiers labored to build stretchers to carry their wounded. They sang songs of mourning and lamentation. Some shot piercing glances at the prisoners as they shuffled by, while others howled in rage.[38]

Diotti, a corporal who had fought in the Dabormida brigade, had an experience rare in war—he had to face the women whose men he had helped to kill. Women rarely accompanied nineteenth-century European armies and, when they did, they were rarely family members. Not so in Ethiopia, where wives and other household members served as support staff for fighting men. As soldiers and captives marched toward camp, some women saluted the prisoners' captors, kissing their hands in gratitude.[39] Others frantically scanned the faces of the returning Ethiopians, anxious for a glimpse of a loved one. Finally, in despair, they turned on the captive Italians with cries of rage. For once, the object of a war widow's rage was not abstract.

Redemption came in strange forms. Ethiopian captors loaded their Italian prisoners with the spoils of war, balancing bundles of clothing and gear on their heads. Diotti stumbled and fell under his burden. Refusing to rise, he asked his captors to end his life—"to end my martyrdom," as he recalled it. He closed his eyes and a shot rang out. His captor had missed, likely deliberately, shooting a spray of dirt into Diotti's face and mouth. When Diotti opened his eyes, an Ethiopian officer on a mule stood before him. The officer was wounded in the leg.

Diotti recognized the man from the distinctive red dressing of his horse. The officer addressed Diotti as "Ali"—a joke because the Italians had used the name "Ali" abusively as a nickname for the Ethiopians, any Ethiopian, just as "Tommy" and "Jerry" would later be names ascribed to British and German soldiers in Europe. The Ethiopians, having turned the tables on the battlefield, now turned the tables in the game of abuse; Ali became a common nickname for any European, not only the Italians.[40]

The officer asked Diotti to dress his wound. Diotti, who had no medical expertise but was willing to pretend that he did, promptly complied. The gesture saved his life. To the chagrin of his tormentors, the enterprising Diotti was led away, holding on to the tail of his savior's mule. He glanced back and grinned as he bounded off, clinging to the tail as if to his very life.[41]

The turn of events allowed Diotti to shake off his gloomy fatalism. Minutes earlier Diotti had been begging for death; now Diotti asked his new patron for something to drink. His patron gestured to a subordinate, who duly dipped his shield in a pool of muddy water. Diotti drank greedily, until mud filled his mouth and he was unable to drink any more.

As his walk into captivity continued, Diotto came up over a rise and for the first time grasped the true dimensions of the Ethiopian army. "An immense valley stretched out before me, with an infinity of tents, other encampments were scattered on the heights, others still could be glimpsed fading into more distant valleys. So many! So many! Immense!"[42]

In camp, askari were separated from their Italian officers; it was as captives that the survivors found one another. Unable to think of anything better to say, they muttered, "You here, too!" Giovanni Tedone encountered Second Lieutenant Gritti, an officer in the *alpini* he had met over dinner at Adigrat a few weeks earlier. Defeated in battle, Gritti failed even at suicide. Gritti had saved the last round of his officer's pistol for himself but missed. He managed only to give himself a powder burn, leaving a black spot on his cheek, "which only made him more endearing."[43]

Survivors recall encountering other prisoners with a mix of pain and relief, eventually finding comfort in companionship. At first Gherardo Pantano reproached himself "for having failed to find a way to kill myself." In the end, however, most gave in to "the drunken feeling of being alive."[44] The prisoners also gave in to fatigue. Francesco Frisina's captor led him, along with several others, into a tent in Menelik's camp. As Frisina and other prisoners settled in for the night, their captor lay down across the opening of the tent, a sleeping sentry.

In the Presence of the Negus

In the morning, the most sought-after personage was the emperor himself. Around ten o'clock the Italian prisoners—hundreds of them—were herded toward Menelik's compound. The emperor's tent was easily identifiable thanks to the cluster of several tents, including the red tent and the *adderach*—large enough for dozens to stand—where Menelik held court. Menelik had agreed to convert his reception tent—the largest covered space available—into a makeshift hospital where Italian medics treated Ethiopian wounded. Italians who sought medical attention were rebuffed by their compatriots: "Later, later! Not now!"[45]

As the prisoners waited, they became acquainted with the only European to witness Adwa from the winning side, the retired French officer Captain Clochette. Clochette had been among the European agents/merchants/advisors who had cultivated a relationship with Menelik. He was an associate of Mondon-Vidailhet, the man who had functioned as Menelik's publicist and done so much to craft Menelik's image in Europe. Clochette had facilitated the sale of eight thousand rifles to Menelik. Now he would witness the results of Menelik's dogged persistence. As the prisoners awaited their audience with Menelik, Clochette sat beneath a canopy, smiling contentedly at the Italians.[46] The prisoners were dispersed after three hours without seeing Menelik.

The following day, 3 March, the prisoners witnessed the Ethiopian court in all of its splendor. Men, women, and children from the Ethiopian camp and the surrounding villages converged on the imperial tent complex, where a procession was about to begin. Clergy took the lead role. They chanted and carried *tabot*. They were followed by a group of

At the court of Menelik. From *L'Illustrazione italiana,* 1 March 1896.

musicians sounding drums and horns. It was the equivalent of what Europeans would call a *Te Deum*—a ritual thanks to God for victory.[47]

At the center of it all was Menelik. The man who engineered modern Africa's greatest military triumph—and one of the great military victories of all time—was forty-nine years old. Finally, the prisoners could see in the flesh the man some had dismissed as a myth. By 3 March, Menelik had already joined the community of great men about whom great rumors abound. To the Ethiopians, he was a legend. To the Europeans, and not just the Italians, he was a figure to whom had been attributed "all the vices and all the virtues," including divine inspiration and cannibalism.[48]

Some of the prisoners were taken before Menelik. Many approached the tent of the *negus* in fear, expecting to find him brutal and haughty, qualities only exaggerated in victory. Instead, they discovered that Menelik, in person, was disarmingly human. As they were ushered into the emperor's presence, they found a calm man with a peaceful demeanor, a man who smiled frequently. His eyes revealed his "lively intelligence," and his pensive countenance gave him an air of quiet confidence.[49]

The greatest challenge that Menelik faced after Adwa was what to do with the prisoners.[50] By Ethiopian custom, the vanquished were at the disposal of the victors. Starting with Ethiopian victory at Harar, followed by the campaign against the Welayta, the Ethiopian pattern was clear. Many defeated soldiers paid with their lives. Captives were rare, except if they were to be enslaved. The property of the vanquished, including noncombatants, was up for grabs.

Adwa was already an exception in that so many prisoners were taken. The remark attributed to Menelik, "Bring me the man, not the testicles," was clearly part of a directive not only against emasculation but also in favor of taking the enemy soldiers alive.[51] Menelik didn't want slaughter; he wanted prisoners.

He got them. On 2 March, Menelik had nineteen hundred Italian prisoners and as many as fifteen hundred askari prisoners.[52] Menelik immediately came under heavy pressure from his advisors to make an example of the vanquished Italians.[53] In the evening following the battle and on into the wee hours of 2 March, a heated debate took place in Menelik's inner circle. Inside the emperor's tent, Empress Taytu and Ras Mangasha, possibly with the support of Taytu's brother Ras Wele, adopted a maximalist position: the Italian soldiers should die and the askari should be punished.[54] It was an elementary justice that Menelik's soldiers—indeed, all of Ethiopia—demanded. Ras Alula, a figure whose name was synonymous with the astonishing slaughter at Dogali, needed no coaxing to side with the maximalists. Such a dramatic gesture—Dogali, but on a massive scale—would send a powerful message that Ethiopia was not to be trifled with.

Ras Makonnen argued in favor of moderation. His voice was important, but his status was complicated. For many at court, Makonnen was compromised. He was seen as soft on Europeans and even as secretly Italophile—the opposite of Taytu and Alula, both of whom saw any dealing with Europeans as risky, a step on the slippery path to betrayal. But along with Makonnen, Tekle Haimanot, the king of Gojjam, and Ras Michael counseled forbearance.[55] So did Clochette, the retired French army officer who served as advisor to Menelik.[56]

What saved the Italians was their redemption value. Italy's soldiers were worth much more to Menelik alive than dead. Alive, Italy's sons were a powerful lever in the negotiations that were sure to follow, and Italy just might be persuaded to pay for their safe return. Thus any mistreatment of Italian soldiers was taken off the table.

The fate of the askari was more complicated. Somewhere between twelve hundred and fifteen hundred askari were taken prisoner after the battle.[57] Those on the winning side who demanded punishment were unyielding. What rankled the court and underpinned the bitterness against the askari was their importance to Italian success. Mangasha, for one, believed the askari had cost him his throne. Without the askari, Baratieri never would have turned back Mangasha at Coatit or caught him in retreat at Senafé.[58] And indeed, the Italian aggression against Ethiopia would have been impossible without the askari. In combat against Mangasha, Bahta Hagos, Alula, and others, the askari had served as the rank and file, the foot soldiers of Italian aggression.[59] In the end, that was their treason.[60]

By all accounts, Menelik represented the voice of moderation. As Paul Lauribar put it, "His natural goodness inclined him toward forgiveness."[61] In the end, Menelik took the counsel of Abuna Matewos, who sided with Taytu, Alula, Mangasha, and the others demanding punishment.[62] In addition to the sheer numbers of advocates of punishment, it was the deep

sense of betrayal the askari inspired in the Ethiopians that invited a settling of accounts. Ras Alula—who always favored straight talk—articulated
this best in a remark he made to askari taken prisoner after Amba Alage.
"You are Abyssinian, you have a *negus*, you have an emperor. And yet you
have sought another in the king of Italy, [you are] fighting against your
brothers. For that, I will punish you and I will cut off your hands."[63]

Judged as traitors rather than enemy combatants, the askari were subject to the most severe penalties. The askari's lives would be spared, but
they would lose their right hand and left foot—they would not fight or betray again.[64] Of the estimated twelve hundred to fifteen hundred askari
prisoners, some three hundred would return to Eritrea, where they would
be fitted with prosthetic devices and given odd jobs.[65] The precise fate of
the others—many presumably dead from infection or loss of blood—will
never be known.

The scene was horrific. Giovanni Tedone walked past hundreds of
askari, many of whom recognized him as their commanding officer and
called out to him, "Meschin meschin, taliano, moia moia! Pity on us! Italians! Water, water!" Long lines of askari submitted to their fate, stepping
forward with right hand presented in resignation. Truncated limbs were
cauterized.[66] Severed hands and feet rose in macabre mounds. Tedone
tried to turn away, but one of the askari forcibly turned him back toward the
spectacle, while another gestured that perhaps Tedone would suffer
the same fate.[67]

Carlo Diotti ran a similar gauntlet, forced to witness the suffering of
askari who had fought beside him, and powerless to answer their calls for
help. He passed by "poor askari" who let out "heartrending cries" as they
rolled in agony in the sand beside his path. "Italian brother!" they cried.
"Water, to drink!" "There's no water!" "I'm dying!"

In this regard, it is worth pointing out that askari who deserted in order to fight for Menelik—and there were some—were treated as traitors
by the Italians if captured. They were subject to the European punishment
for treason, which was death. In one case, an askari who survived Amba
Alage joined the insurgency against the Italians. He was given safe haven
by the clergy of Mekele. When he was discovered by the Italians, he was
hauled back to the fort, tried, and executed. In comparison, the Ethiopian mutilations seem mild, if pitiless.[68] Of course, Italian executions for

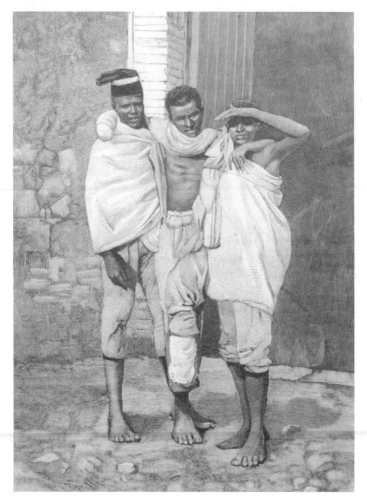

Askari amputee. From *L'Illustrazione italiana,* 3 May 1896.

treason were not carried out on anything like the hellish scale of the post-Adwa amputations.

It was Menelik's worst decision in the aftermath of the battle. Menelik claimed descent from Solomon, the Hebrew king renowned for his discerning judgments, but he was unable to prevent the further shedding of blood, blood that was now carving a chasm between these men and his own. As Menelik undoubtedly understood, the resentments of the askari would stand between any easy reconciliation of Ethiopia and Eritrea, a point Augustus Wylde presciently observed in the immediate aftermath of the battle.[69] The antipathy generated that day poisoned Eritrean-Ethiopian relations for years to come. Gabra Iyasus would try to mitigate the damage by emphasizing Mangasha's role in the decision, thus shielding Menelik somewhat as the reluctant decision maker.[70] In the end, Menelik did what any real leader would do—he took responsibility. When a British journalist asked him about the mutilations, he offered the most vigorous defense he could. "Have you heard what they did?" he asked. "They had committed sacrilege, looted churches, sacked villages and towns, stolen cattle and killed my subjects. . . . [T]hey [were] treated as thieves and receive[d] the punishment of thieves. . . . Tell this in England."[71]

Meanwhile, Menelik's enemies, and the enemies of Ethiopia, would use the image of mutilated askari to buttress the image of "barbaric Ethiopia," undermining Ethiopia's standing among nations and laying the rhetorical groundwork for future incursions.[72]

CHAPTER 16

The Long March

I N THE LATE 1830s, Ras Wube of Tigray received a group of European explorers. Wube had doubts about the visitors' intentions, but
they came prepared with a gift in the hope that it might allay his suspi-
cions.[1] Wube accepted the gift—a framed portrait of the French king
Louis-Philippe—but it did nothing to soften Wube's unwelcoming message. "Take care never to set foot on my country," he warned his startled
French visitors. "You and the English, you are penned up on cursed
land and you covet our healthy climate: one of you gathers our plants,
another our stones; I do not know what you are looking for, but I do not
want it to be *chez moi* that you find it."[2]

Sixty years later, the message hadn't changed. Yet the triumph of Adwa
posed a troubling and fundamental question: was the fighting over, or
should Menelik, in the spirit of Wube, follow up his victory by driving
the Italians into the sea? The Ethiopian claim on what the Italians called
Eritrea had a long history; Ethiopian trade followed a highly trafficked
route through Eritrea with Massawa as its terminus.[3] In the 1880s,
Yohannes and his lieutenants had bitterly resisted the Italian incursions,
just as they had pushed back the Egyptians before them.[4]

In Menelik's court, Alula and Taytu, as northerners, took the lead in
pressing for a campaign to drive the Italians from Eritrea. Menelik knew

better. His army was overextended. The rainy season was approaching. The cultural nexus would shift perceptibly, too, as he moved into Eritrea. The Eritrean highlands rise above the Sudan to the west and the Red Sea coastal lowlands to the east, both areas deeply influenced by Islam. If Menelik's army were to continue northward, it would advance into a more complicated cultural territory.

An invasion of Eritrea would change the strategic dynamic, too—with every step north from the Tigray highlands, he would take himself farther from his base of support. And he would be pressing closer to the Italian garrisons, which were rapidly filling with fresh recruits from Italy.[5]

As decisive as Adwa had been, Menelik knew that the Italians might be out for revenge. Far better for any future confrontation to take place in conditions like those that had led to victory at Adwa, with the Italians far from their resources and home base. To his great credit, Menelik decided not to risk his magnificent triumph by plunging into an adventure with an uncertain outcome. He chose to take his most precious resource—his Italian prisoners—and begin the long march home.

Control of nearly nineteen hundred prisoners gave Menelik some singular advantages. For starters, those prisoners put a number on the Adwa disaster for the world to see. Nineteen hundred prisoners, thousands dead—until the story of Ethiopia's victory could be told in detail, raw numbers would have to do.[6] Beyond that, the prisoners meant that the Ethiopian army had protection as it marched south; any attempt at pursuit, rescue, or revenge would put these men at risk. Just as Galliano's men provided coverage to Menelik as his army moved north, the prisoners would help cover his march southward.

Menelik's return posed challenges of its own. What was to be done with all of these captives? The answer was to divide them up. Badly wounded soldiers were spared the rigors of the long march. They were left in the north, in Mangasha's care.[7] A very large group of prisoners, about eight hundred, remained with Menelik. Most of the remainder were divided into groups of fifty to a hundred, doled out to Menelik's lieutenants. High-ranking officers were paired with Ethiopian commanders, who served as guide and guardian.[8] Tekle Haimanot, king of Gojjam, accepted custody of Major Giovanni Gamerra. Menelik's minister of justice, Afa Negus Nesibu, took Lieutenant Gherardo Pantano into his care, launching what was to become one of the warmest Italo-Ethiopian relationships.[9] Menelik made it clear that he would hold his chiefs accountable: "Bring them back to me alive!"[10]

A Topsy-Turvy World

Menelik's warning resonated among soldiers whose memories of combat were still fresh. Ethiopian soldiers, ripe with resentment over the loss of friends and comrades, lorded their authority over their new subjects. Some sought revenge. Augustus Wylde tells of three hundred prisoners entrusted to Dejazmatch Besheer. Besheer had suffered severe wounds in the fight and hovered near death for hours. When Besheer died, his men became enraged and massacred the three hundred men—Italians and askari—entrusted to their care.[11]

There was also the matter of race. On one level, Adwa—indeed, the entire campaign—had been a racial drama. Adwa was the triumph of black over white; it created a power that was sometimes exercised gleefully. Carlo Diotti wrote that the evident "satisfaction of commanding a company of whites" led to rule by "an iron hand."[12] Some prisoners experienced this new topsy-turvy world in modest but practical ways. At water stops, the Ethiopians drank first, then they watered the animals. The prisoners drank last.

The first few days of marching were long, as long as there was daylight. The army needed to move beyond the resource-depleted fields of Adwa. They also feared Italian pursuit. The pattern repeated for four days, maximizing the distance between the prisoners and any possible Italian rescue. In those first days and nights, the army and its wards encountered challenges procuring the basics—food, shelter, warmth—and these difficulties would dog their journey in the weeks to come. Many soldiers had been stripped in the aftermath of battle or forced to hand over their clothing. They began the march half naked, many without shoes or other foot covering.[13] Prisoners had little or nothing to protect them from the cool night air of high-altitude Ethiopia. A few were given a cowhide wrap as bed and blanket.[14] Many slept without tent or fire.

Able-bodied prisoners were expected to work, to bear the loot—clothing and gear—taken from their fallen comrades. Discipline was simple. Laggards were beaten; they quickly learned to stay near the front of the group.

While most prisoners learned to cooperate with their captors, some resisted. Lieutenant Cesare Pini, who had fought in the Albertone Brigade, was among the ringleaders who, from the earliest days of captivity, aimed to boost morale by encouraging subtle signs of resistance. His captors eventually tamed him by hitting him in the crotch with sticks.[15]

Some prisoners contemplated escape; a few succeeded. Complexion was an obvious marker. Given that black prisoners could more easily travel undetected, their guardians watched them closely. Many captive askari were chained wrist-to-wrist to their captors. European captives were another matter; any escape would need the cover of darkness. As a precaution, the Ethiopians collected the prisoners' shoes at the end of the day's march.[16] Without shoes, the Ethiopians reasoned, escapees wouldn't get far. Even so, five Italian prisoners—all Calabrians—escaped camp in a nighttime dash. Hiding by day and traveling by night, they reached the Italian fort at Adigrat without incident.[17]

Other prisoners experienced hardship not as maltreatment but as something unavoidable in the circumstances. Addis Ababa, the ultimate destination for the court and many of its prisoners, was more than 350 miles from Adwa as the crow flies, but more than 600 miles by the twisting paths of the Ethiopian highlands. Many officers were given mules, but most   Italian and Ethiopian—traveled on foot for five or six hours a day.[18]

There were logistical problems. There had barely been enough food even for the Ethiopian army, and now it had grown by nineteen hundred prisoners. The typical food ration consisted of a handful of chickpeas or barley, to be crushed and mixed with water, then baked over the fire or eaten raw. To their credit, Ethiopian leaders insisted that their men share the hardships of their prisoners, with identical rations for prisoner and guardian.[19] Nicola d'Amato witnessed an Ethiopian officer's complaint to Menelik that he could barely feed himself, let alone the prisoners with which Menelik saddled him. The officer had fasted for two days—not for religious reasons—and said bitterly to Menelik, "I have a handful of corn—not enough for one!"

The scarcity of food also hastened the breakdown of discipline among the Italians. A soldier named Di Salvo stole from an officer at knifepoint. During the distribution of food, one soldier returned to the line for a second ration. When an officer sought to discipline him, the soldier beat the officer on the head with a stick. In yet another episode, a soldier berated an officer who tried to correct him. "We're done with that racket! We're not in Italy anymore! We are all equal! There are no ranks!"[20]

Menelik knew that the lands he had traversed on his northward march were depleted and that for farmers and shepherds the reappearance of his starved army, even in victory, would not be an occasion for rejoicing.[21] To the extent the terrain allowed, he dispersed his forces, along with their allocation of prisoners, into separate columns. Some traveled directly south from Adwa, taking the western road to Sekota by way of the Tembien and Lasta regions. The main column—Menelik, Taytu, their court, and most of the prisoners—headed east from Adwa to Adigrat and then south along the eastern road via Mekele and Lake Ashenge to Addis.[22] This route avoided the lands the army had devastated on its northward march until it reached Mekele. From Mekele south to Ashenge was undoubtedly the most difficult part of the journey.

Thus it was not a single march but many, spread out over two and a half months—from 1 March to 22 May, when Menelik's long column would at last parade into Addis Ababa.[23] For those traveling farther—to Harar or elsewhere—the journey would last until the end of July.[24]

Although survivors of the battle and march reported an array of experiences—and those in Menelik's direct care undoubtedly had the best treatment—even the most Ethiophilic of them remembered the march as "a Calvary."[25] Between forty and sixty prisoners would die en route, 2 to 3 percent of those who had set out from Adwa.[26] Although some of these deaths were the result of abuse, in general they were the result of wounds, cold, and malnourishment—conditions that preyed on Ethiopians and Italians alike. The best evidence of a shared misery is that many Ethiopians died en route, too. Captors expired alongside prisoners, Ethiopians alongside Italians. One soldier who would go on to experience prison camps during World War I compared his experience in Ethiopia favorably to his experience in German prisoner camps.[27]

Humanizing the Enemy

One group of two hundred prisoners marched for four days with little to eat but hard grain, beans, and chicken scraps from their captors. Finally, after four days, they rested. It was Saturday evening. Ethiopian soldiers built a fire between two giant sycamore trees, then set out cowhides in a circular pattern around the fire—a warm campfire for their prisoners. Soon a group of women approached with a feast of *enjera* and raw beef seasoned with ground pepper and other spices.

An Ethiopian soldier who spoke Italian offered reassuring words to his prisoners—they should take courage, for Menelik was good and they would eventually be freed. Then the men, their bellies full and their bodies exhausted from four days on the march, stretched out by the fire and drifted off to sleep.

The halt also brought the first occasion for Ethiopians and Europeans to begin to see each other in more human terms. Ethiopian captors amused themselves by teaching the Italians the Amharic vocabulary for parts of the body; they laughed at the sound of the Italian equivalents.[28] In the morning, women circled the Italians, eager to get a closer look at the first white men they had ever seen. Some were mocking and scornful; others beat their chests in a gesture of compassion and pity. Breakfast arrived in the form of dried beans and peas, followed by *enjera* and pepper in the evening. In the middle of the day, some of the prisoners spied the head of one of the cattle that had been butchered the night before. They borrowed a pot and boiled the head for broth.[29]

It was the first cycle in a parade of feast and famine they endured on the long march to Addis. In one desperate moment, prisoners dug holes in dry creekbeds in anxious search of water.[30] In another, they butchered a lame mule, wasting nothing and consuming the whole, including the intestines.[31]

The march was also an occasion to learn about culinary differences. The main Ethiopian meat proteins come from poultry and cattle. There are strict rules regarding the slaughter of animals: the butcher prays as he cuts the throat of the animal. The Ethiopians were appalled when one of the Italians, Captain Maggi, killed a chicken by twisting its neck. What was a common practice in Europe was ritual defilement in Ethiopia, the barbarous taking of life from one of God's creations without pity or prayer. Repelled by Maggi's act, the Ethiopians insisted that he touch nothing for the remainder of the day, for fear of polluting something or someone else.[32]

Among Ethiopians, butter was used primarily as a lotion, for skin and for hair, rather than as food. But as food supplies diminished, the prisoners improvised. The Italians used the butter, often rancid, to add flavor to *enjera,* which for days was often the only food.[33] One soldier traded his shirt for a chicken.[34]

As the long column of soldiers and prisoners made their way south, they passed through areas where Europeans were rarely if ever seen. Onlookers were curious, repelled, even horrified at the sight of white men. Few could turn away. As the curious approached the wretched prisoners, they held their *shammas* to their noses in anticipation of the odor of these strange men, whom they called "Turks"—exchanging one historical enemy for another.[35] A number of Italians reported similar encounters. Ethiopians, it seems, believed that white people gave off a disagreeable odor.[36]

Menelik's court traveled with music. Prisoners near Menelik marched to the beat of drums.[37] The relentless pace of travel preyed on the weak, and soldiers feared any setback—fever, injury—that might cause them to fall behind, abandoned to recover alone or, more likely, to die. Shoes were shared, with a pair being worn to allow scuffs, scrapes, and sores to heal before being passed on to relieve the suffering of another. At least one officer dismounted to allow a weakened soldier to ride in his place. Giovanni Tedone—exhausted and beset by fever—owed his life to the kindness of Major Giovanni Gamerra, who gave up his mule for five days while Tedone regained his health. "His name will forever be written on my heart," Tedone later wrote in gratitude.[38]

As the train of soldiers and prisoners moved south, hunger and exhaustion began to wear them down. Carlo Diotti's group came across the emaciated body of a sergeant, on whose face could be still be read the agony of his death. When Diotti and a few others stopped to bury him, they were beaten. The army itself was at risk; it must continue to move or others, too, would not survive.[39]

The weakest sat down to die in despair and resignation. Nicola D'Amato's group came across a wasted figure by the side of the road. His muscles had atrophied, and under dry skin that barely covered his bones, one could discern the paths of tendons. The specter made as if to stand, but he could not. "Mi chiamo Golfetto," he gasped. They recognized him as an officer, a lieutenant.[40]

As the column moved south through Tigray, it traversed a land that by tradition was rebellious toward Menelik's southern rule. It was also a land that had been depleted during Menelik's northward march a few months earlier. The landscape was littered with memories, too. At Amba Alage, evidence of Toselli's combat against the forces of Makonnen and Mangasha could be seen everywhere. Partial skeletons lay scattered about, dragged here and there by hyenas.[41]

Although one prisoner recalled receiving a "warm welcome" in village after village, most accounts suggest that there were limits to hospitality toward the army and that relations between soldiers and peasants were typically predatory. Even in the best of times, without tight control, soldiers readily slipped into a form of requisitioning barely distinguishable from marauding.[42] In this regard, the Ethiopian army was very much like modern European armies, who discovered that "war must feed on war."[43] Augustus Wylde, who knew Ethiopia well, described the southward return as an "incessant skirmish between the cultivators and the strangers."

Peasants often gave as well as they got. Some accounts call to mind the harried retreat of the Italian army from Adwa. Wylde describes locals watching the column pass, waiting for an opportunity to prey upon it; they "plundered the transport and murdered the stragglers." Wylde went so far as to claim that in retreat Menelik's army "lost more men in killed and wounded than they had . . . on the field of battle at Adwa."[44]

Some villages grudgingly provided food and shelter but demanded— and received—a three-year dispensation from providing such support again.[45] Peasants everywhere were well schooled in passive forms of resistance, such as burying food or driving off livestock. When a group of soldiers arrived in search of food at a farm, a cagey group of women was ready. They upset beehives, then barricaded themselves in a *tukul*, letting the bees drive off the soldiers.[46]

Still other villages flatly refused. Only iron discipline could prevent thievery by cold and hungry soldiers. Menelik's minister of justice issued a warning that he would execute any soldier caught stealing, and he meant it. An Ethiopian soldier caught taking firewood was brought before him.

"Everybody steals," protested the soldier in defense. The thief was cut down on the spot.[47] Despite such draconian discipline, injustices occurred and produced lasting resentment. A full year later, the road to Addis via Ashenge was deemed unsafe. Travelers from the north were advised to by-pass the area because of raids seeking "revenge for the depredations which Menelik's army had committed among them after the battle of Adwa."[48]

When one village resisted a request for food and shelter, soldiers threatened to burn it down. Peasants reluctantly vacated their huts for the prisoners, who packed in to escape the night chill. Huts that might have slept ten somehow had to accommodate fifty, as prisoners wedged them-selves into them in a desperate to escape the paralyzing cold. They could barely move, let alone lie down. They passed the night leaning against one another for support and warmth.[49]

Some days there would be no village on whom to impose the role of host. At the end of a day of marching, one group found themselves without shelter, without huts to commandeer, in a high, barren valley. With each southward step, the risk of flight had diminished, so the Ethiopians began to leave the Italians to fend for themselves. Exhausted, the prisoners lay on the ground. They shared body heat by aligning themselves chest to back, shins to calves, "like sardines in a can." When it was time to change sides, the group turned in unison, on command. The system provided some protection from the cold but no respite from the howling of hyenas. The men slept fitfully, praying for dawn.[50]

The Return of Plenty

For days, the main food consisted of *enjera* and butter. Finally, at Lake Ashenge, plenty returned. As the day's march ended, the prisoners watched as peasants led cattle and flocks of goats toward the royal kitchens. Lines of women followed bearing round amphoras of *tej* and baskets of *enjera*. Roustabouts put up the *das*—a vast banquet tent without walls. For the first time, the prisoners were to enjoy the warmth of Menelik's paternal embrace and the full measure of Ethiopian bounty in a banquet that sur-passed anything they had yet seen.

The royal party opened the festivities. They dined according to the customary private rituals. Then the *das* was opened to the chiefs and dignitaries, followed by the soldiers. Finally the prisoners were invited to join the banquet. The *das* might well have called to mind the town fairs and itinerant performers of home. Tall tent poles spaced nearly twenty feet apart supported a network of lighter supports carved from branches. Yards of white fabric were draped over to create a covered pavilion. Inside, the late spring daylight filtered through the cloth, giving a soft, shadowless glow to everything within. Portraits of Menelik and Taytu— patrons of the feast, should anyone forget—were affixed to the posts.[51] The prisoners seated themselves in long rows as musicians played horns and flutes.

They gorged themselves on *enjera* and emptied horns of *tej*. For prisoners who were veterans of Eritrea, *tej* was an old friend. But for the hundreds of men who had arrived in the weeks before the campaign, this was likely their first encounter with the drink, certainly any of the quality served at the court of Menelik and Taytu. *Tej* is made by fermenting hops and honey in water. The result is a drink comparable to bitter cider. As with wine and beer, practiced palates easily distinguish varieties by quality and region. Edward Gleichen, who was part of the British delegation to Addis, even noted the preferred styles of the various courts. "Makonnen's best tastes like sweet, strong old Madeira," he noted. He compared Menelik's *tej* to a Riesling. "The inferior kinds," Gleichen observed, "vary between bad sherry and sourish water with dead bees and lumps of wax and bark and earth floating in it."[52] The *tej* served the prisoners was probably somewhere in between, but by the end of the banquet it hardly mattered. Some of the men had trouble finding their way back to their huts, only to find them already stuffed with well-fed Italians. Some had to settle for a piece of bare ground under the stars.[53]

With desperate hunger at bay, in the days that followed, the prisoners could begin to appreciate the rugged and delicate beauty of east-central Ethiopia. To men still traumatized by want, they marveled at the hunter's paradise they traversed, populated with abundant prey. They eyed rabbits, fawns, and iridescent partridges, but they also gazed in wonder at francolins, a species of bird rarely seen outside Africa. They heard the song of the flute bird—smaller than a canary but with an oversized voice "as loud as a pipe organ."[54] They passed

An imperial banquet. From Guèbrè Sellassié, *Chronique du règne de Ménélik II, roi des rois d'Éthiopie.* Paris: Maisonneuve Frères, 1930.

mimosa and towering euphorbia, with pink and yellow flowers; spiny acacia offered a natural defense for nesting birds.

They were amazed, too, at the incessant flow of the Ethiopian army, with its soundtrack of drums, horns, and song. They caught rare glimpses of Empress Taytu, who went about veiled and surrounded by a large entourage. She remained aloof from the prisoners, her inaccessibility adding to an air of mystery.[55] No one gloried more than Taytu in the triumph of Adwa. As a northerner, she felt the Italian occupation keenly, and liberation was all the sweeter.

As the procession of notables and prisoners approached the capital, their ordeal was about to end, though new challenges loomed. The long march was a passage from dearth to plenty, and the risks had been shared by prisoners and guardians. By the end, many prisoners had gone from fear and resentment to relief and gratitude: their keepers had brought them safely through. Those who had traveled with Menelik and

Taytu knew they had experienced a rare privilege, but many lesser personages left the prisoners with abiding memories of kindness. Years later, prisoners readily brought to mind the names of their vigilant guardians: "Who can forget the courtesy of Ligg-Nado, of Ligg-Antali, and of Grasmag-Joseph?"[56]

CHAPTER 17

Sons and Lovers and
Accidental Anthropologists

O N 22 MAY 1896, Francesco Frisina and his group of prisoners reached the heights that rim the Ethiopian capital. The day before had been a day of frenetic activity. Horses were groomed; weapons were festooned. This triumph—a grand victory procession—would exceed the one that followed Menelik's triumph over the Welayta. Menelik had led an army north and defeated an invader. He was bringing back European prisoners—an emblem of prestige, a proof of valor, and, once redeemed, a fountain of wealth.

Addis Ababa sits in a basin more than seven thousand feet above sea level, but the approach from the north, by way of the wooded Entotto hills, reaches over nine thousand feet.[1] It was from this high approach that Menelik, Taytu, their army, and their prisoners entered the city. It was the greatest procession the city had ever seen. Taytu and her retinue were in their best; their bright-hued umbrellas were visible from a great distance. Their main competition came from the many *ras,* who wore splendid velvet capes with gold appliqué and embroidery for the occasion.[2] There was plenty of finery at lower ranks—tiger and leopard skins draped shoulders, while lion's manes formed soldierly halos. Sunlight flashed from harness and tack. Shields dazzled with their radiating strips of metal. Drums and *masenqo* provided a joyful sound track as the court and its army entered the capital to the clamor of voices.

As the emperor's entourage approached the imperial complex—a splendid white in the sunlight—cannon fired a salute. It was answered by celebratory rifle fire from the soldiers, launching a din that would go on for hours. At the palace, artillery pieces seized at Adwa were already in place, standing at attention as an honor guard, a row of trophies. Menelik turned to them as he passed; they answered with their mute testimony of historic triumph.[3]

Some visitors wondered whether "city" or even "town" was the right term for Addis. Edward Gleichen, who visited as part of a diplomatic mission in 1897, insisted on calling Addis a "camp."[4] The observation was fair enough, given that Addis was distinguished mainly not by the grandeur of its buildings or by their scale but by the sheer size of its population, which reached into the tens of thousands. Rome, Italy's capital at the same period, counted more than three hundred thousand. Except for the hilltop placement of the imperial complex, Addis was largely unplanned. There was no distinct commercial district outside the regular market, and there were no streets to speak of. But underneath a superficial randomness was an organization that reflected the system of patronage and favor that underpinned Ethiopian politics. The residences of major personalities at court defined entire neighborhoods. Menelik's advisors and provincial governors, the *ras*, needed to maintain a presence at court. Each kept a residence at Addis—Ras Michael's compound was to the north, Ras Dargé's was to the southeast. These were rather substantial residences, with walls of mud and wood. They, along with dependencies for servants and animals, typically were enclosed by a protective palisade. As there was no permanent housing for an entourage, the palisade was, in turn, surrounded by tents. The capital thus had the appearance of a makeshift, as indeed it should given that it was barely ten years old.[5]

The monumental feature that gave a hint of the importance of Addis was the imperial residence. On a hilltop at the center, visitors could make out a vast compound of white buildings, the *ghebi*—the Imperial Palace and grounds.[6] The main residence, the *elfign*, was an octagonal two-story building with red tile roof. It dominated the capital, with territorial views in all directions. Alongside were a reception hall and dining facility capable of seating more than six hundred guests. Then came the treasury and the post and telegraph office. Finally, there were kitchen gardens, storehouses, and other dependencies, including royal stables and saddlery, barracks for the imperial guard, workshops, storehouses, a clock tower, and a chapel. Eucalyptus trees, ubiquitous today in Addis, had recently been introduced to combat deforestation. They provided shade and relief, but above all wood. Without these fast-growing trees, a scarcity of timber would have obliged the court to abandon the capital after a few years. All around the imperial enclosure were smaller compounds made up of the homes of leading officers in Menelik's government. *Tukul* dotted the hillside below—housing for the thousands of servants to the imperial household.[7]

For much of the decade that Addis Ababa had been Menelik's capital, it was little more than a garrison town. Shoa, the kingdom from which Menelik's rise to imperial power was launched, was in the southernmost reaches of the historic lands of Abyssinia. As it was a frontier town, security was paramount, and as the base for Menelik's expansion plans, it was well situated for the dispatch of armed forces to the east and south.[8] With the conquest of Harar in 1887, Menelik gave his capital breathing space to the east. It also established Addis as the terminus of goods trans-shipped from the coast via Harar. The population boomed.

During the famine of 1889–1892, brought about by a plague among livestock, people from miles around flocked to the capital in search of succor and royal charity.[9] Many remade their lives and stayed. The campaign against the Welayta in 1894 extended Menelik's rule to the southwest, completing a healthy territorial buffer around Shoa. Although turn-of-the-century visitors could still complain that Addis was more a military camp than a city, by the mid-1890s it had the security it needed to develop as the political and economic capital of Shoa and, soon enough, of Ethiopia itself.[10] Trade displaced security among the preoccupations of the capital; the place of the army as the motor of life of Addis diminished.

Merchants—French, Armenian, Jewish, Indian, Greek—began to appear, arriving with the goods they brought up from Obock, Tadjoura, and Djibouti on the Somali coast. By the end of the century, the population had reached fifty thousand.[11]

Captive Residents

With the arrival of the prisoners, life in the capital was considerably enriched. Ethiopia had no experience of prisoners as such. Captives from the successful campaign against the Welayta were enslaved; they served as domestic servants to Menelik, his officers, and their men. The Italians were different. Their value lay in their utility as leverage in peace negotiations and in their redemption value. Menelik knew that he had a valuable asset in the nearly two thousand Italians now in his custody; what to do with them would be a matter of improvisation. There were no prisons or prisoner camps, no institutionalized system for the control and feeding of the Europeans in his care. To concentrate them in one place solved a security problem but raised a host of health and humanitarian concerns.

Menelik decided to billet the prisoners on the population. The Italians would be farmed out. Menelik's closest associates and advisors were tapped for the task of caring for the captives; about one-third of the prisoners remained in the capital.[12] The remainder were dispersed among the wider population—from Lasta to Harar. Over the course of their captivity, a few attempted escape but, as Europeans were hard to miss, all were captured before they reached Harar.[13] Most were content to live out their captivity in relative comfort, waiting for the negotiated release that would allow them to go home.

The result was a rainbow of experiences as, for the first time in colonial-era Africa, Europeans and Africans lived side by side in great numbers as equals. Although the Italians were prisoners and thus subordinate to their Ethiopian hosts, as a practical matter they were accorded great freedom, with the sole proviso that they not leave. In Addis, the prisoners had the run of the city.[14] Some became close to their guardians. A few became lovers.[15] A surprising number confided the details of their experience to journals, diaries, and memoirs. The result is a trove of material that gives us some of our best evidence about personalities, practices, and everyday life in Menelik's Ethiopia.

For Ethiopians and Italians, proximity meant the humanization of the other. Italians found that the Oromo cavalry, who had been elevated in their imaginations to the status of supernatural phantom warriors, were human. The Ethiopians, in turn, overcame their initial dislike for white men and learned that their odors were no more disagreeable than any other. Prejudices and fantasies worked themselves out.[16] Carlo Diotti found that one of his neighbors was fond of touching him—face, feet, arms—marveling at the difference in skin.[17]

The prisoners soon had an established hierarchy among themselves. Businesses were founded; households were established; social invitations went out. Addis Ababa now had a Little Italy. It faithfully reproduced the prejudices of home, in which Calabresi and Sicilians competed with Neapolitans to escape the very bottom of the social scale. It was said that the Neapolitans lost.[18]

As soon as they could, prisoners set out to create the cultural niceties of home. A large *tukul* became a theater. Inside, a team of artists stitched together a backdrop of cardboard and fabric. On either side of the drop were charcoal sketches of the emblems of theater—masks of Comedy and Tragedy, musical instruments, a lyre, books with the titles of famous operas and the names of famous composers. On the drop itself, center top, were the royal arms of the House of Savoy. Below was a charming scene—a panorama of Naples, featuring Posillipo, Capri, the bay, the sea, and mighty Vesuvius belching smoke.[19] Soon the theater had a name—the San Carlino of Addis Ababa, a nod to the Teatro San Carlo of Naples—and a reputation for its comic repertoire. San Carlino was a lifeline for Little Italy during the rainy season.[20]

A theater calls for a bar. Soon enough, one appeared. Within weeks Menelik's Saloon, as it was known informally, emerged as the preferred gathering place in expat Addis.[21] The success of Menelik's Saloon drew the attention of the real Menelik, who decided to get into the restaurant business for himself. He created a very successful trattoria featuring café tables and chairs with seating for forty under a massive tent. Clients were served in the Ethiopian style, that is, without cutlery. The *menu fixe* included a plate of meat, a side dish, bread—the latter reportedly "very good"—and a half liter of *tej*. Total cost? An eighth of a thaler—about a nickel.[22]

Menelik's trattoria also served as an informal popularity index for certain figures. When Casimir Mondon-Vidailhet, Menelik's de facto publicist, started patronizing the trattoria, the place emptied. Mondon's scathing commentaries on Italy and the Italians for the French newspaper *Le Temps* had made him very unpopular among Menelik's core clientele. Mondon had once remarked in print that the Ethiopians were more civilized "than the Egyptians, the Neapolitans, and even other Europeans"—a sly and funny turn on European racism, but also rude and bound to hurt.[23] When Mondon figured out that his presence was undermining Menelik's business, he stopped frequenting it. The boycott ended and the clientele returned.[24]

Shortly after their arrival in Addis, Menelik issued a lamb to each prisoner along with three thalers and small change in the form of seven salt bars. It was enough to barter for or buy clothing and necessities.[25] Ras Michael distributed cash, too. The Addis economy boomed. Prisoners soon discovered the teeming marketplace of Addis Ababa, which was a kilometer in length and nearly a third as wide, already one of the largest open markets in Africa.[26] Although the market operated six days a week from sunup to sundown, Saturday was the day of the grand market, drawing vendors from miles around. At first the prisoners were greeted with insults, as defeated soldiers.[27] Their shabby dress, after days on the march, didn't help. An enterprising Greek merchant took pity on prisoners clothed only in rags. On a hunch, he brought clothes up from the coast and gave them to the prisoners. He sent the bill to the Italian government, which reimbursed him.[28]

Soon enough the presence of the prisoners became commonplace, even desirable, as their role shifted from enemy to buyer. At the market, they elbowed their way between clients in bright *shammas* and ducked as they passed the gaudy parasols preferred by women of standing.[29] When they waded into the chattering mix of sellers and buyers, they could take in the array of goods laid out on blankets and in shallow baskets. There were bananas, eggs, cabbages, tobacco, ground red pepper, and rancid butter. Home furnishings and weapons lay alongside red clay jugs, leather sandals, muslin, sailcloth, rifle ammo, cowhides, and jewelry both decorative and practical (for warding off the evil eye). Goods were organized by type. There were notions of all kinds (thread, buttons, wax) as well as farm animals (goats, chickens, donkeys) and specialty items such as mirrors and leaf tobacco. Those tired of sleeping on straw could find ready vendors of beds made of cowhide stretched over a wooden frame.[30]

There was a lively trade in salvaged castoffs—kerosene tins, slivers of mirror, jam jars (sold as drinking cups), stray buttons—and stolen goods. The market was a place where goods and their former owners could be reunited for a price; whether one saw it as a for-profit lost-and-found or a massive fencing operation depended on one's point of view. Into this gray/black market fell war booty, too, including the unmistakable reminders of fallen comrades. Some were anonymous (a pair of shoes, a helmet, eyeglasses), some traceable to particular individuals (the wallet and spurs of Colonel Airaghi, the monogrammed cape of an artillery officer), some deeply personal (a diary, a family photo, a farewell letter to a loved one). The prisoners were avid buyers; they were keen to keep personal items of fallen friends from becoming mere commodities, but the number of goods was vast, beyond the resources of the soldiers. Sometimes the prisoners' hosts intervened to take things off the market. When Nicola D'Amato discovered the journal of a dear friend for sale, he couldn't afford the asking price. Ato Gabriel, his host, bought it for him.[31]

One prisoner reported that two French merchants, Messieurs Troillet and Stévenin, operated a kind of wholesale business in items taken from the fallen. This allowed those who had harvested helmets, jackets, revolvers, and shoes to convert them to cash immediately, while Troillet and Stévenin doled out the items on the retail market. They also did an extraordinary business in currency conversion. As Ethiopian soldiers brought in cash taken from fallen Italians, Troillet and Stévenin converted these lire to thalers—at a steep discount.[32] Among Italian prisoners, Troillet and Stévenin were some of the least popular European expats, bottom-feeders in a dismal predatory economy.

The prisoners became laborers. The amount of labor expected depended entirely upon the person to whom they were assigned. Some were employed in the backbreaking work of road construction in the provinces; they were paid a modest wage. Those with rare skills in carpentry, blacksmithing, and construction found themselves working directly for Menelik. Though there was some talk that Menelik would use his vast labor reserve of prisoners to build himself a capital city in the European style, the main work focused on the emperor's government complex.[33] Twenty-four prisoners labored as carpenters, building out Menelik's imperial compound.[34] Visitors to Menelik would walk past a furniture shop where a group of prisoners constructed tables, stools, and chairs. There was a forge and, at the end, a tailor's shop where a prisoner labored over a Singer sewing machine.[35]

Still others experienced something akin to house arrest: they had room and board with the single inconvenient limitation that they were forbidden to leave the country.[36] Physicians were particularly prized, a fact that had become abundantly clear during the long march from Adwa. Although the average prisoner was farmed out to the countryside, Menelik kept physicians in Addis for the services they could render him and his soldiers. Once in Addis, Italian physicians enjoyed the high regard and trust of Menelik himself. They were housed within the imperial complex and entrusted with postal operations for the prisoner population. The physicians' *tukul* became the unofficial general delivery address for prisoners.[37]

Prisoners of Love

The perception that captivity in the capital was to be preferred inspired the faking or exaggeration of skills. Sooner or later, faked credentials were exposed. Carlo Diotti didn't claim to be a physician, but he was so desperate to stay in Addis he claimed another prized skill—carpentry. His ineptitude became evident when he was assigned to a work crew. He avoided deportation to the provinces by founding a household with his friend Giovanni Rossi, who made a decent living working for the French merchant Armand Savouré and his import-export business. While Rossi went off each day to work for Savouré or, occasionally, at the imperial complex, Diotti labored as cook, bookkeeper, housemaster, and laundryman. Soon he was making candles, fattening chickens, learning to cook risotto, and dashing off to the market to buy butter, eggs, and soap. "I gave myself completely to the life of the housewife," he noted. With Rossi as breadwinner and Diotti as homemaker, they got by. Thanks to Rossi's solid income, they soon saved enough to buy a bed.

With Rossi away at work, Diotti sought companionship among his neighbors. He became particularly fond of Tuavensc, the Tigrayan wife of a young Shoan often away on business. Tuavensc treated Diotti "like a brother." She listened to his stories of home and shared his tears when he recalled his family. In time, Diotti and Rossi were joined in their household by a third prisoner, known as Orfeo.[38]

The Ethiopian calendar, like the Gregorian calendar, is packed with feast days. Just as the pleasures of life in the capital could be exaggerated, so could the challenges of life outside of Addis. Augustus Wylde recounted seeing a group of five Italians in straw hats walking arm in arm, singing as they went. They were the wards of a man Wylde identified as "Dedjatch Imma"—a tall, jolly, fat man who prided himself on his qualities as a host. Imma was an epicurean. His aim, he explained, was to make his Italian wards as fat as he was. Imma was distressed that Menelik had not allowed him to go to war, judging him too fat to do so. Just the same, he had asked for his quota of prisoners, who surely felt they had done very well by themselves. Imma served a fine meal with "the most excellent *tej* and coffee" and was entirely without the antiwhite prejudice other prisoners encountered.[39]

As Ethiopians of even modest means were expected to take in prisoners, the experience of some prisoners—living as members of Ethiopian families—anticipated the home stays of exchange students. For some, imprisonment was an ethnological exercise. For others, there was unanticipated intimacy. In some cases, deep attachments formed.

The beginning was tentative and sometimes rocky. First, there was the widespread perception among Ethiopians that Europeans, especially Italians, were stinky. Proximity is the enemy of prejudice; the image of the odiferous European crumbled. Moreover, both Ethiopians and Italians are famous for their accommodating standards of intimacy. Soon enough, curiosity and desire won out.

The details of such relationships can be difficult to come by, but certain circumstances overcame discretion. An Italian corporal confined to Addis found friendship with an Ethiopian woman. When the corporal was accused of battery by an Ethiopian, he could prove his innocence only thanks to the testimony of his lover. She assured the court that they were alone together at the time of the alleged offense. Their happy life resumed until her testimony was relayed to her husband.

Francesco Frisina, who passed his imprisonment in the Lasta region, developed a deep affection for Doiomico, the man who hosted him. At the end of his stay, he showered Doiomico with gifts that arrived with the Italian Red Cross. Soap, canned fruit, paper, pencils, cigars, liquor—Frisina couldn't do enough. Years later, he remembered Doiomico "like a father" and promised that he would never be erased from his heart.

Giovanni Tedone was billeted upon an Ethiopian family near Harar. He carried the bitterness of his Adwa battlefield experiences into captivity. In fact, unlike most of his fellow memoirists, he brought them with him back to Italy. And although his contact with Ethiopians was mostly limited to the Oromo, from the south, he was given to broad statements about the Ethiopian character.

"The Abyssinian," he wrote, "is lazy by nature." "He sucks like a vampire everything he can suck." One of the only notes of admiration in Tedone's remarks concerns the talent of the Ethiopian soldier, but even that he offers as a backhanded compliment. "The only exercise to which [the Ethiopians] dedicate themselves with any frequency [is the art of spear throwing]," he noted. The challenge consists of planting a stick in the ground, then trying to hit it with a lance from about 150 feet. "In this kind of fire, they achieve perfection," he admitted. Several times Tedone had witnessed tosses of the lance landing "little more than a finger's width" from the target.

Tedone was assigned to a village in the Harar region. The village—a hamlet, really—consisted of three households. The cock of the walk in the village was a man named Birru, a jealous husband to six wives. Birru's wives had never seen a white man. Once they got over their natural repugnance toward Tedone, they felt a powerful urge to touch him. Tedone—taking counsel from prudence rather than nature—was reluctant to allow himself to be fondled. A wary Birru recommended that Tedone find a wife of his own.

It was the beginning of a vexed relationship, one that turned on questions of manliness. As a prisoner, Tedone's days were full of nothing. This left him without an alibi when Birru suggested that Tedone attend a "lesson" in spear throwing, an art at which Birru excelled. While Tedone witnessed Birru's displays of soldierly *virtù*, Birru would move the conversation around to the subject of Adwa. Tedone chalked this up not to a malicious spirit but only to Birru's lack of tact.

One day, after three expert throws from Birru, Tedone politely expressed his admiration. "At Adwa, I killed eight Italians," Birru boasted. "And I castrated them." Birru proudly raised his tunic to reveal a necklace on which he had strung the irrefutable proof of his conquests.

Tedone found himself plumb out of compliments. "You disgust me," he shouted, and stormed off to his *tukul*. But the conversation wasn't over for Birru. He pursued Tedone. Exasperated, Tedone grabbed some ears of corn, arranged them on the ground in the shape of a fort, and called Birru over. "At Adwa you won with a limitless supply of men," he scolded. "At Mekele, a handful of men kept you at bay for three months; we blew you sky high." As a demonstration, Tedone took some more ears of corn and marched them toward his makeshift fort, only to make them bounce off the corncob walls. Birru shivered. "Yes, but they hid inside!" Birru cried. "We fought in the open." End of conversation.

Eventually Tedone was able to break free of Birru's hospitality and become the guest of another household. There Tedone became the reluctant prize in a different kind of combat. Zandietu, a young woman, wanted Tedone. "Thirsty for love" is how Tedone described her.

Giovanni Tedone was a handsome young man of twenty-four. He had a broad jaw and rugged chin. He preferred to wear his full mustache fashionably upturned at the ends, in the manner made popular by the German emperor Wilhelm II. For his studio portrait he had donned his *bersaglieri* uniform, accessorized with two symbols of leadership—a riding crop and a holstered pistol. Full, bushy eyebrows framed dark, deep-set eyes that suggested a wistful, pensive side. Chiseled, exotic, manly yet sentimental—Tedone was catnip to Zandietu.

While Tedone's style was complicated and thoughtful, Zandietu's emphasized candor. She made a "magnificent declaration" of love to Tedone, a declaration both "clear and explicit." She would be very happy to be his wife. Her intentions were good; she wasn't interested in a dalliance. She was ready to follow him back to Italy. Not only was Tedone good-looking, but he was her ticket out.

Tedone was a hard sell. For reasons of his own, he wasn't interested in Zandietu. But he was afraid that if he snubbed her advances, she would retaliate by making his life miserable. The result was an interminable courtship wherein a coy Tedone gently rebuffed Zandietu's amorous sallies. Tedone was a prisoner of love.

Zandietu redoubled her efforts. She played the attentive spouse. "My every wish was her command," he wrote. When she closed in, Tedone would parry with excuses. Zandietu became impatient and ever more direct. Her flirtations became a lesson in cross-cultural misunderstanding. Everything she did to make herself irresistible backfired. She applied more rancid butter to make her skin soft and silky. She darkened her eyelids and painted her nails (not yet common among European women as marks of beauty).

She tried jealousy. After a particularly emphatic rejection from Tedone, she threatened to take a lover. "I'll call for the son of Fitawrari Gabriel and make him sleep with me," she boasted, thinking that competition from a celebrated soldier would ignite Tedone's desire. "And I'll make you watch!" Nice move, but Tedone wasn't buying. He shrugged off her threat. Just when it seemed that Tedone's only option was to move back in with the merciless Birru, he got word that he was going home.

The Mouth of the Negus

Gherardo Pantano experienced imprisonment as an awakening. He had joined the military as a young man, inspired by a desire to avenge the massacre at Dogali. He was in military school at Modena when he heard the news of the massacre and immediately volunteered for service in Africa. Perhaps because of his cadet status, he was passed over. He noted that Italy lacked a strong "colonial consciousness," as did Pantano himself. Why should Italians leave Italy, he wondered, "to suffer a thousand unpleasant things, in order to undertake pointless enterprises?"[40] While incidentally validating the basic good sense of the Italian people, Pantano confessed that his own motives were personal. As an aspiring officer, he understood that the strenuous pursuit of "pointless enterprises" was precisely how careers could be made.

Pantano's hunch about building a career abroad turned out to be correct; he would retire at the rank of general. In the short run, however, he had his doubts. At Adwa, he had been a lieutenant assigned to an askari battalion in Albertone's brigade. On 1 March his job had been to help hold Albertone's left; he had watched men fall around him but was taken prisoner, apparently unharmed. He was paraded before Menelik by his captors as proof of their valor.[41]

He then had the good fortune to fall into the custody of one of Menelik's most powerful and trusted officers, Nesibu, Menelik's *afa negus,* or

Afa Negus Nesibu. From Guèbrè Sellassié, *Chronique du règne de Ménélik II, roi des rois d'Éthiopie.* Paris: Maisonneuve Frères, 1930.

minister of justice. Pantano knew nothing of the authority of the *afa negus,* but he soon learned. He underwent an interrogation, and when he asked by whose authority he was being questioned, Pantano was told, "You are in the house of Afa Negus Nesibu, minister of justice of the emperor, a powerful and influential leader."[42]

When he finally met Nesibu, he gradually learned to trust him. The elderly Nesibu took a paternal interest in Pantano; he told him that he would do everything in his power to let Pantano's family know that he was alive. He then asked to see Pantano's ring. Pantano gave it to him. Nesibu tried it on all of his fingers, but it was too large for Nesibu's slender hands. He passed it to his wife, who looked it over, then returned it to Pantano.

"Why didn't anyone take this from you?" Nesibu demanded.

"Because I hid it," Pantano responded.

"And why are you wearing it now?" Nesibu asked.

"Because I understand that no one will take it."

The answer pleased Nesibu, who took it as a compliment—even as a providential sign. "You are a son, given to me by God. My house is yours; ask for what you need."

Over the months to come, the relationship deepened. In Addis, Nesibu housed Pantano at his private compound—a minor village of buildings and dependences within the capital. Nesibu gave Pantano a large *tukul* Nesibu typically used as his receiving room. It was a clear honor, in that Pantano enjoyed large private quarters, and it gave Pantano a close look at the everyday life of a major figure in Menelik's government.

Nesibu had a doting mother to thank for a plum appointment in Menelik's government. Nesibu's mother wanted a scholar for a son. As soon as Nesibu was ready to learn, she set before him a series of memory tasks. Soon, in a hothouse education reminiscent of John Stuart Mill, Nesibu put his mind to mastering the Ethiopian legal code. That code, the Fetha Nagast, blended scripture with Roman law and other legal influences.[43] Its association with the dominant religion, the Ethiopian Church, gave it a particular force, as did its apodictic style—the law was given, some of it was even the word of God, and that was that.

The fact of the matter was that the code was too vast for anyone to master entirely. Moreover, as in any legal code, there was room for interpretation. At eighteen, Nesibu was already representing clients at court. With his broad learning and his gift for rhetoric, he won some notable victories—including a few against the government. Nesibu's reputation grew, and his practice flourished. Rather than leave such a formidable talent on the loose, Menelik did what any responsible administrator would do—he hired him.

Or at least he tried. The job Menelik offered was that of *afa negus*, literally "the king's mouth." The title spoke volumes about the sway Nesibu would hold. His functions would blend those of attorney general and minister of justice. The power and wealth were attractive—Nesibu would sit at Menelik's right hand—but Nesibu was proud and feared that the position would cost him his independence, so he resisted. Menelik threw him in jail, setting a single condition for his freedom: that he accept the job. The next day, Nesibu relented.[44]

By custom, the emperor is the ultimate interpreter of the law, and until very late in his reign Menelik frequently sat personally in judgment, rendering justice and embodying the law. As his proxy and standby, Nesibu bore a grave responsibility—to do nothing to diminish the law or the stature of Menelik. Over time, he came to dress like Menelik—black satin cape with embroidered lapel, bandana of white cotton or silk wrapped about the head and tied tightly at the neck, wide-brimmed felt hat.[45] Unlike Menelik, whose pockmarked face gave him a raw, rugged look—a man's man—Nesibu's fine, golden brown complexion and smooth skin gave him a softness that accentuated the perception that this was a man of sophistication and discernment.[46] In a court of strikingly handsome men—Makonnen, Mangasha, Wele—Nesibu could hold his own.

By the time Nesibu adopted Pantano as "the son sent by God," he looked the part of a wealthy man, long accustomed to a life of leisure. He was round, giving him an air of jolliness that belied the gravity of the decisions he handed down.[47]

Pantano impressed his host with his knowledge of scripture. Even Nesibu's chaplain had spotty knowledge regarding some biblical tales. When Pantano could tell the chaplain the names of the three magi—especially the African king—the chaplain was so taken by this evidence of learning that he and Nesibu began to refer to Pantano as *abbatie*, "father"—a title normally reserved for clergy.[48]

One morning Nesibu invited Pantano to accompany him to work. The courthouse was an amphitheater—a semicircle of stairs radiating out from a covered platform where Nesibu sat in judgment as the *afa negus*. Beside the *afa negus* were pages and consultants. Opposite them were the attorneys and their clients along with the accused and the defendant, to the left and right respectively.

Nesibu quickly dispensed with a number of minor cases, handing down decisions involving modest cash payments in restitution or, in injury cases, lashes of the whip. The main case for the day involved a love triangle that resulted in murder. A young woman had been promised in marriage to one man, but she loved another and chose to marry him instead. The jilted fiancé nursed his humiliation and turned it to jealous rage. He pursued his successful rival and killed him with a stone to the temple.

The young widow buried her husband, then sought justice. She had the killer brought before the *afa negus,* where he admitted his guilt. Nesibu offered the widow a choice of compensations—240 thalers in payment or the death of the accused. The sum was huge, but the widow was inconsolable and bent on vengeance. When asked whether she would accept the offer of blood money, she uttered a single word: "No."

Nesibu spoke. "The man is yours. Do with him as you will."

"Let him be taken to Finfinne," the widow responded. Bailiffs appeared, one at each arm, and led the prisoner away.

Finfinne was once the name for the Addis region as a whole. It came to refer to a place of punishment of criminals on the outskirts of the city—a place where an eye is taken for an eye and the hands of thieves are hacked away in scriptural splendor. There, the jilted fiancé begged for forgiveness, throwing himself at the feet of the woman whose husband he had killed. Instead, the widow raised a heavy stone above her head, then let it fall onto the head of the murderer, crushing it. The crowd erupted in shouts. The women ululated, filling the air with the cry of victory.[49] The widow, her *shamma* spattered with blood, walked away in a daze.

That night, the tranquility of Nesibu's household was shattered by the urgent beating of drums, a signal of community alarm. Answering the call of the drums, they came upon an awesome scene. Under a full moon, the widow stood in the middle of a circle formed by her friends. Her hair was cut short in mourning and her *shamma* had fallen to her waist. The movements of her arms and shoulders were sharp, following the rhythm of the drums. She stooped, fell, rose, moved in abrupt dance, then posed as if frozen, letting out cries from time to time.

As Pantano saw it, although justice had been done, it could not touch her anguish, which had now taken hold of her body. Grief owned her. Only by moving could she rid herself of the torment. Her movements became more abrupt, more demonic, until she collapsed. Her family carried her limp body home. The scene was repeatedly nightly until the pain let go and her body was hers again.[50]

Nesibu was frequently called upon to adjudicate disputes between Italians and Ethiopians—some substantial, some trivial. In one case, an Italian soldier brought charges of fraud against an Ethiopian woman. The Italian soldier and the Ethiopian woman appeared before Nesibu. The exchange went as follows:

Nesibu: What did you give to this woman?

Soldier: A thaler, in exchange for five kisses.

Nesibu: And?

Soldier: She gave me four, but then her husband came back. She should give me another kiss or give me back my money.

Nesibu ruled in favor of the soldier, who got back his money.[51]

CHAPTER 18

Menelik Abroad

ONE AFTERNOON late in 1896, Fred Holland Day left his Pinckney Street studio and headed to South Boston. He had an idea for a photograph and he needed a model.

Day had sought out "exotic" models before. They weren't hard to find in late nineteenth-century Boston. Fully one-third of the city's population in the 1890s was foreign-born, and many of them were dependent upon private charity for any hope of personal advancement. Fred Day was from a patrician family and, following his mother's philanthropic lead, he inserted himself into Boston's private charity network. Day volunteered as a tutor and mentor; social workers referred particularly promising young people to him.[1] Day cultivated young talent, and he used his charitable contacts to recruit models for his photographic work. Day had made a striking series of photos of the young Lebanese American immigrant Khalil Gibran, better known today as the author of mystical and sentimental aphorisms published under the title *The Prophet*.[2]

On this day, he was looking for an African American. Back in the studio, Day dressed his African American model as he imagined an African king might dress. For one composition, Day draped his model in a coarse wool wrap and arranged dark pigeon feathers so that they descended from a wide headband. For another series, Day's model stood holding a spear; in yet another, the model wore brass bracelets, chest medallions, and a crown as he sat on leopard skin. For his most striking portrait Day had his model adopt a solemn, confident regard. The model didn't look directly into Day's lens; he looked beyond it, over and beyond the left shoulder of the viewer.

Although some aspects of Day's photos strike us today as naive—the pigeon feather headband, the loose wool wrap, the bronze medallion—if we can look past the comic Africanisms, there's no mistaking where he was going with this work. The titles provide the clue: "Ethiopian Monarch" was one, "Menelek" was another. Day, a privileged but socially aware Bostonian, staged his photos in the weeks following Adwa, as the press and public opinion absorbed the enormity of the event. Day's charged tableaux, like Adwa itself, defied classic categories of Western domination and Oriental submission. His "Menelek" transposed Adwa to the vexed context of post-emancipation America, where it served as a touchstone in the global history of peoples of European and African descent. In the end, what was Adwa if not the story of Africans seeing to their own freedom?

By one of those accidents of timing that feeds ironic juxtaposition, the day before the Adwa story broke stateside, the *Atlanta Constitution* ran a story ridiculing the back-to-Africa aspirations of three hundred African Americans who were to leave Savannah, Georgia, for Africa on 1 March. The article broadened out into a prediction of the collapse of African sovereignty, as Africa was partitioned by Europeans.

It was a point that no doubt made perfect sense the day it was written. It was somewhat less certain after the first of March.

The position articulated by the *Constitution* links the assumptions underpinning Jim Crow and empire. Eighteen ninety-six was the year of *Plessy v. Ferguson,* the Supreme Court decision affirming the constitutionality of "separate but equal," the legal cornerstone of Jim Crow. Atlanta's newspaper embraced a wider vision, a kind of Atlantic dominion—the future of Africa would take shape under European rule, just as contemporary America had taken shape under the rule of European Americans. African Americans, whether committed to an American future or headed back to Africa, faced an equally grim prospect of life under European rule.[3] In short, the culture of Jim Crow thrived in an atmosphere of presumed racial superiority during the age of high empire. Empire was cousin to Jim Crow.

But Adwa shattered the confident assertion of African servitude displayed in the pages of the *Atlanta Constitution,* at least initially. The lead story on 4 March reported little more than that the Abyssinians had killed three thousand Italian soldiers. It also reported the erroneous news that the Italian commanding officer, General Oreste Baratieri, burdened by the shame of defeat, had taken his own life.[4] Subsequent stories featured significant errors of fact, betraying either a prodigious ignorance of Africa or a kind of psychological disarray.[5] An article headed "Italy's Hard Luck" put Ethiopia in South Africa and preferred, as the title suggests, to emphasize Italian misfortune over Ethiopian military prowess.[6]

Finally, the *Atlanta Constitution* began to question how black the Ethiopians really were. An article entitled "The Abyssinian Question" revealed an astonishing mastery of African racial characteristics—a prodigious racial science—and recommended to readers a close study of Ethiopian features. It asserted that the Ethiopians "are not of the flat-footed and splay-nosed Hottentot variety," raised doubts about how much they had in common with Africans of the Congo, and ended by asserting that they were, in fact, "of Phoenician origin," that is to say, not black at all.[7] This view was sustained by some of the images the *Constitution* published with its stories. In fact, the first portrait of Menelik published by the *Constitution* as the story broke revealed a striking similarity between the emperor of Ethiopia and Czar Nicholas II, who had acceded to the throne of imperial Russia a year earlier.[8]

Confusion seemed to increase with news of the scope of the disaster. But rather than leave the impression that the whitening of Menelik was part of a distinctly southern perspective on Adwa, it is worth pointing out that the *New York World* ran a story to similar effect, and the *Chicago Tribune* picked up the *New York World* story and carried it the following day. Thus, major newspapers in the South, in the Midwest, and on the Atlantic seaboard all carried stories regarding Caucasian Ethiopia. The *New York World* flatly stated that "the majority of the inhabitants of Abyssinia are of the Caucasian race," adding for good measure the reassuring claim that they "are well formed and handsome."[9]

ITALIANS FELL,

Abyssinians Killed 3,000 of of Baratieri's Men.

KING MENELIK VICTORIOUS

SECOND ITALIAN FAILURE

Captured Many Prisoners and Sixty Field Pieces.

Baratieri Is Said To Have Committed Suicide.

HE HAD BEEN ORDERED HOME

Abyssinian Campaign Has Proved Most Disastrous—Ministers' Resignation Refused.

Rome, March 3.—The Italian campaign against the Abyssinians threatens to become one of the most disastrous in which the Italian arms have ever taken part, and that the final outcome will be it would be hard to predict.

It was rumored today that the latest defeat of the Italians by the forces of King Menelik had compelled the ministry to resign, owing to the popular disapproval of the government's policy, but tonight this report is denied.

Details received here today of the defeat on Sunday of the Italian army, show

intentions. A persistent rumor circulates that the cabinet will retire. King Humbert today had interviews with Prime Minister Crispi and Signor Farini, president of the senate.

The Italians are said to have lost sixty guns and all their provisions.

Another Crushing Defeat.

This is the second crushing defeat that the Abyssinians have inflicted upon the Italians since the latter attempted to extend their power in the domain of King Menelik.

About three months ago five companies of Italian troops, under command of Major Tosselli, was surprised and surrounded by a force of 25,000 Abyssinians. The Italians made a desperate resistance and fought until their ammunition was ex-

KING MENELIK.

He Is the Monarch, and Commander in Chief of Abyssinnia's Forces.

hausted, when the Abyssinians charged them and massacred nearly the whole force. Fifteen Italian officers and over 700 men were killed.

Only a small number of the Italians succeeded in breaking through the beleaguring lines and making their escape to Makalle. Subsequently the Abyssinians besieged Makalle, and after practically reducing it, allowed the garrison to evacuate the place with their arms and baggage.

Why Baratieri Attacked.

All the available transport steamers have been ordered to assemble at Naples on March 7th to convey re-enforcements to Abyssinia.

General Baldissera, who was recently appointed to succeed General Baratieri in the chief command of the Italian forces in Africa, has arrived in Massowah. It is reported that Baratieri's attack upon the Abyssinian army on Sunday was the re-

A LAW AGAINST GOLD CONTR

Governor McLaurin Sends a Message To Legislature

GIVES HIGH AUT

Asks That Contracts Payabl sively in Gold Be Stopp

THE DANGER THAT IS I

Silver and Gold Should Both Tender, He Says—Full T His Message.

Jackson, Miss., March 3.—Fo a special message from Governor which was read to both houses islature today:

"Executive Office, Jackson, Mi 3.—To the Senate and House sentatives: I respectfully recor your consideration the suggestion enact such law as will prohibit t hereafter of contracts payable in gold. Money is the blood of stroy the money of the people gation of their interests and w of the prosperity of the state.

"By the constitution of the Un (section 8 of article I) the pow gated to congress to coin money late its value. Proceeding unde thority and exercising this p gress has coined a quantity of silver and regulated its value people ought to have the right culation of this coin as the mo state. I say the people ought t right to the circulation of thi cause all the money thus coined in the business of the country, add a great deal more could be utilized.

"I do not suppose it will be se serted by any one that there is in the United States there is no serve the uses of money in order the greatest prosperity to all of this country. Nor do I supp be seriously contended that the money can be materially decreas hurtful results.

Where a Premium Aris

Menelik in America. From the *Atlanta Constitution*, 4 March 1896.

The American press reaction to Adwa in some ways mirrored that of the European press. Upon learning of the Italian defeat at Adwa, the *Times* of London, for example, immediately entered into speculation on the battle's significance for the Triple Alliance, which since 1882 had linked Italy in a defensive agreement with Austria and imperial Germany. The Berlin correspondent to the London *Times* openly asked how Italy could fulfill its treaty obligations in Europe if it could not win in Africa.[10] On the western shores of the Atlantic, the *New York Times* picked up this angle, too, although perhaps we shouldn't read too much into this; in earlier editions it had given equal prominence to alarming reports that Columbia University was about to drop Greek as a required part of its core curriculum.[11]

Marketing Menelik

As for Ethiopia's imperial couple, marketing of their image shifted into high gear. Although neither Taytu nor Menelik ever left Ethiopia, thanks to Adwa their images joined an emerging economy of celebrity culture. In 1897, *Vanity Fair* featured Menelik as the subject of its colored lithograph—a distinction roughly analogous to making the cover of *Time* magazine in twentieth-century America. Thanks to *Vanity Fair,* Menelik was vaulted into the company of such international celebrities as Charles Darwin, Czar Alexander, and Napoleon III; he was tagged "quite an enlightened monarch." The Musée Grevin, Paris's answer to Madame Tussaud's wax museum, assembled a life-sized tableau of the Ethiopian court. Liebig's, a German nutritional firm with a global reach, featured Taytu and Menelik on individual trading cards. And while Liebig's cast the imperial couple as statesmen to promote its meat extract products, the French grocery chain Félix Potin promoted Menelik and Taytu as celebrities, grouping them with five hundred other "collectible" contemporary personalities who could drive traffic to its stores.[12]

The absorption of Ethiopia's royal couple into celebrity culture brought with it now-familiar consequences. It affected the choice of names given newborns: in France, a worker named his son Menelik. The imperial palace at Addis was swamped with fan mail, some of it addressed simply to Menelik in "Byssinie." The false sense of familiarity bred by celebrity culture brought bold and casual requests—for money, for favors.

Menelik in *Vanity Fair*. From *Vanity Fair*, 29 July 1897. Private collection.

One fan asked Menelik for two hundred francs so she could finish her house.[13]

While Taytu and Menelik were joining the ranks of celebrity states-men, more fundamental questions were being posed. Was Ethiopia poised to become modern Africa's first great power? Would political

Taytu trading card. Private collection.

Ethiopia, Africa's Switzerland. Private collection.

unification bring booming demand and a commercial renaissance? Would Menelik, the Lion of Judah, assume leadership of the global black African diaspora? Ethiopia had always attracted its share of foreign adventurers and opportunists. After Adwa, the informal cosmopolitanism of the privateer and the misfit was augmented by the cosmopolitanism of the trade and diplomatic mission. It also drew visionaries eager to cast Ethiopia—black Africa's first nation with a claim to greatness—in a millennial role.

The great powers lost no opportunity to curry favor and sway public opinion. The Vatican touted Menelik as "one of the most important personages, not only in Africa, but in Europe . . . [His] friendship is sought by the greatest of European powers."[14] Shortly after the imperial couple returned to their capital in 1896, a Russian mission appeared. They drew crowds by offering a free musical concert. As a crowd gathered, they handed out tiny medals of the Blessed Virgin, a shrewd way of playing up the affinity of Russian Orthodox and Ethiopian faiths.

Free medical care clinched the deal. The Russians brought medical supplies—tents, sheets, beds, and surgical gear. The Russian Red Cross mission ministered to wounded Ethiopian troops (but turned away Italians); it would soon grow into a permanent hospital facility that dispensed free care and manufactured goodwill—at least among the Ethiopians, who nevertheless were surprised that Europeans would refuse to care for other Europeans. "What?" asked Menelik's minister of justice. "Aren't you whites all brothers?"[15]

European brotherhood, such as it was, occurred *chez* Ilg. As a young man, Alfred Ilg had taken an Ethiopian wife and started a family. At some point they separated, and in 1895 Ilg married Fanny Gattiker, who joined him in Addis.[16] They entertained in a home decorated in the European style—window curtains and drapes, carved wooden door frames, bentwood chairs with caned seats, floral wallpaper. Guests dressed for dinner, which was served in the European style. Conversation over brandy and cigars extended well into the evening. Although Ilg was vaguely francophile in his leanings, in the spirit of Swiss neutrality Fanny and Alfred hosted dinners for businessmen and diplomats from around the world.

The French appeared in January 1897, sending Léonce Lagarde, the governor of Djibouti, as their representative.[17] The French press had been building up Ethiopia as an emerging regional power, on par with

Japan in Asia.[18] A delegation of Spanish Catholics duly appeared, with religious rather than commercial objectives; their presence was likely paired with the Vatican's own initiative.[19]

As for the British, they had some explaining to do. In Ethiopia, the Italians were widely perceived as proxies for British interests in their ongoing struggle with France for mastery of Africa. The Ethiopians were particularly resentful of British complicity in the occupation of Massawa and Eritrea.[20] Sir Rennell Rodd arrived in the spring of 1897, within months of Menelik's return to Addis. It was the most impressive diplomatic performance yet. Rodd was a soldier as well as a diplomat, and he and his party arrived in bright uniforms, supported by a detachment of Sikhs—a scale model of British imperial might. And he brought with him a veteran of the British campaign against Tewodros, the seventy-year-old Captain Charles Sayer Tristram Speedy, a living reminder of Britain's long-standing interest in Ethiopia.[21] They were met by hundreds of Menelik's best soldiers, banners in bright colors of yellow, red, and green streaming from their lances while horns blared; behind them marched thousands more.[22] Rodd's delegation was sandwiched between legions of Adwa's heroes.

Rodd rapidly formed the opinion that Menelik was little interested in trade, less still in cultivating a European business community in Addis. But he was able to clarify Menelik's position with respect to the Sudan and the Mahdi and to deliver a letter from Queen Victoria.[23] Having shown the flag and learned what he could, he departed.

The Americans would follow in due course. In fact, of all the countries jockeying for influence and trade with Menelik's Ethiopia, it was the United States who enjoyed the lead—and it owed nothing to military encroachment or fawning diplomats. Ethiopia bought American cotton, period. Tents, *shammas,* pants, canopies—virtually all of the thread and fabric came from U.S. farms, about $600,000 worth every year.[24] American farmers could thank Greek and Indian merchants for serving as go-betweens, for not a single industry representative, not a single sales call, had generated the business.

The late nineteenth century was a protectionist age, and some thought the thriving trade between Ethiopia and the United States might be at risk, given that it was based on enterprising third parties and mere mutual self-interest. Thus it was not only the vision of new markets but also the concern that some of the existing markets might be taken away that drove Robert Peet Skinner, attached to the American consulate in Marseille, to propose an American mission to Menelik. As a resident of Marseille—the heart and soul of the French colonial enterprise—Skinner could see the forces that might seek to close off American access to an Ethiopian market based on nothing so formal as a treaty. The Djibouti-to-Harar railway—construction had begun a few years earlier—might serve as the choke point for discriminatory trade practices. "At the very least," Skinner reasoned, "we should show our friendship for the Emperor and seek a treaty which should guarantee us the permanent enjoyment of most favored nation privileges."[25]

Skinner pitched his idea for the mission to Teddy Roosevelt, whose penchant for rugged exoticism played in the plan's favor. With little prompting from Skinner, the president's imagination caught fire, imagining Ethiopia as part time machine ("life there must be something similar to life in the time of Christ") and part botany lab ("we must look out for seeds of useful unknown plants"). Roosevelt was especially intrigued by the use of Grévy zebras in the American West: "[Grévy zebras] could go several days without water. Perhaps, with their help, we could breed a new mule that would be enormously valuable in some of our parched western country." Skinner came away wondering if the idea of a mission to Ethiopia hadn't been the president's all along. Soon Skinner was on his way to the War Department "for guns and saddles."[26] Thus was launched one of the most enduring relationships between the United States and Africa.

When Skinner's mission moved up from the Somali coast in 1903, it numbered nearly ninety people, including an escort of U.S. Marines, and forty-eight pack camels. The reception in Addis was grand. A mounted escort of thousands met the Skinner party. Each carried a rifle, a spear, and a shield. Menelik's officers appeared in full parade dress of lion skin capes and lion's mane headgear; they carried shields covered with velvet and studded with gold nails.[27] Music "very much out of tune" added to the splendor. By this time, Menelik had taken to wearing large diamond earrings to complement his usual outfit of gold-trimmed satin cape, white pants, and white cloth wrapped about the head, pulled tightly to the back, and knotted at the neck.[28]

The discussion between Skinner and Menelik ranged widely, touching on imperial ambitions. "America alone was without land in Africa,"

Menelik noted approvingly.[29] Skinner assured the emperor that America had no designs to acquire any. He affirmed that the United States was interested "in the preservation of the independence of Abyssinia, which . . . after the French have absorbed Morocco, will be the only independent State of any consequence in the continent."[30] Meanwhile, Menelik expressed admiration for Abraham Lincoln and the Emancipation Proclamation, promising that slavery in Ethiopia would be abolished within a generation, though incrementally. "I have decreed that, while those at present slaves shall remain such, their children shall be free. Thus slavery will disappear."[31]

Skinner returned both with seeds and with the Grévy zebras coveted by Roosevelt, though the zebras landed in the National Zoo in Washington, D.C., not the high plains of Montana, as did one of two gift lions from Menelik to survive the trip.[32] As for the blossoming of trade between Ethiopia and the United States, it failed to materialize, though not for lack of effort on Skinner's part. Drawing inspiration from Henry Morton Stanley's exploits—and his penchant for publicity—Skinner managed to get press notices of his journey into an astonishing number of American newspapers.[33] Skinner actively promoted the image of independent Ethiopia in newspaper interviews—"Abyssinians the Japanese of Africa" one headline proclaimed.[34] His example inspired at least one farsighted American entrepreneur to make the voyage to the court of Menelik. Emil Gribeschock, whose business was in the line of "Hides, Furs, Wool, Feathers, etc.," took inspiration from Skinner's exploits. Gribeschock announced the creation of the "American-Abyssinian Trading Company," with headquarters at 529 Broadway in New York City. Like most brilliant business ideas, Gribeschock's company started with an order for official letterhead. He solicited letters of introduction from Skinner and made his way to Ethiopia.[35]

Gribeschock thought he was going to get in on the ground floor. During his visit to Harar, he was impressed by Ras Makonnen ("the most intelligent man in Ethiopia") and took a fancy to Afar women, whom he described as "magnificently formed . . . regular small mouth, with nice lips, splendid teeth and well-shaped feet and arms," adding for good measure that they possessed "all the heat and fire of a tropical people." But he was appalled by the filth of Harar, whose residents threw trash into the streets, where "hyenas . . . do the street cleaning." In Addis, he had the honor of an audience with Menelik, to whom he presented the latest model of Winchester rifle, but he seems to have received little more than goodwill in return. On his return to the Somali coast, his caravan nearly ran out of water and his escort led him into a trap. Robbery, he discovered, was an unexpected cost of doing business on caravan routes through Afar lands.[36]

Upon his return to New York, Gribeschock sought to convert his experience into a government post as U.S. consul general to Ethiopia. He even solicited the help of his fellow Masons in a letter campaign on his behalf, but to no avail. He was passed over.[37]

Beneath the level of official delegations driven by politics and trade, Addis hosted a cosmopolitan array of opportunists, adventurers, and "second-chancers." A young Greek styled himself as the capital's mad romantic poet, but eventually he made his career in the Ethiopian military. He Ethiopianized his name to Apteghiorghis and rose to the rank of *fitawrari,* making him the highest-ranking foreigner ever to serve in Menelik's army.[38]

An Armenian by the name of Tigrane insinuated himself into imperial service as a cook and gardener. He was also Menelik's goldsmith. Given that the wearing of gold was a royal privilege, there was only so much money to be made at goldsmithing.[39] He also did a tidy business operating a pawn shop on the side, offering short-term loans to anyone with something precious to put forward as collateral.

From early on, Menelik had encouraged traders, partly because he saw them as a potential source of wealth, partly because he wanted their expertise. Armand Savouré, a portly Frenchman, arrived in Ethiopia in the early 1880s, seeking his fortune as the agent of the Franco-African Company. Fourteen years later, he was still seeking it. Along the way he persuaded a Parisian handyman named Stévenin to assist him. Stévenin oversaw the construction of a factory compound consisting of a two-story circular main building—warehouse and workshop—surrounded by several houses.[40]

More than seventy workers lived in the compound and worked manufacturing rifle ammunition for Savouré's enterprise. Rifle cartridges doubled as small change in Ethiopia, so in a sense Savouré was coining money. He traded his ammunition for gold, elephant tusks, and civet.[41] In effect, Savouré was making money to buy up things for which there was an export market. Foremen were paid in cash, but most workers were paid in food and clothing—Savouré issued new pants and a *shamma* every six months.

The Franco-African Company also imported things for which there might be an Ethiopian market. When Jean Gaston Vanderheym visited in 1894, the real question was what Savouré *wasn't* selling. Savouré's warehouse had become a general store selling, among other things, guns, cartridges, glass, fabric, shoes, socks, gloves, tanned leather, pocketknives, lace, carpet, perfume, wool blankets, oil, vinegar, and liquor.[42]

Despite the appearance of prosperity, Savouré's business struggled. The fortune Savouré had hoped to make in Africa eluded him, but it was a life with its own compensations. He and Stévenin could support themselves and their (European) wives. After fourteen years, they were beyond the point of return. Despite the disappointments, Ethiopia had become their home.[43] Savouré's story was far from unique. It was shared by Arthur Rimbaud and a half dozen other Europeans who were drawn to Ethiopia by stories of its wealth and exoticism. They learned that success soon drew the emperor's attention.

Edward Gleichen, a member of the British mission to Menelik after Adwa, observed that Menelik used his political powers to manipulate or enter successful markets and drive out competitors. He described a Frenchman, a Monsieur Monatte, who had arrived "expecting to find an El Dorado" but instead found his wealth depleted to the point that he was unable to leave. Menelik, Gleichen noted, was not above applying duties on imported goods while exempting his own, to undermine competitors. Menelik relied on the enterprise of Europeans to develop markets from which he might later choose to drive them. Soon enough, all serious commerce passed through his hands. Even though Menelik used some of this wealth for the common good, Gleichen noted, his behavior would discourage investment as long as it continued.[44] Adwa had garnered attention and goodwill for Menelik's Ethiopia, but much of it was squandered. The same fierce independence that made Adwa possible created a hostile environment for foreigners interested in doing business in Ethiopia.

Ethiopia in the African Diaspora

The black African reaction to Adwa was, at first, muted. This undoubtedly owed much to the fact that many newspapers in sub-Saharan Africa were European-owned. The *Lagos Standard* of Nigeria, the *Gold Coast Chronicle,* and the *Sierra Leone Times* had all backed Italy in the 1895–1896 campaign. The motto that graced the masthead of the *Lagos Standard*—"For God, the Queen and the People"—spoke volumes about its intended readership. Though it cannot be said that these newspapers reflected local popular opinion, they remind us just how difficult it could be to gauge African public opinion in the age of European empire. By the time of the Pan-African Congress of 1900, Ethiophilic sentiment was clearer, although Africa itself was underrepresented among the delegates.[45]

Similarly, contemporary African American commentary on Adwa can be difficult to track down. Ida B. Wells passes over Adwa without a word, but she had an iron-clad excuse—she was in the ninth month of her pregnancy, giving birth on 25 March.[46] More puzzling is the silence of African American newspapers of the period, including the *Freeman* and the *Afro-American.*[47] Three weeks after Adwa, the *Freeman* offered a gloomy vision of Africa's future, as if Adwa had not happened: "Except in Haiti, there is now no black race which is not under white sovereignty, or expecting white sovereignty, or preparing itself for a last fight in protest against that encroaching dominion."[48] Although the piece was likely drafted before the news of Adwa broke, it suggests just how much the story of Ethiopia had to fight against a deep pessimism about the future of African sovereignty.

In *The Future of the American Negro,* written shortly after Adwa and published in 1899, Booker T. Washington seems not to have fully absorbed the story of Ethiopia. In a brief survey of Africa meant to emphasize Europe's firm grip on the continent, he duly noted that "Abyssinia is independent" but said nothing about Adwa. Presumably Washington's silence owes something, as his title suggests, to the larger goal of focusing African American attention on an American future, as opposed to African one.[49] It may also reflect the fact that most African Americans were from or had roots in coastal West Africa and, as William Shack has suggested, tended to focus their attention on that part of the continent.[50] Finally, one might venture to observe that in the climate of Jim Crow America—with its racial code enforced by spectacular violence, including lynchings—any discussion of black military triumph or humiliating European defeat might have been discreetly reserved for times and places that escape the historical record.[51]

Accordingly, if we look not for direct references to the triumph of Adwa but instead at less provocative allusions to Ethiopia, a richer and subtler picture emerges. Indeed, although the *Freeman* published no immediate commentary on Adwa, passing over the events in silence, it nevertheless proclaimed from its masthead the scriptural passage from Psalms 68:31: "And Ethiopia shall stretch forth her hand." Throughout the Americas, Ethiopia's elevated status antedated Adwa, as the historian William Scott has shown.[52] The image of Ethiopia as Christian, as a scriptural place, and as the home of an ancient and venerable civilization had already earned the country an elevated rank throughout the diaspora.

So lofty was the status of Ethiopia in the African diaspora that it sometimes was synonymous with Africa itself.[53] Christian churches serving African Americans added "Abyssinian" and "Ethiopian" to their names. The most famous of them all in the United States—the Abyssinian Baptist Church of Harlem—dated from 1808; in Africa, the Ethiopian Church of Pretoria dated from 1892. The image of Ethiopia thus appears to have been as powerful in southern Africa as it was in the Americas. Although these churches did not affiliate with the Ethiopian Orthodox Church or adopt its prayers and rituals, they tapped into an indigenous African Christian tradition—that of Ethiopia—as old and revered as Christianity itself. The post-Adwa image of a strong and independent Ethiopia certainly added to the allure.

Similarly, the connection between Ethiopia and the African American missionaries who fostered the development of the African Methodist Episcopal (AME) Church was conceptual and allusive, rather than actual, with no durable linkages between the AME denomination and Ethiopia's Orthodox Christianity. Pretoria's Ethiopian Church eventually folded into the African Methodist Episcopal Church; the explicit reference to Ethiopia was thus lost. When construction on St. Peter's church in Pretoria began in April 1896, it was to have been known as St. Peter's Ethiopian Church. However, when it was dedicated in late 1897, it had become St. Peter's African Methodist Episcopal Church.[54]

Similarly, in the States, the absorption of the Ethiopian Church into the African Methodist Episcopal Church took place in the immediate aftermath of the Adwa victory. The union under the AME umbrella was decided in May 1896 at a conference in Wilmington, North Carolina. It was ratified ceremonially at Allen Temple in Atlanta in June the same year.[55] Adwa does not appear to have figured in such matters.

Haiti, the Ethiopia of the Americas

More palpably related to Adwa were attempts to link Ethiopia to Haiti, attempts that coincided with the arrival of Benito Sylvain. Sylvain was born in Haiti, but he was in Paris when he heard the news of Menelik's victory. In Paris, Sylvain labored to produce *La Fraternité,* a newspaper devoted since 1889, as its masthead proclaimed, "to the defense of black interests."[56] After the news of Adwa, Sylvain walked away from his newspaper with the determination of "a knight leaving for a crusade."[57] Sylvain was already a pan-African visionary. In Menelik—modern black Africa's first personality with a truly global stature—he imagined a redemptive figure.

He made the journey to Ethiopia in January 1897. His voyage took him from Paris to Marseille and thence to Djibouti and Addis. His mission, as he elaborated it over the course of his trip, was to establish diplomatic relations between Ethiopia and Haiti.[58] Haiti was home to the first successful slave revolt of modern times, and Ethiopia was home to Menelik's independent African empire. Together, they symbolized successful and righteous challenges to the great scourges of African peoples—slavery and colonization. It only made sense that they should be joined.

In all, Sylvain made four voyages to Ethiopia. Though he found in Menelik a reluctant Messiah, Sylvain remained true to his vision. He represented both Haiti and Ethiopia at the first pan-African meeting in 1900, although it is unclear what authorization, if any, he received from either state.

Sylvain made a point of being in Addis in 1904, the hundredth anniversary of Haitian independence. To observe such a momentous occasion in the capital of free Africa would link the two great nations, at least symbolically. His visit happened to coincide with the American diplomatic mission of Robert Skinner, who witnessed an enlightening exchange between Sylvain and Menelik. Sylvain continued to solicit Menelik's leadership for his initiative to improve "the negro race." Menelik listened patiently, then gently declined Sylvain's offer. "Yours is a most excellent idea," Menelik conceded, "the negro should be uplifted. I applaud your theory, and I wish you the greatest possible success. But . . . [y]ou know, I am not a negro at all: I am a Caucasian."[59]

The phrasing sounds more like Skinner, the American from Massillon, Ohio, than like the laconic Menelik we have come to know. But this shouldn't surprise us. Skinner spoke French, as did Sylvain, so while he wouldn't need a translator to understand Sylvain's proposal, both he and Sylvain would have relied on a translator for Menelik's reply.

Still, we have no reason to doubt the gist of Skinner's account. How, then, do we account for Menelik's answer? Menelik may have been influenced by arguments that emphasized the ethnic distinctions between Ethiopia and sub-Saharan Africa, even to the point of positing a Phoenician heritage for Ethiopians. This whitening of Ethiopia would have a durable history. We also know that Menelik was anything but an ideologue; he was a man for whom race—a European category, after all—might remain a supple concept. Such an attitude was reflected in Ethiopian art, to judge from the array of skin tones one finds represented without hierarchical connotation.[60] No doubt race was a more freighted concept for someone such as Sylvain—a native of the Caribbean, with its legacy of racially defined servitude—than it was for Menelik, leader of a country that had never known conquest. It is also possible that regal Menelik, never a populist, was uncomfortable in the role of hero to the broader black African diaspora. One can imagine that Menelik, a practical man interested in what could be achieved locally, thought Sylvain's global idealism tedious. Maybe he just wanted to shake off Sylvain.

For whatever reason, the same man who had courted the Dervishes against Italy in 1895 by appealing to a common blackness ("I am black and you are black—let us unite to hunt our common enemy") now saw fit to decline Sylvain's proffered crown.[61] Undaunted, Sylvain assumed the role of pageant master for a ceremony celebrating the Haitian centenary. Sylvain organized an honor guard of Ethiopian volunteers. They fired several rifle rounds and shouted, "Long live Haiti! Long live the Ethiopia of America!" before Sylvain marched them to Menelik's palace. There, he was disappointed to learn that Menelik had left the night before for his residence at Addis-Alem.

Later that year, Sylvain returned to Haiti, bearing greetings from Menelik to Nord Alexis, president of the Republic of Haiti. Sylvain also carried a gift—a medal and an honorary title for President Alexis from Menelik.[62]

Another pilgrim from the Caribbean was Joseph Vitalien, a physician. In 1903, Ras Makonnen persuaded Vitalien to stay on as director of the hospital in Harar; Vitalien would also attend to Menelik as his personal physician during his long, slow decline.[63] By the 1920s, Vitalien had emerged as a leader in the burgeoning pan-African movement. He met W. E. B. Du Bois at the second Pan-African Congress, where Vitalien represented Ethiopia.[64] As pilgrims to Ethiopia in the aftermath of Adwa, both Vitalien and Sylvain anticipated the later migrations of the Rastafarians, many of whom settled in Ethiopia.[65] They, like Bob Marley and so many others, saw in Ethiopia a new Zion, the fulfillment of an ancient promise of freedom. It was a vision that bestowed upon Ethiopia— Menelik's reservations notwithstanding—the hopes of a global black diaspora.

More than a country, Ethiopia was becoming a place in the imagination, a source of pride and lineage sometimes indistinguishable from Africa itself.[66] The status of Ethiopia, both real and imaginary, grew in the new century. World War I had a radicalizing effect on African American opinion, especially as discrimination in the armed forces showed just how deeply Jim Crow had corrupted the culture and institutions of the Republic. The war also destabilized European rule around the world, just as the anticolonial rhetoric of Woodrow Wilson and Vladimir Lenin fired the imaginations of young leaders as diverse as Ho Chi Minh and Mohandas Gandhi. W. E. B. Du Bois went to Paris in late 1918, knowing that colonial issues—notably the disposition of the former German colonies—would be on the agenda of the peace conference. His proposal, which he was unable to advance, called for the creation of a new African state from remnants of the former German holdings. This state—a showpiece and a training ground for future leaders—would be governed by "Negro leaders from America, Abyssinia, Liberia, [and] Haiti," among others. The proposed name for the model African state? Ethiopian Utopia.[67]

CHAPTER 19

Reckonings

I T WAS 5 June 1896, opening day in the court-martial of Oreste Baratieri. The morning sun threw deep shadows across the town of Asmara as Baratieri stepped into an open carriage. A mounted military escort surrounded the carriage as it moved out, while askari guards on foot provided an outer ring of security.

It was not yet seven o'clock. The early start helped to limit the crowd. A single photographer, ancestor of the modern paparazzo, positioned himself outside the building that would serve as the impromptu courthouse. As the carriage slowed to a halt in front, he captured a photo of the unfortunate general gazing impassively into the lens.[1]

A cordon of soldiers framed Baratieri's path to the entrance as he stepped from the carriage. Inside, a wide table was in place for the magistrates. Two symbols of authority—a portrait of King Umberto and the family crest of the House of Savoy—were mounted on the wall behind the table. At seven-fifteen, a few minutes after General Baratieri and his defense attorney had taken their seats, five magistrates entered the room and sat behind the table. The court-martial of Oreste Baratieri was about to begin.

Many miles away, another grim reckoning was also getting under way. A team of nearly 250 men from the army of Italy were starting another day of work on the battlefields of Adwa. Ras Mangasha, Menelik's ruler of Tigray, had given permission for a team of fourteen officers and 240 members of the engineer corps to return to the sites of combat and bury the dead.

They were led by Lieutenant Colonel Francesco Arimondi. The Arimondis were a military family, and Francesco, as brother of the general who had died at Adwa, had requested the responsibility of visiting the battlefield and burying the dead. Arimondi disembarked at Massawa in May 1896 and began to organize his group. His team was joined by two Capuchin monks, who would provide religious services, and by Gabrè Sghear, a veteran askari who had fought at Adwa and knew the terrain well.[2] In a gracious gesture, Ras Mangasha contributed forty soldiers to serve as armed escort in a territory still openly hostile to the Italians.[3]

Return to Adwa

The progress of the Arimondi mission was followed with rapt attention. Two months after the battle, in May 1896, hundreds of families were still unsure of the fate of loved ones. Survivors of the battle contacted family when they reached the safety of Eritrea, but many families had no word and struggled to interpret the silence. Dead? Wounded? As hundreds of captives marched south with Menelik, many families preferred to cling to the belief that their soldier had been taken prisoner. The Arimondi mission might provide some somber answers.

There were other unresolved issues. Public discussion after Adwa had been rife with accusations—that professional jealousy had doomed the Italian forces, that panic among the askari had compromised the army, that Baratieri had ordered "the attack" in a fit of professional pique. The air was full of theories about why Italy had failed. The Arimondi mission, it was hoped, in tandem with the trial of Baratieri, would provide some answers.

It didn't help that juicy details of an encoded letter Baratieri had sent to Stanislao Mocenni, the minister of war, had been leaked to the press. Baratieri's letter, dated 3 March, was the first summary description of the Adwa catastrophe. It came from an impeccable source, and the language was not kind. The letter was probably drafted by several people, but it went out over Baratieri's signature and he never accepted anything less than full responsibility for it. At one point, Baratieri uses the colorful word *pazzi* ("crazy") to describe the behavior of some of the Italian soldiers during the retreat. Baratieri claimed that he and other officers tried to direct an orderly retreat eastward, back toward the camp at Sauria. Instead, the soldiers ignored orders to regroup; they had retreated toward the north, taking the direct route to Eritrea. As they did, Baratieri wrote, they "threw down their weapons like madmen, in the conviction that if they were taken unarmed they would not be castrated."[4] It was in this disorganized, panicked retreat that "the real losses began."

Besides showing just how effective the fear of castration could be, the remark cast doubt on the valor of Italy's soldiers. Then why was it released? As minister of war, Mocenni had a lot to lose from the disaster; an eagerness to deflect criticism of the campaign fully onto Baratieri likely explains his decision to release it. Baratieri's candid account served his purpose, but it added to the pain of the families of the dead; it took away the consoling thought that the sons of Italy had died valiantly, as heroes. Instead, it strongly suggested that the unsoldierly conduct of some of the men had compromised the retreat and radically increased the loss of life.

As Colonel Arimondi and his team made their way toward Adwa, they retraced the path of the retreat. Their journey provided empirical evidence with which to answer questions about a great tragedy. They learned, for example, that some fifty-five soldiers had eluded capture and made it to safety at Adigrat—one of them had spent thirty-nine days traveling by night, surviving by his wits, before reaching Adigrat on 8 April. There he joined the other refugees of battle, including twenty-seven wounded, seven of whom had been castrated.[5]

Arimondi's group also took custody of some of the prisoners who had remained in the north in the care of Mangasha and his lieutenants. These included soldiers who were too badly wounded to make the journey south with Menelik. One day, as part of the exchange, Arimondi was greeted by Ligg Abraha, barely twenty years old, the young chief of the Entisho region. Abraha's greeting ("Buon giorno, signor colonnello Arimondi!") was uttered in perfect Italian, with a Piedmontese accent, to the astonishment of Arimondi and his entourage.

Ligg Abraha in Turin. From Eduardo Ximenes, *Sul Campo di Adua, marzo-giugno 1896.* Milan: Fratelli Treves Editori, 1897.

Abraha turned to the officers on either side of Arimondi and greeted them: "Buon giorno, signori!" Arimondi responded with an inquiry about the prisoners. "Dunque voi avete degli Italiani prigionieri?"

"Sì, cioè, io no, un qualche sottocapo qui vicino ne ha qualcuno in cura perché ferito."[6] Arimondi was astonished. Many askari had mastered a useful but broken Italian, but this was different. This was flawless.

Abraha was eventually recognized as a boy the Italians had sent to Rome at the age of thirteen. He had been schooled in Turin—hence the Piedmontese accent—where he had mastered Italian, becoming perfectly bicultural. When he returned to Africa, he absconded and joined the resistance to the Italian occupation. He fought for Ethiopia at Adwa and, in recognition, was made chief of the Entisho region.[7] As a gesture of friendship to Italy, Abraha saw to the release of Orrico Rosario, a prisoner from Campania.

As the Arimondi group continued with its work, they kept a careful record both of the number of bodies and of the location. The Ethiopians had already buried their dead—mostly—so the bodies that

remained to be buried were those who had fought on the side of Italy,
Europeans and askari. After working their way along the route of retreat in late May and early June, the Arimondi group reached the battlefield proper, where they buried more than a thousand European
soldiers and thirty-nine askari. Most of the dead were unidentified and
unidentifiable, given that they had been stripped and, in some cases,
burned. Scavengers and eight weeks of decomposition had done the
rest. On 3 June, they interred another 900 whites and 144 askari, and
on the fourth they made their way to Mariam Shavitu, where they identified the body of General Dabormida. On the fifth, they worked on the
flanks of Raio, where Arimondi's brother was presumed to have fallen.
There they erected a rough stone monument, surmounted by a cross.
A memorial mass was offered.[8] The body of General Arimondi was
never found.

It was nasty work burying bodies stripped of clothing, half decom-
posed or torn apart by vultures and hyenas. It was made all the more

Memorial service on Raio. From Eduardo Ximenes, *Sul Campo di Adua, marzo-
giugno 1896.* Milan: Fratelli Treves Editori, 1897.

poignant by the occasional appearance of a personal detail—the gloved hand of an officer, or a *carte de visite* clinging to a bare branch.[9]

Mapping the Dead

When the Arimondi mission returned from its assignment, it presented its accounting. It had buried 3,643 bodies. Given the exigencies of the situation, most were buried in mass graves. It also took care to note where the bodies had been found. By grouping these findings into two broad categories— bodies found on the field of battle and bodies found on the path of retreat—it sought to settle once and for all the question of valor. Had most of the deaths occurred in heroic fighting on the battlefield of Adwa? Or had they occurred during a confused retreat?

As reported by Arimondi, the figures spoke in favor of the scenario of heroism. Of the 3,643 bodies discovered and buried, 3,246 were defined as found on the battlefield, with 397 found on the path of retreat. On closer inspection, however, the results are less clear. A group of 166 bodies is labeled as "on the line of retreat of the Dabormida brigade" with no explanation for why these were included in the battlefield group. And the greatest single location of dead—the 1,267 dead found on the Gundapta plain, on the route from the northern pass to Yeha—was not, properly speaking, part of the battlefield. The notation states, by way of explanation, that this was "where resistance still occurred." But these deaths clearly occurred on the path of retreat. If we shift these figures from the "battlefield" column to the "retreat" column, a much different picture is revealed—nearly equal numbers of deaths, about eighteen hundred, occurred on the path of retreat and on the battlefield. This would tend to confirm Baratieri's remark that the disorderly retreat was where "the real losses began."

Moreover, there is reason to doubt that the Arimondi mission fully accounted for the dead. Augustus Wylde, writing for the *Manchester Guardian,* visited the battle site after the Arimondi mission had left, in July 1896. Wylde knew Adwa well, having first visited in 1884, when it was a thriving market town of fifteen thousand. When he visited four months after the battle, Adwa was "a ruin and a charnel-house." At one house, Wylde found the unburied bodies of three Italians and two askari. He speculated that these men "must have been wounded at the battle and crawled to this shelter to die." At another house there were several bodies "among the vegetable beds" and six more heaped in the corner of the garden. Yet another soul—driven by thirst—had managed to haul himself onto the wall of the well. He died there, slumped over the ledge—a mere skeleton from which scraps of shirt and regimental trousers fluttered.[10]

Wylde explored the battlefield and reported encountering areas that were still "covered with unburied bodies—men, horses, mules, and camels lying everywhere in indistinguishable heaps." Meanwhile, the population of Adwa was beset by typhoid and dysentery, which he attributed to a water supply contaminated by the "dead bodies of men and animals washed into town by the floods."

Wylde concluded that the Arimondi mission had been overwhelmed in its task. He noted that along the roads the dead had been buried, but hundreds more lay where they fell among the fields and streams of Adwa—indeed, he found unburied Italian dead as far away as Axum, thirteen miles to the west of Adwa.[11] Although his graphic reporting offered no comfort to the families of the dead, he sympathized with the Arimondi mission. The proper disposition of thousands of bodies scattered over forty square miles would have required a small army.

Wylde's account does not reflect well on the Ethiopian forces, either. An attempt had been made to bury Ethiopian soldiers in a mass grave at the Church of the Holy Trinity in Adwa, but the bodies were barely covered with earth and the "churchyard was very foul-smelling." Here and there arms and legs rose from the earth, as if in silent rebellion. In one area of the former camp, he found a mound of body parts, "a rotting heap of ghastly remnants"—the amputated hands and feet of askari prisoners. On the battlefield itself, Wylde noted that the Ethiopians had not bothered to bury their Muslim dead: "Not a single body of the Mahommedan Gallas had been touched." Meanwhile, the hyenas "had long ago left the district to procure something more tempting than what the battlefield offered them." As Wylde surveyed the scene, it amounted to a macabre battlefield sculpture in the realist mold—installation art whose tragic and ephemeral material consisted of "putrescent masses held together by ragged clothes."[12]

In the end, Wylde could offer only an epitaph of war. "There are some things . . . that can never be forgotten. . . . [I shudder] when I think of the thousands of white, black and brown men that lay dotted about this lovely country."[13]

Scoundrel Time

The work of the Arimondi mission provided an emotionally charged backdrop to the court-martial of Oreste Baratieri. The commission that sat in judgment represented the finest display of military jurisprudence that Eritrea could muster, though it fell short of what protocol required. Given that the battle of Adwa had taken the lives of so many officers—and that Oreste Baratieri remained Eritrea's highest-ranking officer—it was not obvious who was available to sit in judgment. Shouldn't Baratieri be packed off to Rome?

A trial in Rome made sense. It was the only place where Baratieri could be tried by men of comparable rank and experience. It was the only venue where the full powers of modern journalism could pry loose the facts about the case. It was the only place where the adversarial nature of party politics would provide motivation to pursue the ugly details until they were fully public. For all these reasons, a trial in Rome was both desirable and impossible.

Both military and political leadership were agreed that to return Baratieri to Italy to stand trial would be to invite new humiliations. The case would prolong the disaster, and it would readily turn into a trial of Italian military and political leadership. An official judgment was necessary—public opinion demanded it—but it would be rendered in Eritrea, where the key elements could remain under military control.[14]

At Asmara, Baratieri was given the former residence of Colonel Pianavia as he awaited trial. As a writer and former editor, Baratieri knew that the outcome of his trial depended in part on public opinion.[15] He had been working with General Mariotti, a close friend in Rome, during the Adwa campaign, and they continued their collaboration as the trial approached. Baratieri discussed his plight with Mariotti in his letters, but he also fed his friend with information that could be republished nearly verbatim in *L'Esercito italiano,* the newspaper of the Italian army.[16] The army was fighting for its life (and its budget) in the aftermath of Adwa, and it was closing ranks behind Baratieri. Friends made sure that supportive pieces got published in the regional and popular press—both *Gazzetta del Popolo* and *L'Alto Adige* rushed to defend him.

Baratieri's greatest concern was the letter containing the word *pazzi*, leaked by the minister of war, Stanislao Mocenni. Public opinion in Italy was overwhelmingly sympathetic to the soldiers and victims of Adwa; it could distinguish between the men who had fought at Adwa and the political leadership that had led them there. But Baratieri's thoughtless remark tended to put him at odds with the image of the soldiers as fallen heroes.

Baratieri's supporters questioned the wisdom of racing to hold the trial in the midst of the whirlwind of recrimination that followed the defeat—one defender would later recall that such haste lent itself to "either a great error or a grave injustice." They reached back for precedent and recalled the case of General Girolamo Ramorino, whose incompetence had led to defeat for Italy in 1849. Ramorino had been executed following a brief trial by military court. The precedent was not a good one. In private, even Queen Margherita cited the example approvingly.[17] Baratieri confided to his close friend his certitude that the trial would have one of two outcomes—absolution or death.[18]

At seven-fifteen in the morning on 5 June, General Del Mayno, a count and, at fifty, a mature and trusted member of the old aristocracy of Milan, opened the proceedings.[19] It was anything but a circus. The audience was astonishingly small. The general European press was excluded; they were referred to the Ministry of War in Rome, which is to say they would see only carefully vetted summaries.[20] The Italian press was represented, led by the pro-Africanist *Tribuna* and the skeptical *Corriere della Sera,* but they were forbidden to send telegrams, which prevented the Italian and European public from becoming involved in a blow-by-blow account.[21] Among newspapers, *L'Africa italiana,* based in Eritrea, would offer the most complete coverage, but as it was a product of the colonial administration and because it was a weekly, it offered neither spectacle nor paced drama.

There was dismay at the makeup of the military tribunal. The decision to hold the trial in Eritrea meant that there simply weren't enough officers of sufficient rank available. Six generals would sit in judgment of

Baratieri—Luchino Del Mayno, Nicola Heusch, Filippo Gazzarelli, Tommaso Valles, Luigi Bisesti, and Francesco Mazza. General Francesco Pistoia attended as substitute. Four members of the tribunal, being mere major generals, were of lower rank than the accused. All had experience of combat, but none had commanded units larger than a company. How could these men of inferior rank and experience sit in judgment?[22]

The legal case against Baratieri, as presented by the prosecuting attorney, General Emilio Bacci, centered on two charges. The first concerned the motives behind Baratieri's decision to advance toward Adwa. Baratieri had, the indictment read, "for inexcusable reasons, decided on a military action . . . against the Abyssinian army," thus not only "exposing [the Italian army] to danger but leading [it] to ruin."

The second charge concerned his conduct during the retreat. This charge hinged on the fact that much of the army was left without formal orders from noon of the day of battle until the morning of the third. In effect, Baratieri was accused of abandoning his command.

Baratieri listened to the charges with his arms crossed. His defense attorney, Captain Ernesto Cantoni, raised a number of technical challenges to the proceedings, challenges that would have stopped the trial in its tracks, starting with limitations on court-martial proceedings during time of war. Baratieri thanked his attorney for his zeal but brushed aside these objections so that the trial could proceed. There was also the sticky fact that Baratieri was a member of the Chamber of Deputies, which accorded him legal immunity. But the chamber took the view that the charges bore on his conduct as an officer and not as a member of the legislature; it voted to allow the trial to take place.[23]

The prosecution began with an analysis of the battle of Adwa prepared by General Mario Lamberti, vice governor of Eritrea.[24] Lamberti's report was dry and clinical, deliberately so; he intended merely to lay out the uncontroversial facts regarding the events of the day. Baratieri then embarked on a lengthy statement that focused on the decision to advance to the passes but also included accounts of the battle and the retreat. His testimony filled both the morning and afternoon sessions. Baratieri's testimony, and that of witnesses called in the days that followed, focused on three key issues: the decision to advance, confusion during the advance, the retreat.

Baratieri framed the decision to advance by recounting how the defection of Ras Sebhat and Hagos Tafari marked the beginning of an insurgency, just as the arrival of reinforcements from Italy increased the burden on supply lines. Baratieri recounted how he had considered pulling back, but before making a decision, he had consulted his brigadier generals—Albertone, Arimondi, Dabormida, and Ellena.

Although Baratieri's testimony provided a richer, more complicated picture of the lead-up to Adwa, he was careful not to accuse subordinates or inflame passions. There is no mention of Arimondi's famous prideful ill humor or his justly earned nickname, "Achilles." He didn't mention Albertone's backbiting or how he questioned Baratieri's competence in front of his men. He left out the resentful grudge of privilege that his well-born generals bore against him.

Baratieri rejected disdainfully the accusation that the decision to advance was motivated by his replacement. He defended himself and his army by noting that there was misfortune and error but no dereliction of duty. His conscience was clear.[25]

Under questioning, Baratieri defended his decision to advance. When asked if the advance wouldn't have stretched his supply lines further, Baratieri stated that after advancing on the passes, he had planned to withdraw if Menelik didn't attack.

Had he heard directly or indirectly of his replacement? No.[26]

Were his plans to attack or merely to advance? To advance.

Why hadn't Baratieri ordered Albertone to return to the pass? Albertone was himself held in place by the need to cover Turitto's retreat.

Baratieri received support from Colonel Corticelli, who was called upon to answer questions related to Baratieri's orders and their execution. Corticelli testified that Baratieri's orders had been fine and that the failure was one of execution, specifically in Albertone's failure to occupy the correct position. Similarly, Corticelli faulted Dabormida's execution of Baratieri's order to occupy a certain position in support of Albertone.[27] Giovanni Pittaluga gave a deposition in which he criticized Albertone's failure to stay in contact with the rest of the army. Baratieri's orders required this, as did standard army regulations. Had Albertone stayed in contact, the tragedy might have been avoided. The fact that he had not communicated invited speculation as to his motives.[28]

Gioacchino Valenzano took the stand and provided crucial testimony about the meeting of the generals on 28 February. "Everyone, Albertone, Dabormida, Arimondi, Ellena, showed themselves to be against retreat." They were convinced that after Amba Alage and Mekele, "Italy wanted revenge."[29] Dabormida was the most insistent, seemingly preoccupied with questions of honor. According to Valenzano, Dabormida hotly asserted that "None of us can return to Italy without having attacked the enemy!"[30]

The generals also had believed the most optimistic intelligence about the condition of Menelik's army: the Ethiopians were out of food; morale was low; large detachments had to go on raid, leaving the army weak; dissension and rancor reigned; Menelik's constant movement indicated a fear of combat; the optimal moment to fight had arrived.[31] Valenzano had earlier supported retreat, but on the stand he confessed that after the meeting he was impressed by the vigorous and unanimous advice of the generals. Valenzano recounted that when Baratieri had asked his advice after the meeting, he told Baratieri that he agreed with the generals.[32]

Valenzano was closely questioned about the map distributed to the generals. Was he aware that there were two locations with similar names? No, responded Valenzano, but the sketch was clear about the characteristics of the locations the columns were to occupy.[33] By the time Valenzano's testimony ended, he had left the court with a clear impression of Baratieri as a lonely voice for prudence among a chorus of hotheads.

Graver questions concerning the behavior of Albertone and Dabormida came up only obliquely. What was known prior to the battle was that both men were eager to fight Menelik's army and that they were scornful of Baratieri's caution. Albertone's headlong push beyond the passes precipitated the battle. Was the act deliberate? Was he motivated by the fear that unless he provoked a fight, an encounter would never happen? Did he believe, as Dabormida believed, that Menelik's army would scatter in the face of a sudden attack?[34] As the story of the battle unfolded, such questions were skirted.

And what of Dabormida's diversion of his forces far to the right, in contradiction to Baratieri's order that he should support Albertone by taking up position directly to his right? Was it a simple blunder? Or did Dabormida—either alone or in concert with Albertone—seek to draw the entire army forward by leaving a brigade-sized gap in the center, between Albertone's position on the left and Dabormida's on the right?

Emilio Bellavita, a colonel who had served under General Dabormida, testified that Dabormida—who had never seen combat and had arrived in Eritrea for the first time only six weeks before the battle—had spoken frequently of a desire for battle. Moreover, although Baratieri and Dabormida had conferred for a quarter of an hour at the pass before Dabormida's brigade moved out, the aloof and crusty Dabormida never revealed a thing about their orders or destination.[35] Such conduct was irresponsible—the loss of Dabormida would have left his men confused and without orders. It's hard to know whether Dabormida's behavior was merely a function of personality—the haughty stubbornness of a man highly born—or something more sinister, part of a deliberate act of insubordination.

When the trial resumed on 11 June, after a weekend recess, the taking of depositions was interrupted for some grim information. Colonel Arimondi filed a series of dispatches from the Adwa battlefield regarding the interment of the dead. It is unclear whether this litany of the dead hurt Baratieri's case. It may be that rather than whet the appetite for punishment, these grim reports merely shrouded the proceedings in the pall of shared tragedy. Both Baratieri and the presiding judge, Del Mayno, offered words of praise for the fallen. Then the session was suspended as the participants gathered their composure.[36]

The summary of the defense case was scheduled for 12 June. At precisely eight in the morning, General Del Mayno offered the floor to Captain Cantoni, the defense attorney for General Baratieri. Cantoni dispensed with a lengthy recounting of the Baratieri's distinguished career. He emphasized instead Baratieri's constancy and devotion to duty—qualities prized by his military colleagues now sitting in judgment.

Cantoni attacked the accusation that Baratieri had acted precipitously—for any reason, personal or military—on 29 February.[37] Court testimony had made it amply clear that in the days leading up to Adwa, Baratieri's preference had been to withdraw toward Eritrea; if anyone was disposed to risky, aggressive behavior, it was his brigadier generals.

Cantoni represented Baratieri as a judicious commander, a role fitting Baratieri's temperament and the circumstances in which he found himself in late February. Given the disproportion of forces, Baratieri simply *could not* attack; he could only maintain contact with the enemy and hope that Menelik would attack him. These considerations informed his actions throughout February and on 1 March.[38] Against the charge that Baratieri had recklessly ordered an attack, Cantoni remarked, "Never did the idea of attacking enemy positions enter [Baratieri's] mind."[39] By moving his forces to the passes, Baratieri aimed not to attack Menelik but to present him with a painful choice—to attack Baratieri's forces in a disadvantageous position or commence a humiliating withdrawal. If there was a problem, it was not in Baratieri's plan but in its execution.

Finally, Cantoni turned to Crispi's telegram and the charge that Crispi's rebuke had pushed Baratieri into a reckless act.[40] In his memoirs, Baratieri acknowledged that the telegram had been "a burning reproach" and "a cruel shove."[41] But the key question was not whether Crispi's rebuke hurt or whether Baratieri was aware of his imminent dismissal, but whether Baratieri's decision to move toward the Ethiopian forces was part of a go-for-broke decision to save his position. In other words, did Baratieri act knowing that if he gave battle and won, no one would dare dismiss him?

Cantoni put such speculation into the context of Baratieri's conduct throughout the campaign. As the strength of Menelik's forces became clear, Baratieri had been the picture of prudence and caution. "The action on the first of March conformed to the strategic principles . . . adopted throughout the campaign." He added, "No personal motive drove General Baratieri."[42]

It was a strong defense and a credible one, turning on its head the idea that an angry and bitter Baratieri had acted impetuously, pushing his army into a go-for-broke confrontation in the hope of saving his career. Instead, Cantoni argued that Baratieri showed the utmost respect for the capabilities of the Ethiopian army and a clear inclination to withdraw to defend Eritrea, rather than risk everything in an attack. If there was recklessness, it was on the side of his brigadier generals, who had cast Baratieri's prudence as cowardice and incompetence. In an emotional summing up, Cantoni turned on Baratieri's accusers. "General Baratieri is not guilty of inexcusable motives for exposing our army to danger," he said. "The motives belong to four brigadier generals . . . and the Ministry of War!"

And while Cantoni took care to avoid saying so directly, no one in attendance at the tribunal could quite shake the notion that Albertone and Dabormida had—by reckless accident or by deliberate intent—turned the advance of 29 February into an attack. Of course, neither man was available to state otherwise—Albertone was a prisoner of Menelik and Dabormida was dead—but questions from the tribunal had created opportunities for plausible alternative narratives to emerge. They hadn't.

Cantoni then turned to the second charge, that of negligence during the retreat—in effect, abandonment of command. Cantoni treated the charge categorically. It was true that orders to retreat had not been sent to General Dabormida. Similarly, the camp at Sauria had been left without orders, as had the forces ensconced in the fort at Adigrat. Communications had been effectively cut by the persistence and fury of the pursuit, leaving no real possibility of giving new orders until 3 March, when Baratieri arrived at Adi Caie in Eritrea. It was a matter not of negligence, Cantoni argued, but of *forza maggiore*. The overwhelming power of the Ethiopian attack and pursuit had rendered further communication impossible. That Baratieri had issued no orders was not a dereliction of duty; it was sheer impossibility.[43]

In a dramatic closing, Cantoni invoked the memory of the dead and the words of Baratieri himself. "Remember the words of General Baratieri," he said. " 'Not one of the fallen would accuse me of having sacrificed them to vanity.' " He asked the tribunal to absolve General Baratieri of both charges. The prosecution decided to drop the abandonment-of-command charges.[44]

The Verdict

The verdict came two days later, on the morning of Sunday, 14 June.

Judgment took the form of a lengthy disquisition on the battle. On the question of responsibility, the tribunal exonerated Baratieri. It accepted the argument that Baratieri was not the force behind the decision to advance to the passes, let alone attack. Instead, he "gave in to the too generous instincts of his subordinates" and decided to advance. It was an ingenious way to finesse the problem of responsibility. Without putting a heavy burden of guilt on the shoulders of the brigadier generals, the weight was lifted from Baratieri's.[45] Thanks to the magical power of words, the reckless behavior of the generals became mere patriotic zeal— admirable but misplaced.

In Italy, public reaction was muted. In private, there was anger. Senator Cesare Ricotti offered the contradictory observation that while he was glad that Baratieri had been exonerated, he should have been shot for the *pazzi* remark.[46] Queen Margherita condoned similar views.[47] King Umberto, who seems to have favored conspiracy theories, noted that those in favor of exoneration were members of the Masonic Order.[48] The newspaper *Il Popolo Romano* speculated that the government had intervened to protect Baratieri. Subsequent commentators have echoed this view, observing that at the bottom of the process lay "un meccanismo molto italiano."[49]

It may be amusing to think such a scheme true, just as it can be hard to let go of clichés. But though a claim may be credible, it can also be untrue. Certainly what stands out from the trial, other than the exoneration of Baratieri, was the studied avoidance of politics. There seems to have been a shared resolve not to talk about issues of finance, about policy debates, about the responsibility of political actors. The minister of war's decision to release Baratieri's famous *pazzi* telegram never came up directly at trial, thus preventing the proceedings from turning into an indictment of Italy's political class.[50]

What argues most effectively against a political deal of any kind was the fact that the verdict to absolve Baratieri was arrived at only at the last minute, and even then by a split vote.[51] Alessandro Sapelli, an old hand in Eritrea, an eyewitness, and a man who knew many of the principals, noted that the tribunal was ready to hand down a guilty verdict as late as the final day of testimony. At the last minute they drew back. "After Adwa," noted Sapelli, "a whirlwind of atrocious and ingenerous accusations was let loose. Everyone sought to saddle the defeated man with their own responsibilities." Sapelli credited Antonio Baldissera, Baratieri's successor as governor-general, with persuading the military tribunal of the wisdom of acquittal. On the morning of the verdict, rather than permit "an enormous injustice" to occur, Baldissera appealed to the members of the tribunal on behalf of a fellow soldier.[52]

Baldissera's persuasive appeal to the brotherhood of soldiers saved the life of Oreste Baratieri. The trial of Baratieri might well have been a grand drama on the themes of hubris and betrayal. Instead, the themes were adapted to the modest scale of a trial hidden away in Eritrea. The army—wounded, humiliated, grieving—gathered around one of its own.

CHAPTER 20

Rescues

CHICAGO'S LITTLE ITALY reeled. The dreadful rumors were relayed among the bakeries and grocery stands of the Near West Side—the Italian army routed, Baratieri dead! News raced down Van Buren and up Halsted—hundreds taken prisoner![1]

For days the *Chicago Tribune* ran articles about raw nerves and tender sensibilities among Italian Americans in the aftermath of Adwa. Tradesmen from Basilicata, bachelors from Calabria—it seemed that everyone had a stake in the outcome. The *Tribune* carried early reports that the Italian government would widen the draft and redouble the effort at conquest. Italy would avenge the defeat at Adwa by sending additional troops, who would complete the subjection of Ethiopia.

In the broader Italian diaspora, the sons of Italy apparently felt the same way—only an aggressive counterattack could salvage Italian pride and manhood. Oscar Durante, the owner and editor of *L'Italia,* Chicago's Italian-language newspaper, had openly pushed a pro-Africanist slant in the lead-up to Adwa. "Victory upon Victory!" *L'Italia* crowed as Italy suffered defeat upon defeat at Amba Alage and Mekele. But there was no way to finesse Adwa. "Horrendous and Colossal Slaughter of Italian Troops in Africa!" ran the banner headline for 7 March.[2] They were words to inspire not just compassion but also a desire for revenge.

Prominent Italian Americans in Chicago called a meeting for 8 March at the Hull House gymnasium for the ostensible purpose of collecting money for the Italian Red Cross. At the meeting, however, it was decided also to collect men. Durante, editor of *L'Italia,* announced that a volunteer force was being organized, with the support of the Italian consulate, to return to Italy in order to prepare to avenge Adwa.[3] Forty members of the Italia Club stepped forward—they would go and defend Italian honor. Later, their ardor was cooled by sobering reports from Italy, where crowds were rioting to resist government call-ups. Railroad tracks were being pried up to halt troop departures.[4] Roads to the French and Austrian frontiers were clogged with young men leaving Italy. While Italian Americans were itching for a fight, in Italy men would rather flee than be called to fight the war in Ethiopia.[5]

Everything turned on context, it seemed. In the United States, the story of Italy's defeat—the "shame" of Adwa—threatened the status of Italian immigrants within the emerging hierarchy of race and ethnicity in late nineteenth-century America.[6] The intensity of the Italian American reaction to such a seemingly remote event reveals their precarious status among other recent immigrants, including the Irish, the Greeks, various eastern Europeans, recent arrivals from Asia, and—perhaps most tellingly—the first generation of African Americans to be born and come of age in post-emancipation America. Adwa mattered because it felt so close to home. It was a battle the Italians had lost, but it was also a battle that Italian Americans couldn't win, either. No sooner had they clamorously volunteered to return to Italy to rescue their honor as sons of Italy than the *Chicago Tribune* implicitly ridiculed their divided loyalties with an article entitled "Only One Flag and One Country."[7]

Public opinion in Italy with respect to the vision of an Italian East Africa had been tepid at best.[8] Northern newspapers voiced an emphatic skepticism. The Milan-based *Corriere della Sera,* mouthpiece of the Italian bourgeoisie, was openly skeptical of the grand vision of Italian East Africa. The vision fared little better in the south. The port city of Naples had a more Mediterranean outlook, and pro-colonial points of view could get a more sympathetic hearing there, but among the general population, especially in the countryside, illiteracy and meager subsistence living kept horizons close.[9]

Individual soldiers and officers complained of a distinct lack of enthusiasm among the population at large. Major Marcello Prestinari observed
a "grand, general apathy" among Italians—and he was right.[10] If Italy was
in Africa, it was not because the Italian people clamored for it. At election time, there were plenty of reasons for voters to go to the polls. For
most voters, Africa was not one of them. In an era of jingoism, Italy was
largely immune.

It was an apathy that events did little to change. When Italy's forces
routed Mangasha in 1895, Baratieri enjoyed a brief celebrity, but he
failed to fire the imperial imagination. And although the setbacks during
Menelik's march—Amba Alage, Mekele—did prompt calls for revenge,
they did not notably swell the ranks of the pro-colonialists. On the
contrary, following Amba Alage, students at the University of Rome took
to the streets shouting, "Viva Menelik!"[11] It was quite possibly Europe's
first anticolonial demonstration.

Rather than stir up support for the vision of an Italian empire in Africa, defeat at Adwa emboldened its enemies. Within days of Adwa there
were legislative initiatives to abandon Africa altogether.[12] Within hours,
angry demonstrators in Rome filled the Piazza Colonna. Once again
there were cries of "Viva Menelik!"[13] Students threw rocks through windows of Crispi's house. At Montecitorio, home of the Chamber of Deputies, students shouted, "Death to the deputies!" Bands of demonstrators
attacked the offices of *La Tribuna,* the pro-Crispi, pro-Africanist newspaper based in Rome; they shattered windows and scattered paper.
Demonstrators confronted Prince Odescalchi—a member of the Italian
nobility—and tried to make him join them in the choruses of "Viva
Menelik!" He refused.[14]

In Venice, Antonio Vigo launched a petition drive urging the Chamber of Deputies to get out of Eritrea altogether. The colony, Vigo stated,
"devours dignity, goods, men, and the good name of Italy." "Italy," the
petition continued, "should want [for Africa] what it wants for itself,
freedom from foreign hegemony." With such a shrewd reference to Italy's own history of foreign domination at the hands of the Spanish, the
Ottomans, the French, and the Austrians, Vigo made anticolonialism a
patriotic value. "Leave Africa to the Africans," he urged. "Let us turn
our attention to *bella Italia.*"[15]

The Fate of the Prisoners

Throughout the great global Italian diaspora, hearts and wallets opened for the soldiers and their families. The Giuseppe Garibaldi Mutual Aid Society of Curitiba (Brazil) sent 1,104 lire. Montevideo, Uruguay, sent more than 50,000 lire for the families of soldiers wounded and dead. Guatemala, Argentina, and Bolivia all sent checks, some directly to King Umberto, some to the Ministry of War. The Italian community of Lima, Peru, collected more than 43,000 lire. Sydney, Malta, Hamburg, Trieste, Gibraltar, and Melbourne all checked in, as did the Italian communities of Turkey, Russia, France, and Spain. In New York, "*il cavaliere* Carlo Barsotti," who had spearheaded the drive for the Columbus statue at Columbus Circle in 1892, lent his name and newspaper to the effort on behalf of the families of Adwa fallen. His *Progresso Italo-Americano* netted 55,000 lire. New Jersey stepped up, too—Katie Dughi, Lina Franchi, and Rocchina Belfatto canvassed Newark and netted $428 (2,405 lire) for the Italian Red Cross.[16]

All the goodwill in the world couldn't touch the anxiety of the families of soldiers, desperate for news of their loved ones. In the immediate aftermath of the battle, there was plenty of misinformation to go around, starting with the principals. It was said that Baratieri had committed suicide, that he had died in battle, that he and all of his brigadier generals were dead—none of which turned out to be true. But while some of the basic facts about the battle—the where, when, and how, the fate of the commanders—came out within a week or so, it took much longer for reliable information regarding ordinary soldiers to appear. The prisoners' long march from Adwa to Addis effectively occurred within a news blackout that lasted nearly three months. Some journalists gave in to the demand for news about the fate of soldiers by hatching stories. Tales of heroic and perfidious deeds abounded.

Once in Addis, where European newspapers caught up with them, many soldiers were astonished to read accounts of their own deaths, often glorious. When Giuseppe Pantano reached Addis Ababa, he was gratified to learn that he had died a fine, soldierly death. Surrounded by amused friends, he relished the gripping journalistic fantasy of his final moments on earth. The story obeyed the conventions of patriotic

martyrdom, recounting how a badly wounded Pantano refused to surrender. As a group of Ethiopians closed in, he squeezed off the final
rounds from his officer's pistol, taking with him as many as he could.
Then he pulled a saber from a fallen comrade and rushed at the Ethiopians, hacking and slicing before falling with a thousand wounds. Pantano
died a hero's death and lived to tell about it.

Along with Italian valor and heroism, there were tales of Ethiopian cruelty. Prisoners were astonished to read that they had all been emasculated
and that they would never know the sweetness of fatherhood and family.
Poor Lieutenant Giacomo Sacconi—it was said that he had had his limbs
hacked off and switched around, so that his legs were coming out of shoulders and arms at the hips. When Sacconi read of his cruel fate, he checked
his legs and arms, just to be sure they were where they belonged.[17]

Some families grew tired of waiting for news of loved ones from official
sources and pursued their own leads. Giuseppe Treboldi, a lieutenant,
was reported missing after Adwa. His family was desperate for clarity—
was Giuseppe dead? A prisoner? Anguish drove the family to contact
Anna D'Amico, a celebrated mystic. D'Amico asked the family for a token
object, something that belonged to Giuseppe. She gripped the object,
reading the emanations from it to divine Giuseppe's fate. After a suspen-
seful, silence she proclaimed the good news. "Your Giuseppe lives and
walks!"

A short time later, the Treboldi family received official notice of
Giuseppe's death from the War Ministry. The family turned on D'Amico,
accusing her of profiting from their misery. The mystic stood her ground.
"The Ministry can say what it likes; your Giuseppe lives!" Soon enough
a letter postmarked Addis Ababa arrived to confirm D'Amico's fine
hunch. It was from Giuseppe, who was a prisoner. D'Amico's mystical
gift—termed "television" by contemporaries—had sustained his family's
hopes.[18]

Families of the dead grieved.[19] Families of those taken prisoner felt
relief, but relief soon turned to wonder. When would loved ones return?

In Ethiopian warfare, the victors took spoils among the vanquished.
In European warfare, the victors demanded reparations from the van-
quished. In the last major European war prior to Adwa, the Franco-Prussian
War of 1870, victorious Germany demanded and received five billion

francs as indemnity from defeated France. If Menelik had been unaware of this, Ilg and others surely would have informed him. Italy would have to pay.

Acute public anxiety about the rapid and safe return of the prisoners created political opportunity. If Italy had been apathetic about the colonial project, it was deeply engaged by the plight of the prisoners. Their story would dominate the press for months to come, especially as the prisoners' letters home—in envelopes bearing the new Menelik postage stamps—began to reach Italy.[20] Menelik and Taytu understood that the redemption of the Italian prisoners of war would bring a significant amount of cash; it also brought the negotiating weight required to secure Italian recognition of Ethiopian sovereignty and independence.

The Vatican Reacts

Within Italy, the prisoners became a marvelous new weapon in old political battles. The Catholic Church was still nursing a grudge against the Italian state over issues dating back to the unification of Italy in the 1850s and 1860s. Italy had wrested the Papal States—a vast stretch of land across the middle of the Italian peninsula—from the pope's control. In 1870, the papal city of Rome was taken by armed force. It became the capital of a newly unified Italy, while the pope retreated to the grounds of the Vatican.

After the disaster of Amba Alage, the Vatican censured clergy who had offered the conventional soothing patriotic remarks at memorial services. Why? Because to remark that Italians had "died for their country" validated the status quo, effectively sanctioning the seizure of the Papal States. After Adwa, the bishop of Nardo, in Puglia, requested guidance from the Vatican. He feared that honoring the fallen would glorify the "usurper"— the new Italy—when in fact Adwa showed the tragic consequences of its politics.[21] The bishop hammered away on the theme of usurpation, linking the Italian land grab in Africa with its predation against the papal lands in Italy. Adwa showed the folly of Italian colonial expansion into Ethiopia, which the Vatican had opposed, while it underscored the ineptitude of the political and military leadership.

As for the prisoners, even before the Vatican could act, Michelangelo Gona and Giuseppe Scuderi launched a lay campaign, calling upon the generosity of Catholics to secure the release of Italy's young men. Pope Leo XIII soon authorized a parallel initiative of public collections to be made to buy the prisoners' freedom. It featured printed forms that required donors to fill in relevant details: diocese, town, parish. Respondents sent pledges and small change, along with thousands of petitions in support of the pope's "magnanimous initiative for the redemption of our prisoners in Africa."[22]

Any papal initiative was fraught with risk for the Italian state, which the Vatican newspaper *Osservatore Romano* depicted as riddled with faithless Freemasons eager to crush Africa's only Christian state.[23] The intervention of the Catholic Church on behalf of the prisoners might fall fully within its apostolic and charitable missions, but it also held the promise of a major public relations victory for the pope—and a blow to his secular antagonists.[24] Italian political leadership was trapped. Success for the Vatican would mean yet another embarrassing defeat for Italy, but there was no way they could stand in the way of the benevolent intervention of the pope. Italy wanted its sons back by any means. A pro-Vatican newspaper, anticipating a triumph for the Vatican initiative and a release of the prisoners, crowed ominously, "Long Live Leo XIII, father of the nation!"[25]

Indeed, the Vatican made use of its connections with the Coptic Orthodox Church, on which Ethiopia was dependent for its religious leaders, to pursue the prisoners' release. The Vatican organized a mission to Ethiopia, led by the patriarchal vicar of Alexandria (Egypt), Cyril Macarios.

Monsignor Macarios was young, blond, and "pleasantly round." Much rested on his shoulders. He represented the best efforts of the Catholic Church to secure the release of the Italian prisoners from Ethiopia in the name of shared Christian values. Macarios was received with great pomp when he arrived in Addis Ababa on 14 August. Menelik had a wry sense of humor. He assigned Baratieri's head cook, taken prisoner at Adwa, to Macarios for the duration of his stay.[26]

There were rumors that Macarios carried not one plea from the pope but two. The first, a written message, called upon Menelik to release all the prisoners. A second, communicated in person, was more modest but at least as dangerous—it asked for the release of prisoners from the former Papal States. If true, and if Menelik had acted on it, it would have represented Ethiopia's de facto recognition of papal sovereignty over the former Papal States—and a devastating setback for Italy.[27] Such a shrewd

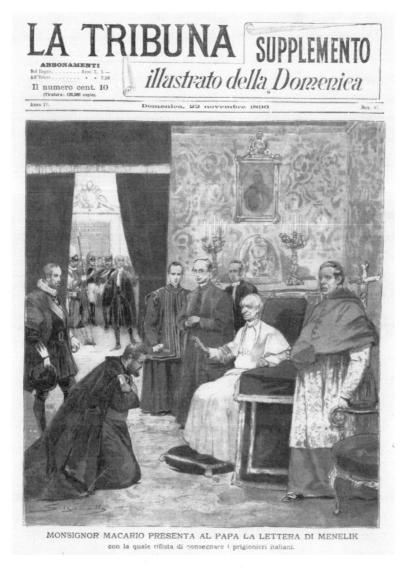

LA TRIBUNA | SUPPLEMENTO
illustrato della Domenica

MONSIGNOR MACARIO PRESENTA AL PAPA LA LETTERA DI MENELIK
con la quale rifiuta di consegnare i prigionieri italiani.

Monsignor Macario returns from Ethiopia. From *La Tribuna Illustrata,*
22 November 1896.

move might have torn Italy apart just as Menelik's Ethiopia was coming
together—brilliant symmetry, cruel payback. Dominico Farini, a well-
connected political leader, confided his worst fears to his diary. Coming
on the heels of defeat at Adwa, success for the papal initiative would be
fatal to Italy. *"Finis Italiae!"* he wrote—"Italy is finished."[28]

Whether Macarios carried one plea or two, neither was going anywhere.
At the urging of the Italian government, Augusto Franzoj contacted Alfred

Ilg, then in Switzerland, and asked him to intervene. Friendship between Franzoj and Ilg went back to the 1880s, when Franzoj had visited Ethiopia as a journalist explorer. Franzoj hired Ilg to turn Menelik against the Macarios mission. In series of letters and telegrams, Franzoj arranged for Ilg to return to Addis immediately to scuttle the papal initiative. It's unclear how much Ilg charged for his services, but the final figure was at least in the tens of thousands of lire. How do we know? Because years later, Franzoj took the government to court for nonpayment of expenses. Whether this was extortion or a mere billing dispute, we'll never know, but given the incendiary potential of such a case—the government paying to subvert a mission to release Italy's sons—the parties agreed that the prudent thing was to settle out of court. Franzoj turned over all documents related to the case in exchange for a cash settlement.[29]

In the end, Ilg's intercession might have been unnecessary. Upon his arrival, Macarios got into a nasty precedence battle with the local authority of the Ethiopian church, the *abuna* Matewos. Historically, Ethiopia had gotten its prelates from Alexandria, to which they were thus symbolically subordinate. When Macarios arrived he insisted on precedence, thus antagonizing not only the *abuna* but also much of Menelik's court, including Taytu.[30]

Nikolai Leontiev: Scoundrel, Impresario, Self-Made Diplomat

Menelik knew the PR value of the prisoners. Unfortunately, so did everyone else. Every swindler with an eye for the main chance, every huckster bent on self-promotion, wanted to get in on the game.

Nikolai Stefanovic Leontiev was one of those classic figures—rogue, scamp, outrageous self-promoter—of which the European nineteenth century had an abundance, just like our own. Leontiev was a native of Kherson, Ukraine. He had sought to make a career for himself in the Russian officer corps. Leontiev traveled. He loved the night life, racked up debts, and very soon was bounced out of the army, though not before drawing down the family patrimony.[31] Somehow, in 1895, he made his way to Ethiopia.

The origins of what became known as the Leontiev mission are obscure, but some things are clear. In St. Petersburg, Leontiev talked up his experience in Persia and India to the Russian Geographic Society.

He also befriended the son of Aleksei Suvorin, editor of *Novoye Vremya,* a St. Petersburg daily. It's possible that he had a conversion experience. It's also possible that he used contrite promises of self-reform to insinuate himself among religiously inspired patriots. In the end, he successfully promoted a vision of a globally engaged Russia to merchants and religious leaders in the Russian capital. It is unclear how Ethiopia specifically became the objective of his campaign, but the ongoing scramble for Africa, along with the perceived affinities between Russian and Ethiopian Orthodoxy, presumably had something to do with it. What is certain is that Leontiev embarked on his mission to Ethiopia in January 1895 without telling the Russian government.[32]

Once in Addis, Leontiev used his looks, charm, and gregarious nature to insinuate himself at court. Leontiev also cut a figure in expat Addis society, serving champagne and cranking up his gramophone to play "Schon nahen sich die Edlen meiner Lande" from Wagner's *Tannhäuser*. A slight stammer softened an otherwise overwhelming impression that this tall, blond, rugged beast might bowl over anyone who got in his way. When asked about his plans, one of his answers was that he intended to establish a mission of the Orthodox Church. Another was that Russia intended to help Ethiopia defend itself. Two weeks into his stay in Addis, Leontiev produced what he claimed was a letter for Menelik from the czar of Russia.[33]

Soon Menelik had Leontiev packed off back to Moscow for the ostensible purpose of placing a wreath on the tomb of Alexander III, who had died in November 1894. It's unclear whether Menelik just wanted to get the lumbering Russian out and so lunged at the pretext or actually believed Leontiev's claims of connections to the czar. Either way, Leontiev had secured a place for himself at the head of an Ethiopian delegation of clergy and notables.

No one bothered to tell the czar. The group was in Cairo by the time St. Petersburg learned of its imminent arrival—too late to unmask Leontiev or to turn the delegation back without embarrassment. In St. Petersburg, the government had no choice but to accord the Ethiopian delegation the usual diplomatic honors. After making landfall in Odessa and a stopover in Moscow, the group arrived in St. Petersburg in early July 1895. Nicholas himself received the group at Peterhof Palace on July 13.[34]

Leontiev pumped up the rank of the delegation along the way. One member gained the title of prince, while a priest, Gebre Egziabeher, was

The Leontiev mission to Russia. From *L'Illustrazione italiana,* 22 July 1895.

elevated to bishop—a title that does not exist in the Ethiopian church.[35] Leontiev himself, although drummed out of the Russian army at the rank of lieutenant, acquired the rank of colonel. He let it be known that Menelik had promoted him to the rank of general in the Ethiopian army—a fiction duly repeated by the St. Petersburg press.[36]

The delegation made the most of its status as guests of the czar; in Petersburg its members were lodged at the Hotel Europa, the city's finest. There, it was said, prodigious quantities of champagne were consumed. The mission was received by a number of high-ranking government and church officials. Cavalry exercises, balloon launches, and Cossack parades were performed for their pleasure and edification.[37] As a gesture of thanks to hosts and dignitaries, the Ethiopian prince started handing out jewelry with very large emeralds; the jewelry was touted as an example of Ethiopian mineral wealth and artisanal skill.

The fairy tale came to an end when the St. Petersburg press began to ask questions, starting with "Who is Leontiev?" An investigation into the emerald jewelry revealed the emerald stones to be colored glass; the jewelry itself—promoted as the apex of Ethiopian skill—had been crafted in St. Petersburg. In the face of the breaking scandal, the government hastened the departure of the mission. Unfortunately, this meant creating a second Leontiev mission to Menelik.[38]

In such a manner, Leontiev had gone from debt-ridden scoundrel to respected diplomat in a single round trip. Having bluffed his way into high diplomatic circles, Leontiev was the czar's obvious choice to lead a return delegation to Addis. Unlike the first mission to Menelik, this one was official. It departed Odessa on 9 August 1895, bearing 135 late-model Berdan rifles as a gift to Menelik.[39]

The historical record did not capture Menelik's reaction to the news of Leontiev's return to Addis, though it must have come as a shock; Menelik probably had thought he was rid of the Russian. Leontiev came prepared for a cool reception: in a feat worthy of Professor Harold Hill, Leontiev arrived in Addis with a caravan load of musical instruments—forty in all—with which to form Ethiopia's first brass band.[40]

In Leontiev, Italy saw sinister designs, a European rivalry transposed to Africa. The French were in Addis, and now the Russians, too? This was too much. Just as Italy faced France and Russia as potential enemies in its alliance with Germany in a European war that threatened to break out at any time, now the war had moved to Africa. Lively imaginations had Leontiev, who had flunked out of the Russian military, actively coaching Menelik's army—on the eve of his campaign against Italy—in the very latest European military techniques.[41] Still others saw in Leontiev's lack of credentials a sure sign of covert Russian involvement, likely with French connivance.[42]

Even worse, what if Ethiopia became a wider European concern, thanks to French and Russian meddling? Everything would be lost if the major powers intervened.[43] Italy's man in Addis, Luigi Capucci, was desperate to know what Leontiev was telling Menelik. He went after the interpreter—the only other man in the room during their conferences—and made liberal use of alcohol, to which the interpreter was known to be partial. Capucci learned that Leontiev was talking down Italy as "poor and weak." He also made grand promises of arms and ammunition from Russia. In exchange, Leontiev suggested, Russia might welcome territory among the Afar.[44] The Afar, who controlled the caravan routes up from the sea, had a long working arrangement with Menelik, who was in no position simply to turn over their territory.

Italian anxiety only furthered Leontiev's efforts at self-promotion by inflating his importance. At one point, Italian diplomats were trying to pin down a rumor that Leontiev had journeyed to Addis with a Cossack regiment to fight for Menelik.[45] In Addis, Capucci knew better. He was aware that Leontiev was an operator, but it took time to convince Rome that the more Italy fretted over Leontiev, the more important he became.

In late 1895, as Menelik prepared to leave Addis on the campaign that would take him to Adwa, Leontiev voyaged to Europe. There he offered his services as peace intermediary between Ethiopia and Italy. Through third parties, he approached Alberto de Blanc, Italy's foreign minister, with an offer of peace. It was Leontiev's bluff and bluster at its best. He claimed that Menelik regarded him "as a god" and that Menelik would do whatever he told him. In return for his good offices, Leontiev asked only for expenses. The request got as far as the Treasury office, where Sidney Sonnino announced he "would have nothing to do with this adventurer" and turned him down.[46] Later, back in St. Petersburg, Leontiev would pad his résumé with the claim that the Italians had offered him two million lire to secure an agreement.[47]

After Adwa, Leontiev returned to Addis. Menelik had released fifty prisoners in honor of Queen Margherita of Italy as a birthday gift. He released another fifty in July, ostensibly in honor of the coronation of the czar of Russia. His real motive was likely to rid himself of Leontiev yet again, for the Russian was chosen to escort the prisoners to the coast.[48] Leontiev then contacted the Italians claiming to have authority from Menelik to negotiate the release of the remaining prisoners. It was another brilliant bid, but the Italians refused to play along.[49]

Menelik the Magnanimous; Nerazzini Deals

Menelik's release of groups of prisoners showed him to be charitable and magnanimous but did nothing to reduce the importance of the hundreds of prisoners he still held. Presumably the Vatican mission led by Macarios would have benefited from a similar gesture: he would have been turned down in his formal request for all of the prisoners but allowed to depart Addis with a compensatory contingent. It would have been a victory for Menelik and the pope, another defeat for Italy. Through back channels Italy made it clear that a release of prisoners to anyone other than a representative of Italy would only deprive Menelik of the means to achieve a lasting peace with Italy.[50] After fifty days in Addis, Macarios left empty-handed, or nearly so.[51] He departed Addis on 1 October 1896 with two sick prisoners and a letter for the pope.[52]

In his letter to Pope Leo XIII, Menelik expressed his "profound regret" that he could not do what his conscience "as a Christian and a monarch" told him he should do. As father of his people, he was "forbidden to sacrifice the sole guarantee of peace."[53] However appealing the prospect of a grand gesture in response to the pope, Menelik knew that the prisoners were worth more than goodwill. They represented his best assurance of peace and secure frontiers.

Although Menelik denied the pope, he favored the simple pleas of mothers. A batch of mail intended for prisoners included an envelope addressed simply "To My Son Antonio, Prisoner in Abyssinia." The letter was opened so that it could be delivered to the intended recipient. The Italian officers who opened the letter were deeply moved by it. They sent it along to Ilg, who passed it on to Menelik himself.

In her letter, Antonio's mother explained that she had traveled to Pompeii, where she lighted a candle before the statue of Our Lady of Pompeii, a devotion greatly in vogue in the 1890s, and prayed for the safe return of her son. Menelik was so impressed by "her simple and certain faith" that he had Antonio brought to him. "Your mother is a holy lady; my wish is that her prayers be answered," Menelik said. "You are free. Her are fifty thalers for your journey. I will give you a mule; you will leave with the first caravan." Antonio was on his way home.[54]

After the launch of the Vatican-sponsored mission, a second nongovernmental mission got under way. Two great matrons of the Roman aristocracy, Marchesa di Rende and Marchesa Perrotti, in collaboration with the Sisters of Mercy, organized a delegation. It was led by

Count Wersowitz, a clergyman of Polish extraction, and included Raynald de Choiseul, Casimiro Jakowski, and Luigi Fagiuoli. They left Naples on 20 May and encountered the usual difficulties organizing a caravan up from the Somali coast. There were still in Djibouti in early July when Count Wersowitz died of sunstroke. The remainder of the party carried on, eventually making their way to Addis, bearing food, medicine, liquor, tobacco, and soap. Intangible needs were also met— each prisoner received a pack of playing cards and a rosary.[55] Then came mail call in the form of 2,626 letters from parents and loved ones.[56]

Menelik was holding out for more than papal goodwill and care packages. Cesare Nerazzini arrived in Addis on 6 October to negotiate for the release of the prisoners.[57] He offered encouragement to the prisoners in the form of fresh uniforms, cigars, and grappa.[58] By 26 October, the negotiations were complete.[59] The breakthrough had come when Nerazzini made a "spontaneous" declaration that Italy would absorb the costs Menelik incurred as host of the prisoners. The final document recognized that the prisoners "had been the object of the greatest solicitude of His Majesty the Emperor of Ethiopia." Menelik did not specify a figure, but the document recognized that the maintenance of the prisoners had led to "considerable expenditures."

Italy was anxious to avoid the appearance of paying indemnity or ransom; Menelik was happy to oblige. Accordingly, the agreement specified no figure for Ethiopian hospitality, claiming instead to rely entirely upon the "sense of fairness" of the Italian government. In fact, the round number of ten million lire, to be paid in three installments, was eventually decided upon.[60] It was a royal figure, about 6,301 lire per prisoner, or 27 lire per prisoner per day. In a country where two lire would buy a whole chicken and a liter of wine, this was gracious hospitality indeed.[61]

Nerazzini departed to prepare the delivery of the agreed-upon sum. As the British delegation arrived a few months later, they spotted Nerazzini on his return trip to Addis; he accompanied a caravan of mules bearing boxes stuffed with money—an installment of the ransom/ reimbursement.[62]

Repatriation of the prisoners required a logistical plan. Men who had spent the year outside the capital were called in. Those already east of the capital were convened at Harar; the rest gathered at Addis. The departures were organized in stages of 100–150 prisoners, separated by several weeks, so as not to overwhelm the water and food resources along the route to the coast. The journey home took six to eight weeks— Addis to Harar, Harar to Zeila on the Somali coast, then by boat to Massawa for a brief layover before the voyage through the Suez Canal to the Mediterranean and back to Naples.

Along the way, the main attraction was Harar, where the Italian Red Cross was ready with wine, liquor, cigars, and European food. This was undoubtedly the high point of their journey. It would stand in marked contrast to their reception upon arrival in Italy. When they made landfall at Naples, the men were loaded into wagons and whisked from the waterfront to the barracks at Granili. At Granili, they underwent a debriefing that left them feeling, some commented, like criminals or bearers of plague.[63]

The first group left Addis on 24 November 1896, a month after the conclusion of the peace treaty. The final group, led by General Albertone as the ranking officer, docked at Naples in late May 1897.

Departure from Ethiopia aroused complicated feelings. Many prisoners were eager to leave. Their memoirs suggest an enthusiasm to be done with Ethiopia and return to Italy as soon as possible. Giovanni Tedone had passed his captivity near Harar, where he had spent much of his time defending Italian soldierly valor against the mockery of his host, Birru. When he wasn't tangling with Birru he was fending off the ardent advances of Zandietu. With the announcement of his departure, the contests ended. All that remained was for Tedone, as the good guest, to listen as his hosts pressed upon him their wishes. As soon as he got back to Italy, he must send them gifts! The women wanted fine fabric from Italy—linens, blouses, lingerie, gold jewelry, perfume. As for the men, they didn't care about trifles. They wanted armaments—a new rifle, an officer's revolver, a small cannon—nothing special.

Zandietu was inconsolable; she wanted Tedone to stay. When he refused, she insisted that he return one day—and bring gifts.[64]

Despite the overwhelming impatience of most to leave, a few prisoners showed no hurry, having found themselves attached, or perhaps having no one to return to. By an estimate of the Italian Red Cross, some nine Italians remained in Ethiopia at the end of 1897, no longer prisoners but lingering all the same, somehow—sentimentally or otherwise—captivated.[65]

The feelings worked in the other direction as well. By the end of their stay, the Italians had become rather popular. When significant numbers of them gathered in the capital, they would be approached by young Ethiopians, some of whom imagined a better future for themselves in Eritrea. Some inquired about service as askari.[66]

Many departures were painful. On 13 February, as Francesco Frisina left Addis by the southern road, he stopped and turned for a final look at the city. A flood of memories washed over him. He knew that he was seeing the city for the last time. He turned and walked away in silence.

Sergeant Ludovico Barbieri, leaving two weeks later, had a similar reaction:

> The sun was just setting behind the hills [that ring the city] and the roof of the Imperial Palace was gold from the dying sun. . . . Plumes of smoke rose from some of the larger *tukul* that appeared as little more than dark spots while a bluish haze settled over the city, enveloping everything.

Some spoke of anguished departures, of leaving a piece of themselves behind though few, in the end, elected to stay.[67]

Saddest of all were those Ethiopians who had entered into relationships with the Italians; they now faced abandonment. These were not relationships born of stark imbalances in colonial power—as prisoners, these men had none—but affairs born of curiosity and desire. After the prisoners arrived, an illusion of durable happiness had settled in as the companionship of days and weeks turned to months.

The idyll vanished with the arrival of the peace. It seems never to have occurred to the prisoners to take their lovers with them. Some women—stubborn in their denial—refused to say goodbye in Addis. They trailed the caravan of men for days, unable to give in to separation, until finally, miles from home, they let go in wrenching scenes of loss.[68]

CHAPTER 21

Passings

L ATE IN 1896, Nicola D'Amato was among a group of prisoners to witness an extraordinary ceremony. Upon their arrival at the imperial compound that day, they found Menelik uncharacteristically somber, speaking in monosyllables. A gesture prompted them to look behind. They turned to see a seemingly infinite line of children, women, and elderly winding up the hillside to the palace. They were the survivors of the fallen—the children, wives, siblings, and parents of the men who had died in Ethiopia's war of independence.

Many wore hooded capes made of coarse wool in chestnut red. Their measured gait and silent resignation spoke of an abiding sorrow. Menelik took his place on the dais, available to them and their grief. Each stopped before the emperor, bowed deeply, received an utterance of recognition (*"Id!"* "Go!") of an individual sorrow, then resumed their solemn course. Menelik and the Italians were witnessing—were made to witness—the full impact of the war, what an observer called "a sigh at the foot of the sovereign." The somber cortege continued through the day and resumed the next. Five days in all were given over to a reckoning of the dead, a grim accounting of incalculable loss.[1]

After Adwa, Menelik's reputation as one of Africa's greatest leaders of all time was secure. Resentments in the north would linger; Tigray was unhappy to be ruled by a Shoan. But there was no mistaking the fact that, thanks to Ethiopia, the question of Africa's future remained open. The battle of Adwa was the battle for Africa. Over the next hundred years, European domination would gradually unravel. The history of African sovereignty in the modern era started at Adwa.

As for Ethiopia itself, Adwa secured an independent future, to be sure. Adwa was a great victory, but it was a victory that obscured a paradox, for in saving Ethiopia, Adwa gave monarchy renewed life. In that regard, the story of Ethiopia is comparable to that of Germany, where unity came through military victory, presided over by a monarchy. Similarly, contemporary Ethiopia took shape in the heroic national campaign of 1895–1896, culminating at Adwa. Menelik and Taytu staked everything on that campaign—in defeat, they certainly would have been overthrown, by the Italians if not by their own people. Even the horrific loss of life during the fighting of 1895–1896 failed to shake their thrones. Victory and Ethiopian unity rendered such losses acceptable, at least to those who survived. In triumph, their status as patrons of modern Ethiopia became unassailable.

Ethiopian art on Adwa captured the grandeur of the event, but also some of its political afterlife. Ethiopia has a great painterly tradition, thanks to the patronage of the Ethiopian Church. Because military victory was regarded as a sacred triumph—thanks to the presence of the clergy carrying the *tabot*—as well as a triumph of arms, it meant that Adwa qualified as a suitable subject for sacred art.[2] Almost immediately after Adwa, the battle became a favorite among artists, who depicted *tabot*-bearing clergy in the same frame as artillerymen and sharpshooters. Their presence constituted the equivalent of a withering spiritual fire.

The paintings observe certain conventions. Typically, the battle scene is split down the middle, with Ethiopians on the left and Italian forces on the right. The wicked Italians are presented in profile, while the righteous Ethiopians are full-face. Between them are individual combat tableaux—the dead and the dying, feats of heroism—and above it all St. George riding his steed with spear in hand, aiming at the Italian forces.

As the battle had occurred on the feast of St. George, Menelik ordered the construction of a monumental church in the saint's honor upon his return to Addis. It was consecrated a year later, in 1897—a tangible sign of royal gratitude.[3] Inside, beneath frescoes depicting the Last Supper and Jesus washing the feet of his disciples, was an Adwa battle scene.[4] In this, it was very much in the Ethiopian artistic tradition of works mingling sacred themes with profane events. Far from Addis, in a monastery church on Lake Tana, a fresco turns a scene from Exodus—the Hebrew flight from Egypt—into a comment on the defeat of the enemies of Ethiopia. It depicts Pharaoh's soldiers drowning in the Red Sea, but instead of chariots, bows, and arrows, they bear rifles and wear modern military dress.

Over time, Adwa battle scenes revealed shifting political fortunes. By the 1920s, artists featured Empress Taytu unveiled, wielding and often firing a revolver. Makonnen, too, began to figure more prominently, a trend that mirrored the rise of his son Haile Selassie to the imperial throne.[5]

The Duelist

When the Haitian intellectual Benito Sylvain made his way to Addis to celebrate the victory of Adwa, he came upon one of the battle's major figures. It was Matteo Albertone, the Italian general. Sylvain noted that Albertone seemed to be "carrying the entire weight of the defeat of Adwa."[6]

Albertone had some explaining to do, and he knew it. No one bore greater responsibility for the battle of Adwa and the horrific loss of life it brought to both sides. It was Albertone who had recklessly pushed his advance guard toward Menelik's camp, convinced that a weakened and demoralized Ethiopian army was ripe for defeat. Albertone's choice dragged the entire Italian army—divided and outnumbered—into battle.

In his first recorded commentary after the battle, Albertone was remorseful. In the early days of captivity, the prospect of a return to Italy seemed especially bleak, and he had some things he wanted to get off his chest. In a quiet moment shared with a fellow prisoner, the young lieutenant Gherardo Pantano, Albertone spoke candidly about his responsibility. "You are young," Albertone noted, "and you have a better chance than I of returning to Italy. Remember well what your general is telling you." Pantano listened intently. "Tell them that General Baratieri was betrayed by his officers."[7]

Later, Albertone sharply modified his view. He no longer spoke of "betrayal," perhaps because the hope of return to Italy improved as

negotiations for the release of the prisoners progressed. Although Baratieri had been careful in his court-martial testimony not to lay blame, in
the court's final judgment the "too eager" conduct of Albertone and
Dabormida—an excess of soldierly ardor—constituted a key argument
in favor of Baratieri's exoneration.

Albertone dropped the contrite demeanor. He began to offer an alternative account of how the day should have played out. He shifted responsibility onto Arimondi. It was said that as a prisoner in Addis, he
blamed Arimondi for not moving forward to occupy the gap between
Dabormida on the right and Albertone on the left. And he floated a possible motive—Arimondi resented the fact that Albertone had been given
command of Arimondi's beloved askari units.[8]

Was there an agreement among the generals to move aggressively
against the Ethiopian positions, against Baratieri's orders? The behavior of Albertone and Dabormida suggests as much. In fact, it is the sup-
position that best accounts for their behavior on the morning of 1 March.
The first rule of warfare is never to divide one's forces; it is a rule that
mere foot soldiers, let alone generals such as Albertone and Dabormida, certainly knew. Why, then, would they have left a gap between
their respective positions except if they expected Arimondi's troops to
fill it?

Albertone's repentant remark after the battle—"Tell them that General Baratieri was betrayed by his officers"—implies such collusion. Of
course, Dabormida and Arimondi were in no position to contradict or
confirm; they died at Adwa. Baratieri might well have had his suspi-
cions, but he was careful to avoid the kind of debate that would have torn
the army apart. At his trial and ever after, he chose simply to describe
what the others did, without attributing motives.

Albertone never faced charges. Back in Italy, he resumed his military
career for a time, continuing to serve as brigadier general. Newspapers
and memoirs continued to raise doubts about his conduct on 1 March.[9]
An oblique recognition of Albertone's disobedience came from Cesare
Pini, a close friend and confidant. "It's pointless to discuss here whether
he obeyed or disobeyed," he wrote in his memoirs. "What is above discussion is the soldierly valor of General Albertone." If he was guilty of
anything, Pini explained, it was that he "burned with a flaming desire to

lead his beautiful troops into battle."[10] In effect, Albertone's only fault was his desire to fight, even if it compromised an army.

A candid charge of disobedience, though private, came from General Giuseppe Ellena, who commanded the reserve brigade at Adwa. Not only was General Ellena part of the pre-battle debates, but he survived the battle and the retreat and was among the first of the participants to return to Italy—a hasty departure for which he was criticized. Months after the battle, in private correspondence with Baratieri, General Ellena wrote candidly about "the generals who disobeyed"—meaning Albertone, Arimondi, and Dabormida—as if the fact were well understood by the two men.[11]

As speculation swirled, Albertone found other ways of defending himself. He changed the subject by getting into a duel to uphold the honor of Italy and its army, taking on a pretender to the French throne.

France was a republic in the 1890s, but Henri d'Orléans was in line to occupy the throne of France should the French Republic fail. For the sake of his political career, he kept himself before the public eye through a series of exploits—there was nothing like travel abroad to demonstrate one's worldliness and capacity for rule. In 1897, Orléans journeyed to Addis to meet Menelik and Taytu, the world's newest celebrity statesmen.

His voyage was chronicled by the European press. Orléans served as his own publicist. He regularly dispatched letters to the newspaper *Figaro,* which was only happy to publish accounts of his exploits in faraway lands. In one of his letters, Orléans had made disparaging remarks about the performance of the Italian army at Adwa. General Albertone took offense; he challenged Orléans to a duel.

Upon his return to Paris in early August, Orléans responded that he would accept the challenge to a duel, but only from a social equal. He insisted on dueling a member of the Italian ruling family. The Count of Turin accepted, and the duel took place on 14 August 1897 at Vaucresson, a leafy village west of Paris.

Orléans chose as his seconds Raoul Mourichon, a traveling companion, and Nikolai Leontiev. Leontiev had befriended Orléans in Ethiopia and had followed him back to Paris.

Orléans and the Count of Turin agreed to duel with swords. The first two clashes ended inconclusively. In the third round, the Count of Turin suffered a superficial wound on the right hand. In the fifth assault, Orléans received an abdominal wound, serious but survivable. As he lay wounded, Orléans extended his hand to the Count of Turin. They shook hands.[12] Honor had been preserved.

Albertone, who had been the first to challenge Orléans, rescued his own honor with that of Italy. As soon as he learned of the outcome of the duel, he dashed off a note to Orléans stating that he considered the matter closed.[13] He retired and announced that he would work on his memoirs. They never appeared.

On the Beach in Djibouti

Italian fantasies of Leontiev's power and influence continued to inflate his importance. Though Leontiev was never more than a charlatan and a self-promoter, some Italians continued to believe he was part of a vast anti-Italian conspiracy.[14] It was even said that he had directed Ethiopian artillery fire at the battle of Adwa—a fiction, but a tribute to his ability to create the illusion of power.[15]

Leontiev found it congenial to stay in Addis, where he served an ornamental role at court. Menelik liked to have a clutch of Europeans on his right in the reception hall whenever foreign delegations visited. Leontiev had become a fixture, an accessory, part of the imperial spectacle. Menelik gave Leontiev the title of count—a title that did not exist in Ethiopia. Having found a station in life, Leontiev barely knew what to do. In his spare time, he hunted; he racked up a record number of elephant kills. Like Leontiev, Alfred Ilg was an avid hunter, and after a successful elephant hunt, Ras Makonnen dashed off congratulations to Ilg: "It is good that you killed an elephant before Count Leontiev exterminated [them all]."[16] Leontiev was becoming a punch line.

Still restless, the Russian inquired among diplomatic missions about their itineraries and destination. He sought to charm the British diplomat Edward Gleichen, letting on that he was pondering a journey to Omdurman but was ready "to go anywhere" at a moment's notice.[17]

Rebuffed in his attempts to refashion himself as freelance diplomat, Leontiev turned to the world of finance. By early 1898, Leontiev was back in Europe, at the center of a major investment scheme. Leontiev claimed that Menelik had appointed him governor-general of "the Equatorial Provinces of Ethiopia" thanks to a decree dated June 1897. Leontiev shuttled between London, Paris, and Brussels rounding up investors to buy shares in a syndicate to which Leontiev would transfer the "benefits and advantages" of Menelik's decree. The syndicate would "open up and develop the commercial, agricultural, mining, industrial and all other resources" of the Equatorial Provinces.[18] In consideration for his role in organizing the syndicate and transferring his rights to it, Leontiev received 25,000 pounds at the creation of the syndicate and another 100,000 pounds once the syndicate had completed a second round of fundraising.[19] Leontiev was becoming very wealthy.

Leontiev's timing was good. The long depression that had beset the European economy since the 1870s was giving way to the sunny world of the Belle Époque. Investor materials compared Leontiev's Equatorial Provinces syndicate to the wildly profitable Belgian Congo Company and the India Rubber Company. Leontiev had little trouble drumming up investors. It was even said that Leopold himself, king of Belgium, had bought in.

Patriotism played a role for British and French investors as they came to see Leontiev's Equatorial Provinces as a strategic piece in plans to link territories across Africa. After a sales visit to London, Leontiev moved on to Paris, deepening British anxiety that French investors might dominate Leontiev's Equatorial Provinces and, through them, Africa itself. "Tell Leontiev we leave for Paris Tuesday night with cash," wrote one group via telegram from London, eager to close the deal before it slipped away. "We rely upon his parole," they added innocently.[20] Once British investors were on the hook, Leontiev and associates were ready to play the French. Nicolas Notovitch, a Leontiev associate, warned investors, "It's the stranglehold of England, not only on Abyssinia, but on all of Africa." By the time the *Moniteur Belge* printed the official notice of the formation of the syndicate in May 1898, it boasted an honor roll of fifty major investors from Britain, France, and Belgium.[21]

The scheme came unraveled shortly thereafter. The territories claimed by Leontiev—and thus the rights transferred to the syndicate—did not belong to him. They weren't even, in fact, part of Ethiopia. Leontiev's Equatorial Provinces included nearly three million acres beyond Ethiopia's southwest frontier, including the southernmost reaches of the Nile and the Lake Rudolph region, parts of modern Sudan and Kenya.

We may never know whether Menelik actually conferred the title of governor-general on Leontiev or, if he had, whether it was part of a massive practical joke designed to get the troublesome Russian out of Addis. What *is* known is that Leontiev had found a way to spin gold from straw. Soon he was moving into a grand residence on the Avenue MacMahon, just off the Champs-Elysées, near the Arc de Triomphe. The mineral riches of the Equatorial Provinces made Leontiev a wealthy man, and he never even picked up a shovel.

In 1900 he published a richly illustrated volume based on an expedition he had led to the Equatorial Provinces after the first round of funding closed. The expedition included a company of Senegalese riflemen, some Cossacks, and fifty Arab scouts mounted on camels, as well as hundreds of Ethiopian soldiers and their spouses. Their ostensible purpose was to explore and settle the region, forming "definitive establishments"—although what became of these establishments is unclear.[22] The book details the natural riches that would be extracted once the railway from Djibouti to Addis was completed, but there are so many illustrations and photos that it is easy to overlook just how short on text—and detail—the book really is. The cover illustration features a dramatic hunting scene in full color. An elephant rears—he has just been shot—and smoke drifts from the barrel of Leontiev's rifle.

What is astonishing is that Leontiev got as far as he did. By 1900, official diplomatic correspondence—generally circumspect in its language—openly referred to him as "a common criminal."[23] But this did not stop Leontiev from organizing a second investment scheme based on his supposed authority. In 1901, Leontiev sold a fifty-year concession to the mining rights in the Equatorial Provinces to a new group of investors for 85,000 pounds.

A few years later, the house of cards was coming down. In 1904, the original group of investors was writing to Menelik himself, in the desperate hope that he would make good on their loss of nearly two million francs. In a statement that must rank among the silliest excuses for a bad investment, they admitted that they had invested "with eyes closed." Why? Because "we were assured of the support of a power and an authority such as Your Majesty."[24]

By then, Leontiev had been on the run for some time. Shortly after closing the second sale of concessions in the Equatorial Provinces in 1901, he had hatched a new scheme. He repackaged the provinces as "the emperor's gold mines" and sold them—a third time—to a group of British investors.

In due course, Europe was no longer hospitable to Leontiev. In late 1901 he found himself back in East Africa with a bounty hunter hot on his trail. An angry group of investors in one of his earlier schemes had sent a certain Monsieur Lagardère in pursuit of Leontiev. Lagardère's assignment was to bring Leontiev back to face trial for fraud. Lagardère arrived in Addis to learn that Leontiev had very recently sold all his worldly belongings and had even put a property in Djibouti up for sale. Leontiev himself was nowhere to be found.

Leontiev was on his way to the coast. Lagardère gave pursuit, hoping to reach Djibouti before Leontiev escaped. Leontiev arrived in Djibouti on 5 December 1902. No doubt clued in to his status as prey, he booked passage on the *Annam,* a steamer scheduled to leave that evening. But the *Annam* was delayed. With his situation becoming more desperate by the minute, Leontiev arranged for his bags to be forwarded to Aden. To avoid suspicion, they would be shipped under the name Zaleswski.[25] Knowing that every second might count, Leontiev decided to sleep on the beach so that he could board the next departing vessel as soon as it appeared. At five in the morning, a coal steamer dispatched from Aden arrived. Leontiev boarded, and the vessel—which never completed the usual formalities of visiting vessels—departed.

The French diplomatic representative at Djibouti recounted the entire comic episode in a tone that alternated between outrage and grudging admiration. He added as a postscript that just two weeks after Leontiev's hasty departure, a group of British investors disembarked at Djibouti, full of enthusiasm and eager to keep an appointment with Leontiev. They were the proud owners of the emperor's gold mines.

By the Canals of Venice

In the quiet of an early June morning in the year 1900, a portly gentleman strolled along the Grand Canal of Venice. Unable to sleep, he had risen early and dressed, seeking distraction in a walk along the canals.

He was the only witness to a woman's desperate act. Her husband had been found guilty of a crime. In her despair she sought death; she threw herself into the water. As she flailed desperately in the canal, the gentleman rushed to her rescue, lifting her to safety.

A crowd, attracted by the commotion, gathered around the woman and her rescuer. As the woman gasped and recovered her breath, attention turned to the hero, her rescuer. "It's Oreste Baratieri!" someone whispered. But before the crowd could react to the notorious person in their midst, he slipped off.[26]

Following his acquittal by the court-martial in 1896, Baratieri did his best to slide into obscurity. The army had rallied around him; his acquittal was a stark refusal by the tribunal to make Baratieri—and through him, the army—shoulder the responsibility for defeat. Baratieri's own conscience was unable to make such a distinction. When a friend tried to cheer up Baratieri by recalling his heroic rescue of the drowning woman in Venice, Baratieri was inconsolable. "What can it mean to save one person when, through my fault, so many are dead in battle?" he asked.

He took up residence in Arco, near his hometown in Trentino. After Adwa, some fifty residents had signed a letter expressing sympathy at his misfortune. He took this as a signal that he would be welcomed home. As Trentino remained under Austrian rule, the frontier helped to keep unpleasantness at bay. He resigned from his seat in the national legislature, where he had represented Brescia for twenty years. "Men pass; the nation remains," he noted in his letter of resignation.[27]

In Arco, Baratieri lived a solitary existence. His sister Luisa and his niece Maria Conzatti, whose letters had sustained him in Africa, grounded him in family.

Baratieri immediately set about the task of setting the record straight. As an intellectual as well as a soldier, this meant setting down his story in print. He wrote at a brisk pace; he was eager to engage ongoing debates about Adwa and empire. In 1898, mere months after his return from Eritrea, he published *Memoirs of Africa,* nearly five hundred pages of biography and self-defense.

In the years that followed, Baratieri lived a vagabond existence. Partly it was an ingrained restlessness—he had rarely enjoyed a settled existence after leaving home as a teenager to fight with Garibaldi. Partly it was a response to chronic insomnia. As regrets and grim memories haunted his nights, he sought out distraction. Prying questions haunted, too.

Baratieri frequented the spa towns and tourist capitals of Europe—Madrid, Baden Baden, Nice, Carlsbad, Trieste, Wiesbaden, Venice, Montecatini, Paris—where he could plunge himself into the quasi anonymity of a cosmopolitan clientele.[28]

In between, he exchanged letters with friends. Judging by the volume and intimacy of the surviving correspondence, his deepest friendship was with Geremia Bonomelli, bishop of Cremona. Although Baratieri's military record shows that he married in 1867, his wife is mentioned nowhere in his correspondence; she seems to have dropped out of his life without a trace shortly after entering it. His most enduring relationship was with Bonomelli; the two men met in 1885 when, as a young officer, Baratieri was posted to Cremona. They became close enough to pose together for a photo portrait in Cremona—two young men about to embark on their careers, one in the church, the other in the military. Years later, Bonomelli remained Baratieri's confidant. "Before the tribunal," Baratieri wrote while facing his court-martial, "I am limited to a simple narration of military fact, taking every precaution to avoid assigning blame to others."[29] At Baratieri's death, Bonomelli would write the epitaph inscribed on his tomb.

From time to time, Baratieri was reminded of an unforgiving public. In 1901, weakened by an illness that would kill him, Baratieri sought refuge in Sterzing, an alpine town under Habsburg rule. An anonymous letter found him there, shortly after news of his illness reached the press. "I learned from the newspapers that you are gravely ill," went the letter. "I am pleased, but I do not wish you to die, that would be too easy a punishment for you. I hope you endure a thousand torments as long as possible."

In fact, the illness was mercifully brief. A short time after receiving the letter, the illness took Oreste Baratieri. He died alone. Oreste Baratieri had a lengthy afterlife, however. After 1922, as the Fascist government of Benito Mussolini began the drumbeat that would culminate in a second Italian invasion of Ethiopia, Baratieri's name was recovered from history as part of an honor roll of revenge.[30] Dabormida, Albertone, Arimondi, Ellena, Toselli, Galliano—the ghosts of all of the celebrated figures from the Adwa epoch were made to labor on behalf of Fascist ambition. When Ethiopia fell in 1936, a massive bust of Mussolini was erected at the Adwa battlefield.

Makonnen, Ilg, Menelik: A Heroic Generation Fades

Ras Alula, the scourge of Ethiopia's enemies, was the first of Ethiopia's heroic generation to pass on. Early in 1897, Alula got into a dispute over land. The dispute turned violent; Alula fell wounded and died shortly thereafter, mere weeks before the first anniversary of Adwa. By then he had earned the grudging respect of Europeans and even the admiration of a few. Gherardo Pantano, who encountered much of the Ethiopian leadership as a high-ranking prisoner, regarded Alula as "the most notable and esteemed" of the figures at court. "Short, lively, full of energy," the dashing Alula was "a kind of Ethiopian d'Artagnan."[31] The British journalist and diplomat Augustus Wylde knew Alula well and loved him as a leader and patriot. For Wylde, it wasn't only Alula's military skills that set him apart; it was his character. Wylde was a friend of Ethiopia, but he didn't admire its court culture. The "honorable and fearless" Alula stood in singular relief against "the background of intrigue and fraud" of Ethiopian political life.

Ras Makonnen only grew in esteem after Adwa. His conduct in battle was above reproach. Shrapnel had ripped through his thigh in combat, giving him a nasty wound that took weeks to heal. His heroism and his injury silenced his detractors at court who had depicted him as a man in the pocket of the Italians.[32]

After Adwa, no less than before, Makonnen was "the emperor's favorite."[33] Even during the dark hours of the siege of Mekele, Menelik's trust never wavered. After Adwa, Menelik continued to rely on Makonnen as the public face of Ethiopia abroad. In 1898, Makonnen journeyed to Paris, where he was received at the Elysée Palace. Two years later, he was back in Paris on a tour that eventually would take him to Jerusalem. In 1901, he led a delegation to London, where he represented Ethiopia at the coronation of King Edward VII.[34]

Makonnen was widely regarded as Menelik's successor. Such speculation ended with Makonnen himself. Makonnen was the first major figure at court among Ethiopia's heroic generation to pass on. He died in 1906 after a short illness.[35] By then, Menelik's health was also in decline, showing symptoms of stroke or, perhaps, the advanced effects of syphilis contracted years before.[36] Alfred Ilg, whose devotion to Menelik included

Makonnen at the coronation of King Edward VII. From Richard Pankhurst and Denis Gérard, *Ethiopia Photographed: Historic Photographs of the Country and Its People Taken between 1867 and 1935.* London: Kegan Paul International, 1996.

naming a son for him, found that his influence decayed with the emperor's health. In 1906, he and his wife, Fanny, packed up their things and their children—Alfred, Menelik, Fanny, and Felix—and retired to Switzerland. He died there ten years later.[37]

Of the heroic figures of the Adwa generation, Empress Taytu proved the most durable. For a time, as Menelik's health faded, she assumed greater political responsibility. Ultimately she was perceived as a threat, and by 1910 she had been pushed away from the levers of power and reduced to caring for her invalid husband. Upon Menelik's death in 1913, she took up residence at Entotto, at a safe remove from the capital. She died in 1918.

While Taytu and Menelik enjoyed a remarkable afterlife as the founding figures of modern Ethiopia, they were rivaled, even eclipsed, by

The Lion of Judah in winter. From Lincoln de Castro, *Nella terra dei negus, pagine raccolte in Abissinia*. Milan: Fratelli Treves, 1915.

Makonnen and his progeny. Makonnen's image—that of the urbane, cosmopolitan, multilingual statesman—endured. By the 1960s he had become the hero of Adwa—his reputation puffed up by a hagiographical literature that undoubtedly owed much to dynastic considerations and the rise of Rastafarianism.[38] Indeed, Makonnen's reputation was surpassed by that of his son, Tafari Makonnen, who would enjoy the greatest global celebrity of all. Tafari acquired the title of *ras*. As Ras Tafari, he became the divine object of a cult that emerged out of Jamaica, although he remained ambivalent toward the Rasta cult that put him at its center. In the political realm, Ras Tafari would be better known by the name Haile Selassie, a name he assumed when he ascended the Ethiopian throne in 1930.

That Ras Tafari—a monarch—would be venerated as a redeemer and emblem of freedom in the African diaspora is understandable, but it only underlines the paradox of Adwa. Rastafarianism captured the spirit and some of the dignity of free Ethiopia, but as politics it was a muddle; Adwa was a victory for Ethiopia and its people, but also for sacred monarchy. Rastafarian veneration of Haile Selassie as the Lion of Judah and the champion of oppressed peoples buttressed an old regime in Ethiopia that was justifiably a source of pride—the modern extension of a proud and ancient civilization. But it was also a regime—a church and state—that presided over decades where progress rarely kept pace with an evident demographic dynamism. The Rastafari cult perpetuated the paradox of Adwa, undoubtedly one of the reasons that many Ethiopians regarded Rastafarianism with a mix of incomprehension and disdain. It was a paradox later generations of Ethiopians would have to unravel.

But the core message of Adwa was clear. It was a national epic, the founding event in the modern life of the nation. The stately northward march of Menelik and Taytu not only consolidated their rule but called upon the Ethiopian people—Tigrayans, Shoans, Oromo, Welayta, and others—to set aside their differences and, in recognizing a common enemy, recognize a common nationhood. Nations, if they are to endure, are defined not by religion, ethnicity, or race but by the scale at which freedom can reliably be defended. Only on the scale of Ethiopia itself could resistance have succeeded.

Adwa reminds us that the only freedom we truly possess is the freedom we are able to defend. But it is not only for what it secured but also for how it secured it that Adwa deserves to be ranked among the great military campaigns of modern history. Its greatness starts with the fact that it was never just a campaign of guns, blood, and steel. Ethiopia pioneered key "soft power" techniques that would became part of the repertoire of anti-colonial warfare in the new century. By the time the actual military campaign began, Ethiopia had won over a significant portion of enemy public opinion thanks to a well-orchestrated "hearts and minds" campaign.

Even as a conventional military campaign, Adwa deserves a place among the great campaigns of modern times. Take scale alone: Robert

E. Lee's campaign from Chancellorsville to Gettysburg covered about 135 miles. Sherman's March to the Sea from Atlanta to Savannah traversed 300 miles. The Adwa campaign spanned five months and 580 miles. It was rivaled among nineteenth century military campaigns only by Napoleon's Russian campaign, which took three months and logged 490 miles from Vilnius to Moscow. Unlike Napoleon's Russian campaign, the Adwa campaign ended in victory. This is greatness.

But the greatest battle of all is the battle that isn't fought. One of the measures of the greatness of the Adwa campaign was that it made the actual *battle* of Adwa unnecessary. Menelik had staged a brilliant campaign and achieved strategic victory weeks before the battle, by the middle of February. When Menelik bypassed Adigrat and threatened Eritrea, it was the military equivalent of checkmate. He showed that he didn't need to fight Baratieri to defeat him. Baratieri knew this. He understood that his only real option was to abandon the conquered territories, save his army, and defend Eritrea from invasion. Only relentless pressure from his brigadier generals—scornful of Baratieri's leadership and anxious for a decisive encounter with an enemy they underestimated—touched off the cascade of events that ended in ruin for Baratieri and his army. The responsibility for everything that followed, from the tragic loss of life to the horrors that followed the fighting, must be shared by those whose recklessness brought it to pass.

Finally, Adwa was a victory not only for Ethiopia but also for Africa and for people everywhere who stood athwart the presumed path of history. On the eve of Adwa, the capitulation of Africa to European expansion truly seemed inevitable, a manifest destiny transplanted to Africa. Indeed, in the United States, Adwa might have served as an object lesson to a nation about to close out one chapter in its history of expansion and conquest, that of Manifest Destiny, and contemplating another—global empire—in the run-up to the Spanish-American War. Africa might have been far from the minds of many Americans. Empire, however, was not. Adwa occurred at a critical moment in the history of the United States, at the apogee of Jim Crow and on the eve of America's foray into global empire. Just as the Manifest Destiny of westward expansion was drawing to a close, the Spanish-American War of 1898 left the United States—the world's first great postcolonial power—as an imperial power for the first time.[39] In 1896, however, the story of Menelik and Ethiopia had to compete for newspaper space with stories related to Spain and Cuba—a war already looming. The sobering lesson of Adwa, the cautionary tale of hubris, empire, and race, was lost in the din of jingoism.

Historians sometimes refer to the twentieth century as the American century, as it witnessed the relative decline of Europe and the emergence of the United States as a global power. It has even been said that the American century got under way a few years early when, in 1898, the United States gathered in the remnants of the "decadent" Spanish empire in the Philippines.[40] This moment—Spain's defeat by the United States—is sometimes considered the signal event in the history of European global hegemony because it was the first time that a European power had been defeated, without allies or aid, by a non-European power. It was followed in 1905 by Russian defeat in the Russo-Japanese War of 1905. Together, these events are taken to have jolted old certainties about empire and the hierarchies of nation and race. We now know better. The signal moment for our times, the event that reopened previously settled questions for a new century, occurred not in 1905 or even in 1898. It took place in 1896 at a place called Adwa.

Notes

A complete bibliography may be found at BattleofAdwa.org.

1. See "The Misfortune of a Race" in *The Atlanta Constitution,* 2 March 1896.
2. Robert Hill says that Vitalien was from Martinique. However, Chris Prouty and Bahru Zewde, respectively, describe him as from Guadeloupe or Haiti. See Robert A. Hill, ed., *The Marcus Garvey and Universal Negro Improvement Association Papers: Africa for the Africans, 1923–1945* (Berkeley: University of California Press, 2006), 80n; Chris Prouty, "The Medical History of Menilek II, Emperor of Ethiopia (1844–1913): A Case of Medical Diplomacy," *Munger Africana Library Notes* 45/46 (October 1978): 14; Bahru Zewde, "The Italo-Ethiopian War of 1895–1896 and the Russo-Japanese War of 1904–1905; A Comparative Essay," in *Adwa Victory Centenary Conference, 26 February–2 March 1996,* ed. Abdussamad Ahmad and Richard Pankhurst (Addis Ababa: Institute of Ethiopian Studies, Addis Ababa University, 1998), 302.

1. COURTLY AMBITIONS

1. Nicola D'Amato, *Da Adua ad Addis-Abeba ricordi d'un prigioniero* (Salerno: A. Volpe, 1898), 46; "Guerra in Abissinia," *L'Illustrazione italiana,* 1 March 1896; Edward Gleichen, *With the Mission to Menelik, 1897* (London: E. Arnold, 1898), 128.
2. Heribert Küng, *Staatsminister Alfred Ilg (1854–1916): Ein Thurgauer Am Hof Kaiser Meneliks II von Äthiopien* (Zurich: Thesis-Verlag, 1999), 35; "L'ingegnere Alfredo Ilg," *L'Illustrazione italiana,* 29 March 1896; Gleichen, *Mission to Menelik,* 118–129.

337

3. Alphonse Aubry, "Une mission au Choa et dans les pays Galla," *Compte rendu des séances de la société de géographie,* 1886, 323.

4. Capitaine Longbois, "Souvenirs d'un voyage au Choa," *Compte rendu des séances de la société de géographie,* 1886, 567.

5. Augustus Blandy Wylde, *Modern Abyssinia* (London: Methuen, 1901), 249.

6. On Ireland, see Piers Brendon, *The Decline and Fall of the British Empire, 1781–1997* (New York: Knopf, 2008), 302.

7. James Rennell Rodd, *Social and Diplomatic Memories, 1894–1901, Egypt and Abyssinia* (London: Arnold, 1923), 150, 162.

8. Jules Borelli, *Ethiopie méridionale: journal de mon voyage aux pays Amhara, Oromo et Sidama, septembre 1885 à novembre 1888* (Paris: Ancienne Maison Quantin, 1890), 109; Augusto Salimbeni, *Crispi e Menelich nel diario inedito del conte Augusto Salimbeni* (Turin: Industria libraria tipografica editrice, 1956), 146, 192; Jean Gaston Vanderheym, *Une expédition avec le négous Ménélik: vingt mois en Abyssinie* (Paris: Hachette, 1896), 29; Hugues LeRoux, *Ménélik et nous* (Paris: Nilsson, 1901), 223.

9. Elisabeth Biasio, *Prunk und Pracht am Hofe Menileks: Alfred Ilgs Äthiopien um 1900* (Zurich: Neue Züricher Zeitung, 2004), 13.

10. Willi Loepfe, *Alfred Ilg und die äthiopische Eisenbahn* (Zurich: Atlantis Verlag, 1974), 9; Wylde, *Modern Abyssinia,* 22–25.

11. Küng, *Staatsminister Alfred Ilg,* 35.

12. Ibid., 77.

13. Guèbrè Sellassié, *Chronique du règne de Ménélik II, roi des rois d'Éthiopie,* ed. Maurice de Coppet, trans. Tèsfa Sellassié (Paris: Maisonneuve Frères, 1930), 341.

14. Taytu Betul to Alfred Ilg, 18 June 1891, in *Ethiopian Records of the Menilek Era: Selected Amharic Documents from the Nachlass of Alfred Ilg, 1884–1900,* ed. Bairu Tafla (Wiesbaden: Harrassowitz, 2000), 401–402.

15. See Taytu Betul to Alfred Ilg, 13 November 1891, and Taytu Betul to Alfred Ilg, 18 June 1891, in *Ethiopian Records,* 401–402, 415. Taytu's tag played upon a pun in her name. See Richard Pankhurst, "The Battle of Adwa (1896) as Depicted by Traditional Ethiopian Artists," *Proceedings of the First International Conference on the History of Ethiopian Art Sponsored by the Royal Asiatic Society,* 1989, 84.

16. Küng, *Staatsminister Alfred Ilg,* 94; Sellassié, *Chronique,* 341; letter from Ilg to Menelik, 18 April 1889, in *Ethiopian Records,* 379.

17. Francesco Frisina, *L'Italia in Abissinia e nel Sudan: dall'acquisto di Assab, 1869, alla cessione di Cassala, 1897* (Alexandria: Molco Petrini, 1919), 329.

18. See, among others, Adam Hochschild, *King Leopold's Ghost: A Story of Greed, Terror, and Heroism in Colonial Africa* (Boston: Houghton Mifflin, 1998); Tim Jeal, *Stanley: The Impossible Life of Africa's Greatest Explorer* (New Haven, CT: Yale University Press, 2007).

19. Bahru Zewde, "The Historical Context of the Dogali Encounter," in *The Centenary of Dogali,* ed. Taddesse Beyene, Taddesse Tamrat, and Richard Pankhurst (Addis Ababa: Institute of Ethiopian Studies, Addis Ababa University, 1988), 109.

20. Sven Rubenson, *King of Kings: Tewodros of Ethiopia* (Addis Ababa: Haile Sellassie I University, 1966), 31, 46; Harold G. Marcus, *The Life and Times of Menelik II:*

Ethiopia, 1844–1913 (Oxford: Clarendon Press, 1975), 13, 16; Raymond A. Silverman, "Qes Adamu Tesfaw—A Priest Who Paints: Painting in the Ethiopian Orthodox Church," in *Ethiopia: Traditions of Creativity,* ed. Raymond A. Silverman (Seattle: University of Washington Press, 1999), 180–181; Eric Hobsbawm, *Bandits* (London: Weidenfeld & Nicolson, 2000).

21. Letter from Consul Plowden to Lord J. Russell, 28 July 1853, in *Parliamentary Papers, Correspondence Respecting Abyssinia, 1846–1868* (London: Harrison and Sons, 1868), 77. For Plowden, see also Clements R. Markham, *A History of the Abyssinian Expedition* (London: Macmillan, 1869), 59–60.

22. Letter from Consul Plowden to the Earl of Clarendon, 3 March 1855, in *Parliamentary Papers, Correspondence Respecting Abyssinia, 1846–1868,* 146.

23. Markham, *History of the Abyssinian Expedition,* 59–60, 63–74; Mordechai Abir, *Ethiopia: The Era of the Princes: The Challenge of Islam and Re-unification of the Christian Empire, 1769–1855* (New York: Praeger, 1968), 183–185; Marcus, *Life and Times of Menelik II,* 18–19; Harold G. Marcus, *A History of Ethiopia* (Berkeley: University of California Press, 1994), 66–67.

24. Donald Crummey, "Banditry and Resistance: Noble and Peasant in Nineteenth-Century Ethiopia," in *Banditry, Rebellion, and Social Protest in Africa,* ed. Donald Crummey (London: J. Currey, 1986), 139–142.

25. British policy had turned pro-Ottoman in the Red Sea. See Girma-Selassie Asfa and David L. Appleyard, *The Amharic Letters of Emperor Theodore of Ethiopia to Queen Victoria and Her Special Envoy Preserved in the India Office Library and the Public Record Office* (Oxford: Oxford University Press, 1979), 12–13.

26. India Office Library MSS Eur F 103, f. 53, Theodore to Rassam, n.d. [17 April 1866], in Asfa and Appleyard, *Amharic Letters of Emperor Theodore,* 25b.

27. Asfa Yilma, *Haile Selassie Emperor of Ethiopia: With a Brief Account of the History of Ethiopia* (London: Sampson Low, Marston, 1936), 89–90; Bahru Zewde, *A History of Modern Ethiopia, 1855–1974* (London: J. Currey, 1991), 28.

28. Markham, *History of the Abyssinian Expedition,* 81–82.

29. Gleichen, *Mission to Menelik,* 321.

30. Asfa Yilma, *Haile Selassie,* 92; Chris Prouty, *Empress Taytu and Menelik II: Ethiopia, 1883–1910* (London: Ravens, 1986), 9; Marcus, *A History of Ethiopia,* 70–71.

31. Roger Acton, *The Abyssinian Expedition and the Life and Reign of King Theodore* (London: Illustrated London News, 1868).

32. Some artifacts from the court of Tewodros found their way to the British Museum. See Graham Robb, *Rimbaud* (New York: W. W. Norton, 2000), 260. See also photographs of the British Expeditionary Force in Abyssinia at the Department of Special Collections, UCLA.

33. Luigi Sambon, *L'esercito abissino: usi e costumi* (Rome: V. Enrico, 1896), 27; Bairu Tafla, "Two of the Last Provincial Kings of Ethiopia," *Journal of Ethiopian Studies* 11 (1973): 35.

34. Augustus Blandy Wylde, *Modern Abyssinia* (London: Methuen 1901), 25.

35. Richard Caulk, "Menilek II and the Diplomacy of Commerce: Prelude to an Imperial Foreign Policy," *Journal of Ethiopian Studies* 17 (1984): 66.

36. One of the leading American figures was Alexander Macomb Mason, a member of the Egyptian chiefs of staff, governor at Massawa as of 1883, and Egypt's representative during the negotiations of the Hewett treaty. See his obituary in the *Bulletin de la Société Khédiviale de Géographie* (Cairo), 1898, 2–5. See also his papers and personal correspondence, "Alexander Macomb Mason, 1841–1897," Library of Congress, Manuscript Division, 79-5433.

37. Haggai Erlich, *The Cross and the River: Ethiopia, Egypt, and the Nile* (Boulder, CO: Rienner, 2002), 10.

38. Ibid., 70.

39. Wylde, *Modern Abyssinia,* 25; Vico Mantegazza, *Gli Italiani in Africa: L'assedio di Macalle* (Florence: Successori Le Monnier, 1896), 128; John Dunn, *Khedive Ismail's Army* (London: Routledge, 2005), 113–124.

40. Haggai Erlich, "Egyptian Reactions," in *Adwa Victory Centenary Conference, 26 February–2 March 1996,* ed. Abdussamad Ahmad and Richard Pankhurst (Addis Ababa: Institute of Ethiopian Studies, Addis Ababa University, 1998), 429–430; Marcus, *A History of Ethiopia,* 73–74.

41. Prouty, *Empress Taytu and Menelik,* 14; Erlich, *The Cross and the River,* 71; Dunn, *Khedive Ismail's Army,* 152.

42. Haggai Erlich, "The Battle of Dogali, 1887: Strength and Weakness in Late 19th Century Ethiopia," in *The Centenary of Dogali,* ed. Taddesse Beyene, Taddesse Tamrat, and Richard Pankhurst (Addis Ababa: Institute of Ethiopian Studies, Addis Ababa University, 1987), 113–114; Hussein Ahmed, "The Military Aspect of the Battle of Dogali," in *The Centenary of Dogali,* ed. Taddesse Beyene, Taddesse Tamrat, and Richard Pankhurst (Addis Ababa: Institute of Ethiopian Studies, Addis Ababa University, 1987), 46.

43. Erlich, *The Cross and the River,* 83–90; Carlo Zaghi, *Rimbaud in Africa: con documenti inediti* (Naples: Guida editori, 1993), 74.

44. Borelli, *Ethiopie méridionale,* 116.

45. Rubenson, *King of Kings,* 48.

46. Vanderheym, *Une expédition,* 72–75; on serial matrimony, see Alberto Pollera, *La donna in Etiopia* (Rome: Grafia, 1922), 20.

47. Gleichen, *Mission to Menelik,* 146; Prouty, *Empress Taytu and Menelik,* 111; Sellassié, *Chronique du Règne de Menelik II,* 448n; Rodd, *Social and Diplomatic Memories,* 154–155; Alexander Bulatovich, *Ethiopia Through Russian Eyes: Country in Transition, 1896–1898,* trans. Richard Seltzer (Lawrenceville, NJ: Red Sea Press, 2000), 118.

48. D'Amato, *Da Adua ad Addis-Abeba,* 69; Biasio, *Prunk und Pracht,* 57.

49. Giovanni Tedone, *Angera: i ricordi di un prigioniero di Menelik* (Milan: Giordano, 1964), 100; D'Amato, *Da Adua ad Addis-Abeba,* 63–64; Paul de Lauribar, *Douze ans en Abyssinie* (Paris: Flammarion, 1898), 571–572; Gleichen, *Mission to Menelik,* 322; Francesco Crispi, *Francesco Crispi: La prima guerra d'Africa: documenti e memorie dell'Archivio Crispi* (Milan: Fratelli Treves, 1914), 74; Prouty, *Empress Taytu and Menelik,* 16–17.

50. Marcus, *A History of Ethiopia,* 80–81.

51. Prouty, *Empress Taytu and Menelik,* 49.

52. Vanderheym, *Une expédition,* 72–75; D'Amato, *Da Adua,* 70; Asfa Yilma, *Haile Selassie,* 104–105.

53. Borelli, *Ethiopie méridionale,* 128.

54. D'Amato, *Da Adua ad Addis-Abeba,* 72.

55. Ibid., 63–69.

2. LISTING TOWARD ADWA

1. Francesco Frisina, *L'Italia in Abissinia e nel Sudan: dall'acquisto di Assab, 1869, alla cessione di Cassala, 1897* (Alexandria: Molco Petrini, 1919), 123.

2. Gherardo Pantano, *Ventitré anni di vita africana* (Florence: Casa editrice militare italiana, 1932), 5.

3. Frisina, *L'Italia in Abissinia,* 229–231; Pantano, *Ventitré anni,* 5.

4. Vico Mantegazza, *Da Massua a Saati: narrazione della spedizione italiana del 1888 in Abissinia* (Milan: Treves, 1888), 3.

5. Diary entry for 29 August 1894 in Francesco Lemmi, ed., *Lettere e diari d'Africa, 1895–96* (Rome: Edizioni Roma, 1938), 137–138.

6. Mantegazza, *Da Massaua,* 12.

7. Luigi Goj, *Adua e prigionia fra i galla* (Milan: Scuola Tipografica Salesiana, 1901), 1.

8. "Arrivo dei rinforzi a Massaua," *l'Illustrazione,* 26 January 1896.

9. Pantano, *Ventitré anni,* 5.

10. Ibid.; Goj, *Adua,* 3.

11. Goj, *Adua,* 5.

12. Ibid., 5.

13. Jonathan Miran, *Red Sea Citizens: Cosmopolitan Society and Cultural Change in Massawa* (Bloomington: Indiana University Press, 2009), 4.

14. Hussein Ahmed, "The Military Aspect of the Battle of Dogali," in *The Centenary of Dogali,* ed. Taddesse Beyene, Taddesse Tamrat, and Richard Pankhurst (Addis Ababa: Institute of Ethiopian Studies, Addis Ababa University, 1987), 42; Harold G. Marcus, *A History of Ethiopia* (Berkeley: University of California Press, 1994), 74, 83.

15. Cesare Pini, *Frammenti de'miei ricordi d'Affrica* (Rome: S. Lapi, 1912), 63–64.

16. Alessandro Sapelli, *Memorie d'Africa* (Bologna: Zanichelli, 1935), 8.

17. Ibid., 12.

18. Rosalia Pianavia Vivaldi, *Tre anni in Eritrea* (Milan: Cogliati, 1901), 14–15.

19. Vico Mantegazza, *Gli Italiani in Africa: L'assedio di Macalle* (Florence: Successori Le Monnier, 1896), 497–498.

20. Pini, *Frammenti,* 20–21.

21. Eugenio Dolciotti, *Da Napoli a Adua: Bozzetti e ricordi della campagna d'Africa, 1895–96* (Tivoli: A. Chicca, 1913), 22; Carlo Diotti, *Prigioniero d'Africa: la battaglia di Adua e l'impresa coloniale del 1895–96 nel diario di un caporale italiano* (Como: Nodolibri, 2006), 35.

22. Pianavia Vivaldi, *Tre anni in Eritrea,* 12.

23. Dolciotti, *Da Napoli,* 23.

24. Sapelli, *Memorie,* 7.

25. Mantegazza, *Da Massaua,* 24.

26. Sapelli, *Memorie,* 17; on nakedness in Massawa, see Diotti, *Prigioniero,* 37; on commerce (and the pearl trade) more broadly, see Miran, *Red Sea Citizens,* 73, 101–111.

27. "An Unofficial Mission to Abyssinia," *Manchester Guardian,* 12 May 1896.

28. Gerald H. Portal, *My Mission to Abyssinia* (London: Edward Arnold, 1892), 249–250.

29. Diotti, *Prigioniero,* 37.

30. Dolciotti, *Da Napoli,* 23.

31. Ibid., 24.

32. Roberto Battaglia, *La Prima guerra d'Africa* (Turin: Einaudi, 1958), 497.

33. Dolciotti, *Da Napoli,* 24–25.

34. Giuseppe Micali, "Piazzetta del Bazar Arabo a Massaua," in *La Tribuna illustrata,* 400–401.

35. Dolciotti, *Da Napoli,* 25.

36. Ibid., 26–27.

37. Sapelli, *Memorie,* 16.

38. Silvana Palma, *L'Italia coloniale* (Rome: Editori Riuniti, 1999).

3. ITALY IN AFRICA

1. On earlier expansion, see Jonathan Miran, *Red Sea Citizens: Cosmopolitan Society and Cultural Change in Massawa* (Bloomington: Indiana University Press, 2009), 54.

2. Daniel Ghebrekidan, "Dogali and Ethiopia's Continuing Struggle on the Red Sea Coast," in *The Centenary of Dogali,* ed. Taddesse Beyene, Taddesse Tamrat, and Richard Pankhurst (Addis Ababa: Institute of Ethiopian Studies, Addis Ababa University, 1987), 29–30; Haggai Erlich, *The Cross and the River: Ethiopia, Egypt, and the Nile* (Boulder, CO: Rienner, 2002), 41; John Dunn, *Khedive Ismail's Army* (London: Routledge, 2005), 107–109.

3. Richard Smith, *Mercenaries and Mandarins: The Ever-Victorious Army in Nineteenth Century China* (Millwood, NY: KTO Press, 1978).

4. Richard Pankhurst, "Ras Alula, Dogali and the Beginnings of Italian Colonialism on the Horn of Africa," in *The Centenary of Dogali,* ed. Taddesse Beyene, Taddesse Tamrat, and Richard Pankhurst (Addis Ababa: Institute of Ethiopian Studies, Addis Ababa University, 1987), 123–124; Harold G. Marcus, *A History of Ethiopia* (Berkeley: University of California Press, 1994), 80–81; Erlich, *The Cross and the River,* 43; Richard Hill, *Egypt in the Sudan, 1820–1881* (London: Oxford University Press, 1959), 165.

5. Gerald H. Portal, *My Mission to Abyssinia* (London: Edward Arnold, 1892), 3.

6. Erlich, *The Cross and the River,* 83–90; Carlo Zaghi, *Rimbaud in Africa: con documenti inediti* (Naples: Guida editori, 1993), 74.

7. "Mort de Mason bey," *Bulletin de la Société Khédiviale de Géographie* 5, no. 1 (1898): 3–5; Portal, *My Mission*, 3; Augustus Blandy Wylde, *Modern Abyssinia* (London: Methuen, 1901), 472–473; Haggai Erlich, *Ras Alula and the Scramble for Africa: A Political Biography: Ethiopia and Eritrea, 1875–1897* (Lawrenceville, NJ: Red Sea Press, 1996), 47.

8. For the long-term view, see Ralph Austen, *Trans-Saharan Africa in World History* (New York: Oxford University Press, 2010).

9. T. C. S. Speedy, "Letter from T. C. S. Speedy to Alexander Macomb Mason," 30 October 1884, Alexander Macomb Mason Papers, 1871–1898, Library of Congress Manuscript Division.

10. See Miran, *Red Sea Citizens,* 77–90, 136–144. Miran emphasizes the broad and complicated ties linking Massawa with other parts of a vast trade network.

11. For the text of the treaty, see Wylde, *Modern Abyssinia,* 472–473.

12. See letters of 29 July and 30 October in Alexander Macomb Mason Papers, 1871–1898, Library of Congress, Manuscript Division.

13. See the correspondence of "Il R. Agente e Console Generale in Egitto al Ministro Degli Affari Esteri, Cairo, 9 febbraio 1885," in Vico Mantegazza, *De Massua a Saati: narrazione della spedizione italiana del 1888 in Abissinia* (Milan: Treves, 1888), appendixes VII–VIII; Emilio Bellavita, *Adua: i precedenti—la battaglia—le conseguenze (1881–1931)* (Genoa: Rivista di Roma, 1931), 17; Hussein Ahmed, "The Military Aspect of the Battle of Dogali," in *The Centenary of Dogali,* ed. Taddesse Beyene, Taddesse Tamrat, and Richard Pankhurst (Addis Ababa: Institute of Ethiopian Studies, Addis Ababa University, 1987), 42–43.

14. John Gooch, *Army, State, and Society in Italy, 1870–1915* (New York: St. Martin's Press, 1989), 75.

15. Mantegazza, *De Massaua a Saati,* appendix IX.

16. Adam Hochschild, *King Leopold's Ghost: A Story of Greed, Terror, and Heroism in Colonial Africa* (Boston: Houghton Mifflin, 1998); Tim Jeal, *Stanley: The Impossible Life of Africa's Greatest Explorer* (New Haven, CT: Yale University Press, 2007).

17. Maria Carazzi, *La Società geografica italiana e l'esplorazione coloniale in Africa (1867–1900)* (Florence: La nuova Italia, 1972), 106, 109.

18. Leopoldo Traversi, *Let Marefia: prima stazione geographica italiana nello Scioa e le nostre relazione con l'Etiopia, 1876–1896* (Milan: Edizioni Alpes, 1931); Mario Matucci, *Le dernier visage de Rimbaud en Afrique: d'après des documents inédits* (Florence: Edizioni Sansoni Antiquariato, 1962), 38n.

19. Raffaele Ciasca, *Storia coloniale dell'Italia contemporanea: da Assab all'impero* (Milan: Ulrico Hoepli, 1938), 116; Zaghi, *Rimbaud in Africa,* 99; Matucci, *Dernier visage de Rimbaud,* 38–39; Robert L. Hess, "Germany and the Anglo-Italian Colonial Entente," in *Britain and Germany in Africa: Imperial Rivalry and Colonial Rule* (New Haven: Yale University Press, 1967), 155.

20. Il Ministro degli Affari Esteri al Ambasciatore in Costantinopoli, Rome, 25 January 1885, in Mantegazza, *De Massaua a Saati;* Hess, "Germany and the Anglo-Italian Colonial Entente," 157; Angelo Del Boca, "Colonialismo," in *Dizionario storico dell'Italia unita,* ed. Bruno Bongiovanni and Nicola Tranfaglia (Rome: Laterza, 1996), 159–160.

21. Portal, *My Mission,* 5; Erlich, *Ras Alula,* 47, 63; James Rennell Rodd, *Social and Diplomatic Memories, 1894–1901, Egypt and Abyssinia* (London: Arnold, 1923), 164.
22. Erlich, *The Cross and the River,* 67–70. Erlich cites FO 78/3004, Lascelles to Salisbury, 5.10.79: "I have received from Gordon pasha [a private letter] pointing out that if a port on the Red Sea were to be given to King John, there would be a great risk of his conceding it to French or Italian adventurers."
23. Rodd, *Social and Diplomatic Memories,* 164; Edward Gleichen, *With the Mission to Menelik, 1897* (London: E. Arnold, 1898), 323; Chris Prouty, *Empress Taytu and Menelik II: Ethiopia, 1883–1910* (London: Ravens, 1986), 46; Marcus, *A History of Ethiopia,* 82–83.
24. Vico Mantegazza had no illusions about this. "Che gl'Inglesi vedano con grande piacere la possibilità di un'espansione del nostro paese in queste regioni, stento a crederlo. Certo, vedono più volentieri noi altri che non i Francesi." See Mantegazza, *De Massaua a Saati,* 71.
25. Wylde, *Modern Abyssinia,* 123; Pankhurst, "Ras Alula," 124.
26. Mantegazza, *De Massaua a Saati,* appendix XXXI.
27. Portal, *My Mission,* 8–9, 57–59; Erlich, *Ras Alula,* 105; Ahmed, "Battle of Dogali," 49; Gooch, *Army, State, and Society,* 76; Francesco Crispi, *Francesco Crispi: La prima guerra d'Africa: documenti e memorie dell'Archivio Crispi* (Milan: Fratelli Treves, 1914), 18.
28. Lucia Stefanelli, "Dogali, January 1887: An Engraved Sapphire by Giorgio Antonio Girardet for a Castellani Brooch," *Burlington Magazine* 144, no. 1191 (2002): 354; on the political aftermaths of Dogali see Christopher Duggan, *Francesco Crispi, 1818–1901: From Nation to Nationalism* (Oxford: Oxford University Press, 2002), 468–472.
29. Bahru Zewde, "The Historical Context of the Dogali Encounter," in *The Centenary of Dogali,* ed. Taddesse Beyene, Taddesse Tamrat, and Richard Pankhurst (Addis Ababa: Institute of Ethiopian Studies, Addis Ababa University, 1987), 103; see also Marco Scardigli, *Il braccio indigeno: ascari, irregolari e bande nella conquista dell'Eritrea: 1885–1911* (Milan: F. Angeli, 1996), 27.
30. Stefanelli, "Shorter Notices—Dogali, January 1887," 354.
31. Krystyna von Henneberg, "Monuments, Public Space, and the Memory of Empire in Modern Italy," *History and Memory* 16 (2004): 37–85.
32. "Cinquecento Monument," n.d., http://www.mmdtkw.org/VCinquecento.html.
33. Portal, *My Mission,* 5–6.
34. See letter from King John of Abyssinia to Her Majesty the Queen, 30 [sic] February, 1887, in Portal, *My Mission,* 6.
35. Parliamentary Papers, *Mr. Portal's Mission to Abyssinia* (London: Harrison and Sons, 1888), 18–19.
36. Portal, *My Mission,* 11.
37. "Sir Gerald Herbert Portal" (obituary), *New York Times,* 26 January 1894.
38. See letter from Her Majesty the Queen to King John of Ethiopia, 11 August 1887, in Parliamentary Papers, *Mr. Portal's Mission,* 7.
39. Lincoln de Castro, *Nella terra dei negus, pagine raccolte in Abissinia* (Milan: Fratelli Treves, 1915), 352a.

40. Wylde, *Modern Abyssinia,* 149.

41. Cesare Pini, *Frammenti de'miei ricordi d'Affrica* (Rome: S. Lapi, 1912), 29.

42. Portal, *My Mission,* 75–77.

43. Ibid., 19.

44. Ibid., 81; Ahmed, "Battle of Dogali," 53.

45. Portal, *My Mission,* 143–145.

46. Ibid., 145–146.

47. Ibid., 19.

48. Ibid., 30–31.

49. Stefanelli, "Shorter Notices—Dogali, January 1887."

50. Ahmed, "Battle of Dogali," 54.

51. Un Eritreo [Pietro Toselli], *Pro Africa italica* (Rome: Casa editrice libraria italiana, 1891), 17; Wylde, *Modern Abyssinia,* 38–39; Zewde, "Dogali Encounter," 108; Crispi, *Prima guerra d'Africa,* 97–98; Richard Caulk, "Menilek II and the Diplomacy of Commerce: Prelude to an Imperial Foreign Policy," *Journal of Ethiopian Studies* 17 (1984): 81.

52. Crispi, *Prima guerra d'Africa,* 97–98.

53. Wylde, *Modern Abyssinia,* 38–39.

54. Jean-Marie Carré, *Lettres de la vie littéraire d'Arthur Rimbaud: 1870–1875* (Paris: Gallimard, 1931), 213–214.

55. Zewde, "Dogali Encounter," 106; Crispi, *Prima guerra d'Africa,* 97–98.

56. Carlo Zaghi, "L'Italia e l'Etiopia alla vigilia di Adua nei dispacci segreti di Luigi Capucci," *Gli annali Africa italiana* 4, no. 2 (1941): 520; Wylde, *Modern Abyssinia,* 496–497.

57. Prouty, *Empress Taytu and Menelik,* 20; Bairu Tafla, "The Political Crisis in Tigray, 1889–1899," *Africa: rivista trimestrale di studi e documentazione* 34 (1979): 110.

58. Wylde, *Modern Abyssinia,* 39–42.

4. THE PRICE OF LIBERTY

1. Jean Gaston Vanderheym, *Une expédition avec le négous Ménélik: vingt mois en Abyssinie* (Paris: Hachette, 1896), 191.

2. Clément de La Jonquière, *Les italiens en Érythrée: quinze ans de politique coloniale* (Paris: H. Charles-Lavauzelle, 1897), 218. Garretson estimates that at least fifteen thousand Welayta slaves lived in the capital as late as 1909; see Peter Garretson, *A History of Addis Abäba from Its Foundation in 1886 to 1910* (Wiesbaden: Harrassowitz, 2000), 98.

3. Lincoln de Castro, *Nella terra dei negus, pagine raccolte in Abissinia* (Milan: Fratelli Treves, 1915), 92a.

4. Report from Capucci to the Ministry of Foreign Affairs, 18 January 1895, in Carlo Zaghi, ed., "L'Italia e l'Etiopia alla vigilia di Adua nei dispacci segreti di Luigi Capucci," *Gli annali dell'Africa italiana* 4, no. 2 (1941): 534. Harold Marcus mentions the campaign in Harold G. Marcus, *The Life and Times of Menelik II: Ethiopia 1844–1913* (Oxford: Clarendon Press, 1975), 156.

5. Vanderheym, *Une expédition,* 146. The Nadar Express Detective was a forebear to the Eastman Kodak Brownie box camera, one of the first mass-market photographic devices.

6. Chris Prouty, *Empress Taytu and Menelik II: Ethiopia, 1883–1910* (London: Ravens Educational and Development Service, 1986), 115.

7. Capucci to Leopoldo Traversi, Addis Ababa, 16 November 1894, and Capucci to Ministry of Foreign Affairs, Addis Ababa, 15 December 1894, in Zaghi, "Dispacci segreti," 530.

8. Capucci to Traversi, 16 November 1894, in Zaghi, "Dispacci segreti," 530. Vanderheym put the total of Michael's advance guard at ten thousand men in Vanderheym, *Une expédition,* 139–140.

9. Vanderheym, *Une expédition,* 146–147.

10. Ibid., 149–150.

11. Ibid., 162–163.

12. Guèbrè Sellassié, *Chronique du régne de Menelik II, roi des rois d'Éthiopie,* ed. Maurice de Coppet, trans. Tésfa Sellassié (Paris: Maisonneuve Fréres, 1930), 362.

13. Vanderheym, *Une expédition,* 142.

14. Ibid., 177–178.

15. Albert Hans, "L'armée de Ménélik," *Revue des Deux Mondes* 135 (1896): 882; Harold Marcus, "Motives, Methods and Some Results of the Unification of Ethiopia during the Reign of Menelik II," *Proceedings of the Third International Conference of Ethiopian Studies* (Addis Ababa: Institute of Ethiopian Studies, University of Addis Ababa, 1966), 1:274.

16. Vanderheym, *Une expédition,* 181–182.

17. Ibid., 172.

18. Capucci to Traversi, 16 November 1894, in Zaghi, "Dispacci segreti," 530; Prouty, *Empress Taytu and Menelik,* 115–116; Sellassié, *Chronique,* 363.

19. Garretson, *History of Addis,* 11–12; Bahru Zewde, "The Historical Context of the Dogali Encounter," in *The Centenary of Dogali,* ed. Taddesse Beyene, Taddesse Tamrat, and Richard Pankhurst (Addis Ababa: Institute of Ethiopian Studies, Addis Ababa University, 1988), 110; Harold G. Marcus, *A History of Ethiopia* (Berkeley: University of California Press, 1994), 93; John Gooch, *Army, State, and Society in Italy, 1870–1915* (New York: St. Martin's Press, 1989), 78–79.

20. Luigi Capucci estimated the population loss at one-third. See "Relazione sommaria delle informazioni da me date al Governo dal giugno 1894 fino al maggio 1895 e mio processo e prigionia," in Archivio storico del Ministero Africa Italiana (ASMAI), pos. 3.7, fasc. 49.

21. Vanderheym, *Une expédition,* 184–186; Carlo Zaghi, *Rimbaud in Africa: con documenti inediti* (Naples: Guida editori, 1993), 389.

22. Vanderheym, *Une expédition,* 185.

23. Report from Capucci to the Ministry of Foreign Affairs, 13 February 1895, in Zaghi, "Dispacci segreti," 539; Capucci notes that Menelik came to prefer American-made Remingtons. See also Giuseppe Bourelly, *La Battaglia di Abba Garima* (Milan: Cogliati, 1901), 669.

24. "Lettres d'Ethiopie," *Le Temps,* 27 April 1895. Mondon arrived in Ethiopia in 1892 as *envoyé spécial* for *Le Temps.* See Alain Rouaud, *Casimir Mondon-Vidailhet: pionnier de l'Amitié franco-éthiopienne (1847–1910)* (Addis Ababa: Maison des études éthiopiennes, 1997), 20.

25. Vanderheym, *Une expédition,* 194.

5. BLACK IN SERVICE OF WHITE

1. James Rennell Rodd, *Social and Diplomatic Memories, 1894–1901, Egypt and Abyssinia* (London: Arnold, 1923), 14.

2. Cesare Pini, *Frammenti de'miei ricordi d'Affrica* (Rome: S. Lapi, 1912), 75–82; Vico Mantegazza, *Gli Italiani in Africa: L'assedio di Macalle* (Florence: Successori Le Monnier, 1896), 321–322; Guido Moltedo, *L'Assedio di Maccalé: campagna d'Africa 1895–96* (Rome: Dante Alighieri, 1901), 151; Richard Pankhurst, "Italian Settlement Policy in Eritrea and Its Repercussions, 1889–1896," in *Boston University Papers in African History* (Boston: Boston University Press, 1964), 138–139; Marco Scardigli, *Il braccio indigeno: ascari, irregolari e bande nella conquista dell'Eritrea: 1885–1911* (Milan: F. Angeli, 1996), 42–43.

3. Cesare Pini, *Frammenti de'miei ricordi d'Affrica* (Rome: S. Lapi, 1912), 76–80; Paul de Lauribar, *Douze ans en Abyssinie* (Paris: Flammarion, 1898), 219.

4. On slavery in East Africa and the Middle East, see Edward Alpers, "Flight to Freedom: Escape from Slavery among Bonded Africans in the Indian Ocean World, c. 1750–1962," *Slavery and Abolition* 24 (2003): 51; Edward Alpers, Gwyn Campbell, and Michael Salman, eds., *Slavery and Resistance in Africa and Asia* (London: Routledge, 2005); Frederick Cooper, *Plantation Slavery on the East Coast of Africa* (New Haven: Yale University Press, 1977); Murray Gordon, *Slavery in the Arab World* (New York: New Amsterdam, 1987); Y. Hakan Erdem, *Slavery in the Ottoman Empire and Its Demise, 1800–1909* (New York: St. Martin's, 1996).

5. Rosalia Pianavia Vivaldi, *Tre anni in Eritrea* (Milan: Cogliati, 1901), 33.

6. Lauribar, *Douze ans,* 231.

7. Scardigli, *Il braccio indigeno,* 18.

8. Lauribar, *Douze ans,* 235.

9. Ibid., 234.

10. Ibid., 237; Alessandro Sapelli, *Memorie d'Africa* (Bologna: Zanichelli, 1935), 14.

11. Some of these innovations were the work of General Baldissera. See Scardigli, *Il braccio indigeno,* 43.

12. Alfonso Riguzzi, *Macalle: Diario di 45 giorni di Assedio* (Palermo: Fratelli Marsala, 1901), 53.

13. Ibid., 18.

14. Lauribar, *Douze ans,* 415–460.

15. Scardigli, *Il braccio indigeno,* 44; on language competencies, see 49.

16. Riguzzi, *Macalle,* 21–22, 25.

17. For counts of European soldiers deployed at Adwa, see Augustus Wylde, "An Unofficial Visit to Abyssinia by Our Special Correspondent," *Manchester Guardian*, 20 May 1897, part 6, page 7; for deployments and arrivals, see Archivio dello Stato Maggiore dell'Esercito, Ufficio storico (ASME) L7 (Eritrea), Cartella 41, "Prospetto della forza partita per l'Africa."

18. For comparative purposes in German South-West Africa, see Jon Bridgman and Leslie J. Worley, "Genocide of the Hereros," in Samuel Totten, William Parsons, and Israel Charny, eds., *Century of Genocide: Eyewitness Accounts and Critical Views* (New York: Garland, 1997), 9; for the account of an officer's spouse, see Pianavia Vivaldi, *Tre anni;* more broadly, see Jennifer Cole and Lynn Thomas, eds., *Love in Africa* (Chicago: University of Chicago Press, 2009).

19. Giovanni Tedone, *Angerà: i ricordi di un prigioniero di Menelik* (Milan: Giordano, 1964), 193.

20. See General Records of the Department of State (RG 59), 449.046, Italian East Africa, 1936–1939, 865d.112–865d.115.

21. Pianavia, *Tre anni*, 19. See also Giulia Barrera, *Dangerous Liaisons: Colonial Concubinage in Eritrea, 1890–1941* (Evanston, IL: Program of African Studies, Northwestern University, 1996), 17.

22. Francesco Frisina, *L'Italia in Abissinia e nel Sudan: dall'acquisto di Assab, 1869, alla cessione di Cassala, 1897* (Alexandria: Molco Petrini, 1919), 282.

23. Pietro Felter, *La vicenda affricana, 1895–1896* (Brescia: Vannini, 1935), 156, 159.

24. Sapelli, *Memorie*, 199.

25. Chris Prouty, *Empress Taytu and Menelik II: Ethiopia, 1883–1910* (London: Ravens, 1986), 233.

26. Pankhurst, "Italian Settlement Policy in Eritrea," 49.

27. See John Taglibue, "Tracing Roots Fostered by War, Severed by Shame," *New York Times*, 9 July 2009.

28. Augustus Wylde, *Modern Abyssinia* (London: Methuen, 1901), 350.

29. Tedone, *Angerà*, 45–46.

30. Silvana Palma, *L'Italia coloniale* (Rome: Editori Riuniti, 1999); Roberto Battaglia, *La prima guerra d'Africa* (Turin: G. Einaudi, 1958), 449.

31. See Palma, *L'Italia coloniale*. On Massawa, see Jonathan Miran, *Red Sea Citizens: Cosmopolitan Society and Cultural Change in Massawa* (Bloomington: Indiana University Press, 2009), 155–156.

32. On colonial power and the transgressive nature of colonial sexual relations, see Ann Laura Stoler, *Carnal Knowledge and Imperial Power: Race and the Intimate in Colonial Rule* (Berkeley: University of California Press, 2002); Ann Stoler, "Making Empire Respectable: The Politics of Race and Sexual Morality in 20th-Century Colonical Cultures," *American Ethnologist* 16 (1989): 634–660.

33. Pianavia, *Tre anni*, 317.

34. Sapelli, *Memorie*, 199.

35. Pianavia, *Tre anni*, 313.

6. AFRICA IN ITALY

1. Cesare Pini, *Frammenti de'miei ricordi d'Affrica* (Rome: S. Lapi, 1912), 275; Carlo Zaghi, "La missione Maconnen in Italia," *Rivista delle colonie italiane* 10, no. 1 (1935): 367; Roberto Battaglia, *La prima guerra d'Africa* (Turin: G. Einaudi, 1958), plate 33; Lincoln De Castro, *Nella terra dei negus, pagine raccolte in Abissinia* (Milan: Fratelli Treves, 1915), 80; Arnoldo Nicoletti-Altimari, *Fra gli abissini: memorie di un prigioniero nel Tigre* (Rome: Voghera, 1898), 116n.

2. "An Unofficial Mission to Abyssinia," *Manchester Guardian,* 10 and 17 May 1897; Augustus Wylde, *Modern Abyssinia* (London: Methuen, 1901), 249, 475–477.

3. The assessment belongs to Augustus Wylde. See Hussein Ahmed, "The Military Aspect of the Battle of Dogali," in *The Centenary of Dogali,* ed. Taddesse Beyene, Taddesse Tamrat, and Richard Pankhurst (Addis Ababa: Institute of Ethiopian Studies, Addis Ababa University, 1987), 47.

4. Un Eritreo [Pietro Toselli], *Pro Africa italica* (Rome: Casa editrice librara italiana, 1891), 36; "An Unofficial Mission to Abyssinia," *Manchester Guardian,* 10 May 1897; Haggai Erlich, *Ras Alula and the Scramble for Africa: A Political Biography: Ethiopia and Eritrea, 1875–1897* (Lawrenceville, NJ: Red Sea Press, 1996), x, 11–13, 35, 41.

5. Edoardo Scarfoglio, *Abissinia 1888–1896: Studi di "Tartarin" durante la prima campagna d'Africa* (Livorno: Edizioni Roma, 1936), 17, 77, 80; Francesco Crispi, *Francesco Crispi: La prima guerra d'Africa: documenti e memorie dell'Archivio Crispi* (Milan: Fratelli Treves, 1914), 70; Giuseppe Puglisi, *Chi è dell'Eritrea: dizionario biografico* (Asmara: Agenzia Regina, 1952), 18–19.

6. Bairu Tafla, ed., *Ethiopian Records of the Menilek Era: Selected Amharic Documents from the Nachlass of Alfred Ilg 1884–1900* (Wiesbaden: Harrassowitz, 2000), 367; Crispi, *Prima guerra d'Africa,* 93, 97–99.

7. "Cronologica storica degli avvenimenti nella colonia Eritrea," *Rivista militare italiana* 41 (1896): 38. On rivalries between Menelik and Tekle Haimanot, see Mohammed Hassen, *The Oromo of Ethiopia: A History, 1570–1860* (Cambridge: Cambridge University Press, 1990), 198–200.

8. See Antonelli's plan in Crispi, *Prima guerra d'Africa,* 91. General Baldissera had a similar take on the effect of the death of Yohannes; see his telegram dated 2 April 1889 on page 135 of Crispi's book.

9. Ibid., 11–12.

10. Ibid., 77.

11. Abebe Hailemelekot, *The Victory of Adowa and What We Owe to Our Heroes: The First Victory of Africa over Colonialists* (Addis Ababa: Abebe Hailemelekot, 1998), 50.

12. "Cronologica storica degli avvenimenti nella colonia Eritrea," 39.

13. Crispi, *Prima guerra d'Africa,* 158–159; Saheed Adejumobi, *The History of Ethiopia* (Westport, CT: Greenwood Press, 2007), 28–32; Richard Pankhurst, *The Ethiopians* (Oxford: Blackwell Publishers, 1998), 183–185; Paulos Milkias and Getachew Metaferia, *The Battle of Adwa: Reflections on Ethiopia's Historic Victory against European Colonialism* (New York: Algora, 2005), 116; Anacleto Bronzuoli, *Adua* (Rome: Instituto Poligrafico dello Stato, 1935), 9; Shepard Bancroft Clough and

Salvatore Saladino, eds., *A History of Modern Italy: Documents, Readings, and Commentary* (New York: Columbia University Press, 1968), 218–220; Luigi Fusella, "Il Dagmawi Menilek di Afawarq Gabra Iyasus," *Rassegna di Studi Etiopici* 19 (1963): 129; Carlo Rossetti, *Storia diplomatica dell'Etiopia durante il regno di Menelik II* (Turin: Societa tipografico-editrice nazionale, 1910), 60, 78–80, 113; "Les Italiens en Afrique," *Revue militaire de l'étranger,* December 1896, 283; Christopher Duggan, *Francesco Crispi, 1818–1901: From Nation to Nationalism* (Oxford: Oxford University Press, 2002), 583–584, 695, 703–704; Sidney Sonnino, *Diario,* 3 vols. (Bari: Laterza, 1972), 1:234; Richard Caulk, "'Black Snake, White Snake': Bahta Hagos and His Revolt Against Italian Overrule in Eritrea, 1894," in *Banditry, Rebellion, and Social Protest in Africa,* ed. Donald Crummey (London: J. Currey, 1986), 298; George F.-H. Berkeley, *The Campaign of Adowa and the Rise of Menelik* (New York: Negro Universities Press, 1969), 18, 31–32; Angelo Del Boca, "Colonialismo," in *Dizionario storico dell'Italia unita,* ed. Bruno Bongiovanni and Nicola Tranfaglia (Rome: Laterza, 1996), 160–161.

14. Chris Prouty, *Empress Taytu and Menelik II: Ethiopia, 1883–1910* (London: Ravens, 1986), 62.

15. Richard Burton, *First Footsteps in East Africa* (New York: Praeger, 1966), 195.

16. Carlo Zaghi, *Rimbaud in Africa: con documenti inediti* (Naples: Guida editori, 1993), 112.

17. Jean Gaston Vanderheym, *Une expédition avec le négous Ménélik: vingt mois en Abyssinie* (Paris: Hachette, 1896), 41–42.

18. Burton, *First Footsteps,* 187.

19. Zaghi, *Rimbaud in Africa,* 123–124.

20. Jules Borelli put the number at thirty-five thousand. See Jules Borelli, *Ethiopie méridionale: journal de mon voyage aux pays Amhara, Oromo et Sidama, septembre 1885 à novembre 1888* (Paris: Ancienne Maison Quantin, 1890), 238.

21. For cloth, see Burton, *First Footsteps,* 194.

22. Casimir Mondon-Vidailhet, "Description de la ville de Harar," *Le Temps,* 29 September 1892.

23. Ottorino Rosa, *L'Impero del Leone di Giuda: note sull'Abissinia alle cui ultime vicende l'autore assistette per 47 anni, dal 1880 al 1927* (Brescia: Apollonio, 1935), plate 73.

24. Zaghi, *Rimbaud in Africa,* 114–115. Coffee houses and brothels rounded out the commercial offerings. See Starkie, *Rimbaud in Abyssinia,* 16.

25. Enid Starkie, *Arthur Rimbaud in Abyssinia* (Oxford: Clarendon Press, 1937), 88.

26. Casimir Mondon-Vidailhet, "Harar, une ville en deuil," *Le Temps,* 12 August 1892; Emil Gribeschock, "The First American Trading Expedition to Ethiopia," n.d., 12, Papers of Emil Gribeschock. 1904–11, New York Public Library; Zaghi, *Rimbaud in Africa,* 114–115.

27. Burton, *First Footsteps,* 178.

28. The Anglo-Ethiopian Treaty of 1897 extended and consolidated these gains. See Burton, *First Footsteps,* xi.

29. Letter from Arthur Rimbaud to Alfred Ilg, 7 August 1889, in Arthur Rimbaud, *Les lettres manuscrites de Rimbaud* (Paris: Textuel, 1997), 3:479–482.

30. Vanderheym, *Une expédition,* 42.

31. Harald Swayne, *Seventeen Trips through Somaliland and a Visit to Abyssinia* (London: Rowland Ward, 1903), 270–271.

32. Ibid., 270.

33. Gribeschock, "The First American Trading Expedition," 10.

34. Edward Gleichen, *With the Mission to Menelik, 1897* (London: E. Arnold, 1898), 42–45.

35. Luigi Goj, *Adua e prigionia fra i galla* (Milan: Scuola Tip. Salesiana, 1901), 151–152.

36. Vico Mantegazza, *La guerra in Africa* (Florence: Successori Le Monnier, 1896), 446.

37. Ibid., 448.

38. James Rennell Rodd, *Social and Diplomatic Memories, 1894–1901, Egypt and Abyssinia* (London: Arnold, 1923), 135, 183.

39. Nicola D'Amato, *Da Adua ad Addis-Abeba ricordi d'un prigioniero* (Salerno: A. Volpe, 1898), 216.

40. Gribeschock, "The First American Trading Expedition," 19–20; Mondon-Vidailhet, "Harar, une ville en deuil"; Guido Moltedo, *L'Assedio di Maccalé: campagna d'Africa 1895–96* (Rome: Dante Alighieri, 1901), 209–210; Rodd, *Social and Diplomatic Memories,* 135, 183; Gleichen, *Mission to Menelik,* 42–43; Augustus Blandy Wylde, *Modern Abyssinia* (London: Methuen, 1901), 430–431; D'Amato, *Da Adua ad Addis-Abeba,* 218; Vanderheym, *Une expédition,* 42; Asfa Yilma, *Haile Selassie, Emperor of Ethiopia: With a Brief Account of the History of Ethiopia* (London: Sampson Low, Marston, 1936), 108; Goj, *Adua e prigionia,* 151–152; Mantegazza, *La guerra in Africa,* 448.

41. Swayne, *Seventeen Trips,* 272.

42. Wylde, *Modern Abyssinia,* 431; Casimir Mondon-Vidailhet, "Une visite au ras Makonen," *Le Temps,* 2 November 1892.

43. See the letter from Monsignor André Jarosseau to André Tian in Mario Matucci, *Le dernier visage de Rimbaud en Afrique: d'après des documents inédits* (Florence: Edizioni Sansoni Antiquariato, 1962), 118–119.

44. Borelli, *Ethiopie méridionale,* 238.

45. Such as Bardey, Stein, Bienenfeld, and Tian. See Zaghi, *Rimbaud in Africa,* 421. On out-of-date merchandise, see Alfred Bardey and Joseph Tubiana, *Barr-Adjam: souvenirs d'Afrique orientale, 1880–1887* (Paris: Editions du Centre national de la recherche scientifique, 1981), 316.

46. Matucci, *Dernier visage de Rimbaud,* 29. For a more optimistic reading of Rimbaud's fortunes, see Graham Robb, *Rimbaud* (New York: W. W. Norton, 2000), 377–387; see also Jean-Jacques Lefrère, *Arthur Rimbaud* (Paris: Fayard, 2001). Also, Marc Fontrier, *Abou-Bakr Ibrahim: pacha de Zeyla, marchand d'esclaves: commerce et diplomatie dans le golfe de Tadjoura, 1840–1885* (Paris: L'Harmattan, 2003), 209.

47. Vanderheym, *Une expédition,* 44.

48. Massawa was another. See Jonathan Miran, *Red Sea Citizens: Cosmopolitan Society and Cultural Change in Massawa* (Bloomington: Indiana University Press, 2009), 16–17, 83.

49. Zaghi, *Rimbaud in Africa,* 82; Starkie, *Rimbaud in Abyssinia,* 76–78. See also John Dunn, *Khedive Ismail's Army* (London: Routledge, 2005), 107–109; Fontrier, *Abou-Bakr Ibrahim;* Philipp Paulitschke, *Ethnographie Nordost-Afrikas* (Berlin: D. Reimer, 1893), 175–176; Richard Pankhurst, *Economic History of Ethiopia, 1800–1935* (Addis Ababa: Haile Sellassie I University Press, 1968), 99–100; M. L. Louis-Lande, "Un Voyageur française dans l'Ethiopie méridionale: une colonie française dans le Choa," *Revue des Deux Mondes* 31 (1879): 392.

50. Bardey and Tubiana, *Barr-Adjam,* 70–71.

51. Zaghi, *Rimbaud in Africa,* 76–77.

52. On camel loads and caravan sizes, see Borelli, *Ethiopie méridionale,* 20, 52.

53. Starkie, *Rimbaud in Abyssinia,* 76–78.

54. Borelli, *Ethiopie méridionale,* 43; on Abu-Bakr's negotiating skills, see Fontrier, *Abou-Bakr Ibrahim,* 192–195.

55. Starkie, *Rimbaud in Abyssinia,* 114–115, 123. In fact, the decline of the port of Zeyla and concomitant rise of Djibouti owe much to this partnership; see Fontrier, *Abou-Bakr Ibrahim,* 202.

56. Borelli, *Ethiopie méridionale,* 50–51; Jules Borelli, "Lettre de M. Jules Borelli sur l'Ethiopie (Ambabo, 6 avril 1886)," *Compte rendu des séances de la société de géographie,* 1886, 8; Fontrier, *Abou-Bakr Ibrahim,* 114–115.

57. Zaghi, *Rimbaud in Africa,* 396, 401, 420; M. L. Louis-Lande, "Un Voyageur française dans l'Ethiopie méridionale: une colonie française dans le Choa," *Revue des Deux Mondes* 30 (1878): 392; Starkie, *Rimbaud in Abyssinia,* 114–115.

58. Rebuilding the Harar economy after the Shoan conquest was another challenge. Scarfoglio, *Abissinia 1888–1896,* 256–261.

59. Menelik seems to have entrusted Makonnen with important banking responsibilities, calling on him to operate, in effect, as imperial treasurer. See letter from Ilg to Menelik, 19 February 1895, in Archivio storico del Ministero Africa Italiana (hereafter cited as ASMAI), pos. 3.7, fasc. 49.

60. Zaghi, *Rimbaud in Africa,* 427.

61. Pankhurst, *Economic History of Ethiopia,* 103, 106.

62. Zaghi, *Rimbaud in Africa,* 434–435.

63. Gleichen, *Mission to Menelik,* 85.

64. Starkie, *Rimbaud in Abyssinia,* 16.

65. Mondon-Vidailhet, "Une visite au ras Makonen."

66. Though not between sub-Saharan Africa and the United States. See Walter L. Williams, "Nineteenth Century Pan-Africanist: John Henry Smyth, United States Minister to Liberia, 1878–1885," *Journal of Negro History* 63, no. 1 (January 1978): 18–25; "Il ritardo dell'arrivo della Missione scioana," *Corriere della sera,* 6 August 1889.

67. Carlo Zaghi, "La missione Maconnen in Italia," *Rivista delle colonie italiane* 10, no. 1 (1935): 371–372; "La Missione scioana," *Osservatore Romano,* 28 August 1889.

68. "I ricevimento della Missione scioana a Napoli," *Corriere della sera,* 22 August 1889. This establishes the existence of the Ethiopian flag earlier than previously thought. For comparison, see Stanisław Chojnacki, "Some Notes on the History of the Ethiopian National Flag," *Journal of Ethiopian Studies* 1 (1963): 49–63; Stanisław

Chojnacki, "A Second Note on the Ethiopian National Flag, with Comments on Its Historical and Sociological Sources," *Proceedings of the Third International Conference of Ethiopian Studies* 1 (1966): 137–153; Stanisław Chojnacki, "Third Note on the History of the Ethiopian National Flag," *Rassegna di studi etiopici* 28 (1980–1981): 23–40.

69. On Naples and more, see Frank Snowden, *Naples in the Time of Cholera, 1884–1911* (Cambridge: Cambridge University Press, 1995), 18.

70. "La Missione scioana," *Corriere della sera,* 23 August 1889.

71. "Il ricevimento"; "Gli Scioani attorno a Napoli," *Corriere della sera,* 25 August 1889.

72. "La Camera per Giordano Bruno," *La Tribuna,* 2 June 1889.

73. Letter from Crispi to Menelik dated 12 September 1888 in Francesco Crispi, *Francesco Crispi: La prima guerra d'Africa: documenti e memorie dell'Archivio Crispi* (Milan: Fratelli Treves, 1914), 108–109; for a more sober view, see letter from Pietro Toselli dated 7 December 1889 in Francesco Lemmi, *Lettere e diari d'Africa, 1895–96: a cura di Francesco Lemmi* (Rome: Edizioni Rome, 1938), 29.

74. "L'occupazione dell'Asmara," *La Tribuna,* 7 August 1889.

75. "L'occupazione dell'Asmara," *Osservatore Romano,* 30 August 1889.

76. "L'arrivo degli scioani," *La Tribuna,* 27 August 1889.

77. Zaghi, "La missione Maconnen in Italia," 372.

78. "L'arrivo della Missione scioana a Roma," *Corriere della sera,* 27 August 1889.

79. "La Missione scioana," *Osservatore Romano,* 28 August 1889.

80. Elsewhere, the delegation paid its respects at the tomb of Cardinal Massaia, a Roman Catholic missionary to Ethiopia and a friend to Menelik. See "L'arrivo della Missione scioana," *Osservatore Romano,* 27 August 1889; Richard Caulk, "Menelik II and the Diplomacy of Commerce: Prelude to an Imperial Foreign Policy," *Journal of Ethiopian Studies* 17 (1984): 65; Chris Prouty, *Empress Taytu and Menelik II: Ethiopia, 1883–1910* (London: Ravens, 1986), 9; Paul Lesourd, *Histoire des missions catholiques* (Paris: Librairie de l'Arc, 1937), 360.

81. "Il protettorato italiano sull'Abissinia," *Osservatore Romano,* 30 August 1889.

82. Zaghi, "La missione Maconnen in Italia," 372.

83. Ibid.; "Protettorato italiano"; "L'occupazione dell'Asmara"; Crispi, *Prima guerra d'Africa,* 159.

84. Berkeley, *The Campaign of Adowa,* 19; indeed, the man who translated Makonnen's invocation, Joseph Negussié, had also translated the protectorate clause of the Wichale treaty. See Zaghi, "La missione Maconnen in Italia," 371–372.

85. Ibid. 373; "L'elefante," *Osservatore Romano,* 3 September 1889.

86. Zaghi, "La missione Maconnen in Italia," 373–374.

87. Carlo Rossetti, *Storia diplomatica dell'Etiopia durante il regno di Menelik II* (Turin: Societa tipografico-editrice nazionale, 1910), 60, 78.

88. Sven Rubenson, "Adwa: The Resounding Protest," in *Protest and Power in Black Africa,* ed. Robert Rotberg and Ali Mazrui (New York: Oxford University Press, 1970), 134.

89. Crispi, *Prima guerra d'Africa,* 152–163; Leopoldo Traversi, *Let Marefia: prima stazione geografica italiana nello Scioa e le nostre relazione con l'Etiopia, 1876–*

1896 (Milan: Alpes, 1947), 313; Rossetti, *Storia diplomatica,* 60; Vico Mantegazza, *La guerra in Africa* (Florence: Successori Le Monnier, 1896), 18–19.

90. "L'elefante," *Osservatore Romano,* 3 September 1889.

7. "SOMETHING HUMILIATING FOR MY KINGDOM"

1. Carlo Rossetti, *Storia diplomatica dell'Etiopia durante il regno di Menelik II* (Turin: Societa tipografico-editrice nazionale, 1910), 78.

2. Richard Pankhurst, "L'esercito etiopico," in *Adua, le ragioni di una sconfitta,* ed. Angelo DelBoca (Rome: Laterza, 1997), 318.

3. "Il protettorato italiano sull'Abissinia," *Osservatore Romano,* 30 August 1889.

4. In the letter of 27 September 1890, Menelik calls Makonnen "mon frère, mon bien-aimé"; see Rossetti, *Storia diplomatica,* 80.

5. Richard Caulk, " 'Black Snake, White Snake': Bahta Hagos and His Revolt against Italian Overrule in Eritrea, 1894," in *Banditry, Rebellion, and Social Protest in Africa,* ed. Donald Crummey (London: J. Currey, 1986), 298.

6. On skepticism as a Baldissera trait, see Marco Scardigli, *Il braccio indigeno: ascari, irregolari e bande nella conquista dell'Eritrea: 1885–1911* (Milan: F. Angeli, 1996), 41.

7. Giuseppe Puglisi, *Chi è dell'Eritrea* (Asmara: Agenzia Regina, 1952), 18–19.

8. Clément de La Jonquière, *Les italiens en Érythrée: quinze ans de politique coloniale* (Paris: H. Charles-Lavauzelle, 1897), 119–122; George F.-H. Berkeley, *The Campaign of Adowa and the Rise of Menelik* (New York: Negro Universities Press, 1969), 18, 22; Bahru Zewde, *A History of Modern Ethiopia, 1855–1974* (London: J. Currey, 1991), 76.

9. Augusto Salimbeni, *Crispi e Menelich nel diario inedito del conte Augusto Salimbeni* (Turin: Industria libraria tipografica editrice, 1956), 218; Silvana Palma, *L'Italia coloniale* (Rome: Editori Riuniti, 1999), 12; Berkeley, *The Campaign of Adowa,* 22.

10. Christopher Duggan, *Francesco Crispi, 1818–1901: From Nation to Nationalism* (Oxford: Oxford University Press, 2002), 582–583.

11. It's also possible that the Greek island city of Eretria was the colony's namesake. Eretria, on the island of Euboea, could lay claim to a place in the origins of Western civilization. See Robin Lane Fox, "Eretria, National Archaeological Museum," *Financial Times,* 3 June 2010.

12. Augustus Blandy Wylde, *Modern Abyssinia* (London: Methuen, 1901), 50; Denis Mack Smith, *Modern Italy: A Political History* (Ann Arbor: University of Michigan Press, 1997), 167; Angelo Del Boca, "Colonialismo," in *Dizionario storico dell'Italia unita,* ed. Bruno Bongiovanni and Nicola Tranfaglia (Rome: Laterza, 1996), 160–161; Palma, *L'Italia coloniale,* 12; Sven Rubenson, "Adwa: The Resounding Protest," in *Protest and Power in Black Africa,* ed. Robert Rotberg and Ali Mazrui (New York: Oxford University Press, 1970), 134; Rossetti, *Storia diplomatica,* 78.

13. See letter to minister of foreign affairs in Francesco Crispi, *Francesco Crispi: la prima guerra d'Africa: documenti e memorie dell'Archivio Crispi* (Milan: Fratelli Treves, 1914), 179.

14. Crispi, *Prima guerra d'Africa,* 187; John Gooch, *Army, State, and Society in Italy, 1870–1915* (New York: St. Martin's Press, 1989), 80.

15. Bairu Tafla, "The Political Crisis in Tigray, 1889–1899," *Africa: rivista trimestrale di studi e documentazione* 34 (1979): 118–119; Guèbrè Sellassié, *Chronique du règne de Menelik II, roi des rois d'Éthiopie,* ed. Maurice de Coppet, trans. Tésfa Sellassié (Paris: Maisonneuve Frères, 1930), 285.

16. Crispi, *Prima guerra d'Africa,* 220–221.

17. Oreste Baratieri, *Pagine d'Africa, 1875–1901* (Trento: Museo del Risorgimento e della lotta per la libertà, 1994), 91.

18. Julian Ralph, "Italy's Fallen Hero," *Boston Globe,* 6 March 1896; Domenico Quirico, *Adua: la battaglia che cambiò la storia d'Italia* (Milan: Mondadori, 2004), 211; Nicola Labanca in preface to Baratieri, *Pagine d'Africa,* xliii; Ernesto Mezzabotta, *Il processo dei generali* (Rome: Edoardo Perino, 1896), 2; Berkeley, *The Campaign of Adowa,* 38–39.

19. Maria Carazzi, *La Società geografica italiana e l'esplorazione coloniale in Africa (1867–1900)* (Florence: La nuova Italia, 1972), 51, 106. On Congo, see Adam Hochschild, *King Leopold's Ghost: A Story of Greed, Terror, and Heroism in Colonial Africa* (Boston: Houghton Mifflin, 1998); Tim Jeal, *Stanley: The Impossible Life of Africa's Greatest Explorer* (New Haven, CT: Yale University Press, 2007).

20. Carazzi, *Società geografica italiana,* 107, 109; Palma, *L'Italia coloniale,* 6–7.

21. Nicola Labanca in Baratieri, *Pagine d'Africa,* 70.

22. Suspicion of Menelik's intentions was rife in Tigray before, during, and after the campaign. See Asnake Ali, "The Environmental Impact of the Campaign," in *Adwa Victory Centenary Conference, 26 February–2 March 1996,* ed. Abdussamad Ahmad and Richard Pankhurst (Addis Ababa: Institute of Ethiopian Studies, Addis Ababa University, 1998), 277.

23. Caulk, "'Black Snake, White Snake,'" 306; Rosalia Pianavia Vivaldi, *Tre anni in Eritrea* (Milan: Cogliati, 1901), 239; Tekeste Negash, *No Medicine for the Bite of a White Serpent: Notes on Nationalism and Resistance in Eritrea, 1890–1940* (Uppsala: Scandinavian Institute of African Studies, 1986).

24. Oreste Baratieri, *Memorie d'Africa, 1892–1896* (Geneva: Dioscuri, 1988), 145; Chris Prouty, *Empress Taytu and Menelik II: Ethiopia, 1883–1910* (London: Ravens, 1986), 116.

25. Pianavia Vivaldi, *Tre anni,* 239–240.

26. Ibid., 240–241.

27. Tekeste Negash, *Italian Colonialism in Eritrea, 1882–1941* (Uppsala: Acta Universitatis Upsaliensis, 1987), 3; *L'Africa italiana al Parlamento nazionale, 1882–1905* (Rome: Tip. dell'Unione cooperativa editrice, 1907), 198; Giacomo Perticone, *La politica coloniale dell'Italia negli atti, documenti e discussioni parlamentari* (Rome: Istituto poligrafico dello Stato, 1965), 18; Richard Pankhurst, "Italian Settlement Policy in Eritrea and Its Repercussions, 1889–1896," in *Boston University Papers in African History* (Boston: Boston University Press, 1964), 126.

28. Negash, *Italian Colonialism in Eritrea,* 35; Palma, *L'Italia coloniale,* 12.

29. Pianavia Vivaldi, *Tre anni,* 169–170; Richard Pankhurst, "Italian Settlement Policy in Eritrea and Its Repercussions, 1889–1896," in *Boston University Papers in African History* (Boston: Boston University Press, 1964), 134.

30. Pianavia Vivaldi, *Tre anni,* 166.

31. Alessandro Sapelli, *Memorie d'Africa* (Bologna: Zanichelli, 1935), 74; Claudio Mario Betti, *Missioni e colonie in Africa orientale* (Rome: Studium, 1999), 269; Baratieri, *Memorie d'Africa, 1892–1896,* 141.

32. Pianavia Vivaldi, *Tre anni,* 180–181.

33. Ibid., 181.

34. "Il dissidio fra il generale Baratieri e l'on. Franchetti," *Corriere della sera,* 26 February 1895; *L'Africa italiana al Parlamento nazionale,* 334. On wages and productivity, see Giovanni Federico and Paolo Malanima, "Progress, Decline, Growth: Product and Productivity in Italian Agriculture, 1000–2000," *Economic History Review* 57 (2004): 437–464; Paolo Malanima, "SAGGI—An Age of Decline. Product and Income in Eighteenth-Nineteenth Century Italy," *Rivista di storia economica* 22, no. 1 (2006): 91.

35. Peter Garretson, *A History of Addis Abäba from Its Foundation in 1886 to 1910* (Wiesbaden: Harrassowitz, 2000), 11–12; Bahru Zewde, "The Historical Context of the Dogali Encounter," in *The Centenary of Dogali,* ed. Taddesse Beyene, Taddesse Tamrat, and Richard Pankhurst (Addis Ababa: Institute of Ethiopian Studies, Addis Ababa University, 1987), 110; Harold G. Marcus, *A History of Ethiopia* (Berkeley: University of California Press, 1994), 93; Gooch, *Army, State, and Society,* 78–79; Pankhurst, "Italian Settlement Policy in Eritrea," 124.

36. Letter from Crispi to Baratieri in Crispi, *Prima guerra d'Africa,* 273.

37. Jean Gaston Vanderheym, *Une expédition avec le négous Ménélik: vingt mois en Abyssinie* (Paris: Hachette, 1896), 125–130.

38. Pianavia Vivaldi, *Tre anni,* 241–242; Zewde, *A History of Modern Ethiopia, 1855–1974,* 76; Pankhurst, "Italian Settlement Policy in Eritrea," 147.

39. Pianavia Vivaldi, *Tre anni,* 242–243. See also *Manchester Guardian,* 12 May 1896.

40. Pankhurst, "Italian Settlement Policy in Eritrea," 148.

41. Caulk, "'Black Snake, White Snake,'" 302; Berkeley, *The Campaign of Adowa,* 64–65; "Les Italiens en Afrique," *Revue militaire de l'étranger,* December 1897: 290–292.

42. Pianavia Vivaldi, *Tre anni,* 242–244.

43. Berkeley, *The Campaign of Adowa,* 67, 70–71.

44. See letter from Capucci to Ministry of Foreign Affairs dated 6 February 1895 in Carlo Zaghi, "L'Italia e l'Etiopia alla vigilia di Adua nei dispacci segreti di Luigi Capucci," *Gli annali Africa italiana* 4, no. 2 (1941): 537.

45. Edoardo Scarfoglio, *Abissinia 1888–1896: Studi di "Tartarin" durante la prima campagna d'Africa* (Livorno: Edizioni Roma, 1936), 1:101; Berkeley, *The Campaign of Adowa,* 70; see Baratieri's dispatch dated 14 January in Crispi, *Prima guerra d'Africa,* 294; Paul de Lauribar, *Douze ans en Abyssinie* (Paris: Flammarion, 1898), 385.

46. Zaghi, "Dispacci segreti di Luigi Capucci," 520; Baratieri to Foreign Affairs, 14 February 1895, in *Documenti diplomatici, XXIII-bis, Avvenimenti d'Africa,* Atti

Parlamentari (Rome: Tipografia della camera dei deputati, 1896), 4; Berkeley, *The Campaign of Adowa*, 78–79.

47. Baratieri to Affari Esteri, "Corrispondenza Ras Mangasha," Massawa, 14 February 1895, Archivio storico del Ministero Africa Italiana (hereafter cited as ASMAI), pos. 3/8, fasc. 55.

48. See letter from Capucci to Ministry of Foreign Affairs dated 14 February 1895 in Zaghi, "Dispacci segreti di Luigi Capucci," 539.

49. Haggai Erlich, *Ras Alula and the Scramble for Africa: A Political Biography: Ethiopia and Eritrea, 1875–1897* (Lawrenceville, NJ: Red Sea Press, 1996), 164, 170.

50. The remark is Cesare Narazzini's, quoted in Baratieri, *Memorie d'Africa, 1892–1896*, 111.

51. "Dimostrazione delle maggiori spese che approssimativamente graveranno sul bilancio dell'esercizio in corso (1894–1895)," in ASMAI, pos. 3/8, fasc. 55.

52. Berkeley, *The Campaign of Adowa*, 81.

53. Telegram from Baratieri to Ministero degli Affari Esteri, 12 October 1895, in *Documenti diplomatici*, 44.

54. Baratieri, *Memorie d'Africa, 1892–1896*, 153.

55. Baratieri to Ministero degli Affari Esteri, Adigrat, 27 March 1895, in *Documenti diplomatici*, 20.

56. Baratieri, *Memorie d'Africa, 1892–1896*, 118.

57. Telegram from Baratieri to Ministero degli Affari Esteri, 9 April 1895, *Documenti diplomatici*, 22.

58. Cesare Nerazzini immediately identified the risks in Baratieri's expansion. See ASMAI, pos. 3/7, fasc. 52.

59. Baratieri, *Memorie d'Africa, 1892–1896*, 118.

60. Telegram, 28 March 1895, in *Documenti diplomatici*, 20.

61. Baratieri, *Memorie d'Africa, 1892–1896*, 140–141, 145. For the report see ASMAI, pos. 3/8 fasc. 55.

62. Ibid., 124.

63. "Oreste Baratieri," in *Il Gazzettino*, 9 August 1936. Regarding medals, one such may be found in Museo Storico Trento (hereafter cited as MST), Baratieri, B3 fasc. 4.

64. Crispi's most direct defense came in the legislative session of 27 July 1895. Camera dei deputati, *Documenti diplomatici*, Atti parlamentari: prima sessione 1895, Legislatura 19 (Rome, 1895), 2155.

65. For photos of Baratieri's sojourn in Trentino, see MST, Baratieri, B3 fasc. 4.

8. MENELIK'S MARCH

1. On the use of heralds at market, see Henri Philippe Marie Orléans, *Une visite à l'empereur Ménélick, notes et impressions de route* (Paris: Librairie Dentu, 1898), 198.

2. Luigi Fusella, "Il Dagmawi Menilek di Afawarq Gabra Iyasus," *Rassegna di Studi Etiopici* 19 (1963): 135. Gabra Iyasus was the Ethiopian ambassador to Rome; he was

thus in a position to assess both European and Ethiopian points of view. See also Vico Mantegazza, *La guerra in Africa* (Florence: Le Monnier, 1896), 386. For "Menelik is a myth," see letter, 7 December 1889, in Francesco Lemmi, ed., *Lettere e diari d'Africa, 1895–1896* (Rome: Edizioni Roma, 1936), 41.

3. Years later, Menelik was still struggling to assert his authority there. In a letter dated 29 April 1901, the missionary priest E. Coulbeaux flatly stated that "the power of the Emperor is not very effective in northern Tigray, a country in a constant state of rebellion." See Archivio Segreto Vaticano Segretaria di Stato 1902, r. 280.

4. See Capucci's summary account dated 15 April 1897 in Carlo Zaghi, "L'Italia e l'Etiopia alla vigilia di Adua nei dispacci segreti di Luigi Capucci," *Gli annali Africa italiana* 4, no. 2 (1941): 553.

5. Guèbrè Sellassié, *Chronique du règne de Ménélik II, roi des rois d'Éthiopie,* II, ed. Maurice de Coppet, trans. Tèsfa Sellassié (Paris: Maisonneuve Frères, 1930), 373. Taytu had once accused Makonnen of "having eaten Italian money." Augusto Salimbeni, *Crispi e Menelich nel diario inedito del conte Augusto Salimbeni,* ed. Carlo Zaghi (Turin: Industria libraria tipografica editrice, 1956), 278.

6. On the organization of the Ethiopian army, see John Dunn, *Khedive Ismail's Army* (London: Routledge, 2005), 125–127.

7. Alexander Bulatovich, *Ethiopia through Russian Eyes: Country in Transition, 1896–1898* (Lawrenceville, NJ: Red Sea Press, 2000), 108.

8. Gleichen noted that Ethiopians were not good about cleaning their rifles; many preferred to stuff the muzzle to keep out dirt. Edward Gleichen, *With the Mission to Menelik, 1897* (London: E. Arnold, 1898), 196.

9. Augustus Blandy Wylde, *Modern Abyssinia* (London: Methuen, 1901), 286.

10. Albert Hans, "L'armée de Ménélik," *Revue des Deux Mondes* 135 (1896): 871.

11. Sellassié, *Chronique,* 374, 374n.

12. Luigi Sambon, *L'esercito abissino: usi e costumi* (Rome: Voghera Enrico, 1896), 35–36.

13. Fusella, "Gabra Iyasus," 136.

14. Nicola D'Amato, *Da Adua ad Addis Ababa: ricordi d'un prigioniero* (Salerno: A. Volpe, 1898), 68. On Begirond Baltcha, see Hans, "L'armée," 882; Pietro Felter, *La vicenda affricana 1895–1896* (Brescia: Vannini, 1935), 47; Sellassié, *Chronique,* 47; Hans, "L'armée," 882; Yaltasamma, *Les amis de Ménélik II, roi des rois d'Ethiopia* (Paris: A. Challamel, 1899), 33; J. G. Vanderheym, *Une expédition avec le négous Ménélik: vingt mois en Abyssinie* (Paris: Hachette, 1896), 112; Pierre Petrides, *Le héros d'Adoua: Ras Makonnen, prince d'Éthiopie* (Paris: Plon, 1963), 149–150; Alberto Pollera, *La donna in Etiopia* (Rome: Grafia, 1922), 16.

15. D'Amato, *Da Adua,* 67; Francis Falceto, *Abyssinie Swing: A Pictorial History of Modern Ethiopian Music* (Addis Ababa: Shama Books, 2001), 10.

16. Sellassié, *Chronique,* 391.

17. Gherardo Pantano, *Ventitré anni di vita africana* (Florence: Casa editrice militare italiana, 1932), 86.

18. Hans, "Armée," 887.

19. Sellassié, *Chronique,* 392.

20. Paul de Lauribar, *Douze ans en Abyssinie* (Paris: Flammarion, 1898), 564. For Fernet-Branca, see Chris Prouty, "The Medical History of Menilek II, Emperor of Ethiopia (1844–1913): A Case of Medical Diplomacy," *Munger Africana Library Notes* 45–46 (October 1978): 16.

21. Sellassié, *Chronique,* 389–390.

22. On the *afa negus,* see Pantano, *Ventitré anni,* esp. 80; Paul de Lauribar, *Douze ans en Abyssinie* (Paris: Flammarion, 1898), 563–564; Harold G. Marcus, *The Life and Times of Menelik II: Ethiopia 1844–1913* (Oxford: Clarendon Press, 1975), 219.

23. Fusella, "Gabra Iyasus," 136.

24. Sellassié, *Chronique,* 407.

25. Wylde, *Modern Abyssinia,* 377.

26. Felter, *La vicenda affricana,* 21.

27. George F.-H. Berkeley, *The Campaign of Adowa and the Rise of Menelik* (New York: Negro Universities Press, 1969), 124–125; Prouty, "Medical History of Menelik II," 14.

9. AMBA ALAGE

1. Vico Mantegazza, *La guerra in Africa* (Florence: Le Monnier, 1896), 463.

2. Letter of 17 January 1895 in Francesco Lemmi, ed., *Lettere e diari d'Africa, 1895–1896* (Rome: Edizioni Roma, 1936), 38–39.

3. "La Guerra d'Africa: il battaglione del Maggiore Toselli," *Illustrazione italiana,* 12 January 1896, 30; Gherardo Pantano, *Ventitré anni di vita africana* (Florence: Casa editrice militare italiana, 1932), 21.

4. For pay, see Marco Scardigli, *Il braccio indigeno: ascari, irregolari e bande nella conquista dell'Eritrea: 1885–1911* (Milan: F. Angeli, 1996), 49.

5. Letter of 2 March 1895 in Lemmi, ed., *Lettere,* 41.

6. Un Eritreo [Pietro Toselli], *Pro Africa italica* (Rome: Casa editrice librara italiana, 1891).

7. Oreste Baratieri, *Memorie d'Africa, 1892–1896* (Torino: Bocca, 1898), 235. On Thala's forces, see Clément de La Jonquière, *Les italiens en Erythrée: quinze ans de politique coloniale* (Paris: H. Charles-Lavauzelle, 1916), 234.

8. See "Commissario d'inchiesta circa la campagna 1895–1896," 13 May 1897 in Archivio dello Stato Maggiore dell'Esercito, Ufficio Storico (ASME), L7 Eritrea, cartella 36, Processo Baratieri.

9. Paul de Lauribar, *Douze ans en Abyssinie* (Paris: Flammarion, 1898), 421; Francesco Frisina, *L'Italia in Abissinia e nel Sudan: dall'acquisto di Assab, 1869, alla cessione di Cassala, 1897* (Alexandria: Molco Petrini, 1919), 105.

10. Letter of 9 July 1895 in Lemmi, ed., *Lettere,* 45.

11. Cesare Nerazzini actively encouraged efforts to win Makonnen over to the Italian side, in hopes of playing him against Menelik. See memo of 26 January 1895 in Archivio storico del Ministero Africa Italiana (hereafter cited as ASMAI), pos. 3/7, fasc. 52.

12. The possibility of treason on the part of Makonnen, Tekle Haimanot, and others is discussed in Luigi Fusella, "Il Dagmawi Menilek di Afawarq Gabra Iyasus," *Rassegna di Studi Etiopici* 19 (1963): 137–138. Baratieri remained convinced that a "mortal hatred" existed between some of the Ethiopian leaders. See ASMAI, pos. 3/10, fasc. 69. Telegram from Baratieri, Massawa, 28 January 1896, in Domenico Farini, *Diario di Domenico Farini, 1891–95* (Milan: Ist. per gli studi di politica internaz., 1942), 747. The possibility of a double game can't be ruled out and shouldn't be surprising. Many Ethiopian leaders—Mangasha, Tekle Haimanot, Makonnen—harbored private ambitions. Makonnen certainly found ways to feed the Italians with soothing information. By means of Pietro Felter he was able to convince Baratieri that "Amba Alage was attacked against [Makonnen's] orders." See ASMAI, pos. 3/9, fasc. 62, telegram from Baratieri, 20 December 1895. Pierre Pétridès argues that Makonnen glosses over the various jealousies and rivalries on the Ethiopian side in his *Le héros d'Adoua, ras Makonnen, prince d'Éthiopie* (Paris: Plon, 1963), esp. 117–121. Pétridès's book is clearly intended to serve the purposes of Haile Selassie, establishing the emperor's credentials and lineage.

13. Although reports of a well-armed force of a hundred thousand were circulating in Rome by July 1895. See Farini, *Diario 1891–1895,* 723.

14. Luigi Capucci to Ministry of Foreign Affairs, 23 April 1895, in Carlo Zaghi, "L'Italia e l'Etiopia alla vigilia di Adua nei dispacci segreti di Luigi Capucci," *Gli annali dell'Africa italiana* 4 (1941): 548.

15. Pietro Felter, *La vicenda affricana, 1895–1896* (Brescia: Giulio Vannini, 1935), 22.

16. Farini, *Diario 1891–1895,* 747.

17. Letter from Toselli to his brother, 9 July 1895, in Lemmi, ed., *Lettere,* 15. In November, Toselli received new information that a much larger force had gathered at Lake Ashenge. See Jonquière, *Les italiens,* 234.

18. Mantegazza, *Guerra in Africa,* 450; Jonquière, *Les italiens,* 234–235. Another message to Arimondi stated the issue less poetically, though no less emphatically: "La situazione è più grave di quanto si crede. I nemici, che sono almeno trenta mila, ci attaccheranno domani. . . . Aspetto i suoi rinforzi." See "Una pagina di storia d'Africa," *Corriere della Sera,* 2–3 January 1896.

19. Mantegazza, *Guerra in Africa,* 449. Gabra Iyasus put a different inflection on it. "I am come against you; as you cannot resist me, flee! Do not remain in my path!" In Fusella, "Il Dagmawi Menilek," 135.

20. Mantegazza, *Guerra in Africa,* 449–450. See also Guido Moltedo, *L'Assedio di Maccalè: campagna d'Africa 1895–96* (Rome: Dante Alighieri, 1901), 65.

21. From Amba Alage, dated 2 December 1895. Printed in Mantegazza, *Guerra in Africa,* 475. See also George Berkeley, *The Campaign of Adowa and the Rise of Menelik* (New York: Negro Universities Press, 1969), 131n.

22. "Una pagina di storia d'Africa," *Corriere della Sera,* 2–3 gennaio 1896.

23. Guido Moltedo notes that an order from Baratieri to hold at Amba Alage or to withdraw northward was truncated in transmission from Arimondi to Toselli, whose orders stopped at "hold Amba Alage." *Assedio,* 56n.

24. Letter from Toselli to General Arimondi, 5 December 1895, in Lemmi, ed., *Lettere*, 48.

25. Report of Lieutenant Bodrero, reported in "Les Italiens en Afrique," *Revue militaire de l'étranger*, December 1896, 313. See also Moltedo, *Assedio*, 67.

26. Berkeley, *Campaign*, 131–132.

27. For the array of forces, see Moltedo, *Assedio*, 82–83.

28. "Les Italiens en Afrique," 314–315.

29. See David Chapple, "The Firearms of Adwa," in *Adwa Victory Centenary Conference*, ed. Abdussamad Ahmad and Richard Pankhurst (Addis Ababa: Institute of Ethiopian Studies, Addis Ababa University, 1998), 47–78.

30. "Les Italiens en Afrique," 316; Mantegazza, *La Guerra in Africa*, 427.

31. Moltedo, *Assedio*, 82–84.

32. Ibid., 95; Berkeley, *Campaign*, 139.

33. Jonquière, *Les italiens*, 237–238.

34. Alfonso Riguzzi, *Macalle: diario 45 giorni di Assedio* (Palermo: Fratelli Marsala, 1901), 14. Riguzzi also described how items taken from the fleeing, the dead, and the wounded ended up being offered for sale after Mekele. Riguzzi reported seeing Toselli's beret, the watch of Captain Ricci, and Captain Canovetti's monogrammed saber—all for sale. Ibid., 74.

35. Nicola d'Amato, *Da Adua ad Addis Abeba: ricordi d'un prigioniero* (Salerno: A. Volpe, 1898), 59; Eduardo Ximenes, *Sul Campo di Adua, marzo-giugno 1896* (Milan: Treves, 1897), 278.

36. Fusella, "Gabra Iyasus," 136. Some soldiers recount being stirred to revenge by accounts of his death. See Frisina, *L'Italia in Abissinia*, 121.

37. Although at least one Italian newspaper reported his death as a suicide. See "Una pagina di storia d'Africa," *Corriere della Sera*, 2–3 January 1896.

38. Mantegazza, *Guerra in Africa*, 58–59.

39. Jonquière, *Les italiens*, 242–243.

40. For examples of the persistent critique of *Corriere della Sera*, see especially 10–11 January 1895, also 19–20 January. On students in Rome, see Mantegazza, *Guerra in Africa*, 47.

41. Guèbrè Sellassié, *Chronique du règne de Menelik II, roi des rois d'Éthiopie*, ed. Maurice de Coppet, trans. Tèsfa Sellassié (Paris: Maisonneuve Frères, 1930), 408.

42. Sellassié, *Chronique*, 413. On the guns of Menelik, see Moltedo, *Assedio*, 98. For context, see Chapple, "The Firearms of Adwa," 47–78. Although Chapple speculates (50–52) that the Hotchkiss guns used by the Ethiopians were Hotchkiss revolving cannon—in effect, machine guns—this is unlikely. Unlike Hotchkiss mountain guns, the 37 mm revolving cannon was not easily dismantled for transport via pack animal. On pack animal transport, see M. F. Parrino, "Development of Pack Artillery and Its Significance in Modern Warfare," *Military Affairs* 20 (1956): 28–34.

43. Sellassié, *Chronique*, 414–415.

44. Fusella, "Gabra Iyasus," 136.

45. Mantegazza, *La guerra in Africa*, 329. On some of the broader implications of Amba Alage, see Christopher Duggan, *Francesco Crispi, 1818–1901: From Nation to Nationalism* (Oxford: Oxford University Press, 2002), 699–700.

46. "Les Italiens en Afrique," 457, 462. A third set of reinforcements would make the same voyage between 6 February and 23 February.

47. *Corriere della Sera,* 2–3 January 1896.

48. On the number of men under Galliano's command at Mekele, see his letter dated 19 December 1895 in Lemmi, ed., *Lettere,* 53.

49. *Corriere della Sera,* 2–3 January 1896; Riguzzi, *Macalle,* 10; Moltedo, *Assedio,* 68–69.

50. Moltedo, *Assedio,* 71.

51. Ibid., 72.

52. Ibid., 79; Riguzzi, *Macalle,* 11.

53. Riguzzi, *Macalle,* 14. Vico Mantegazza reports on an askari from Sudan who returned despite losing blood from twelve wounds, including a castration wound. Mantegazza, *Guerra in Africa,* 321–322.

54. Lauribar, *Douze ans,* 433. On the preparations, see also John Gooch, *Army, State, and Society in Italy, 1870–1915* (New York: St. Martin's Press, 1989), 86.

55. Riguzzi, *Macalle,* 17.

56. On wire, see "Les Italiens en Afrique," 419; Riguzzi, *Macalle,* 19. Berkeley wonders why the glass wasn't used to augment the fort's water supply; *Campaign,* 191.

57. Riguzzi, *Macalle,* 25. For a slightly different account, see Moltedo, *Assedio,* 126–127.

58. Riguzzi, *Macalle,* 21–22.

59. Another modified the lyrics of a song used to mock German soldiers so that it targeted the Ethiopians: "We want to play ball, with the heads of the Abyssinians; fire, keep firing; we will conquer or die." See Riguzzi, *Macalle,* 18.

60. Moltedo, *Assedio,* 89.

61. *Corriere della Sera,* 2–3 January 1896.

62. Moltedo, *Assedio,* 108. Jonquière gives the date as the twentieth. See *Les italiens,* 247–248.

63. At the same time, Makonnen was writing to Baratieri at Adigrat. "As long as you are in the center of Tigray, at Adigrat, it is not possible to make peace." Moltedo, *Assedio,* 122.

64. For elephants, see letter dated 31 December 1895 in Lemmi, ed., *Lettere,* 43; for Tigrayan skepticism regarding Menelik, see Moltedo, *Assedio,* 99.

65. Riguzzi, *Macalle,* 31.

66. Ibid. Jonquière gives the date as 30 December: *Les italiens,* 248.

67. At the conclusion of the siege at Mekele, as he and his fellow soldiers were marching north in Ethiopian custody, Riguzzi would estimate Menelik's forces at 150,000 men. Riguzzi, *Macalle,* 85.

68. Ibid., 40.

69. Ibid., 38; Moltedo, *Assedio,* 91.

70. Moltedo, *Assedio,* 121.

71. Ibid., 123.

72. Ibid., 128.

73. "Lettera diario del Maggiore Galliano con due allegati," in ASME, L7 Eritrea, cartella 55, Fatti d'armi, 1896–1914. Reproduced in Lemmi, ed., *Lettere,* 74.

74. Sellassié, *Chronique,* 419; Moltedo, *Assedio,* 131.

75. Moltedo, *Assedio,* 129.

76. Sellassié, *Chronique,* 416–417.

77. Felter, *Vicenda affricana,* 25.

78. Jonquière, *Les italiens,* 252–253; "Les Italiens en Afrique," 418. The Italians took a keen interest in the Ethiopian artillery. Besides being a game-changer on the battle-field—in colonial warfare, artillery typically constituted one of the advantages of the colonizer—it raised the question of whether France was supplying Ethiopia directly. In fact, they weren't, although French nationals were involved. At least ten of the artillery pieces came to Menelik by way of a deal with Léon Chefneux, a French merchant, who traded the Hotchkiss for the salt concession on Lake Asal. See Augusto Salimbeni, *Crispi e Menelich nel diario inedito del conte Augusto Salimbeni,* ed. Carlo Zaghi (Torino: Industria libraria tipografica editrice, 1956), 175, 247. Another French merchant, M. Savouré, procured an equal number. See Albert Hans, *"L'armée de Ménélik," Revue des Deux Mondes* 135 (1896), 880. Some Italian sources severely underestimate the quality of Ethiopian military equipment. See Luigi Sambon, *L'Esercito abissino: usi e costumi* (Rome: Voghera Enrico, 1896), 28. By 1896, the Italian press was reporting that Menelik had forty 57 mm Hotchkiss cannon. See *La Tribuna,* 12 January 1896. On the choice between artillery assault and siege, see also Augustus Blandy Wylde, *Modern Abyssinia* (London: Methuen, 1901), 53.

79. Letter dated 31 December 1895 in Lemmi, ed., *Lettere,* 43; Moltedo, *Assedio,* 135.

80. Rapporto del cavaliere Pietro Felter, Asmara, 8 avrile 1896, in ASMAI, pos. 3/10, fasc. 69. Felter, a successful Italian merchant who had befriended Makonnen during his many years in Harar, was a guest in Makonnen's camp. On Felter, see Lauribar, *Douze ans,* 416.

81. Jonquière, *Les italiens,* 252; Berkeley, *Campaign,* 209–210.

82. Felter, *Vicenda affricana,* 34.

83. Rapporto del cavaliere Pietro Felter.

84. Felter, *Vicenda affricana,* 37–38.

85. Jonquière, *Les italiens,* 246.

86. Riguzzi, *Macalle,* 20; Moltedo, *Assedio,* 100.

87. Sellassié, *Chronique,* 419. This source gives Taytu particular responsibility for sustaining the morale of soldiers.

88. Riguzzi, *Macalle,* 21.

89. Jonquière, *Les italiens,* 251.

90. Ibid., 254. For the broader context, see Gooch, *Army, State, and Society,* 85–86.

91. Riguzzi, *Macalle,* 61. Galliano journal entry dated 20 January 1896 in Lemmi, ed., *Lettere,* 76.

92. Jonquière, *Les italiens,* 245–246.

93. "At each stage and at every choke point [one] would have to leave a protective force to defend the long line of operations [from Adigrat to Mekele]," Baratieri later wrote, leading to the obvious question of why Baratieri would have let himself get over-extended in the first place. Baratieri, *Memorie d'Africa,* 283.

94. *Corriere della Sera,* 26–27 January 1896.

95. Felter, *Vicenda affricana,* 49.

96. Ibid., 50–51; Sellassié, *Chronique,* 423.

97. These were essentially the terms Menelik offered on or before 13 January. See Baratieri's telegram dated 13 January 1896 in ASMAI, pos. 3/10, fasc. 69.

98. Gabra Iyasus records that Menelik gave Galliano five hundred mules, "half for sale and half for nothing." See Fusella, "Gabra Iyasus," 136. Much later Francesco Frisina would reveal that the "rental" of seven hundred animals carried the price tag of twenty-five thousand thalers. See *Memorie di un prigioniero d'Africa* (Reggio Calabria: Lombardi, 1899), 137.

99. Riguzzi, *Macalle,* 72.

100. "La Guerra in Abissinia," *Illustrazione italiana,* 2 February 1896, 75.

101. Frisina, *L'Italia in Abissinia,* 136.

102. See *Le Petit Journal,* 9 February 1896; also *Chicago Tribune,* 9 March 1896. Not all French opinion was negative. Jonquière recognized that Mekele had produced some significant results; see *Les italiens,* 239–240.

103. Francesco Crispi, *Francesco Crispi: La prima guerra d'Africa: documenti e memorie dell'Archivio Crispi,* ed. T. Palamenghi-Crispi (Milan: Fratelli Treves, 1914), viii.

104. Baratieri's telegram dated 28 January 1896 in ASMAI, pos. 3/10, fasc. 69; Berkeley, *Campaign,* 222.

105. Although some asked how much of a shield some 2,000 men could offer an army of 120,000. Pantano, *Ventitré anni,* 52.

106. Baratieri's telegram dated 30 January 1896 in ASMAI, pos. 3/10, fasc. 69. Riguzzi puts the figure at ten and supplies their names; *Macalle,* 85–6. See also "Les Italiens en Afrique," 463.

107. Lauribar, *Douze ans,* 475.

108. Ibid., 476–477.

10. STALLED AT SAURIA

1. "Un intervista con Ilg," *Corriere della Sera,* 27–28 January 1896. See also *Il Messagero,* 27 January 1896.

2. "Un'altra intervista con Ilg," *Corriere della Sera,* 15–16 February 1896.

3. Cited in Vico Mantegazza, *Gli italiani in Africa: l'assedio di Macalle* (Florence: Successori Le Monnier, 1896), 441.

4. Bruce Vandevort, *Wars of Imperial Conquest in Africa, 1830–1914* (Bloomington: Indiana University Press, 1998), 160.

5. Baratieri understood quite clearly about Menelik: "Per vincere italiani si dovrebbe attirarli in paese pianeggiante come Mekele." Archivio storico del Ministero Africa Italiana (hereafter cited as ASMAI), pos. 3/10, fasc. 71, telegram from Baratieri to Ministero Esteri, 28 January 1896.

6. "La posizione di Gundapta e la battaglia del 1° marzo," note from Baratieri to Mariotti in ASMAI, pos. 3/10, fasc. 75.

7. Telegram, 5 February 1896, ASMAI, pos. 3/10, fasc. 71.

8. See "Prospetto della forza partita per l'Africa," Archivio dello Stato Maggiore dell'Esercito, Ufficio Storico (ASME), L7 Eritrea, C41.

9. Ernesto Cordella, *L'artiglieria della Brigata Albertone ad Adua* (Rome: Sindicato italiano arti grafiche, 1930), 7.

10. Giuseppe Menarini, *La brigata Dabormida alla battaglia d'Adua* (Naples: Detken e Rocholl, 1897), 13.

11. Paul de Lauribar, *Douze ans en Abyssinie* (Paris: Flammarion, 1898), 391.

12. Ibid., 391–392.

13. ASMAI, pos. 3/8, fasc. 58, memorandum, Baratieri to Ministro degli Esteri, Adigrat, 27 March 1895, "Oggetto: occupazione dell'Agame," and Il R. Governatore dell'Eritrea al Ministro degli affari esteri, Adi Ugri, 10 April 1895.

14. ASMAI, pos. 3/8, fasc. 58, memorandum, 27 March 1895, 20.

15. For "nostro amico," see "Il Governatore dell'Eritrea al Ministro degli Affari Esteri (Telegramma), Massaua, 30 gennaio 1896," in *Documenti diplomatici, XXIII-bis, avvenimenti d'Africa,* 2 vols., *Atti Parlamentari* (Rome: Tipografia della camera dei deputati, 1896), 2. Others were less confident. Major Toselli called Hagos Tafari "a nullity, a danger, a burden." See Toselli's remarks in Vico Mantegazza, *La guerra in Africa* (Florence: Le Monnier, 1896), 469.

16. Lauribar, *Douze ans,* 477–478.

17. Giovanni Tedone, *Angerà: i ricordi di un prigioniero di Menelik* (Milan: Giordano, 1964), 154.

18. "Il Governatore dell'Eritrea al Ministro della guerra (Telegramma), Massaua, 13 febbraio 1896," in *Documenti diplomatici,* 127.

19. Chris Prouty, *Empress Taytu and Menelik II: Ethiopia, 1883–1910* (London: Ravens, 1986), 152–153.

20. "Il Governatore dell'Eritrea al Ministro della guerra (Telegramma), Massaua, 17 febbraio 1896," in *Documenti diplomatici,* 129. On the broader situation see Christopher Duggan, *Francesco Crispi, 1818–1901: From Nation to Nationalism* (Oxford: Oxford University Press, 2002), 706.

21. "Ma intanto per la defezione di quei due vili, i quali sono oggetto di scherno e di dileggio anche per gli Amhara, il fuoco della ribellione che covava sotto la cenere divampò tremendo; avvenne l'eccidio di Seetà; le nostre carovane di rifornimento furono saccheggiate e disperse, e le retrovie rese mal sicure. Per essi il corpo di operazione si trovò con nemici sul fronte ed alle spalle; allo stremo di viveri; tagliato fuori, può dirsi, da Massaua!" Giovanni Gamerra, *Ricordi di un prigioniero di guerra nello Scioa (marzo 1896–gennaio 1897)* (Florence: Barbèra, 1897), 26.

22. Luigi Goj, *Adua e prigionia fra i Galla* (Milan: Scuola Tipografica Salesiana, 1901), 14.

23. Emilio Bellavita, *Adua: i precedenti—la battaglia—le conseguenze (1881–1931)* (Genoa: Rivista di Roma, 1931), 304.

24. "Il Governatore dell'Eritrea al Ministro della guerra (Telegramma), Massaua, 17 febbraio 1896," in *Documenti diplomatici,* 130.

25. Goj, *Adua,* 17.

26. Bellavita, *Adua: i precedenti*, 305; Gamerra, *Ricordi*, 26; Francesco Frisina, *L'Italia in Abissinia e nel Sudan* (Alexandria, Egypt: Molco Petrini, 1919), 141.

27. Eugenio Dolciotti, *Da Napoli a Adua: Bozzetti e ricordi della campagna d'Africa, 1895–96* (Tivoli: A. Chicca, 1913), 41–42. Gherardo Pantano reported that the bodies of dead soldiers were burned and that a wounded officer, Lieutenant De Conciliis, had been burned alive; see *Ventitré anni di vita africana* (Florence: Casa editrice militare italiana, 1932), 60. The charge also appears in Francesco Frisina, *Memorie di un prigioniero d'Africa* (Reggio Calabria: P. Lombardi, 1899), 25, and Frisina, *Italia in Abissinia*, 141.

28. Lauribar, *Douze ans*, 484–485.

29. Goj, *Adua*, 11, 14.

30. Carlo Diotti, *Prigioniero d'Africa: La battaglia di Adua e l'impresa coloniale del 1895–1896 nel diario di un caporale italiano* (Como: Nodolibri, 2006), 46–47.

31. Ibid., 47.

32. Frisina, *Memorie*, 26.

33. "Les Italiens en Afrique," *Revue militaire de l'étranger*, December 1896, 479–480.

34. Goj, *Adua*, 18–19.

35. "Il Governatore dell'Eritrea al Ministro della guerra (Telegramma), Massaua, 18 febbraio 1896," in *Documenti diplomatici*, 130.

36. Ibid., 132.

37. Sidney Sonnino, *Diario*, 3 vols. (Bari: Laterza, 1972), 1:218–219.

11. BARATIERI CHOOSES

1. On Menelik calling the shots, see Giuseppe Menarini, *La brigata Dabormida alla battaglia d'Adua (combattimento e ritirata)* (Naples: Detken e Rocholl, 1897), 13.

2. Ibid., 20, 27.

3. Ibid., 34.

4. Abebe Hailemelekot, *The Victory of Adowa and What We Owe to Our Heroes: The First Victory of Africa over Colonialists* (Addis Ababa: Abebe Hailemelekot, 1998), 132.

5. Francesco Crispi, *Francesco Crispi: La prima guerra d'Africa: documenti e memorie dell'Archivio Crispi*, ed. Tommaso Palamenghi-Crispi (Milan: Fratelli Treves, 1914), 393–394.

6. Julian Ralph, "Italy's Fallen Hero," *Boston Globe*, 6 March 1896; Nicola Labanca in preface to Oreste Baratiere, *Pagine d'Africa, 1875–1901* (Trento: Museo del Risorgimento, 1994), xliii; Domenico Quirico, *Adua: La battaglia che cambiò la storia d'Italia* (Milan: Mondadori, 2004), 211.

7. Letter, 6 December 1895, in Francesco Lemmi, ed., *Lettere e diari d'Africa, 1895–1896* (Rome: Edizioni Roma, 1936), 111–112.

8. Letter, 13 December 1895, in Lemmi, ed., *Lettere e diari*, 114. It seems that Arimondi was not alone in this opinion. See the anonymous sketches entitled "Il Generale Baratieri" and "Maggiore Salsa" in Archivio storico del Ministero Africa

Italiana (hereafter cited as ASMAI), pos. 3/8, fasc. 57 (1895). The sketch of Baratieri flatly states of Salsa that "in materia militare e politica ha un assoluto predominio su di lui."

9. Paul de Lauribar, *Douze ans en Abyssinie* (Paris: Flammarion, 1898), 430–431.

10. "Lo chiamavano Achille sotto la tenda." See "Deposizione Brusati" in Archivio dello Stato Maggiore dell'Esercito, Ufficio Storico (hereafter cited as ASME), L7 Eritrea, cartella 36bis, Processo Baratieri.

11. Ministero degli Affari Esteri, Servizio Storico e Documentazione, *Inventario dell'archivio storico del Ministero Africa Italiana,* vol. 1 (1857–1939), Archivio Storico Diplomatico, Rome, 1975, pos. 3/8, fasc. 57 (1895).

12. Letter dated 29 April 1895 in Lemmi, ed., *Lettere e diari,* 43.

13. Oreste Baratieri, *Memorie d'Africa, 1892–1896* (Genoa: Dioscuri, 1988), 279.

14. Ibid., 279.

15. Gherardo Pantano, *Ventitre anni di vita africana* (Florence: Casa editrice militare italiana, 1932), 51–52, 74. Alessandro Sapelli, who fought under Albertone, offers the richest and most balanced portrait; see *Memorie d'Africa* (Bologna: Zanichelli, 1935). For a photo portrait, see Eduardo Ximenes, *Sul Campo di Adua, marzo-giugno 1896* (Milan: Fratelli Treves, 1897), 289.

16. Alessandro Sapelli, *Memorie d'Africa* (Bologna: Zanichelli, 1935), 103.

17. Ximenes, *Sul Campo di Adua,* 270.

18. See Lemmi, ed., *Lettere e diari,* 83.

19. John Gooch, *Army, State, and Society in Italy, 1870–1915* (New York: St. Martin's Press, 1989), 55–56.

20. Emilio Bellavita, *Adua: i precedenti—la battaglia—le conseguenze (1881–1931)* (Genoa: Rivista di Roma, 1931), 375–376.

21. "In Memoria," *Rivista militare italiana* 41 (1896): 772.

22. Menarini, *La brigata Dabormida,* 22.

23. Lemmi, ed., *Lettere e diari,* 83.

24. Ibid.

25. Quirico, *Adua,* 206.

26. Giuseppe Lembo, *Il Processo Baratieri* (Bari: F. Casini e Figlio, 1937), 72–73; Bellavita, *Adua,* 325; Crispi, *Francesco Crispi,* 393; Quirico, *Adua,* 218. See also "Deposizione del maggior generale Giuseppe Ellena, Alti processuali dell'Istruttoria a Massawa," reproduced in Baratieri, *Memorie d'Africa,* 469–471.

27. For Italian indifference, see the entry in Major Prestinari's diary for 29 August 1894 in Lemmi, ed., *Lettere e diari,* 137.

28. Ridolfo Mazzucconi, *La Giornata di Adua (1896)* (Milan: Mondadori, 1935), 122.

29. Illness played a role. See Bellavita, *Adua,* 310.

30. Crispi, *Francesco Crispi,* 378.

31. Ibid. 398. It is unclear whether this news reached Baratieri. Francesco Frisina claims that such a rumor circulated around camp on the twenty-eighth but was discounted, as many prior rumors had proven false. Francesco Frisina, *L'Italia in Abissinia e nel Sudan: dall'acquisto di Assab, 1869, alla cessione di Cassala, 1897* (Alexandria: Molco Petrini, 1919), 143.

32. ASMAI, pos. 3/10, fasc. 69, coded telegram dated 25 February 1896.

33. Letter dated 10 February 1896 in Lemmi, ed., *Lettere,* 90.

34. Bellavita, *Adua,* 322.

35. Pantano, *Ventitre anni,* 72.

36. See the account of Yosef Negusie to Alfred Ilg and Léon Chefneux dated 31 March 1896 in Bairu Tafla, ed., *Ethiopian Records of the Menilek Era: Selected Amharic Documents from the Nachlass of Alfred Ilg, 1884–1900* (Wiesbaden: Harrassowitz, 2000), 459.

37. Cesare Pini, *Frammenti de'miei ricordi d'Affrica* (Rome: S. Lapi, 1912), 157.

38. Menarini, *La brigata Dabormida,* 41.

39. Emilio Bellavita cites the journal of Captain Bassi for February, in which he expresses sympathy for a sick General Baratieri. "Baratieri is very sick and is the victim of great nervous exhaustion. He doesn't eat and has a constant fever. He is physically finished." See Bellavita, *Adua,* 310, 312.

40. Baratieri, *Memorie d'Africa,* 363. See also "Deposizione Valenzano," *L'Africa italiana,* 14 June 1896, in ASME, L7 Eritrea, cartella 36 bis, Processo Baratieri. Also Mazzucconi, *La Giornata di Adua,* 166.

41. Carlo Diotti, *Prigioniero d'Africa: La battaglia di Adua e l'impresa coloniale del 1895–1896 nel diario di un caporale italiano* (Como: Nodolibri, 2006), 47.

42. See "Deposizione Spreafico," *L'Africa italiana,* 14 June 1896, in ASME, L7 Eritrea, cartella 36 bis, Processo Baratieri; also see Quirico, *Adua,* 214. In fact, there was no food to be bought; see Sapelli, *Memorie d'Africa.*

43. Giuseppe Bourelly, *La Battaglia di Abba Garima* (Milan: Cogliati, 1901), 178–181.

44. Lembo, *Il Processo Baratieri,* 71–72; Baratieri, *Memorie d'Africa,* 364.

45. See "Seduta pomeridiana [5 giugno 1896]," *Africa italiana,* 7 June 1896, in ASME, L7 Eritrea, cartella 36 bis, Processo Baratieri.

46. Mazzucconi states that Albertone was convinced that the Italians were facing a rear guard of no more than twenty to twenty-five thousand men; see *Giornata di Adua,* 200–201. According to traditional Ethiopian sources, an old man approached Baratieri and told him, "All the Army has gone to fetch grain; he's sitting there alone for you." See Sven Rubenson, "Adwa 1896: The Resounding Protest," in *Protest and Power in Black Africa,* ed. Robert I. Rotberg and Ali Mazrui (New York: Oxford University Press, 1970), 121. Bellavita points out that the Italians tended to undervalue the effectiveness of Shoan (southern Ethiopian) soldiers, believing them to be "small, effeminate, timid"; *Adua,* 322.

47. Mazzucconi, *Giornata di Adua,* 173; "Deposizione Valenzano."

48. Lembo, *Il Processo Baratieri,* 72; Mazzucconi, *Giornata di Adua,* 175; Bellavita, *Adua,* 322.

49. Lembo, *Il Processo Baratieri,* 72–73.

50. "Deposizione Valenzano."

51. Lembo, *Il Processo Baratieri,* 73.

12. ARMIES MEET

1. On this distinction, see also Pietro Felter, *La vicenda affricana, 1895–1896* (Brescia: Giulio Vannini, 1935), 84.

2. Colonel Valenzano, Baratieri's chief of staff, reported at Baratieri's court-martial that the plan was to advance and, if the Ethiopians did not attack, begin the retreat the following day. See "Deposizione Valenzano," *L'Africa italiana*, 14 June 1896, Archivio dello Stato Maggiore dell'Esercito, Ufficio Storico (hereafter cited as ASME), L7 Eritrea, cartella 36 bis, Processo Baratieri. See also Francesco Crispi, *Francesco Crispi: La prima guerra d'Africa: documenti e memorie dell'Archivio Crispi,* ed. Tommaso Palamenghi-Crispi (Milan: Fratelli Treves, 1914), 400; Alberto Pollera, *La battaglia di Adua del 1 marzo 1896, narrata nei luoghi ove fu combattuta* (Florence: Carpigiani e Zipoli, 1928), 42.

3. Giuseppe Menarini, *La brigata Dabormida alla battaglia d'Adua (combattimento e ritirata)* (Naples: Detken e Rocholl, 1897), 44.

4. Ernesto Cordella, *L'artiglieria della Brigata Albertone ad Adua (1 marzo 1896)* (Rome: Sindicato italiano arti grafiche, 1930), 7.

5. Francesco Frisina, *L'Italia in Abissinia e nel Sudan: dall'acquisto di Assab, 1869, alla cessione di Cassala, 1897* (Alexandria: Molco Petrini, 1919), 146.

6. Carlo Diotti, *Prigioniero d'Africa: La battaglia di Adua e l'impresa coloniale del 1895–1896 nel diario di un caporale italiano* (Como: Nodolibri, 2006), 49.

7. Anonymous letter dated 14 March 1896 [Massawa], in Francesco Lemmi, ed., *Lettere e diari d'Africa, 1895–1896* (Rome: Edizioni Roma, 1936), 100.

8. Diotti, *Prigioniero d'Africa*, 48–49.

9. Paul de Lauribar, *Douze ans en Abyssinie* (Paris: Flammarion, 1898), 219.

10. Diotti, *Prigioniero d'Africa*, 49.

11. For the makeup of the units, their numbers, and names, see A. B. Wylde, "An Unofficial Visit to Abyssinia by Our Special Correspondent," *Manchester Guardian*, 20 May 1897, part 6, page 7; Oreste Baratieri, *Memorie d'Africa, 1892–1896* (Genoa: Dioscuri, 1988), 383–384; Pollera, *Battaglia*.

12. Cordella, *Artiglieria*, 7.

13. Giovanni Tedone, *Angerà: i ricordi di un prigioniero di Menelik* (Milan: Giordano, 1964), 7.

14. Giovanni Gamerra, *Ricordi di un prigioniero di guerra allo Scioa (Marzo 1896–gennaio 1897)* (Florence: Barbèra, 1897), 29.

15. Menarini, *La brigata Dabormida*, 49.

16. Ibid., 48.

17. Luigi Fusella, "Il Dagmawi Menilek di Afawarq Gabra Iyasus," *Rassegna di Studi Etiopici* 17 (1961): 141.

18. See ASME, L7 Eritrea, C55, Fatti d'armi, 1896–1914, for a copy of the map. "La Posizione di Gundapta e la Battaglia del 1° Marzo," note from Baratieri to Mariotti, Archivio storico del Ministero Africa Italiana (hereafter cited as ASMAI), pos. 3/10, fasc. 75.

19. Giuseppe Bourelly, *La Battaglia di Abba Garima* (Milan: Cogliati, 1901), 315.

20. Alessandro Sapelli, who fought under Albertone, offers the richest and most balanced portrait. See his *Memorie d'Africa* (Bologna: Zanichelli, 1935). See also Gherardo Pantano's account in *Ventitre anni di vita africana* (Florence: Casa editrice militare italiana, 1932), 51–52. For a photo portrait, see Eduardo Ximenes, *Sul Campo di Adua, marzo-giugno 1896* (Milan: Fratelli Treves, 1897), 289.

21. Cesare Pini, *Frammenti de'miei ricordi d'Affrica* (Rome: S. Lapi, 1912), 142–143.

22. "Deposizione Valenzano," *L'Africa italiana*, 14 June 1896, ASME, L7 Eritrea, cartella 36 bis, Processo Baratieri.

23. Ridolfo Mazzucconi, *La Giornata di Adua (1896)* (Milan: Mondadori, 1935), 225; Aldo Valori in Pollera, *Battaglia*, x, 55. Francesco Frisina offers a more complicated account that confirms the general idea that Turitto was pushed; see *L'Italia in Abissinia*, 161.

    There is no doubt that Albertone seriously underestimated his opponent—as did many Italians. A book published in Italy in 1896 pretended to describe the Ethiopian army, but it described an army making a transition from sabers and spears to firearms—a description that was at least five and probably ten years out of date. See Luigi Sambon, *L'esercito abissino: usi e costumi* (Rome: Voghera Enrico, 1896).

24. See Giovanni Pittaluga, *Atti processuali del Tribunale dell'Asmara,* reprinted in Baratieri, *Memorie d'Africa*, 473–479.

25. Ximenes, *Sul Campo di Adua*, 286.

26. See Chris Prouty, *Empress Taytu and Menelik II: Ethiopia, 1883–1910* (London: Ravens, 1986), 155. This account is apparently drawn from "La Bataille d'Adowa d'après un récit Abyssin," *Revue française de l'étranger et des colonies* 21 (1896): 656. This French-language source is the only primary source to mention the incident, though even the claim to eyewitness status cannot be verified; the "Abyssinian" in the title is never identified. The account is reproduced in Ridolfo Mazzucconi, *Giornata*, 238. It is also repeated, without attribution, in Pierre Pétridès, *Le Héros d'Adoua, ras Makonen, prince d'Éthiopie* (Paris: Plon 1963), 158–159, although the hour is given as five in the morning, perhaps because the earlier hour calls into question the reliability of the account as a whole. Pétridès is, in general, unreliable; his book contains lengthy quotations without citation or supporting evidence. Pétridès seems to have been inspired by a series of pieces published in 1935 by the royalist *Action française;* see 171n.

27. See Guèbrè Sellassié, *Chronique du règne de Ménélik II, roi des rois d'Ethiopie*, ed. Maurice de Coppet, trans. Tesfà Sellassié (Paris: Maisonneuve, 1930), 438–439.

28. See report of Yosef Negussié to Alfred Ilg and Léon Chefneux, 31 March 1896, in Bairu Tafla, ed., *Ethiopian Records of the Menilek Era* (Wiesbaden: Harrassowitz, 2000), 460. Still, we cannot rule out that the Ethiopian camp had warnings of the Italian advance; Ras Alula told Augustus Wylde that his spies in the Italian camp had warned him. See Augustus Blandy Wylde, *Modern Abyssinia* (London: Methuen, 1901), 148–149, 204. Assuming this to be true, however, begs the question of how Alula might have acted on this information, especially as Albertone's forces did not encounter resistance until they were well beyond the passes, their rendezvous point.

29. Sellassié, *Chronique,* 440–441.

30. For pictorial representations of the battle of Adwa featuring the *tabot,* see Raymond A. Silverman, *Painting Ethiopia: The Life and Work of Qes Adamu Tesfaw* (Los Angeles: UCLA Fowler Museum of Cultural History, 2005), 84. On Menelik and the *tabot* of St. George, see Sellassié, *Chronique,* 243. See also Richard Pankhurst, "The Battle of Adwa (1896) as Depicted by Traditional Ethiopian Artists," in *Proceedings of the First International Conference on the History of Ethiopian Art* (London: Pindar, 1989), 78–103.

31. The official Ethiopian chronicle relates that Turitto first encountered the troops of Ras Mangasha. See Sellassié, *Chronique,* 438–439. Giuseppe Puglisi reports that Baltcha's troops were the first encountered. See *Chi è dell'Eritrea, 1952: dizionario biografico* (Asmara: Agenzia Regina, 1952), 289–290.

32. Pollera, *Battaglia,* 56; Bourelly, *Battaglia di Abba Garima,* 606.

33. In Fusella, "Il Dagmawi Menilek," 141.

34. Ximenes, *Sul Campo di Adua,* 287. Mazzucconi puts the figure at seven thousand; see Mazzucconi, *Giornata,* 228.

35. Anacleto Bronzuoli, *Adua* (Rome: Instituto Poligrafico dello Stato, 1935), 35.

36. Ximenes, *Sul Campo di Adua,* 287–288.

37. Pantano, *Ventitré anni,* 64; *Guerra d'Africa: documenti sulla battaglia di Adua e sulla operazione per la liberazione di Cassala* (Rome: E. Voghera, 1896), 15.

38. Ximenes, *Sul Campo di Adua,* 286.

39. Cordella, *Artiglieria,* 9.

40. Mazzucconi, *Giornata,* 248.

41. Bourelly, *Battaglia di Abba Garima,* 358.

42. However, David Chapple notes that the effectiveness of Ethiopian artillery was questionable, especially given that ammunition shortages made practice expensive and rare. See David Chapple, "The Firearms of Adwa," in *Adwa Victory Centenary Conference,* eds. Abdussamad Ahmad and Richard Pankhurst (Addis Ababa: Institute of Ethiopian Studies, Addis Ababa University, 1998), 50.

43. Pollera, *Battaglia,* 60; Mazzucconi, *Giornata,* 245.

44. Lauribar states that her forces included five Hotchkiss artillery pieces; *Douze ans,* 436. Accounts of Taytu's conduct at Adwa are highly variable. Some accounts have her exhorting the Ethiopian soldiers. Others have her locked away in anxious prayer until the outcome became clear. Nicola d'Amato, *Da Adua ad Addis Abeba: ricordi d'un prigioniero* (Salerno: Volpe, 1898), 66–67. See also Sellassié, *Chronique,* 441; report of Yosef Negussié to Alfred Ilg and Léon Chefneux, 31 March 1896, in Tafla, ed., *Ethiopian Records,* 458–463.

45. For a rough map of the disposition of forces, see the annotated map published in the *Manchester Guardian* of 20 May 1897. It largely concurs with the array of Ethiopian forces described by Yosef Negussié in Tafla, ed., *Ethiopian Records,* 459–460.

46. Mazzucconi, *Giornata,* 246; Tafla, ed., *Ethiopian Records,* 459–460; Clément de La Jonquière, *Les italiens en Erythrée: quinze ans de politique coloniale* (Paris: H. Charles-Lavauzelle, 1916).

47. Alberto Woctt, *Battaglia di Adua, 1 marzo 1896: memorie vive ed inedite di un ufficiale superstite* (Parma: Albertelli, 1991), 63.

48. Giuseppe Bourelly specifies that the position was "a spur about 700 meters forward from the pass, on the road to Mariam Shavitu"; *Battaglia di Abba Garima*, 435–436. Francesco Frisina of the Arimondi brigade puts the location about 800 meters from the pass; *Memorie di un prigioniero d'Africa* (Reggio Calabria: Tip. de P. Lombardi, 1899), 8. Such a location would not be far enough forward to provide support to Albertone. Baratieri himself gives no precise distance. See Baratieri, *Memorie d'Africa*, 414–415.

49. Francesco Frisina, a soldier in General Arimondi's brigade, would later claim that Baratieri ordered Albertone to fall back from his advanced position. There is no evidence to support the claim that Baratieri ever advocated such a risky move. Albertone was simply too deeply engaged to extract himself. See Frisina, *Memorie*, 8. For Baratieri's orders to Arimondi, see Eugenio Dolciotti, *Da Napoli a Adua: Bozzetti e ricordi della campagna d'Africa, 1895–96* (Tivoli: A. Chicca, 1913), 64.

50. Baratieri, *Memorie d'Africa*, 423–424.

51. Mazzucconi, *Giornata*, 282.

52. This was Baratieri's view, as expressed in a note to his friend General Mariotti. See the several undated *note esattissime* sent by Baratieri to Mariotti in ASMAI, pos. 3/10, fasc. 75.

53. Baratieri, *Memorie d'Africa*, 419; Bourelly, *Battaglia*, 345; Quirico, *Adua*, 260.

54. Baratieri, *Memorie d'Africa*, 420–421; Bourelly, *Battaglia*, 344.

55. Baratieri, *Memorie d'Africa*, 418–419.

56. Mazzucconi, *Giornata*, 282.

57. Diotti, *Prigioniero d'Africa*, 44.

58. Ibid., 54.

59. *Guerra d'Africa*, 15; Baratieri, *Memorie d'Africa*, 409.

60. *Guerra d'Africa*, 18; Menarini, *La brigata Dabormida*, 58.

13. THE CENTER CRUMBLES

1. Augustus B. Wylde, "An Unofficial Mission to Abyssinia," *Manchester Guardian*, 20 May 1897, 8.

2. Antonio Baldissera, *Guerra d'Africa: relazione sulle operazioni militari nel secondo periodo della Campagna d'Africa 1895–6* (Rome: E. Voghera, 1896), 20.

3. Ibid., 21.

4. Alberto Pollera, *La battaglia di Adua del 1 marzo 1896, narrata nei luoghi ove fu combattuta* (Florence: Carpigiani e Zipoli, 1928), 71.

5. Anonymous letter dated 14 March 1896 (Massawa) in Francesco Lemmi, ed, *Lettere e diari d'Africa, 1895–1896* (Rome: Edizioni Roma, 1936), 100.

6. Giovanni Tedone, *Angerà: i ricordi di un prigioniero di Menelik* (Milan: Giordano, 1964), 8.

7. Francesco Frisina, *L'Italia in Abissinia e nel Sudan: dall'acquisto di Assab, 1869, alla cessione di Cassala, 1897* (Alexandria: Molco Petrini, 1919), 149, 150.

8. Colonel Brusati would later claim that Arimondi's troops were not fully in their positions until ten-fifteen, fully two hours after Baratieri's order. See "Deposizione

Brusati" in *L'Africa italiana,* 14 June 1896, in Archivio dello Stato Maggiore dell'Esercito, Ufficio Storico (hereafter cited as ASME), L7 Eritrea, cartella 36 bis, Processo Baratieri.

9. All the same, the Ethiopians were taking hellish fire. Lieutenant Fuso, a member of Turitto's battalion, was captured at nine o'clock. Taken to the Ethiopian position facing Albertone, he had to get behind a rock to avoid being hit by dense Italian fire. Nicola d'Amato, *Da Adua ad Addis Abeba: ricordi d'un prigioniero* (Salerno: A. Volpe, 1898), 5.

10. Ernesto Cordella, *L'artiglieria della Brigata Albertone ad Adua (1 marzo 1896)* (Rome: Sindicato italiano arti grafiche, 1930), 9–10.

11. Ibid., 10–11.

12. Ibid., 11, 15.

13. Gherardo Pantano, *Ventitré anni di vita africana* (Florence: Casa editrice militare italiana, 1932), 64.

14. Cordella, *L'artiglieria della Brigata Albertone,* 11. Major Giorgio Cossu, commander of the Sixth Native Battalion in the Albertone Brigade, also put the time of the retreat at ten-thirty. See his deposition in *L'Africa italiana,* 14 June 1896, in ASME, L7 Eritrea, cartella 36 bis, Processo Baratieri.

15. Cordella, *L'artiglieria della Brigata Albertone,* 15.

16. One exception were the men under the command of Captain Spreafico, who organized some sixty-five askari and led them back to the passes, where they fought alongside Colonel Brusati's men on the flanks of Raio. See "Deposizione Spreafico" in *L'Africa italiana,* 14 June 1896, in ASME, L7 Eritrea, cartella 36 bis, Processo Baratieri.

17. For the retreat, see *Guerra d'Africa,* 24. For deaths during the retreat, see detailed figures in the appendix of Eduardo Ximenes, *Sul Campo di Adua, marzo-giugno 1896* (Milano: Fratelli Treves, 1897).

18. Cordella, *L'artiglieria della Brigata Albertone,* 14.

19. Ximenes, *Sul Campo,* 289 and appendix.

20. Francesco Frisina, *Memorie di un prigioniero d'Africa* (Reggio Calabria: P. Lombardi, 1899), 8.

21. Anacleto Bronzuoli, *Adua* (Rome: Instituto Poligrafico dello Stato, 1935), 58.

22. Francesco Frisina, *L'Italia in Abissinia e nel Sudan: dall'acquisto di Assab, 1869, alla cessione di Cassala, 1897* (Alexandria: Molco Petrini, 1919), 168.

23. Baldissera, *Guerra d'Africa,* 26.

24. Tedone, *Angerà,* 10. For officer casualties, see Giuseppe Bourelly, *La Battaglia di Abba Garima* (Milan: Cogliati, 1901), 662. Out of the total complement of officers, 295 died and 57 were taken prisoner.

25. Anonymous letter dated 14 March 1896, published in *Illustrazione popolare* and reprinted in Lemmi, ed., *Lettere e diari d'Africa,* 100.

26. Tedone, *Angerà,* 14–15.

27. Ibid., 19.

28. Baldissera, *Guerra d'Africa,* 26.

29. Ibid., 29.

30. Ximenes, *Sul Campo,* 264; Bronzuoli, *Adua,* 46.

31. Ridolfo Mazzucconi, *La Giornata di Adua (1896)* (Milan: Mondadori, 1935), 282.

32. Baldissera, *Guerra d'Africa,* 30.

33. Ibid.

34. Menarini, *La brigata Dabormida,* 64.

35. Ximenes, *Sul Campo,* 265, 289; Menarini, *La brigata Dabormida,* 64.

36. Emilio Bellavita, *Adua: i precedenti—la battaglia—le conseguenze (1881–1931)* (Genoa: I. Dioscuri, 1931), 377.

37. Archivio storico del Ministero Africa Italiana (hereafter cited as ASMAI), pos. 3/10, fasc. 75, note from Baratieri to Mariotti, speculating on Dabormida's motives. See also Mazzucconi, *La Giornata di Adua,* 197. "Più attendibile potrebbe sembrare l'intenzione segreta del Comandante la prima Brigata di operare un audace diversivo sul campo scioano di Gherrà, in fondo al vallone di Mariam Sciavitú, al fine d'alleggerire, per via indiretta, la pressione nemica contro Albertone; ma di ciò cadrà in acconcio di parlare a suo luogo"; Menarini, *La brigata Dabormida,* 66n.

38. Baldissera, *Guerra d'Africa,* 15.

39. Alberto Woctt, *Battaglia di Adua, 1 marzo 1896: memorie vive ed inedite di un ufficiale superstite* (Parma: Albertelli, 1991), 72; Menarini, *La brigata Dabormida,* 76.

40. Woctt, *Battaglia di Adua,* 73. But note that other accounts state that the smoke from Ethiopian firearms provided cover for their movements. Carlo Diotti, *Prigioniero d'Africa: La battaglia di Adua e l'impresa coloniale del 1895–1896 nel diario di un caporale italiano* (Como: Nodolibri, 2006), 57.

41. Woctt, *Battaglia di Adua,* 74.

42. Baldissera, *Guerra d'Africa,* 32.

43. Menarini, *La brigata Dabormida,* 83.

44. Ibid., 77.

45. Ibid., 84.

46. Diotti, *Prigioniero d'Africa,* 59; Woctt, *Battaglia di Adua,* 78; Menarini, *La brigata Dabormida,* 85.

47. Menarini, *La brigata Dabormida,* 85.

48. See ASME, L7 Eritrea, cartella 55, Fatti d'armi, 1896–1914. From the diary of Capitano Vencenzo Tolas, taken prisoner after the battle. Augustus Wylde gives a similar account in "The Battle of Adwa," *Manchester Guardian,* 20 May 1897, 7, and *Modern Abyssinia* (London: Methuen, 1901), 220. General Albertone recounts a less detailed version of Dabormida's death in a letter to Dabormida's family in 1901. See letter, "Alla famiglia Dabormida," in Lemmi, ed., *Lettere e diari d'Africa,* 86. Of course, Albertone was a prisoner, so he could not have witnessed Dabormida's death. There were also reports that Dabormida had taken his own life. See Henri d'Orléans, *Une visite à l'Empereur Ménélick: Notes et impressions de route* (Paris: Dentu, 1898), 189.

49. Domenico Quirico, *Adua: La battaglia che cambiò la storia d'Italia* (Milan: Mondadori, 2004), 216–217.

50. Menelik would later give Dabormida's saber and officer's sash to General Albertone, who would return them to Dabormida's family. See General Albertone's letter, "Alla famiglia Dabormida," in Lemmi, ed., *Lettere e diari d'Africa*, 86.

14. DESPAIR, PANIC, PURSUIT

1. Arnoldo Nicoletti-Altimari, *Fra gli abissini: memorie di un prigioniero nel Tigre* (Rome: Voghera, 1898), 171–173.
2. Francesco Frisina, *Memorie di un prigioniero d'Africa* (Reggio Calabria: Tipografica de P. Lombardi, 1899), 8.
3. Ibid., 29.
4. "Udienza del giorno 6 giugno 1896" (Processo Baratieri), *L'Africa italiana,* 7 June 1896. One of the difficulties was the lack of leadership. Ethiopian soldiers targeted officers, with the result that many rank-and-file soldiers were leaderless. "Deposizione Brusati," *L'Africa italiana,* 14 June 1896.
5. Luigi Goj, *Adua e prigionia fra i galla* (Milan: Scuola Tipografica Salesiana, 1901), 25. Giovanni Tedone also recalls Baratieri's attempt to control the retreat and pursuit. See Giovanni Tedone, *Angerà: i ricordi di un prigioniero di Menelik* (Milan: Giordano, 1964), 19.
6. Alessandro Sapelli, *Memorie d'Africa* (Bologna: Zanichelli, 1935), 122.
7. Alberto Woctt, *Battaglia di Adua, 1. Marzo 1896: memorie vive e d inedite di un ufficiale superstite* (Parma: Albertelli, 1991), 100.
8. See the drawing by Eduardo Ximenes on page 214, which was widely reproduced, including for the cover of *l'Illustrazione* of 22 March 1896. Tedone's remarks can be found in Tedone, *Angerà,* 19.
9. Telegram from General Baratieri to Ministry of War, Massawa, 3 March 1896. Reproduced in *Documenti diplomatici,* XXIII-bis, *Avvenimenti d'Africa,* 2 vols, *Atti Parlamentari* (Rome: Tipografia della camera dei deputati, 1896), 151. Baratieri's coded message to the government was leaked to the press. Baratieri regretted the release of the remark, but not his candor. See Archivio storico del Ministero Africa Italiana (ASMAI), pos. 3/10, fasc. 75, letter from Baratieri to Mariotti, Massawa, 27 May 1896.
10. Giuseppe Menarini, *La brigata Dabormida alla battaglia d'Adua* (Napoli: Libreria Detken & Rocholl, 1897), 118.
11. Eugenio Dolciotti, *Da Napoli a Adua: Bozzetti e ricordi della campagna d'Africa, 1895–96* (Tivoli: A. Chicca, 1913), 66.
12. Tedone, *Angerà,* 20.
13. Francesco Frisina, *L'Italia in Abissinia e nel Sudan: dall'acquisto di Assab, 1869, alla cessione di Cassala, 1897* (Alexandria: Molco Petrini, 1919), 174.
14. Tedone, *Angerà,* 21.
15. Giuseppe Bourelly, *La Battaglia di Abba Garima* (Milan: F. Cogliati, 1901), 487.
16. Carlo Diotti, *Prigioniero d'Africa; La battaglia di Adua e l'impresa coloniale del 1895–1896 nel diario di un caporale italiano* (Como: Nodo Libri, 2006), 59; Woctt, *Battaglia di Adua,* 89.

17. Diotti, *Prigioniero d'Africa,* 59–60.

18. Woctt, *Battaglia di Adua,* 85–86.

19. Ibid., 89–90.

20. Ibid., 76.

21. Ibid., 89.

22. Anonymous letter dated 14 March 1896, published in *Illustrazione popolare* and re-printed in Francesco Lemmi, ed., *Lettere e diari d'Africa, 1895–1896* (Rome: Ed-izioni Roma, 1936), 100.

23. Pietro Felter, *La vicenda affricana 1895–1896* (Brescia: Vannini, 1935), 81.

24. Ibid., 82. See also Girma Fisseha, "Ethiopian Paintings on Adwa," in *Adwa Victory Centenary Conference,* ed. Abdussamad Ahmad and Richard Pankhurst (Addis Ababa: Institute of Ethiopian Studies, Addis Ababa University, 1998), 653.

25. Fisseha, "Ethiopian Paintings on Adwa," 82.

26. Sapelli, *Memorie,* 119–120.

27. Nicoletti-Altimari, *Fra gli abissini,* 19.

28. Anonymous letter dated 14 March 1896 in Lemmi, ed., *Lettere,* 102–103.

29. Nicoletti-Altimari, *Fra gli abissini,* 10.

30. "Udienza del giorno 6 giugno 1896" (Processo Baratieri), *L'Africa italiana,* 7 June 1896.

31. Nicoletti-Altimari, *Fra gli abissini,* 14.

32. Augustus B. Wylde, "An Unofficial Mission to Abyssinia," *Manchester Guardian,* 20 May 1897.

33. Anonymous letter dated 14 March 1896 in Lemmi, ed., *Lettere,* 104.

15. THE HARVEST

1. Chris Prouty, *Empress Taytu and Menelik II: Ethiopia, 1883–1910* (London: Ravens, 1986), 158.

2. During the Egyptian campaign of 1798–1801, for example, Napoleon's soldiers were particularly keen to strip the bodies of fallen Mamluks. Mamluks, they had learned, kept gold coins and other valuables stitched inside their clothing. See Paul Strath-ern, *Napoleon in Egypt* (New York: Bantam, 2007), 305.

3. Gian Carlo Stella, *Battaglia di Adua, 1 marzo 1896: memorie vive ed inedite di un ufficiale superstite* (Parma: E. Albertelli, 1991), 91.

4. Giovanni Tedone, *Angerà: i ricordi di un prigioniero di Menelik* (Milan: Giordano, 1964), 28.

5. Tedone, *Angerà,* 25. Tedone also witnessed the execution of an Italian soldier who refused to carry scrotums piled in a blanket; *Angerà,* 27.

6. Luigi Goj, *Adua e prigionia fra i galla* (Milan: Scuola Tip. Salesiana, 1901), 28. Francesco Frisina describes a similar scene in *Memorie di un prigioniero d'Africa* (Reggio Calabria: P. Lombardi, 1899), 29.

7. Consul Plowden to the Earl of Clarendon. Massawa, 3 March 1855. In *Parliamen-tary Papers, Correspondence Respecting Abyssinia, 1846–1868* (London: Harrison

and Sons, 1868), 146. See also Sven Rubenson, *King of Kings: Tewodros of Ethiopia* (Addis Ababa: Haile Selassie I University, 1966), esp. 55.

8. For a suggestive interpretation of such issues in West Africa, see Florence Bernault, "Body, Power and Sacrifice in Equatorial Africa," *Journal of African History* 47 (2006): 207–239.

9. Augustus Blandy Wylde, *Modern Abyssinia* (London: Methuen, 1901), 310.

10. Augustus B. Wylde, "An Unofficial Mission to Abyssinia," *Manchester Guardian*, 24 May 1897, 5.

11. It was not unknown for Europeans to take trophies of their own—more often the head of a vanquished opponent. See Edgar V. Winans, "The Head of the King: Museums and the Path to Resistance," *Comparative Studies in Society and History* 36 (1994): 221–241, and David Thomas, *Skull Wars: Kennewick Man, Archaeology, and the Battle for Native American Identity* (New York: Basic Books, 2000).

12. "Lorsqu'on demande au Abyssiniens pourquoi ils coupent ce membre plutôt qu'un autre, ils répondent sans hésiter que c'est là seulement ce qui caractérise l'homme." See Edmond Combes and Maurice Tamisier, *Voyage en Abyssinie, dans le pays des Galla, de Choa et d'Ifat: précédé d'une excursion dans l'Arabie-heureuse, et accompagné d'une carte de ces diverses contrées* (Paris: L. Desessart, 1838), 1:221–222.

13. Nicola d'Amato read the act in these terms. See *Da Adua ad Addis-Abeba ricordi d'un prigioniero* (Salerno: A. Volpe, 1898), 6.

14. See Gary Taylor, *Castration: An Abbreviated History of Western Manhood* (New York: Routledge, 2000), 57.

15. Ibid., 57. On Coligny and the St. Bartholomew's Day massacre more broadly, see Barbara Diefendorf, *Beneath the Cross: Catholics and Huguenots in Sixteenth Century Paris* (New York: Oxford University Press, 1991).

16. Jacqueline Murray, "Sexual Mutilation and Castration Anxiety: A Medieval Perspective," in *The Boswell Thesis: Essays on Christianity, Social Tolerance, and Homosexuality,* ed. Mathew Kuefler (Chicago: University of Chicago Press, 2006), 254–272, esp. 257.

17. For a gloss on the episode, see Taylor, *Castration,* 136. That a similar logic (that the perpetrators were carrying out the work of God) was at work in the massacres of the wars of religion is the contention of Denis Crouzet in *Les Guerriers de Dieu: la violence au temps des troubles de religion,* 2 vols. (Paris: Champ Vallon, 1990).

18. On the whiteness of the Irish, see Noel Ignatiev, *How the Irish Became White* (New York: Routledge, 1995).

19. For the lynching of Italians, see "Di Rudini as Cabinet Chief," *New York Times,* 9 March 1896. On French fairs, see Yves-Marie Bercé, *History of Peasant Revolts: The Social Origins of Rebellion in Early Modern France* (Ithaca: Cornell University Press, 1990), 21. Alain Corbin, *The Village of Cannibals: Rage and Murder in France, 1870* (Cambridge: Cambridge University Press, 1992) describes an extraordinary scene during the Franco-Prussian War.

20. From Jean Martet, *Le silence de M. Clemenceau* (Paris: Albin Michel, 1929), 293–299.

21. Tedone, *Angerà,* 59.

22. Sometimes the mutilations went well beyond castration to a kind of torture of the defeated body. See Stella, *Battaglia di Adua*, 92.

23. See Telegram from General Baratieri to Ministry of War, Massawa, 3 March 1896. Reproduced in *Documenti diplomatici*, XXIII-bis, *Avvenimenti d'Africa*, 2 vols, *Atti Parlamentari* (Rome: Tipografia della camera dei deputati, 1896), 151.

24. Tedone, *Angerà*, 94. On the collection of trophies, see Prouty, *Empress Taytu and Menelik II*, 158–159.

25. J. G. Vanderheym, *Une expédition avec le négous Ménélik: vingt mois en Abyssinie* (Paris: Hachette, 1896), 71. See the comments of Harold G. Marcus in *The Modern History of Ethiopia and the Horn of Africa: A Selected and Annotated Bibliography* (Stanford: Stanford University Press, 1972) as well as those of Richard A. Caulk in his review of Marcus's book in *International Journal of African Historical Studies* 8 (1975): 26.

26. See Richard Pankhurst, "The Saint-Simonians and Ethiopia," in *Proceedings of the Third International Conference of Ethiopian Studies* (Addis Ababa: Institute of Ethiopian Studies, University of Addis Ababa, 1969), 169–223.

27. Combes and Tamisier, *Voyage en Abyssinie*, 1:221–222. Years later, Henri d'Orléans mentioned daisy-chained scrotums dangling ornamentally from the grip of a soldier's saber. See Henri d'Orléans, *Une visite à l'Empereur Ménélick: Notes et impressions de route* (Paris: Dentu, 1898), 158.

28. Combes and Tamisier, *Voyage en Abyssinie*, 2:322.

29. Ibid., 2:322–323.

30. Eduardo Ximenes, *Sul Campo di Adua, marzo-giugno 1896* (Milan: Fratelli Treves, 1897), 200.

31. Raffaele Ciasca, *Storia coloniale dell'Italia contemporanea: da Assab all'impero* (Milan: Ulrico Hoepli, 1938), 210n. This figure is not far from the twenty-eight to thirty reported by Stella. See *Battaglia di Adua*, 91n.

32. "And in that regard there could be fraud, as in the taking of trophies not from the enemy, but from the dead among one's fellow soldiers." That is how Augustus Wylde—almost certainly the European most familiar with, and most sympathetic to, Ethiopia—describes one such incident. Wylde returned to Ethiopia after Adwa and wrote a series of articles for the *Manchester Guardian*. His voyage later provided the material for a book, *Modern Abyssinia*, published in 1901. In his book, he recounts a story whereby the head man of Woro Eilu had been wounded at Adwa. As he lay dazed and in shock, he was very nearly castrated by a soldier from Shoa. The would-be trophy taker was beaten and put into chains. See Wylde, *Modern Abyssinia*, 388–389.

33. Guido Moltedo, *L'Assedio di Maccalè, campagna d'Africa 1895-96* (Rome: Dante Alighieri, 1901), 8–9n.

34. Richard Pankhurst, *The Ethiopians* (Oxford: Blackwell, 1998), 192–193.

35. Frisina, *Memorie*, 31. For details regarding the layout of the Ethiopian camp, see the map accompanying Augustus B. Wylde's piece for the *Manchester Guardian* dated 20 May 1897.

36. Tedone, *Angerà*, 29–30; Prouty, *Empress Taytu and Menelik II*, 158.

37. Lieutenant Guglielmo Pini recounts a similar experience in a letter to a friend, reproduced in Giuseppe Canuti, *L'Italia in Africa e le guerre con l'abissinia: dall'occupazione di Massaua alla resa dei prigionieri dopo la battaglia d'Adua* (Florence: Adriano Salani, 1911), 237–238.

38. Carlo Diotti, *Prigioniero d'Africa: La battaglia di Adua e l'impresa coloniale del 1895–1896 nel diario di un caporale italiano* (Como: Nodolibri, 2006), 60–61.

39. Ibid., 60.

40. Edward Gleichen, *With the Mission to Menelik, 1897* (London: E. Arnold, 1898), 216–217.

41. Diotti, *Prigioniero d'Africa*, 61.

42. Ibid., 66.

43. Tedone, *Angerà*, 33.

44. Gherardo Pantano, *Ventitré anni di vita africana* (Florence: Casa editrice militare italiana, 1932), 73.

45. Francesco Frisina, *L'Italia in Abissinia e nel Sudan: dall'acquisto di Assab, 1869, alla cessione di Cassala, 1897* (Alexandria: Molco Petrini, 1919), 201.

46. Frisina, *Memorie*, 32, and *L'Italia in Abissinia*, 202. On the sale of rifles, see Luigi Capucci's dispatch of 15 December 1894 in Carlo Zaghi, "L'Italia e l'Etiopia alla vigilia di Adua nei dispacci segreti di Luigi Capucci: contributo alla biografia di un grande pioniere," *Gli annali dell'Africa italiana* 4 (1941): 533, 536.

47. Frisina, *Memorie*, 34, and *L'Italia in Abissinia*, 205.

48. D'Amato, *Da Adua ad Addis-Abeba*, 45.

49. Ibid., 45–46.

50. On the general situation after the battle, see Harold Marcus, *The Life and Times of Menelik II, Ethiopia 1844–1913* (Oxford: Clarendon, 1975), 174ff.

51. Molteo, *l'Assedio di Maccalè*, 8–9n.

52. Although many sources refer to 1,900 prisoners or occasionally 2,000, the final count of prisoners released under the Treaty of Addis Ababa was 1,587. See Carlo Rossetti, *Storia diplomatica dell'Etiopia durante il regno di Menelik II* (Turin: Società tipografico—editrice nazionale, 1910), 210. Although there is no official accounting of the difference, a number of factors would help to explain the discrepancy, including escape and death from wounds. George Berkeley starts with the figure of 1,865 prisoners but identifies 106 as dying subsequently, leaving 172 unaccounted for. George F.-H. Berkeley, *The Campaign of Adowa and the Rise of Menelik* (New York: Negro Universities Press, 1969), 346–347. There were accounts of deaths among prisoners, although not enough to account for the discrepancy. The diverse and scattered nature of the southward march may account for some of this; so would the allocation of prisoners to Mangasha, prisoners who did not make the journey south. See Archivio storico del Ministero Africa Italiana (ASMAI), Eritrea Questioni Politico Militare, pos. 3/16, fasc. 130; Arnoldo Nicoletti-Altimari, *Fra gli abissini: memorie di un prigioniero nel Tigre* (Rome: Voghera, 1898), 214–215, 222. The number of askari prisoners is harder to determine with precision. See Prouty, *Empress Taytu and Menelik II*, 158; John Gooch, *Army, State, and Society in Italy, 1870–1915* (New York: St. Martin's Press, 1989), 94; Bruce Vandevort, *Wars of*

Imperial Conquest in Africa, 1830–1914 (Bloomington: Indiana University Press, 1998), 164.

53. Prouty, *Empress Taytu and Menelik II,* 336.

54. Giovanni Gamerra, *Ricordi di un prigioniero di guerra allo Scioa (Marzo 1896-gennaio 1897)* (Firenze: Barbera, 1897), 45; Tedone, *Angerà,* 35–36; D'Amato, *Da Adua ad Addis-Abeba,* 69.

55. Frisina, *L'Italia in Abissinia,* 202.

56. Tedone, *Angerà,* 35–36.

57. Paul Lauribar puts the figure at 1,200. Augustus Wylde states that "they could not have numbered less than 1500." See Paul Lauribar, *Douze ans en Abyssinie* (Paris: Flammarion, 1898), 623, and Wylde, *Modern Abyssinia,* 132.

58. On Afawarq Gabra Iyasus and Mangasha, see Luigi Fusella, trans., "Il Dagmawi Menilek di Afawarq Gabra Iyasus," *Rassegna di Studi Etiopici* 17 (1961): 143.

59. When the Italians had entered Adwa in April 1895, askari had played a prominent role in acts of pillaging. This, too, may have fed the animus against them, although, of course, no effort was made to distinguish between askari who had participated in that campaign and those captured following the battle of Adwa. See Guèbrè Sellassié, *Chronique du règne de Ménélik II, roi des rois d'Ethiopie,* II, ed. Maurice de Coppet, trans. Tèsfa Sellassié (Paris: Maisonneuve, 1930), 369n, citing Wylde, *Modern Abyssinia,* 51.

60. See also Lauribar, *Douze ans,* 623.

61. Ibid.

62. Albert Hans claimed that this aspect of Ethiopian law could be traced back to the code of Justinian. See Albert Hans, "L'armée de Ménélik," *Revue des Deux Mondes* 135 (1896): 873.

63. Moltedo, *l'Assedio di Maccalè,* 117.

64. Silvana Palma claims that only Christian askari suffered amputation. See *L'Italia coloniale* (Rome: Editori Riuniti, 1999), 69. The evidence doesn't bear this out. The vast majority of askari were Muslim, and there is ample evidence that they were not spared. See, for example, the fate of Mohamed Aga Adam, Sultan Aga Amed, and Idris Tutai as related in Ernesto Cordella, *L'artiglieria della Brigata Albertone ad Adua (1 marzo 1896)* (Rome: Sindicato italiano arti grafiche, 1930), 14. See also Archivio dello Stato Maggiore dell'Esercito, Ufficio Storico (ASME), L7 Eritrea, cartella 41, f. 22.

65. Palma, *L'Italia coloniale,* 69. The amputations were carried out in several locations. Augustus B. Wylde noted the location where some eight hundred had lost limbs in *Modern Abyssinia,* 213.

66. On cauterization, see Gerald H. Portal, *My Mission to Abyssinia* (London: E. Arnold, 1892), 151.

67. Tedone, *Angerà,* 36. Giovanni Gamerra recounted a similar experience as his former soldiers cried out "Major! Major!" to him. Gamerra, *Ricordi di un prigioniero,* 54.

68. Moltedo, *Assedio di Maccalè,* 102–103.

69. "The punishment of the native Abyssinians, according to the laws of the country, was perfectly just, but the horrible part was that the offence of the majority of the

prisoners was their first, and no distinction was made between Moslem and Christian. There are many Moslem soldiers in Italian employ who have never been Abyssinian subjects, and the harsh way in which they were treated has made the whole Mahomedan population of the north lasting enemies to King Menelek and to the Abyssinian Christians of the south, and no doubt in the future they will have their revenge." Wylde, *Modern Abyssinia,* 213.

70. Fusella, trans., "Il Dagmawi Menilek," 143–145. He also argues in favor of abandoning such punishments as inhumane.

71. Augustus B. Wylde, "An Unofficial Mission to Abyssinia," *Manchester Guardian,* 28 May 1897, 10.

72. Palma, *L'Italia coloniale,* 69. Augustus B. Wylde, Ethiopia's most effective advocate in Europe, sought to mitigate the impact, emphasizing a tone of pity rather than outrage. Wylde, *Modern Abyssinia,* 132, 422–423. On the status of the askari generally, see Vandevort, *Wars of Imperial Conquest,* 43.

16. THE LONG MARCH

1. Stuart Munro-Hay, *Ethiopia: The Unknown Land* (London: I. B. Tauris, 2002), 110. Jules Borelli claimed to have been inspired by d'Abbadie in *Ethiopie méridionale: journal de mon voyage aux pays Amhara, Oromo et Sidama, septembre 1885 à novembre 1888* (Paris: Ancien Maison Quantun, 1890), 1–2. D'Abbadie's son—"a man full of vices," according to Wylde—became a business partner of Ilg and Clochette in the 1880s. For Wylde's commentary, see the *Manchester Guardian* of 27 May 1897, where Wylde relates learning that d'Abbadie arrived at Addis dressed as a Jesuit. See also letter from Antoine d'Abbadie to the minister of foreign affairs, 8 July 1839, in Archives du ministère des affaires étrangères (quai d'Orsay), Mémoires et documents, Afrique, 13 documents postérieurs à 1814.

2. Richard Pankhurst, "The Saint-Simonians and Ethiopia," in *Proceedings of the Third International Conference of Ethiopian Studies* (Addis Ababa: Institute of Ethiopian Studies, 1969), 203; Cornelius Jaenen, "The Combes-Tamisier Mission to Ethiopia, 1835–37: Saint-Simonian Precursors of Colonialism," *French Colonial History* 3 (2003): 150–151.

3. William Gervase Clarence-Smith, *The Economics of the Indian Ocean Slave Trade in the Nineteenth Century* (London: Frank Cass, 1989), 93; Jonathan Miran, *Red Sea Citizens: Cosmopolitan Society and Cultural Change in Massawa* (Bloomington: Indiana University Press, 2009), esp. 119–165.

4. Vico Mantegazza, *Gli Italiani in Africa: L'assedio di Macalle* (Florence: Successori Le Monnier, 1896), 441.

5. For the departures of troop ships, see Archivio dello Stato Maggiore dell'Esercito, Ufficio Storico (hereafter cited as ASME), L7 Eritrea, C41, "Dati intorno alla partenza di reinforzi in Africa."

6. The best full "instant history" of the battle in any language was written by Augustus Wylde for the *Manchester Guardian.* Like any instant history, Wylde's account has

its errors. Wylde's great contributions include the fact that he interviewed many of the participants—Alula and Albertone, among others—and he knew Ethiopia well.

7. For an account of this experience, see Arnoldo Nicoletti-Altimari, *Fra gli abissini: memorie di un prigioniero nel Tigre* (Rome: Voghera, 1898).

8. Paul de Lauribar credits Major Salsa with the suggestion that the captives be placed in the care of individual Ethiopian leaders. Paul de Lauribar, *Douze ans en Abyssinie* (Paris: Flammarion, 1898), 561; Giovanni Tedone, *Angerà: i ricordi di un prigioniero di Menelik* (Milan: Giordano, 1964), 34, 39.

9. Giovanni Gamerra, *Ricordi di un prigioniero di guerra allo Scioa* (Marzo 1896–gennaio 1897) (Florence: Barberà, 1897), 54; Gherardo Pantano, *Ventitré anni di vita africana* (Florence: Casa editrice militare italiana, 1932), 80–81. On the role of the *afa negus,* see Harold G. Marcus, *The Life and Times of Menelik II: Ethiopia 1844–1913* (Oxford: Clarendon Press, 1975), 219. For an overview, see Angelo Del Boca, *Adua: le ragioni di una sconfitta* (Rome: Laterza, 1997), 13.

10. Nicola d'Amato, *Da Adua ad Addis-Abeba: ricordi d'un prigioniero* (Salerno: A. Volpe, 1898), 8. See also Albert Gleichen, *With the Mission to Menelik* (London: E. Arnold, 1898), 207. On doling out, see Tedone, *Angerà,* 39.

11. Wylde witnessed the mound of bodies when he visited Adwa in the aftermath of the fight. Augustus Blandy Wylde, *Modern Abyssinia* (London: Methuen, 1901), 214. See also Guèbrè Sellassié, *Chronique du règne de Menelik II, roi des rois d'Éthiopie,* ed. Maurice de Coppet, trans. Tèsfa Sellassié (Paris: Maisonneuve, 1931), 445–446. Gherardo Pantano described such an episode in *Ventitré anni,* 75–76.

12. Carlo Diotti, *Prigioniero d'Africa: La battaglia di Adua e l'impresa coloniale del 1895–1896 nel diario di un caporale italiano* (Como: Nodolibri, 2006), 69. After their arrival in Addis, Menelik issued a decree regarding the treatment of prisoners. See Gleichen, *Mission to Menelik,* 26.

13. Diotti, *Prigioniero,* 70; Francesco Frisina, *L'Italia in Abissinia e nel Sudan: dall'acquisto di Assab, 1869, alla cessione di Cassala, 1897* (Alexandria: Molco Petrini, 1919), 199.

14. Pantano received a cowhide and a *shamma*. As an officer—and as the ward of the afa negus, his experience was probably not typical. See *Ventitré anni,* 81.

15. Tedone, *Angerà,* 74, 93. For more on Pini, see Cesare Pini, *Frammenti de'miei ricordi d'Affrica* (Rome: S. Lapi, 1912).

16. Frisina, *L'Italia in Abissinia,* 207.

17. Tedone, *Angerà,* 42. Prisoners in Mangasha's care were very near Eritrea, making escape easier to contemplate. For the story of one such escape, see Nicoletti-Altimari, *Fra gli abissini.*

18. Frisina, *L'Italia in Abissinia,* 208.

19. Ibid., 208–209.

20. "Sommario delle notizie raccolte dallo scaglione dei prigionieri condotto del capitano sig Tolas," 6 May 1897, ASME, L7 Eritrea, cartella 55, Fatti d'armi, 1896–1914.

21. Asnake Ali, "The Environmental Impact of the Campaign," in *Adwa Victory Centenary Conference,* ed. Abdussamad Ahmad and Richard Pankhurst (Addis Ababa: Institute of Ethiopian Studies, Addis Ababa University, 1998), 277–280.

22. There were rumors that the entire army might travel by the western road. They turned out to be incorrect. See Alessandro Sapelli, *Memorie d'Africa* (Bologna: Zanichelli, 1935), 106.

23. D'Amato, *Da Adua,* 28–29.

24. Tedone, *Angerà,* 39.

25. D'Amato, *Da Adua,* 29; Guido Moltedo, *L'Assedio di Maccalé: campagna d'Africa 1895–96* (Rome: Dante Alighieri, 1901), 8–9n.

26. Gherardo Pantano, gives the figure of forty dead en route; Nicola D'Amato gives sixty. See Pantano, *Ventitré anni,* 93; D'Amato, *Da Adua,* 8–9.

27. Pantano, *Ventitré anni,* 95.

28. Frisina, *L'Italia in Abissinia,* 211.

29. Diotti, *Prigioniero,* 82–85.

30. Ibid., 91.

31. D'Amato, *Da Adua,* 9.

32. Diotti, *Prigioniero,* 86. For a similar account, see D'Amato, *Da Adua,* 11.

33. Diotti, *Prigioniero,* 83.

34. James Rennell Rodd, *Social and Diplomatic Memories, 1894–1901, Egypt and Abyssinia* (London: Arnold, 1923), 128.

35. Diotti, *Prigioniero,* 71–72.

36. Tedone, *Angerà,* 71.

37. D'Amato, *Da Adua,* 39.

38. Tedone, *Angerà,* 83.

39. Diotti, *Prigioniero,* 76; Gamerra, *Ricordi di un prigioniero,* 80.

40. D'Amato, *Da Adua,* 34.

41. Ibid., 36.

42. Gleichen, *Mission to Menelik,* 68; see also pages 204–205, where Gleichen talks of "the raiding of villages in search of food as a natural privilege of the soldier's profession." Asnake Ali, "The Environmental Impact of the Campaign," in *Adwa Victory Centenary Conference,* ed. Abdussamad Ahmad and Richard Pankhurst (Addis Ababa: Institute of Ethiopian Studies, Addis Ababa University, 1998), 277.

43. The expression is from François-Apolline Guibert, *Essai général de tactique* (London: Chez les libraires associés, 772). Cited in Felix Markham, *Napoléon and the Awakening of Europe* (London: English Universities Press, 1954).

44. Wylde, *Modern Abyssinia,* 53.

45. D'Amato, *Da Adua,* 8, 58.

46. Wylde, *Modern Abyssinia,* 350.

47. Pantano, *Ventitre anni,* 89.

48. Augustus B. Wylde, "An Unofficial Mission to Abyssinia," *Manchester Guardian,* 24 May 1897.

49. Diotti, *Prigioniero,* 102–103.

50. Ibid., 77–78.

51. Sellassié, *Chronique,* plate XIX.

52. Gleichen, *Mission to Menelik,* 41.

53. D'Amato, *Da Adua,* 58; Diotti, *Prigioniero,* 83.

54. D'Amato, *Da Adua,* 35.

55. Ibid., 68. On Bejirond Baltcha, see Albert Hans, "L'armée de Ménélik," *Revue des Deux Mondes* 135 (1896), 882; Pietro Felter, *La vicenda affricana 1895–1896* (Brescia: Vannini, 1935), 47; Sellassié, *Chronique,* 47; Albert Hans, "L'armée de Ménélik," *Revue des Deux Mondes,* 1896: 882; Yaltasamma, *Les amis de Ménélik II, roi des rois d'Ethiopia* (Paris: A. Challamel, 1899), 33; J. G. Vanderheym, *Une expédition avec le négous Ménélik: vingt mois en Abyssinie* (Paris: Hachette, 1896), 112; S. P. Pétridès, *Le héros d'Adoua: Ras Makonnen, prince d'Éthiopie* (Paris: Plon, 1963), 149–150.

56. D'Amato, *Da Adua,* 8.

17. SONS AND LOVERS AND ACCIDENTAL ANTHROPOLOGISTS

1. James Rennell Rodd, *Social and Diplomatic Memories, 1894–1901, Egypt and Abyssinia* (London: Arnold, 1923), 1:148–149; Harold Marcus, "The Rodd Mission of 1897," *Journal of Ethiopian Studies* 3 (1965): 25–36.

2. Francesco Frisina, *L'Italia in Abissinia e nel Sudan: dall'acquisto di Assab, 1869, alla cessione di Cassala, 1897* (Alexandria: Molco Petrini, 1919), 243.

3. Ibid.

4. Edward Gleichen, *With the Mission to Menelik, 1897* (London: E. Arnold, 1898), 156.

5. Elisabeth Biasio, *Prunk und Pracht am Hofe Menileks: Alfred Ilgs Äthiopien um 1900* (Zurich: Neue Züricher Zeitung, 2004), 70.

6. Carlo Diotti, *Prigioniero d'Africa: la battaglia di Adua e l'impresa coloniale del 1895–96 nel diario di un caporale italiano* (Como: Nodolibri, 2006), 87.

7. Biasio, *Prunk und Pracht,* 72, 76; Gleichen, *Mission to Menelik,* 156–157; Richard Pankhurst and Denis Gerard, *Ethiopia Photographed: Historic Photographs of the Country and Its People Taken between 1867 and 1935* (London: Kegan Paul International, 1996), 63; Frisina, *L'Italia in Abissinia,* 243; *Manchester Guardian,* 28 May 1897.

8. Peter Garretson, *A History of Addis Abäba from Its Foundation in 1886 to 1910* (Wiesbaden: Harrassowitz, 2000), xix.

9. Harold G. Marcus, *A History of Ethiopia* (Berkeley: University of California Press, 1994), 93; John Gooch, *Army, State, and Society in Italy, 1870–1915* (New York: St. Martin's Press, 1989), 78–79; Garretson, *History of Addis,* 11; Bahru Zewde, "The Historical Context of the Dogali Encounter," in *The Centenary of Dogali,* ed. Taddesse Beyene, Taddesse Tamrat, and Richard Pankhurst (Addis Ababa: Institute of Ethiopian Studies, Addis Ababa University, 1987), 103–111.

10. On Addis as a military camp, see Henri Philippe Marie Orléans, *Une visite à l'empereur Ménélick: notes et impressions de route* (Paris: Dentu, 1898), 141.

11. Robert Peet Skinner, *Abyssinia of Today: An Account of the First Mission Sent by the American Government to the Court of the King of Kings, 1903–1904* (London: Edward Arnold, 1906), 87.

12. The estimate is from Augustus B. Wylde in *Manchester Guardian,* 27 May 1897, 12. See also Frisina, *Italia in Abissinia,* 258.

13. Francesco Frisina reported eight prisoners captured in flight and returned to the capital. *Italia in Abissinia,* 313.

14. Ibid., 248–249.

15. Ibid., 330. Gherardo Pantano reported that female companions were "given" to prisoners held outside of Addis—"una schiava per ciascuno" is how he put it. Although Pantano is the only source to mention this, he took careful notes during his service and imprisonment and appears to have been an especially acute observer. See Gherardo Pantano, *Ventitré anni di vita africana* (Firenze: Casa editrice militare italiana, 1932), 154. See also Frisina, *Italia in Abissinia,* 280, 285.

16. Nicola D'Amato, *Da Adua ad Addis-Abeba ricordi d'un prigioniero* (Salerno: A. Volpe, 1898), 5.

17. Diotti, *Prigioniero,* 98.

18. D'Amato, *Da Adua,* 19–21, 23.

19. Ibid., 22.

20. Frisina, *Italia in Abissinia,* 308.

21. Pantano, *Ventitré anni,* 164.

22. For currency conversion, see M. L. Louis-Lande, "Un Voyageur française dans l'Ethiopie méridionale: une colonie française dans le Choa," *Revue des Deux Mondes* 30 (1878): 377; Jules Borelli, *Ethiopie méridionale: journal de mon voyage aux pays Amhara, Oromo et Sidama, septembre 1885 à novembre 1888* (Paris: Ancienne Maison Quantin, 1890), 3n; on the restaurant, see Frisina, *L'Italia in Abissinia,* 328.

23. Casimir Mondon-Vidailhet, "Aux environs de Harar," *Le Temps,* 18 April 1892.

24. Pantano, *Ventitré anni,* 164.

25. Frisina, *Italia in Abissinia,* 255; Diotti, *Prigioniero,* 87, 89.

26. Biasio, *Prunk und Pracht,* 73.

27. D'Amato, *Da Adua,* 3.

28. Augustus Blandy Wylde, *Modern Abyssinia* (London: Methuen, 1901), 402.

29. A. B. Wylde describes finding artifacts taken from General Dabormida in Augustus Blandy Wylde, "An Unofficial Visit to Abyssinia by Our Special Correspondent," *Manchester Guardian,* 20 May 1897; for Airaghi, see Archivio dello Stato Maggiore dell'Esercito, Ufficio Storico (hereafter cited as ASME), L7 Eritrea, cartella 55, Fatti d'armi, 1896–1914; for the cape, see Giovanni Tedone, *Angerà: i ricordi di un prigioniero di Menelik* (Milano: Giordano, 1964), 180; see also "Sommario delle notizie raccolte dallo scaglione dei prigionieri condotto del capitano sig Tolas," 6 May 1897 in ASME, L7 Eritrea, cartella 55, Fatti d'armi, 1896–1914; D'Amato, *Da Adua.*

30. Henri Rebeaud, *Chez le roi des rois d'Ethiopie* (Neuchatel: V. Attincer, 1934), 86–88; Orléans, *Une visite à l'empereur Ménélick,* 132; Frisina, *L'Italia in Abissinia,* 246–247.

31. D'Amato, *Da Adua,* 184; D'Amato reproduced portions of the journal in his own memoir.

32. Ibid., 101; Frisina, *L'Italia in Abissinia,* 252.

33. See letter from Baldissera dated 18 April 1896 in Archivo storico del Ministero Africa Italiana (ASMAI), Eritrea, Questioni Politico Militare, pos. 3/16, fasc. 130.

34. Diotti, *Prigioniero,* 93.

35. Ibid., 90–91.

36. Garretson, *History of Addis,* 103.

37. Frisina, *Italia in Abissinia,* 305; Diotti, *Prigioniero,* 91.

38. Diotti, *Prigioniero,* 93, 95, 100, 106.

39. Wylde, *Modern Abyssinia,* 386.

40. Pantano, *Ventitré anni,* 3.

41. Ibid., 68.

42. Ibid., 80.

43. Richard Pankhurst, *Economic History of Ethiopia, 1800–1935* (Addis Ababa: Haile Selassie I University Press, 1968), 73; Alain Rouaud, *Le négus contre l'esclavage: les édits abolitionnistes du ras Täfäri: contexte et circonstances* (Paris: Aresae, 1998), 8; Chris Prouty, *Empress Taytu and Menelik II: Ethiopia, 1883–1910* (London: Ravens, 1986), 227; Skinner, *Abyssinia of Today,* 151.

44. Pantano, *Ventitré anni,* 140.

45. The fact that two leading figures in Ethiopian society wore European-style felt hats helps to explain their extraordinary popularity in Ethiopia. See Gleichen, *Mission to Menelik,* 54–55.

46. Guèbrè Sellassié, *Chronique du règne de Menelik II, roi des rois d'Éthiopie,* ed. Maurice de Coppet, trans. Tèsfa Sellassié (Paris: Maisonneuve, 1930), plate 28.

47. Paul de Lauribar, *Douze ans en Abyssinie* (Paris: Flammarion, 1898), 681; S. Pierre Pétridès, *Le heros d'Adoua: Ras Makonnen, prince d'Etiopie* (Paris: Plon, 1963), 149–150.

48. Pantano, *Ventitré anni,* 102.

49. Ibid., 143. For Finfinne, see Marcus, *A History of Ethiopia,* 64; Edoardo Scarfoglio, *Abissinia 1888–1896: Studi di "Tartarin" durante la prima campagna d'Africa* (Livorno: Edizioni Roma, 1936), 106–107. On crime and punishment, see also Frisina, *L'Italia in Abissinia,* 250–251.

50. Pantano, *Ventitré anni,* 146.

51. D'Amato, *Da Adua,* 14–15.

18. MENELIK ABROAD

1. F. Holland Day, Verna Posever Curtis, and Jane Van Nimmen, *Fred Holland Day: Selected Texts and Bibliography* (New York: G. K. Hall, 1995), xxi. For insight on Day's mentoring and models, see Verna Posever Curtis, "F. Holland Day and the Staging of Orpheus," *New Perspectives on F. Holland Day* (North Easton, MA: Stonehill College Press, 1998), 51–60.

2. Pam Roberts, *F. Holland Day* (Zwolle: Waanders, 2000), 17.

3. George Fredrickson, following Rayford Logan, has called the years between the end of Reconstruction and World War I the nadir of the African American experience. See George Fredrickson, *Racism: A Short History* (Princeton: Princeton University Press, 2002), 81.

4. "Italy's Hard Luck," *Atlanta Constitution,* 4 March 1896.

5. On misperceptions of Africa in late nineteenth-century America, see Christopher Robert Reed, *"All the World Is Here!": The Black Presence at White City* (Bloomington: Indiana University Press, 2000), esp. 144, where Dahomey represents all of sub-Saharan Africa. On the problems of bias and advocacy in American journalism, see Matthew Gentzkow, Edward L. Glaeser, and Claudia Goldin, "The Rise of the Fourth Estate: How Newspapers Became Informative and Why It Mattered," in *Corruption and Reform: Lessons from America's Economic History,* ed. Edward L. Glaeser and Claudia Goldin (Chicago: University of Chicago Press, 2006): 187–230.

6. "Italians Fell," *Atlanta Constitution,* 4 March 1896.

7. "The Abyssinian Question," *Atlanta Constitution,* 8 March 1896. Jules Borelli had argued that Menelik's people were "of semitic family" who had crossed the Red Sea. Their "racial" heritage had been broken down through mixing with slaves and native Africans. See Jules Borelli, *Ethiopie méridionale: journal de mon voyage aux pays Amhara, Oromo et Sidama, septembre 1885 à novembre 1888* (Paris: Ancien Maison Quantun, 1890), 210–211. An Italian summary of Ethiopian ideas about color, race, and ethnicity can be found in Alberto Pollera, *La donna in Etiopia* (Rome: Grafia, 1922), 74. For a perspective on these issues in the ancient world, see Frank M. Snowden Jr., *Blacks in Antiquity: Ethiopians in the Greco-Roman Experience* (Cambridge, MA: Belknap Press, 1970) and his "Bernal's 'Blacks' and the Afrocentrists," in *Black Athena Revisited,* ed. Mary R. Lefkowitz and Guy MacLean Rogers (Chapel Hill: University of North Carolina Press, 1996), 112–128.

8. Photo caption from *Atlanta Constitution:* "King Menelik; He is the Monarch and Commander in Chief of Abyssinia's Forces."

9. See "Notes on Abyssinia," *Chicago Tribune,* 9 March 1896. The story is reprinted from the *New York World.*

10. "Our Own Correspondent, Berlin, March 3," *Times* (London), 4 March 1896. See also Robert L. Hess, "Germany and the Anglo-Italian Colonial Entente," in *Britain and Germany in Africa: Imperial Rivalry and Colonial Rule,* ed. Prosser Gifford and Wm. Roger Louis (New Haven: Yale University Press, 1967), 153–178; Mack Smith, *Modern Italy: A Political History* (Ann Arbor: University of Michigan Press, 1997), 114–115; Aldo Valori's preface in Alberto Pollera, *La battaglia di Adua del 1 marzo 1896, narrata nei luoghi ove fu combattuta* (Florence: Carpigiani e Zipoli, 1928), iv.

11. "London and Italian Ire," *New York Times,* 8 March 1896; "Changes at Columbia: Greek Not to Be Required under the New Curriculum," *New York Times,* 3 March 1896.

12. Private collection.

13. Henri Philippe Marie Orléans, *Une visite à l'empereur Ménélick: notes et impressions de route* (Paris: Librairie Dentu, 1898), 166.

14. "Il Negus Menelik," *Osservatore Romano,* 12 January 1897.

15. Robert Peet Skinner, *Abyssinia of Today: An Account of the First Mission Sent by the American Government to the Court of the King of Kings, 1903–1904* (London: Edward Arnold, 1906), 89; Gherardo Pantano, *Ventitré anni di vita africana* (Florence: Casa editrice militare italiana, 1932), 122. A second Russian mission, including twenty-two

Cossacks, followed in 1898. See Leonid Artamonov, L. K. Artamonov Papers, n.d., Library of Congress Manuscript Division.

16. Elisabeth Biasio, *Prunk und Pracht am Hofe Menileks: Alfred Ilgs Äthiopien um 1900* (Zurich: Neue Zürcher Zeitung, Völkerkundemuseum der Universität, 2004), 14–15.

17. Harold G. Marcus, *The Life and Times of Menelik II: Ethiopia 1844–1913* (Oxford: Clarendon Press, 1975), 179–180; Angelo Del Boca, *Adua: le ragioni di una sconfitta* (Rome: Laterza, 1997), 179.

18. David Levering Lewis, *The Race to Fashoda: European Colonialism and African Resistance in the Scramble for Africa* (New York: Weidenfeld and Nicolson, 1987), 121; Orléans, *Une visite*, 3, 5–6.

19. Augustus Blandy Wylde, *Modern Abyssinia* (London: Methuen, 1901), 61.

20. James Rennell Rodd, *Social and Diplomatic Memories, 1894–1901, Egypt and Abyssinia* (London: Arnold, 1923), 1:164; on Rennell Rodd, see also Lewis, *Race to Fashoda*, 7–8; Marcus, *Life and Times of Menelik II*, 181–183.

21. Chris Prouty, *Empress Taytu and Menelik II: Ethiopia, 1883–1910* (London: Ravens, 1986), 195.

22. Marcus, *Life and Times of Menelik II*, 182.

23. Ibid., 181–182; "Missione inglese nello Scioa, anno 1897," n.d., Archivio dello Stato Maggiore dell'Esercito, Ufficio Storico (ASME), L7 Eritrea, cartella 75, n. 25.

24. The estimate is from "Commerce of Abyssinia: Is It of Proportions Worthy of Encouragement? Facts Relative and Associated," ca. 1904, Papers of Emil Gribeschock. 1904–11, New York Public Library.

25. Robert Peet Skinner, "Untitled manuscript, 415 pages, relating the diplomatic career of Robert P. Skinner," n.d., 45–46, Massillon [Ohio] Museum.

26. Ibid., 46–47.

27. Ibid., 54.

28. "The Visit to King Menelik," *New York Sun,* 2 April 1904.

29. *Kansas State Journal,* 18 December 1903.

30. *Philadelphia Public Ledger,* 18 October 1903.

31. *Boston Transcript,* 17 December 1903.

32. "The Visit to King Menelik," *New York Sun,* 2 April 1904; Records of the National Zoological Park, Smithsonian Institution Archives.

33. For newspaper accounts of Skinner's voyage see the Papers of Robert P. Skinner at the Massillon Public Library.

34. For the Japanese of Africa see "Back from Abyssinia; Consul Skinner Tells of His Visit with Menelik," *New Jersey Record,* 1 February 1904.

35. Gribeschock, "Commerce of Abyssinia."

36. Emil Gribeschock, "The First American Trading Expedition to Ethiopia," Papers of Emil Gribeschock, 1904–11, New York Public Library.

37. See the letter from Townsend Scudder of the Free and Accepted Masons of the State of New York, Papers of Emil Gribeschock, 1904–11, New York Public Library.

38. Pantano, *Ventitré anni,* 120.

39. Edward Gleichen, *With the Mission to Menelik, 1897* (London: E. Arnold, 1898), 248.

40. Jean Gaston Vanderheym, *Une expédition avec le négous Ménélik: vingt mois en Abyssinie* (Paris: Hachette, 1896), 51–52.

41. Francesco Frisina, *L'Italia in Abissinia e nel Sudan: dall'acquisto di Assab, 1869, alla cessione di Cassala, 1897* (Alexandria: Molco Petrini, 1919), 252.

42. Vanderheym, *Une expédition*, 54.

43. See letter, Capucci to Ministry of Foreign Affairs, 13 February 1895, in Carlo Zaghi, ed., "L'Italia e l'Etiopia alla vigilia di Adua nei dispacci segreti di Luigi Capucci," *Gli annali dell'Africa italiana* 4, no. 2 (1941): 539. Garretson claims that some Italian prisoners were assigned to Stévenin as laborers; see Peter Garretson, *A History of Addis Abäba from Its Foundation in 1886 to 1910* (Wiesbaden: Harrassowitz, 2000), 103.

44. Gleichen, *Mission to Menelik*, 245–247, 314.

45. Hosea Jaffe, "The African Dimension of the Battle," in *Adwa Victory Centenary Conference,* ed. Abdussamad Ahmad and Richard Pankhurst (Addis Ababa: Institute of Ethiopian Studies, Addis Ababa University, 1998), 407.

46. Paula Giddings, *Ida: A Sword Among Lions: Ida B. Wells and the Campaign against Lynching* (New York: Amistad, 2008), 370.

47. See Ida B. Wells-Barnett, *Selected Works of Ida B. Wells-Barnett,* ed. Trudier Harris (New York: Oxford University Press, 1991). The announcement that Wells-Barnett had a baby boy is in *Freeman, an Illustrated Colored Newspaper,* 11 April 1896.

48. "White Blood in Africa!" *Freeman, an Illustrated Colored Newspaper,* 21 March 1896.

49. Booker T. Washington, *The Future of the American Negro* (Boston: Small, Maynard, 1899); see also Norrell, *Up from History.*

50. William A. Shack, "Ethiopia and Afro-Americans: Some Historical Notes, 1920–1970," *Phylon* 35 (1974): 142.

51. W. E. B. Du Bois had plenty to say about Ethiopia. By his time, however, the circumstances were different. His commentary was not about Adwa itself but a brilliant defense of African independence against the background to the Ethiopian crisis of the 1930s and the threat of Italian invasion under Fascist leadership. See William E. B. Du Bois, "Inter-Racial Implications of the Ethiopian Crisis," *Foreign Affairs* 14 (1935): 82–92.

52. William Scott, *The Sons of Sheba's Race: African-Americans and the Italo-Ethiopian War, 1935–1941* (Bloomington: Indiana University Press, 1993), 11.

53. Sylvia Jacobs, *The African Nexus: Black American Perspectives on the European Partitioning of Africa, 1880–1920* (Westport, CT: Greenwood, 1981), 192–193.

54. Josephus Coan, *The Expansion of Missions of the African Methodist Episcopal Church in South Africa, 1896–1908* (Hartford, CT: Hartford Seminary Foundation, 1961), 94, 132.

55. Ibid., 107.

56. Antoine Bervin, *Benito Sylvain, apôtre du relévement social des noirs* (Port-au-Prince: La Phalange, 1969), 9.

57. Ibid., 14.

58. Giulia Bonacci, *Exodus! L'histoire du retour des rastafariens en Éthiopie* (Paris: Scali, 2008), 135.

59. Skinner, *Abyssinia of Today,* 130–131.
60. Today, highland Ethiopians do not see themselves as black; when asked, they will say their skin is red. I am grateful to an anonymous reader for pointing this out. The key question for the historian is whether such a view would have been current in Menelik's time.
61. Menelik's remark was recorded by Luigi Capucci. See Zaghi, ed., "L'Italia e l'Etiopia," 553.
62. Bervin, *Benito Sylvain,* 68–69, 144–146.
63. Prouty, *Empress Taytu and Menelik,* 283–284, 292–293; see also Vitalien's commentary in Joseph Vitalien, *Pour l'indépendance de l'Ethiopie* (Paris: Éditions de l'Effort, 1919).
64. Robert A. Hill, ed., *The Marcus Garvey and Universal Negro Improvement Association Papers: Africa for the Africans, 1923–1945* (Berkeley: University of California Press, 2006), 80n.
65. Bonacci, *Exodus!*
66. Dennis Hickey, *An Enchanting Darkness: The American Vision of Africa in the Twentieth Century* (East Lansing: Michigan State University Press, 1993), esp. 253.
67. William E. B. Du Bois, "The Pan-African Movement," in *History of the Pan-African Congress: Colonial and Coloured Unity, a Programme of Action,* ed. George Padmore (London: Hammersmith Bookshop, 1963), 13.

19. RECKONINGS

1. Istituto Italiano per l'Africa e l'Oriente (IsIAO) Sezione 2 (Ex Schedaria), Eritrea 22/A—Storico, Prima Guerra d'Africa, 53, "L'arrivo del Generale Baratieri ad Asmara per essere giudicato dal Tribunale."
2. Eduardo Ximenes, *Sul Campo di Adua, marzo-giugno 1896* (Milan: Fratelli Treves, 1897), 162.
3. Clément de La Jonquière, *Les Italiens en Erythrée: quinze ans de politique coloniale* (Paris: H. Charles-Lavauzelle, 1916).
4. Telegram, Baratieri to Minister of War, Massaua, 3 March 1896, in *Documenti Diplomatici,* XXIII—bis, *Avvenimenti d'Africa, Atti Parlamentari* (Rome: Tipografia della camera dei deputati, 1896), 151; on the drafting of the telegram, see Gian Carlo Stella, "La Battaglia nelle prime notizie, dispacci, telegrammi, relazioni, inchieste e negli scritti editi dai militari italiani superstiti," in *Adwa Victory Centenary Conference,* ed. Abdussamad Ahmad and Richard Pankhurst (Addis Ababa: Institute of Ethiopian Studies, Addis Ababa University, 1998), 659–660.
5. Ximenes, *Sul Campo di Adua,* 99.
6. Ibid., 162.
7. Ibid., 179.
8. Francesco Frisina, *L'Italia in Abissinia e nel Sudan: dall'acquisto di Assab, 1869, alla cessione di Cassala, 1897* (Alexandria: Molco Petrini, 1919), 183.
9. Ximenes, *Sul Campo di Adua,* 212, 215–216.

10. *Manchester Guardian,* 17 May 1897, 7; Frisina, *Italia in Abissinia,* 182.

11. Augustus Wylde, *Modern Abyssinia* (London: Methuen, 1901), 147–148.

12. Ibid., 172, 213.

13. Ibid., 173.

14. Giuseppe Lembo, *Il Processo Baratieri* (Bari: Casini e Figlio, 1937), 33.

15. Baratieri was editor of *La Rivista militare,* which he used, along with his post on the governing council of the Italian Geographical Society, to promote colonial expansion. Maria Carazzi, *La Società geografica italiana e l'esplorazione coloniale in Africa (1867–1900)* (Florence: La nuova Italia, 1972), 51; "Italy's Fallen Hero," *Boston Globe,* 6 March 1896.

16. See "Carteggio Baratieri-Mariotti," in Archivio storico del Ministero Africa Italiana (hereafter cited as ASMAI), pos. 3/10, fasc. 75.

17. Domenico Farini, *Diario di fine secolo* (Rome: Bardi, 1962), 904. Later in 1896, Ernesto Mezzabotta would rush into print a book comparing the Ramorino and Baratieri trials under the title *Il Processo dei Generali: resoconto del processo contro Oreste Baratieri* (Rome: Edoardo Perino, 1896).

18. Letter from Baratieri to Mariotti, Massawa, 27 May 1896, in ASMAI, Eritrea, Questioni Politico Militare, pos. 3/10, fasc. 75. Many political insiders expected that he would be absolved. "Sarà assolto," commented Domenico Farini on 4 June, halfway through the trial; see *Diario,* 951.

19. Ridolfo Mazzucconi, *La Giornata di Adua (1896)* (Milan: Mondadori, 1935), 335.

20. Wylde, *Modern Abyssinia,* 102.

21. *L'Africa italiana,* 7 June 1896.

22. "Breve aggiunta alle parole premesse dall'editore all'autodifesa del generale Baratieri," *L'Alto Adige,* 24–25 July 1896, in ASMAI, Eritrea, Questioni Politico Militare, pos. 3/10, fasc. 75. See also Domenico Quirico, *Adua: La battaglia che cambiò la storia d'Italia* (Milan: Mondadori, 2004), 341.

23. *L'Africa italiana,* 7 June 1896; Mazzucconi, *Giornata,* 335–336.

24. *L'Illustrazione italiana,* 28 January 1896; Mario Lamberti, *Rapport sur la bataille d'Adoua, 1er mars 1896* (Paris: H. Charles-Lavauzell, 1896).

25. Ibid.

26. "Udienza del giorno 6 giugno 1896," *L'Africa italiana,* 14 June 1896. Francesco Frisina claims that the rumor circulated openly at Sauria; *Italia in Abissinia,* 195. Of course, the knowledge of his dismissal does not necessarily explain his actions and motives.

27. "L'inchiesta Tecnico-Militare del colonello Corticelli," *L'Africa italiana,* 14 June 1896.

28. Giovanni Pittaluga, *Atti processuali del Tribunale dell'Asmara,* reprinted in Baratieri, *Memorie d'Africa* (Genoa: Dioscuri, 1898), 473–479.

29. "Deposizione Valenzano," *L'Africa italiana,* 14 June 1896.

30. "Le ultime deposizioni," *L'Africa italiana,* 21 June 1896.

31. "Deposizione Valenzano."

32. Ibid.

33. Ibid.

34. Letter dated 10 February 1896 in Francesco Lemmi, ed., *Lettere e diari d'Africa, 1895–1896* (Rome: Edizioni Roma, 1936), 90.
35. "Udienza del giorno 11 giugno 1896," *L'Africa italiana,* 21 June 1896.
36. Ibid.
37. Francesco Frisina notes that rumors of Baratieri's dismissal were rampant in camp. Frisina, *L'Italia in Abissinia,* 195.
38. "Udienza del giorno 12 giugno 1896—La Difesa," *L'Africa italiana,* 21 June 1896.
39. Ibid.; Frisina, *L'Italia in Abissinia,* 195.
40. For the text, see telegram, Rome, 25 February 1896, in ASMAI, pos. 3/10, fasc. 69; also *Documenti Diplomatici,* 353.
41. Francesco Crispi, *Francesco Crispi: La prima guerra d'Africa; documenti e memorie dell'Archivio Crispi* (Milan: Fratelli Treves, 1914), viii; Quirico, *Adua,* 211; Baratieri, *Memorie,* 354. See also Mazzucconi, *Giornata,* 157 and Ernesto Ragionieri, *Storia d'Italia* (Turin: Einaudi, 1976), 1821–1829.
42. "Udienza del giorno 12 giugno 1896—La Difesa," *L'Africa italiana,* 21 June 1896. See also Mazzucconi, *Giornata,* 157.
43. "Udienza del giorno 12 giugno 1896—La Difesa," *L'Africa italiana,* 21 June 1896.
44. Lembo, *Il Processo Baratieri,* 74.
45. "La Sentenza," *L'Africa italiana,* 21 June 1896.
46. Farini, *Diario,* 961.
47. Ibid., 903.
48. Ibid., 1016–1017.
49. Quirico, *Adua,* 341.
50. In a private letter, Baratieri discussed the extreme caution with which he would address Mocenni's handling of the telegram. ASMAI, pos 3.10, fasc. 75, letter from Baratieri to Mariotti, 27 May 1896. He followed through on this promise. See "Udienza del giorno 5 giugno 1896," *L'Africa italiana,* 7 June 1896.
51. Farini, *Diario,* 961.
52. Alessandro Sapelli, *Memorie d'Africa* (Bologna: Zanichelli, 1935), 124.

20. RESCUES

1. "L'orrendo e colossale carneficina delle truppe italiane in Africa!" *L'Italia—Giornale del Popolo,* 7 March 1896; Humbert Nelli, *Italians in Chicago, 1880–1930: A Study in Ethnic Mobility* (New York: Oxford University Press, 1970), 24–25.
2. "Vittorie sopra vittorie," *L'Italia,* 18–19 January 1896.
3. "Italians in Chicago Are Aroused," *Chicago Tribune,* 7 March 1896.
4. Francesco Frisina, *L'Italia in Abissinia e nel Sudan: dall'acquisto di Assab, 1869, alla cessione di Cassala,* 1897 (Alexandria: Molco Petrini, 1919), 185; Mark Choate, *Emigrant Nation: The Making of Italy Abroad* (Cambridge, MA: Harvard University Press, 2008), 38.
5. "Youth of Italy Fleeing," *Chicago Tribune,* 8 March 1896.

6. On race and the precarious status of Irish immigrants to America, see Noel Ignatiev, *How the Irish Became White* (New York: Routledge, 1995), esp. 112.

7. See "Only One Flag and One Country," *Chicago Tribune*, 7 March 1896. The piece is about a decision not to allow Confederate Army veterans to parade in uniform behind the Confederate flag; however, it appears in the same column as the story regarding the Italian American volunteers, immediately following it. The article's title, "Only One Flag and One Country," serves as oblique commentary on the preceding piece.

8. Crispi had himself harbored such doubts, but he overcame them to become one of Italian imperialism's most ardent supporters. In a speech before the Italian legislature on 7 May 1885, Crispi characterized Assab as "an ugly legacy" of earlier governments. He expressed the wish that Italy had never ventured into the Red Sea. He acknowledged grudgingly, however, that Italy was already "engaged" at Assab and Massawa and should seek "to extract a profit from a mistake." See Francesco Crispi, *Francesco Crispi: La prima guerra d'Africa: documenti e memorie dell'Archivio Crispi*, ed. Tomasso Palamenghi-Crispi (Milan: Fratelli Treves, 1914), 2.

9. Although Amba Alage and Mekele did inspire demonstrations wherein it was difficult to disentangle patriotism from a desire for revenge. See Choate, *Emigrant Nation*, 36–37.

10. Diary entry for 29 August 1894 in Francesco Lemmi, ed., *Lettere e diari d'Africa, 1895–1896* (Rome: Edizioni Roma, 1896), 137.

11. Vica Mantegazza, *Gli Italiani in Africa: L'assedio di Macalle* (Florence: Successori Le Monnier, 1896), 47.

12. On 17 March, after Di Rudinì presented his new government to the Chamber.

13. *La Tribuna,* 3 March 1896.

14. See "Le Dimostrazioni a Roma," *Il Mattino*, 8 March 1896, in Edoardo Scarfoglio, *Viaggio in Abissinia: nascita del colonialismo italiano* (Palermo: L'Epos, 2003), 213–214; Ernesto Ragionieri, *Storia d'Italia,* vol. 3: *Dall'Unità a oggi* (Turin: Einaudi, 1976), 1821–1829; Silvana Palma, *L'Italia coloniale* (Rome: Editori Riuniti, 1999), 14; Emilio Bellavita, *Adua: i precedenti—la battaglia—le conseguenze 1881–1931* (Genoa: Rivista di Roma, 1931), 394.

15. See *Il Senza Pretese,* 13 May 1896, in Archivio Segreto Vaticano (ASV), Segretaria di Stato, 1900.R165.f5.

16. Archivio storico del Ministero Africa Italiana (hereafter cited as ASMAI), Eritrea, Questioni Politico Militare, pos. 3/13, contains several dossiers on the response from the diaspora. For Latin America, see fasc. 95; for Australia, see fasc. 102; for Lisbon, Malta, and Hamburg, see fasc. 138; for New York and New Jersey, see fasc. 96. For the diaspora more broadly, see Choate, *Emigrant Nation*.

17. Gherardo Pantano, *Ventitré anni di vita africana* (Florence: Casa editrice militare italiana, 1932), 163–164. For examples of highly speculative journalistic profiles, see *La Tribuna illustrata,* 19 July 1896.

18. Pantano, *Ventitré anni,* 130.

19. Some grieved, only to find their loved ones had survived. Frisina, *L'Italia in Abissinia,* 141.

20. For letters and stamps, see "Consolato di S. M. Il Re d'Italia in Aden," 11 June 1896, in ASMAI, Eritrea, Questioni Politico Militare, pos. 3/13, fasc. 103. See also Henri Tristant, *Histoire postale de l'Éthiopie sous le régne de l'empereur Ménélik II* (Paris: H. Tristant, 1977), 67–68; Alain Rouaud, *Casimir Mondon-Vidailhet: pionnier de l'amitié franco-éthiopienne (1847–1910)* (Addis Ababa: Maison des études éthiopiennes, 1997), 29.

21. Letter, Monsignor G. Ricciardi, vescovo di Nardò a S. Eminenza Sig. Cardinal Rampolla, in ASV, Segretaria di Stato, 1900.R165.f5. For remarks of Carlo Mola, see undated letter sent from Pisa to Rampolla. Printed instructions were circulated, apparently to all dioceses, with strict instructions: "Cavendum omnino, ne haec omnia in politicos sensus detorqueantur."

22. See memo dated 7 June 1896, ASV, Segretaria di Stato, 1900.R165.f6.

23. "La bandiera dittatoriale," *Osservatore Romano,* 6 March 1896; "Il Negus Menelik," *Osservatore Romano,* 12 January 1897; see also "Unione Antimassonica, Consiglio Direttivo Generale, Roma," printed brochure in ASV, Segretario di Stato, 1900.R165.f6.

24. Farini, *Diario,* 947.

25. "Viva Leone XIII padre della Patria!" The paper was the *Unione* of Bologna. Farini, *Diario,* 951.

26. *Osservatore Romano,* 23 September 1896.

27. Giovanni Tedone, *Angerà: i ricordi di un prigioniero di Menelik* (Milan: Giordano, 1964), 93.

28. Farini, *Diario,* 948.

29. The documents, along with the key to the lockbox in which Franzoj delivered them, may be found in the archives of the Ministry of Foreign Affairs. ASMAI, Eritrea, pos. 3/15, fasc. 126.

30. Pantano, *Ventitré anni,* 133.

31. Carlo Zaghi, *I russi in Etiopia* (Napoli: Guida, 1972), 1:237, 245.

32. Ibid., 1:245–246.

33. Ibid., 1:251.

34. Ibid., 1:269; Prouty, *Empress Taytu,* 124.

35. *Journal de Saint Petersbourg,* 13 July 1895; Prouty, *Empress Taytu,* 125.

36. *Journal de Saint Petersbourg,* 16 July 1895.

37. Ibid., 21 and 24 July 1895.

38. Zaghi, *I russi in Etiopia,* 2:158–159.

39. Ibid., 2:166.

40. Edward Gleichen, *With the Mission to Menelik, 1897* (London: E. Arnold, 1898), 161–162.

41. Albert Hans, "L'armée de Ménélik," *Revue des Deux Mondes* 135 (1896), 889n.

42. "I Russi sono positivamente venuti dietro invito del Governo francese." Luigi Capucci report to Pietro Felter, 4 April 1895, in Carlo Zaghi, "L'Italia e l'Etiopia alla vigilia di Adua nei dispacci segreti di Luigi Capucci: contributo alla biografia di un grande pioniere," *Gli annali dell'Africa italiana* 4 (1941): 545.

43. Note from Capucci to Ministry of Foreign Affairs, 23 April 1895, in Zaghi, "L'Italia e l'Etiopia," 548.

44. ASMAI, Eritrea, pos. 3.7, fasc. 49, Luigi Capucci, "Relazione sommaria."

45. ASMAI, Eritrea, Questioni Politico Militare, pos. 3/16, fasc. 129.

46. Sidney Sonnino, *Diario* (Bari: Laterza, 1972), 200; see also Jacques Léotard, "Chronique géographique," *Bulletin de la société de géographie de Marseille* 20 (1896): 62–99.

47. Maffei to Ministry of Foreign Affairs, 14 February 1896, in Crispi, *Francesco Crispi*, 370.

48. On the release of the prisoners in honor of the czar, see letter, Lamberti to minister of war, Massawa, 31 July 1896, in Archivio dello Stato Maggiore dell'Esercito, Ufficio Storico (hereafter cited as ASME), L7 Eritrea, cartella 36; also Carlo Rossetti, *Storia diplomatica dell'Etiopia durante il regno di Menelik II* (Torino: STEN, 1910), 191.

49. ASMAI, Eritrea, pos. 3/11, f. 79, "le trattative de pace di Leontieff"; Prouty, *Empress Taytu*, 184–186.

50. ASV, Segretario di Stato 1900.R165.f6, unsigned, undated memo.

51. Pantano, *Ventitre anni*, 134; Carlo Diotti, *Prigioniero d'Africa: la battaglia di Adua e l'impresa coloniale del 1895-96 nel diario di un caporale italiano* (Como: Nodolibri, 2006), 13.

52. Prouty, *Empress Taytu and Menelik II*, 184; "Monsignor Macario presente al Papa la lettera di Menelik," *La Tribuna*, 22 November 1896.

53. Giuseppe Canuti, *L'Italia in Africa e le guerre con l'abissinia: dall'occupazione di Massaua alla resa dei prigionieri dopo la battaglia d'Adua* (Florence: Adriano Salani, 1911), 244–245.

54. Pantano, *Ventitré anni*, 134–135; Frisina, *L'Italia in Abissinia*, 328.

55. Frisina, *L'Italia in Abissinia*, 330.

56. On the marchesas, see ASV, Segretaria di Stato, 1900.R165.f5. See also Diotti, *Prigionieri*, 13; Pantano, *Ventitré anni*, 175; Canuti, *L'Italia in Africa*, 242; "La Morte del sacerdote Conte Wersowitz-Rey," *La Tribuna*, 19 July 1896.

57. Salvatore Tedeschi, "Santa Sede ed Etiopia dopo Adua (1896)," *Africa: Rivista trimestrale di studi e documentazione* 40 (1985): 521.

58. Diotti, *Prigioniero d'Africa*, 104; Frisina, *L'Italia in Abissinia*, 325.

59. Carlo Rossetti, *Storia diplomatica dell'Etiopia durante il regno di Menelik II* (Turin: Società tipografico—editrice nazionale, 1910), 210; Salvatore Tedeschi, "Santa Sede ed Etiopia dopo Adua (1896)," *Africa: Rivista trimestrale di studi e documentazione* 40 (1985): 519; "La Pace fra l'Italia e l'Abissinia," *Osservatore Romano*, 17 November 1896.

60. ASMAI, Eritrea, pos. 3/15, fasc. 115, "Pagamento a Menelik della indennità per i prigionieri"; Frisina, *L'Italia in Abissinia, 307.* Apparently Ilg had prepared Nerazzini's expectations regarding the negotiations and the indemnity amount, having first mentioned the figure of forty million and the forfeit of Asmara. See *La Tribuna*, 5 January 1897, in Museo Storico Trento (herafter cited as MST), Baratieri, b. 3, f. 1.

61. For wine and chickens, see Diotti, *Prigioniero d'Africa, 38.*

62. Gleichen, *With the Mission to Menelik*, 266.

63. Frisina, *L'Italia in Abissinia*, 357–358; Diotti, Prigioniero d'Africa, 118.

64. Tedone, *Angerà,* 187.
65. Gleichen, *With the Mission to Menelik,* 247–248. See also ASMAI, L7 Eritrea, cartella 55, Fatti d'armi, 1896–1914, which describes a soldier refusing repatriation.
66. Pantano, *Ventitré anni,* 165.
67. Frisina, *L'Italia in Abissinia,* 337.
68. Ibid., 322–323.

21. PASSINGS

1. Nicola D'Amato, *Da Adua ad Addis-Abeba ricordi d'un prigioniero* (Salerno: A. Volpe, 1898), 61–62.
2. Girma Fisseha, "Ethiopian Paintings on Adwa," in *Adwa Victory Centenary Conference,* ed. Abdussamad Ahmad and Richard Pankhurst (Addis Ababa: Institute of Ethiopian Studies, Addis Ababa University, 1998), 691.
3. Edward Gleichen, *With the Mission to Menelik, 1897* (London: E. Arnold, 1898), 131; Elisabeth Biasio, *Prunk und Pracht am Hofe Menileks: Alfred Ilgs Äthiopien um 1900* (Zurich: Neue Züricher Zeitung, 2004), 73; James Rennell Rodd, *Social and Diplomatic Memories, 1894–1901, Egypt and Abyssinia* (London: Arnold, 1923), 151; Peter Garretson, *A History of Addis Abäba from its Foundation in 1886 to 1910* (Wiesbaden: Harrassowitz, 2000), 15.
4. Lincoln di Castro, *Nella terra dei negus, pagine raccolte in Abissinia* (Milan: Fratelli Treves, 1915), 92a.
5. Richard Pankhurst, "The Battle of Adwa (1896) as Depicted by Traditional Ethiopian Artists" in *Proceedings of the First International Conference on the History of Ethiopian Art* (London: Pindar, 1989), 86. Pankhurst notes in particular Makonnen's prominence in the painting reproduced in S. Pierre Pétridès, *Le heros d'Adoua: Ras Makonnen, prince d'Etiopie* (Paris: Plon, 1963), 86, a book Pankhurst terms "a work of adulation."
6. Antoine Bervin, *Benito Sylvain, apôtre du relèvement social des noirs* (Port-au-Prince: La Phalange, 1969), 43.
7. Gherardo Pantano, *Ventitre anni di vita africana* (Florence: Casa editrice militare italiana, 1932), 97. Albertone made a similar remark to Major Tommaso Salsa. The remark was reported in "Il Processo Baratieri," *Corriere della Sera,* 13–14 June 1896.
8. Pantano, *Ventitré anni,* 50–52; see also a letter from Pantano dated October 1933 in Museo Storico Trento (hereafter cited as MST), Baratieri, busta 1, fasc. 2; *Manchester Guardian,* 20 May 1897; Augustus Blandy Wylde, *Modern Abyssinia* (London: Methuen, 1901), 122–123, 206–208, 211; Domenico Farini, *Diario di fine secolo* (Rome: Bardi, 1962), 971.
9. Francesco Frisina, *L'Italia in Abissinia e nel Sudan: dall'acquisto di Assab, 1869, alla cessione di Cassala, 1897* (Alexandria: Molco Petrini, 1919), 198.
10. Cesare Pini, *Frammenti de'miei ricordi d'Affrica* (Rome: S. Lapi, 1912), 142–143.
11. Letter from Ellena to Baratieri, 9 October 1896 in MST, Baratieri b. 1, f. 2.

12. See Archivio storico del Ministero Africa Italiana (hereafter cited as ASMAI), Eritrea, Questioni Politico Militare, pos. 3/15, fasc. 117 Calunnie del Principe d'Orleans; Farini, *Diario di fine secolo,* 1199–1200; *L'Esercito Italiano,* 9 June 1897, "I prigionieri italiani in Africa e le asserzioni del Duca d'Orléans"; "La vertenza Orleans-Savoia," *Osservatore Romano,* 16–17 August 1897.

13. "Il duello Savoia-Orléans," *Osservatore Romano,* 18 August 1897. Not everyone was fooled. Mariotti, Baratieri's friend at the Ministry of War, wrote a skeptical letter to Baratieri regarding Albertone's conduct since his return from Ethiopia. See MST, Baratieri, b. 2, f. 4a. On the broader context of dueling, see Robert Nye, *Masculinity and Male Codes of Honor in Modern France* (New York: Oxford University Press, 1993).

14. Giovanni Tedone, *Angera: i ricordi di un prigioniero di Menelik* (Milan: Giordano, 1964), 35.

15. Alessandro Sapelli, *Memorie d'Africa* (Bologna: Zanichelli, 1935), 116; Angelo Del Boca, *Adua: le ragioni di una sconfitta* (Rome: Laterza, 1997), 127.

16. Rodd, *Social and Diplomatic Memories,* 157; Bairu Tafla, ed., *Ethiopian Records of the Menilek Era: Selected Amharic Documents from the Nachlass of Alfred Ilg 1884–1900* (Wiesbaden: Harrassowitz, 2000), 528.

17. Gleichen, *With the Mission to Menelik,* 161–162.

18. For the text of Leontiev's offering, see France, Ministry of Foreign Affairs, Correspondance politique 1897–1901, NS 59, Ethiopie, finances privées, Affaires Léontieff, 1897–1901.

19. For details, see ibid.

20. See telegrams from March and April 1898 in ibid.

21. See "Société anonyme belge pour le Développement de l'Industrie et du Commerce dans les provinces equatoriales d'Abyssinie," supplement to *Moniteur Belge,* 23–24 May 1898, in France, Ministry of Foreign Affairs, Correspondance politique 1897–1901, NS 59 Ethiopie, finances privées, Affaires Léontieff, 1897–1901.

22. Nikolai Leontieff, *Provinces equatoriales d'Abyssinie* (Paris: Chambrelent, 1900), 24.

23. Letter from French ambassador to British minister of foreign affairs, 12 March 1900, in France, Ministry of Foreign Affairs, Correspondance politique 1897–1901, NS 59, Ethiopie, finances privées, Affaires Léontieff, 1897–1901.

24. See letter dated 15 May 1904 in France, Ministry of Foreign Affairs, Correspondance politique 1897–1901, NS 60, Ethiopie, finances privées, Affaires Léontieff, 1897–1901.

25. The French diplomatic representative at Djibouti recounted the episode in a tone that blended admiration and outrage. See Ormières to ministre des colonies, 14 July 1902, in France, Ministry of Foreign Affairs, Correspondance politique 1897–1901, NS 60, Ethiopie, finances privées, Affaires Léontieff, 1897–1901.

26. "Un Vinto," *Vita Internazionale,* 20 August 1901, in MST, Baratieri, b. 2, f. 4a.

27. "Le dimissioni dell'On. Baratieri," in MST, Baratieri, b. 2, f. 4a.

28. MST, Baratieri, b. 1, fasc. 1 for Madrid; MST, Baratieri, b. 2, fasc. 4a for Wiesbaden, Carlsbad, Montecatini, Paris, Madrid, Trieste, Burgos. For Nice, see *Petit Niçois,* 6 November 1899, in MST, Baratieri, b. 3, f. 1.

29. Bice Rizzi, "Il Generale Baratieri ed il Vescovo Bonomelli in un Carteggio espistolare," *Quaderno della rivista Trentino* 6 (1934): n.p., in MST, Baratieri, b. 2, f. 4.

30. MST, Oreste Baratieri, b. 3, f. 2 and 4.

31. Wylde, *Modern Abyssinia,* 29, 149; Pantano, *Ventitré anni,* 98; for Alula, memory, and much more, see Haggai Erlich, *Ras Alula and the Scramble for Africa: A Political Biography: Ethiopia and Eritrea, 1875–1897* (Lawrenceville, NJ: Red Sea Press, 1996), 197–203.

32. For Makonnen's post-Adwa ascent, see the remarks of Nerazzini, who visited with Makonnen shortly after the battle; MST, Baratieri, b. 3, f. 1. On accusations of treason, see ASMAI, Eritrea, pos. 3/10, fasc. 69. Not always reliable, Henri d'Orléans writes that Makonnen was wounded in the arm by a rifle shot. See his *Une visite à l'empereur Ménélick notes et impressions de route* (Paris: Librairie Dentu, 1898), 71–72.

33. See "Un invervista con Nerazzini," in MST, Baratieri, b. 3, f. 1.

34. On Paris, see *Le Petit Journal* of 24 July 1898; for London, see Rodd, *Social and Diplomatic Memories,* 135; for Jerusalem, see Alain Rouaud, *Casimir Mondon-Vidailhet: pionnier de l'amitié franco-éthiopienne (1847–1910)* (Addis Ababa: Maison des études éthiopiennes, 1997), 44.

35. His obituary was widely noted, although not always promptly. See *Colored American Magazine,* September 1909, 167–168. If one looks beyond the court, Ras Alula was the first of the historic generation to die, mere months after Adwa. See Wylde, *Modern Abyssinia,* 148–149.

36. On venereal disease, see Chris Prouty, "The Medical History of Menilek II, Emperor of Ethiopia (1844–1913): A Case of Medical Diplomacy," *Munger Africana Library Notes* 45/46 (October 1978): 15–16.

37. Biasio, *Prunk und Pracht,* 14–15.

38. See, for example, Pétridès, *Le heros d'Adoua.*

39. For a recent overview, see Warren Zimmerman, *First Great Triumph: How Five Americans Made Their Country a World Power* (New York: Farrar, Straus and Giroux, 2002).

40. See the introduction to Claude Fohlen, *Les États-Unis au XXe siècle* (Paris: Aubier, 1988).

Acknowledgments

Friends helped me to begin this book. New friends helped me to complete it. Dear colleagues at the University of Washington—Lynn Thomas, Stephanie Camp, Quintard Taylor—provided critical early research leads, especially as I pursued the Adwa story from Africa to Europe to the Americas.

A topic that spans three continents inevitably involves considerable travel and expense. Early support came from the Royalty Research Fund and the Center for West European Studies at the University of Washington. Funding from the National Endowment for the Humanities provided a year of sustained research. Residency at the Institute for Advanced Study in Princeton provided safe haven and fine colleagues as I began writing. I want to thank in particular Avishai Margalit, Caroline Bynum, Joan Scott, Herman Bennett, Karl Shoemaker, Carl Levy, Han Baltussen, and Tom Phillips. The Giovanni and Amne Costigan Professorship in History provided critical ongoing support. Final research trips were funded by the Howard and Frances Keller Fellowship and the Lenore Hanauer Fellowship.

More than ever, scholarship in the digital age requires savvy archivists, curators, and librarians. I wish to recognize the contributions of Theresa Mudrock of the University of Washington, Caterina Tomasi of the Museo Storico Trento, Alessandro Gionfrida of the Ufficio Storico dello Stato Maggiore dell'Esercito, Elizabeth Wolde Giorgis of the Institute for Ethiopian Studies, Antonella Martellucci of the Istituto Italiano per l'Africa e l'Oriente, Professor Patricia Fanning of the Fred Holland Day House, Alexandra Nicholis of the Massillon Museum, and Mary Yearwood of the Schomburg Center for Research in Black Culture. I also owe a debt to Marianne LaBatto and the Special Collections staff of the Brooklyn College Library.

Portions of this work were presented at conferences in the United States and Ethiopia or discussed informally over coffee. I thank Judith Byfield, Linda Heywood, Giulia Bonacci,

Solomon Addis Getahun, Elizabeth Wolde Giorgis, Paul Halliday, Vanessa Schwartz, Assaye Abunie, Kay Kaufman Shelemay, and Steven Kaplan for advice, encouragement, and commentary.

For help with orthography and translation, I wish to thank Albert Sbragia (Italian) and Azmera Melashu (Amharic). Ray Silverman alerted me to the visual dimensions of the story. Jere Bacharach helped me figure out how *Tannhäuser* might have played in Addis. Victoria Scarlett and Joseph Anderson are always full of good ideas. Kathleen Clark Bracco and Jeff Bracco hosted me during a final research stint in Paris.

Jean-Clément Martin, an old friend, warmly encouraged new questions and new directions. He, along with Kent Guy, Lynn Hunt, Robert Stacey, and Tom Kselman, provided words when they counted most. A special thanks to Dan O'Connell, who believed in the project and found a home for it. I owe a large debt to Kathleen McDermott, who championed the book at Harvard University Press.

Scholars accumulate intergenerational debts that can never be repaid—all we can do is acknowledge them and pay them forward in a lineage of gratitude. Thanks to Lynn Hunt, the late Tony Judt, and the late David Pinkney.

Hank Scarlett listened to my earliest attempts at telling the Adwa story. Annie reminded me when it was time to work and when it was time to stop. Patty, Elizabeth, Katherine, Anthony, and Krissy provided companionship and the sustaining hope of family.

Index

The letter *f* following a page number denotes a figure.

among Napier's men. Having failed at a show of force, Tewodros tried negotiation. He released some of the hostages and made a gift of a thousand cattle and five hundred sheep in peace and friendship.[30] Napier declined any peace offer that did not include the emperor himself. As Napier's expeditionary force closed in on the imperial redoubt at Magdala, Tewodros's authority vanished. When British forces moved up the mountainside and raced to free the hostages, Tewodros put the barrel of a pistol in his mouth and pulled the trigger.[31]

Britain had no interest in the conquest of Ethiopia. There was no ulterior motive, no secret plan to occupy Ethiopia. Britain's gripe was with Tewodros, not the Ethiopian people. After the rescue of the hostages, Napier packed up his things and left.[32]

When the British departed, they left behind two things—weapons and a blueprint for conquest. Kassa of Tigray, a local collaborator, had offered safe passage to Napier's forces and secure supply lines in the pursuit of Tewodros. The predations of Tewodros had created a population that was ready for a champion, and Kassa found that the role of champion suited his imperial ambitions. The departing British rewarded Kassa with a healthy stock of rifles and ammunition.[33] With Tewodros out of the way, the British gift of guns and ammo was enough to tip the ensuing succession battle in Kassa's favor.

But although the British were themselves not interested in Ethiopia, Napier's mission set an example for Egypt and Italy, who were. The British had shown how to take down an Ethiopian emperor by allying themselves with an internal rival. By using Kassa against Tewodros, the Napier mission drafted the blueprint for subsequent campaigns. One might add that the relative ease of the Napier rescue mission gave a quite false impression of the tenacity and fighting skills of Ethiopians, a misapprehension that would cost others dearly.

Egypt Moves against Ethiopia

Over the next three years, and thanks to his hefty arsenal, Kassa consolidated his power and dispatched his rivals. In January 1872, he assumed the imperial throne. He took the title of Yohannes IV when he received the crown in a coronation ceremony in the holy city of Axum.

While Ethiopia was distracted by the Napier mission and its after-maths, Egypt pursued its vision of grandeur. Khedive Ismail imagined a modern Egypt that would recapture the glory of ancient Egypt through aggressive expansion into Sudan, Ethiopia, and the Somali coasts. Egyptian forces pushed south along the Red Sea coast, seizing Massawa in 1865. Ismail installed Werner Munzinger, a Swiss adventurer, voyager, and agent for hire, as governor of Massawa.[34]

Following Napier's lead, Ismail sought an internal Ethiopian ally who might challenge Yohannes. Menelik had already demonstrated a stubborn independence, withholding recognition of Yohannes and his claim to the title of emperor. And Menelik's location—at Yohannes's back as he faced the Egyptians in the north—would distract Yohannes as the Egyptians maneuvered against him.[35] Menelik would serve nicely as an ally to Egypt.

In 1875, the Egyptians occupied Harar, a major trading station and the end point of caravans coming up to Shoa from Djibouti. With Harar, Egypt had control of Menelik's main outlet to the sea. Very little left Shoa except by way of Harar, and very little entered. The Egyptians thus had considerable leverage over Menelik. At the same time they began to offer Menelik the firearms that would be useful in his ongoing quarrel with Yohannes, they consolidated control over a position that could choke off Menelik's access to the wider world.

Yohannes represented a significant obstacle to Egyptian ambitions, both because his power base was close at hand, in northern Ethiopia, and because Yohannes took seriously his role as defender of the Christian faith. Yohannes cast the Egyptian incursions both as territorial aggression and as the return of a conquering Islam. And, indeed, Egypt went after areas—Massawa, the Red Sea coast, Harar—where Islam had been durably established.

In 1875, Egypt organized a large force against Yohannes. It consisted of some fifteen thousand Egyptian soldiers commanded by veterans of the German wars of the 1860s (Danes, Germans, and Austrians) as well as veterans of the American Civil War.[36] The objective of this force was to bring about the downfall of Yohannes by threatening the area north of the Mareb River and west of the Red Sea—roughly speaking, the territory that would become Eritrea.[37]

At the same time, Werner Munzinger, Egypt's governor of Massawa, accompanied a shipment of firearms to Menelik. However, Munzinger's group of four hundred never reached Menelik. On 7 November 1875, Munzinger and his party, including his Ethiopian wife and child, were annihilated by Afar, who preyed on trade to Shoa.[38] The very same day, the Egyptian force invading from the north was checked by Yohannes at Gundet.[39]

A few months later, Yohannes's advance guard, led by a bright and brave young commander named Alula, engaged the Egyptians at Gura. The Egyptians suffered a devastating defeat—a rout and a massacre—losing half their men in battle.[40] Defeat at Gura shattered Ismail's dream of an African empire for Egypt. Indeed, it set in motion events that would lead to his downfall three years later. It solidified Ethiopia's claim on what would become Eritrea.

Victory at Gura secured Alula's reputation as Ethiopia's fiercest defender.[41] Yohannes conferred upon Alula the lofty title of *ras* and installed Alula in the town of Asmara, in the highlands above Massawa, thus making the man and the town the hub of his defense against any future threats.[42]

Then Yohannes turned against his perceived enemies. Egypt's Muslim strategy made him wary of Ethiopia's Islamic minority. In 1880, he issued a proclamation in which he invited Ethiopian Muslims either to convert to Christianity or leave.[43] Then he moved against Menelik and forced him to pay homage. Yohannes sealed the deal by marrying his son to Menelik's daughter in 1882. This patched up relations, though the animosity never really subsided. Menelik never renounced his ambition to topple Yohannes and rule Ethiopia. Rather, Menelik pursued the imperial crown by other means. At about the time that Menelik was marrying off his daughter to the son of Yohannes, he began to court the woman who would serve as his most important political ally.

Ethiopia's Power Couple: Menelik and Taytu

Taytu Betul had a restless heart and an iron will. When Menelik courted Taytu, he was merely king of Shoa, but he articulated loftier ambitions. Menelik laid claim to the Ethiopian throne thanks to lineage reaching back to King Solomon and the queen of Sheba.[44] According to the *Kebre Negast,* a compendium of tradition and law, Ethiopia must be ruled by someone of such descent, so Menelik was both conforming to tradition and staking a claim, as had Tewodros and Yohannes before him.[45] As for Taytu, marriage to Menelik would fulfill a prophecy of royal destiny.[46]

Empress Taytu. From *Le Petit Journal*, 29 March 1896.

An early photograph shows a woman with high, full cheeks, full lips, and a narrow jaw. She wore her hair in cornrow braids that followed the arc of her ears and were collected in a ponytail at the back. She was famous for her slender fingers and her light complexion—a gift of her Oromo "Arab" descent. She was also known for her wealth, including holdings in farmland and pasture. She was connected to an extensive network of wealth and power through relatives.[47]